READING SPECIALISTS IN THE *REAL* WORLD

A Sociocultural View

MARYELLEN VOGT

California State University, Long Beach

BRENDA A. SHEARER

University of Wisconsin, Oshkosh

Boston   New York   San Francisco
Mexico City   Montreal   Toronto   London   Madrid   Munich   Paris
Hong Kong   Singapore   Tokyo   Cape Town   Sydney

Series Editor: *Aurora Martínez Ramos*
Editorial Assistant: *Beth Slater*
Marketing Manager: *Elizabeth Fogarty*
Production Editor: *Christine Tridente*
Editorial-Production Service: *Chestnut Hill Enterprises, Inc.*
Composition Buyer: *Linda Cox*
Manufacturing Buyer: *JoAnne Sweeney*
Cover Administrator: *Kristina Mose-Libon*
Electronic Composition: *Galley Graphics, Ltd.*

For related titles and support materials, visit our online catalog at www.ablongman.com.

Between the time Website information is gathered and then published, it is not unusual for some sites to have closed. Also, the transcription of URLs can result in unintended typographical errors. The publisher would appreciate notification where these occur so that they may be corrected in subsequent editions.

Library of Congress Cataloging-in-Publication Data

Vogt, MaryEllen
    Reading specialists in the real world : a sociocultural view /
MaryEllen Vogt, Brenda A. Shearer.— 1st ed.
        p.   cm.
    Includes bibliographical references and indexes.
    ISBN 0-205-34256-6
        1. Reading—Social aspects—United States.   2. Reading
    teachers—United States.   3. Literacy—United States.   I. Shearer,
    Brenda A.   II. Title.
    LB1050.2 .V64 2003
    306.4′88—dc21

                                                                    2002027651

Printed in the United States of America

10 9 8 7 6 5   RRD-IN 07 06 05 04

To the following reading specialists (and professors) who served as my mentors and models of leadership:

Dr. Jack A. Graves, California State University, Stanislaus (Emeritus)
Dr. Deborah Osen Hancock, California State University, Bakersfield (Emeritus)
Dr. Robert B. Ruddell, University of California, Berkeley (Emeritus)

MEV

To the women who taught me who I am and inspire me to be the best I can be:
Regina Terranova Benzschawel, my mother
Ann Delia Podlich, my daughter

BAS

And, to Dr. Martha Rapp Ruddell, our mentor and friend.

MEV and BAS

CONTENTS

CHAPTER THREE

Assessing Literacy Needs, Establishing Goals, and Developing a Plan   51

CHAPTER FOUR

Matching Context to Students: Assessment as Inquiry   75

CHAPTER FIVE

Adapting Instruction to Learners' Needs: Reframing Literacy Intervention   98

CHAPTER SIX

Addressing Issues of Culture and Language   121

CHAPTER ELEVEN
Planning and Providing Professional Development   221

PART IV   THE READING SPECIALIST: PROFESSIONALISM
AND ADVOCACY   245

CHAPTER TWELVE
Working with Families and Adult Literacy   247

CHAPTER THIRTEEN
Moving the Field Forward as Leaders, Researchers, and Advocates   263

APPENDIXES

LIST OF FIGURES

PREFACE

You just opened this book and, as a reader, you have expectations for what it holds and what it can do for you; otherwise, you wouldn't be here with us. If you are preparing to really read it (rather than just thumbing through it), most likely you are either a teacher studying to become a reading specialist, or you already are one. As such, you are part of a unique group of educators, those who care passionately about reading, books, literacy, and ensuring that all children, adolescents, and adults read well enough to assume a place in our society. Although we reading specialists are relatively few in number, individually and collectively we hold tremendous potential for shaping our world.

For example, we have the responsibility to foster collaboration among the literacy stakeholders in our schools, districts, universities, and communities. People look to us for advice and assistance about anything related to reading and language arts. We are expected to assist during textbook adoptions, schoolwide literacy celebrations, and in mentoring new teachers. The community and popular media also require that we undo years of damage caused by poverty, discrimination, and inequity. It is expected that we take the very young child who has never been read a story nor seen a book nor laughed at a silly limerick or poem, and turn her into a reader. The community relies on us to know how to motivate the adolescent who sees little connection between school and life, and whose lack of literacy ability has taken its toll on identity and hope for the future. And, if this isn't enough, we are also perceived as having answers for how to make schools better and how to raise test scores. We believe that well-prepared, knowledgeable, culturally responsive, and caring reading specialists can make an incredible difference in schools, school districts, and communities. They can fill many and varied roles with professionalism, knowledge, insight, and purpose. One very visible way to begin is to open the literacy club, as Frank Smith (1987) described it, to every child, adolescent, and adult who enters our schools . . . and to extend that invitation beyond the schools and into the community.

ABOUT THIS BOOK

Throughout this book you will find a number of practical suggestions, examples, and step-by-step guides for establishing a literacy team, assessing school literacy needs, developing longitudinal plans, designing assessment and curriculum for all learners, providing professional development, and seeking grants. Each of these illustrates evolving and emerging roles of today's reading specialists.

In the following section, we introduce the concepts and theories that guided the writing of this book. As you read about them, reflect on and relate each one to your own classrooms, contexts, and communities.

A Sociocultural Perspective

You've probably noticed the second part of this book's title, *A Sociocultural View*. And, you may wonder why we have adopted a sociocultural stance and why it is important. The idea grew from our search for an appropriate textbook for our graduate courses in leadership and supervision of reading and literacy programs. We were looking for a text that reflects the exciting changes in pedagogy, complexity, and diversity that are reshaping literacy education as we know it. Because MaryEllen teaches in California and Brenda in Wisconsin, we have learned that one-size-fits-all approaches to the job of Reading Specialist will not accommodate the needs of a small monolingual rural school in Wisconsin, an urban Los Angeles school in which students speak several dozen languages, and your own particular school. Thus, in *Reading Specialists in the Real World: A Sociocultural View*, we discuss the traditional issues of roles, programs, and decisions integral to the world of the reading specialist. But, we also adopt a lens through which we can examine our work. A sociocultural perspective recognizes the importance of the school, community, and family contexts in which literacy events occur—ultimately using that knowledge to enhance literacy learning.

Multiple Literacies.   Historically, schools have defined language and literacy practices in rather narrow ways, privileging certain literacies above or in exclusion of others. When we broaden our definitions to include the numerous ways in which humans convey meaning, for example, symbolically, through pop culture, story, song, and ritual, we can then provide and develop resources that connect to the lives of our students. We need not alter the goals of literacy relative to standards or abandon our responsibility to prepare our students to function within existing power structures. Instead, we can better use these multiple literacies within existing structures to meet the goals of schools, districts, and communities.

Multiple Contexts, Multiple Communities, and Discourse Theory.   We all belong to a number of complex literacy communities, many of which overlap. Think of the communities in which you participate, such as your fellow graduate students, high school friends, neighbors, church congregation, cultural and ethnic groups, or even fellow computer users. By gaining insight into our own literacy communities and those of our students, we can create programs that are much more culturally responsive.

Critical Literacy, Activity Theory, and Reader Response Theory.   These three theories extend the constructivist ideas that literacy events are situated in social contexts and that meaning is socially constructed. Adopting a critical stance includes leading students to evaluate historical factors, personal beliefs, purposes for reading, reactions to reading, the author's stances, clues to bias, and information included and excluded in texts.

New Perspectives on Adolescent Literacy.   Until recently, the emphasis on literacy in middle and secondary schools focused on a cognitive strategies approach with an emphasis on the various content areas. The term *adolescent literacy* involves a much more integrated approach. It includes the flexible use of strategies and recognizes the social contexts of learning. It incorporates many of the new perspectives and theories previously described.

New Perspectives on Leadership and Advocacy.   New models of leadership recognize the complexity of change and do not seek to silence dissent or to coerce individuals into consensus. It is our intention to help reading specialists develop advocacy skills necessary to deal with the difficult and long-term aspects of change and school reform.

Tensions as Opportunities for Inquiry.   Rather than trying to oversimplify the process of change or pretend that everyone will put aside ideological differences and act as one, we provide insight into the ways in which tensions and differences are fundamental to the change process.

Our Own Voices as Authors.   Reading involves interactions between the reader and the author. Therefore, consistent with a sociocultural perspective, we drop the masks used in textbook writing and use first person, presenting our opinions and biases. Note, however, that we also ground our writing in research and theory. Our approach to writing this book illustrates how we continually question our work and our world as we seek answers related to literacy teaching.

OVERVIEW OF THE BOOK

This book is divided into four parts. The first part, The Reading Specialist: Teacher and School Literacy Leader, begins with Chapter 1 (Examining the Historical Context for Teaching Reading). The chapter includes a brief history of reading instruction and the reading specialist's role in the United States.

The second chapter (Establishing a Literacy Team and Developing a Vision Statement) addresses the formation of a dynamic and effective school literacy team, while Chapter 3 (Assessing Literacy Needs, Establishing Goals, and Developing a Plan), includes a framework for determining programmatic needs and creating a comprehensive two-year plan for implementing and evaluating school literacy programs. In Chapter 4 (Matching Contexts to Students: Assessment as Inquiry), we focus on identifying students' needs in order to plan and implement appropriate literacy instruction for them within a sociocultural perspective. In Chapter 5 (Adapting Instruction to Learner's Needs: Reframing Literacy Intervention), we concentrate on models of intervention for children and adolescents. In Chapter 6 (Addressing Issues of Culture and Language) we focus on the design and implementation of appropriate instruction for English language learners, and those whose culture may differ from the majority.

In Part II, The Reading Specialist: Resource Teacher and Curriculum Developer, we focus on other leadership responsibilities. In Chapter 7 (Implementing a Reading/Language Arts Program in the Elementary School), we describe and discuss literacy development and instruction for young children. Chapter 8 (Meeting the Literacy Needs of Adolescent Learners) describes new, culturally responsive models of middle and high school literacy programs, including content area literacy. A primary role of reading specialists is described in Chapter 9 (Selecting and Evaluating Instructional Materials and Technology Resources), where we discuss how to make informed decisions about appropriate instructional materials for teaching reading and language arts.

Part III, The Reading Specialist: Coach, Supervisor, and Professional Developer, focuses on the relationship of reading specialists and teachers within a community of learners. Chapter 10 (Serving as Peer Partner, Cognitive Coach, and Supervisor) discusses how to develop relationships among reading specialists and classroom teachers that establish and maintain trust, facilitate mutual learning, and enhance the growth of participants to act both autonomously and interdependently within the group. In Chapter 11 (Planning and Providing Professional Development) the emphasis is on shared ownership of the content, implementation, evaluation, and follow-through of professional development based on teachers' self-assessed needs.

The final section of the book, Part IV, The Reading Specialist: Professionalism and Advocacy, examines the reading specialist's roles beyond the school and into the community. In Chapter 12 (Working with Families and Adult Literacy) we explore the role of the reading specialist in family literacy programs and adult literacy. Chapter 13 (Moving the Field Forward as Leaders, Researchers, and Advocates) discusses teacher research, grant writing, professionalism, professional organizations, and advocacy. Finally, we challenge reading specialists to serve as agents of change within the ever-changing field of reading and language arts.

ACKNOWLEDGMENTS

We express appreciation to our graduate students who have helped us with this book, both in terms of their critiques of manuscripts we've used in our classes in supervision and leadership and in their willingness to test our ideas. They've also shared written case problems that helped focus our vignettes, as well as their Needs Assessments, Two-Year Plans, and Literacy Assessment Profiles completed for course requirements. In particular, we wish to thank Jose Avila, Carnella Bey, Erica Bowers, Diana Escalante, Leslie Gloyne, Shirley Guthrie, Denise Hagen, Elisa Hagen, Wendy Hansen, Lisa Holbrook, Laurie Manzo, June Matt, Marci McGolden, Alison Mitchell, Jenny Morelli, Lorri Oliver, Lisa Parra, Claudio Ribas, Kelly Riggs, Susan Thompson, Gretchen Tuthill, and Stacy Westling from California State University, Long Beach. From the University of Wisconsin, Oshkosh, we thank Lynn Betts, Barb Cummings, Julie Dilts, Tera Ellison, Terra Kind, Kristin Klemme, Kari Koerner, Karla Koslowski, Marcia Morgan, Jennifer Mursau, Maggie Patton, Kristen Petersen, Marilyn Rankin, Stacey Reese, Jann Rohloff, Deb Rupnow, Heidi Schmidt, Julie Schmudde, Becky Schuler, Amy Sippert, Karen Sprangers, Norah Vandermolen, Carla Witkowski, and Christine Wright.

We also acknowledge Dr. Michael Nelipovich, Principal Tom Westermeyer, Dr. Pat Scanlan, Deb Zarling, Susan Smith, Vonnie Harness, Sandy Johnson, Katrina Mraz, John Brekke, and Keith Vogt, individuals who provided information, feedback, encouragement, and wise counsel. To our colleagues who served as reviewers, Dr. Deb Carr,

King's College and Hazleton Area School District; Dr. Martha Rapp Ruddell, Sonoma State University; Dr. Patty Schmidt, LeMoyne College; Dr. Karen Thomas, Western Michigan University, we express appreciation for their thoughtful, critical, and most helpful comments. We're also grateful for the assistance, patience, and support of our editorial team at Allyn & Bacon, including Aurora Martínez Ramos, Beth Slater, Arnis Burvikovs, and Virginia Lanigan.

WELCOME TO THE WORLD OF READING SPECIALISTS

Finally, we'd like to welcome you to our exciting, rewarding, and challenging profession. As a reading specialist, you'll never be bored or without something that needs to be done. You'll find yourself worrying in the middle of the night about kids' reading problems, instructional materials, and that new teacher who needs your help. At times, you may question yourself and your ability to perform all the responsibilities required of you. And, you may quickly learn to avoid any conversation about reading, reading problems, and the latest trends in reading while riding on an airplane or attending a cocktail party, because you'll quickly be targeted as someone who has the knowledge and information that others want to talk about. Also, some of you may be in districts where reading specialist positions are few and far between, and you'll never work in a room that has Reading Specialist on the door. But, remember . . . once you are a reading specialist, you'll always be a reading specialist. And, best of all, you'll find yourself in an area of specialization that is intellectually stimulating, immensely rewarding, always challenging, and forever changing. Welcome aboard!

MEV   BAS

ABOUT THE AUTHORS

MaryEllen Vogt is a Professor of Education at California State University, Long Beach, and Co-Director of the CSU Center for the Advancement of Reading. A former public school reading specialist and district reading resource teacher, Dr. Vogt served as president of the California Reading Association, and will serve as president of the International Reading Association in 2004–2005. She was inducted into the California Reading Hall of Fame and received her university's Distinguished Faculty Teaching Award. Dr. Vogt received her doctorate in Language and Literacy from the University of California, Berkeley.

Brenda A. Shearer, Associate Professor of Reading Education at the University of Wisconsin, Oshkosh, has over 30 years of experience as a teacher, reading specialist, professor, and researcher in urban and rural Wisconsin. Her publications include articles in *The Reading Teacher, Journal of Educational Psychology, Journal of Adolescent and Adult Literacy,* and *NRC Yearbook,* and several book chapters.

PART I

THE READING SPECIALIST: TEACHER AND SCHOOL LITERACY LEADER

CHAPTER ONE

EXAMINING THE HISTORICAL CONTEXT FOR TEACHING READING

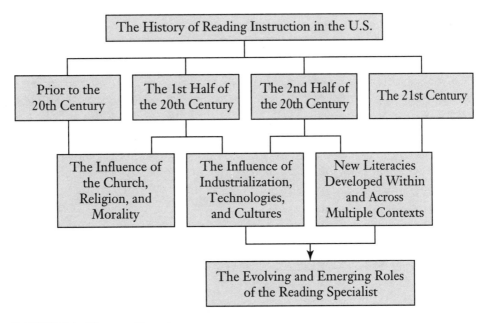

FIGURE 1.1 Chapter Overview

LEARNING GOALS

After reading, discussing, and engaging in activities related to this chapter, you will be able to:

1. relate the history of reading instruction to your own development as a reader;
2. explain why reading specialists need to understand the influences of methods and approaches to teaching reading that have been used in the United States;

3. define and describe historical terminology, methods, and materials used for teaching reading in the United States;

4. explain how the roles of the reading teacher and specialist have evolved over the past fifty years;

5. Personal Learning Goal: In a three-minute brainstorming session, share what you know about the history of reading instruction. Write a goal or a question that reflects something you want to learn about this topic. Share this with others in your group.

Vignette

Barbara Johnson has recently been hired as her district's reading coordinator. She is responsible for overseeing the literacy instructional programs in the twenty-four elementary and middle schools in the district. For the past five years, she has served as her school's reading specialist. Her supervisor, the Assistant Superintendent for Curriculum and Instruction, has expressed concern about the district's lack of a cohesive reading program for the elementary grades, and he has been pushing Barbara to "get teachers on the same page for reading."

The community has experienced a gradual increase in the number of English language learners over the past ten years, *as well as a number of new teachers. District standardized test scores have dipped in comparison to comparable districts in the state, and teachers, administrators, parents, and the school board have all expressed concern.*

District policy permits the teachers in each school to adopt whatever commercial reading series they wish. As a result, there are currently several integrated reading series in use in the elementary grades, as well as supplemental programs for teaching phonics and spelling. Some upper-grade teachers have chosen to use class sets of chapter books for their reading instruction rather than any commercial reading series.

Thinking Points

1. What do you suspect are the underlying tensions and problems Barbara may want to investigate?
2. Which issue should she address first?

Expanding the Vignette: Exploring the Tensions

Barbara decided that her first step was to meet with teachers and reading specialists at each of the twenty-four schools. Almost immediately she became aware of the strong prejudices some teachers held for the reading approaches they were currently using. She frequently heard comments from veteran teachers such as: "I've been doing this for years, and my students all became readers. Why should I think about changing how I *teach?" "Look, reading programs and approaches come and go, and we just jump on any bandwagon that comes along. Yes, I teach phonics, and, yes, I teach comprehension. I've been through all the phases and I've seen all the trends. What I've learned is that what I use to teach reading isn't nearly as important as how I teach it."*

However, several new teachers expressed concerns, such as: "I'm just trying to figure out what I'm doing. At the university, my professors said I should be teaching in a particular way, but I don't see the teachers at my school doing that. I don't know what to do or what I should use. I just want to survive this school year."

After discussing these issues with the teachers and reading specialists throughout her district, Barbara felt overwhelmed. She wondered how she could possibly unify everyone and "get them on the same page." She even questioned whether they should be on the same page. She knew the Assistant Superintendent was expecting a plan of action, and she knew he wanted it immediately. However, she didn't know where to begin.

Thinking Points

1. What additional tensions and questions have you identified in the vignette?
2. What are some short-term suggestions you would give Barbara?
3. What long-term measures should Barbara consider, given the district policies and the teachers with whom she is working?
4. What are some proactive measures a reading specialist, either at the school or district level, could take to avoid the problems you identified?

Keep your answers to these questions in mind as you read. We will revisit the vignette at the end of this chapter.

What Barbara is experiencing is not uncommon. She works in a district in which the reading program is loosely defined. Consequently, teachers are all doing what they believe works best, based on their experience, resources, and student population. As an experienced reading specialist and teacher, she, too, has used a number of innovative approaches, materials, and trends. However, she has also seen these same approaches and materials fall into disfavor and disappear when the new tidal wave of methods and instructional resources hits.

WHY CHANGE?

We find it amazing that between the two of us, we have nearly sixty years of teaching experience, and during this time, we've survived a variety of trends and approaches. Throughout, we've adjusted our instruction, learned new methods, and adapted to "the latest."

Although we "old timers" like to say, "kids don't change," the reality is that they *do* change. Society changes, the school population changes, parents change, teachers change, and reading curriculum changes. It's part of the teacher's life . . . and the more that reading specialists understand the change process, including what's come before, the better we are able to make sound instructional decisions about what children and adolescents need to become proficient readers and writers in a complex world.

In this chapter we provide a historical synopsis of some of the approaches and methods that have been used for teaching reading during the twentieth century. We attempt to situate them in the political, cultural, social, and historical contexts that shaped them. Think about how you learned to read. If you and your parents share your memories together, you will most likely discover that their memories of learning to read are different from yours. If you are a "seasoned" teacher and have taught for twenty to thirty years, you have probably gone through at least three major cycles in reading instructional approaches and materials. In the following section, we'll explore some of these and how theory, research, political, and sociocultural factors have influenced the methods, approaches, and materials used in schools.

EXPLORING READING INSTRUCTION OVER TIME

> *Tears must be shed—by tender little creatures liable to so many accidents and diseases;*
> *Tears must be shed—by eager little creatures so often refused desired toys;*
> *Tears must be shed—by affectionate little creatures, forced to part from a charming playmate;*
> *But tears need not be shed—by little creatures, ignorant and playful*
> *though they be, while learning to read*
> —*Reading without Tears*, Preface, p. vii

Not long ago, one of our graduate students shared an old book his grandmother had stored in her attic. The book was written for teachers and was an early attempt at providing methodology instruction for teaching children to read. The title of the book is *Reading without Tears: A Pleasant Mode of Learning to Read*. There is no author's name listed, and the publisher was Harper & Brothers in New York. There is no publication date given, but on the inside cover of the book in beautiful old penmanship is the following: "Harriet Ely, July 3, 1867." Was Harriet a reading teacher? A principal? A mother or grandmother who wanted to help her children or grandchildren to read? In the opening section, the author of this book suggests that the act of teaching reading should occur only under certain conditions:

> Only let them not begin too soon (never before four, sometimes not till five); only—let not the lessons be too long; and only—let them be omitted altogether, when the little learners are sick, though only from a cold; or when they are wearied from walking or playing; or when they are excited by promised pleasures . . ." (*Reading without Tears*, p. vii).

From the title of this book, and from the author's expressed concerns, it appears that, when this book was written, certainly before 1867, there were reading methods that inspired tears in young children. We wonder about the reading instructional approaches that have come and gone during our own teaching careers, and which, if any, have evoked frustration to the point of eliciting children's (and sometimes teachers') tears!

The suggested approach in *Reading without Tears* relies heavily on phonics[1] and the gradual introduction of sound–letter correspondences. For example, the first lesson after introducing the alphabet consists of simple phonetically regular sentences in large, dark type (see Figure 1.2). The remainder of the old text includes gradually more difficult sentences that carry more meaning. Note the complexity of the sentences that are found in Figure 1.3 (midway through the book) and then in Figure 1.4, the final story of the book, "The Beggar Boy" (p. 130).

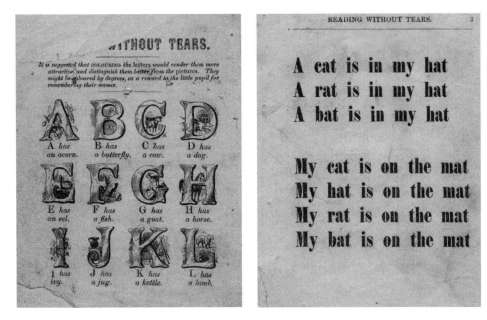

FIGURE 1.2   *Reading without Tears:* **The Alphabet and First Story**

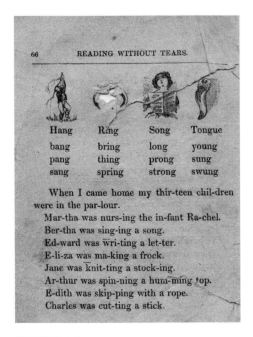

FIGURE 1.3
Reading without Tears: **Page 66**

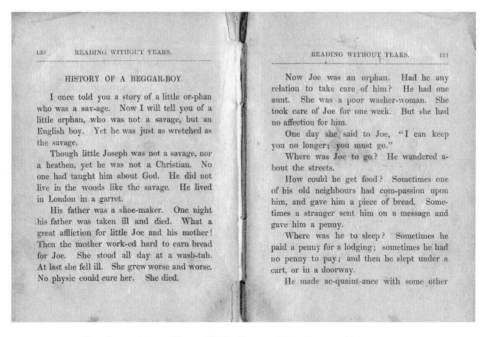

FIGURE 1.4   *Reading without Tears:* "The Beggar Boy," page 130

The methods suggested in this 140+ year-old book parallel many of those recommended today, and they demonstrate that the search for the most effective ways to teach children to read has preoccupied reading teachers and specialists for a long time.

The Early Years of the United States

The earliest "textbook" used in the Jamestown settlement in 1607 was the Horn Book, a paddle-shaped piece of wood with a transparent sheet of animal horn that protected the alphabet and verses written on the wood (Ruddell, 2002). Later, The *New England Primer* (1790–1850) was published, with grim admonitions for children to behave themselves or suffer the consequences. This early textbook included the alphabet, verses, rhymes, and stories, such as the following:

> *In the burying place may see*
> *Graves shorter there than I;*
> *From Death's arrest no age is free,*
> *Young children too may die.*
> *My god, may such an awful sight,*
> *Awakening be to me!*
> *Oh! That by early grace I might*
> *For Death prepared be.*

Religious and patriotic views dominated instruction in the country during the years of 1607–1840. The instructional emphasis was on knowledge of the alphabet, recitation, memorization of Bible verses, spelling bees, oral reading, and elocution. Teachers were most often men with a "good moral character who were able to read and write" (Ruddell, 2002, p. 16).

In the mid and late 1800s, the Civil War, Gold Rush, westward expansion, and industrial revolution increased the need for an educated populace. In 1841, Rev. William Holmes McGuffey published the first *McGuffey Reader* with fifty-five lessons that introduced a strict ethical code that required children to be prompt, good, kind, honest, and truthful. The first two readers focused on alphabet knowledge, phonics, syllables, and sight words, and the stories were written at increasingly difficult reading levels with some comprehension questions. The second reader included 85 lessons with160 pages that outlined history, biology, astronomy, zoology, and botany, along with table manners and attitudes toward God, teachers, parents, and the poor. In all, there were six readers, with the third through sixth intended for what would be today's middle and secondary students. The sixth was published in 1885, with 186 selections that quoted great authors such as Longfellow, Shakespeare, and Dickens (Payne, 2001). The "eclectic" readers (so-called because they included selections from a variety of sources) were very moralistic and presented a picture of a White Protestant America (see Figure 1.5).

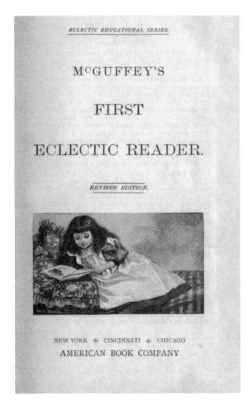

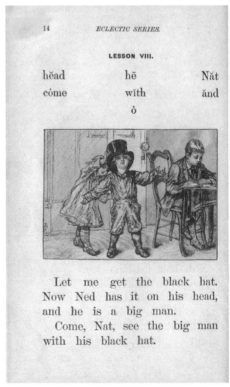

FIGURE 1.5 *McGuffey Reader* **Excerpt**

The First Half of the Twentieth Century

In 1908, E. B. Huey published *The Psychology and Pedagogy of Reading*, an influential and progressive text that examined the reading process using the scientific method (Huey, 1908/1968). At about this time, universal education in the United States was gaining momentum with an enormous increase in those attending school and with the support of federal and state legislatures. However, as waves of immigrants from Western Europe were landing on Ellis Island, children of immigrants, descendants of former slaves, and the sons and daughters of the poor continued to labor in factories, fields, and sweatshops, with little access to formal education.

In the schools, reading for information and commerce replaced the primary purpose of reading during the eighteenth and nineteenth centuries, which was reading the Bible. As the United States entered World War I, the armed forces needed to identify young men who demonstrated leadership. Because this had to be accomplished rapidly, the decision was made to use newly developed "scientific testing." The intent was to identify both the "leaders" and the "followers." The result was the country's first large-scale testing program (Ruddell, 2001) and the development of a constellation of instruments, a number of which, though revised, are still in use today. Thorndike's 1917 measure of reading comprehension, which he described as ability in reading, Binet's IQ test, and Gray's (1915) *Standardized Oral Reading Paragraphs* are among the early "scientifically constructed" tests that attempted to measure complex cognitive abilities and processes.

During the first half of the twentieth century, educators explored a variety of approaches for teaching reading, including phonics. Whether to teach phonics was not argued; what was debated was when and how phonics should be taught. There were those who advocated for synthetic phonics instruction (students learn the parts and blend them into words), and there were those who recommended analytic phonics instruction (students learn words and then analyze the parts). Analytic phonics was popularly referred to as a "look–say" approach, later to be skewered in the popular press.

In the late 1930s through the 1960s, publishers provided a variety of leveled readers that were used to teach children to read. Instructional approaches reflected the dominance of behaviorism[2] and the quest to produce scripted teachers' guides. Remember that, during the first half of the century, the majority of teachers received less than two years of preparation in regional "Normal Schools." The leveled readers also reflected the work of researchers such as Thorndike (1921) and Dolch (1942), who identified the words most frequently used in books. Publishers then produced children's "readers" with stories written according to these word lists. The resulting books included contrived stories with carefully controlled vocabulary, and sight words that were frequently repeated so that a child eventually achieved independence in reading them.

Throughout the United States from the mid-1930s until the 1980s, millions of children came to know a "typical" American family and its members: Father, Mother, Dick, Jane, Sally, and, of course, their pets, Puff and Spot (see Figures 1.6, 1.7, 1.8). If children were not reading about Dick and Jane, they most likely were reading in other books about Alice and Jerry, Ann and David, or Janet and Mark, all who lived in white,

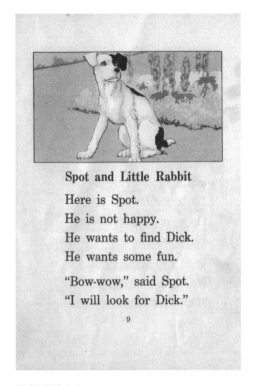

Spot and Little Rabbit

Here is Spot.

He is not happy.

He wants to find Dick.

He wants some fun.

"Bow-wow," said Spot.

"I will look for Dick."

9

Dick said, "See Puff.

Puff can play.

Puff can run and jump."

Jane said, "Oh, oh.

Spot can not play.

Spot can not run.

Spot can not jump.

Spot is funny."

FIGURE 1.6
Dick and Jane: 1935

(Reprinted with permission of SRA/Scott Foresman.)

FIGURE 1.7
Dick and Jane: 1945

(Reprinted with permission of SRA/Scott Foresman.)

middle-class families and communities like Dick and Jane's. The homogenization of American culture and the resulting lack of diversity in some of the early readers characterized the instructional materials that were used in classrooms for over forty years. Later editions of this series included illustrations of children of different ethnicities. These were portrayed as classmates, neighbors, and friends of Dick, Jane, and Sally, or their counterparts in the other readers.

The Second Half of the Twentieth Century

During World War II, educators and the public discovered once again that many soldiers were unable to read well enough to comprehend training manuals and other related texts. The advent of content area reading, teaching students how to read informational and expository texts, was a direct result. Post-World War II was a time of increased prosperity and political conservatism as the United States entered the Cold War. Along with the growing nationalism during the two World Wars and the notion of America as the melting pot, immigrant and Native American children were strongly encouraged

FIGURE 1.8 Dick and Jane: 1962
(Reprinted with permission of SRA/Scott Foresman.)

to assimilate, often losing most of their cultural heritage in one generation. When the Russians launched Sputnik, the "Race for Space" brought millions of dollars to the task of reforming the science, mathematics, and reading programs in schools. Laws were passed to increase the age of mandatory school attendance. Although the United States offered "education to all," many inequities remained between the quality of education for the rich and poor, particularly in racially segregated schools.

During this time, phonics was taught in many schools, and debate continued about the best approach, synthetic or analytic. Rudolph Flesch's (1955) famous publication *Why Johnny Can't Read* mobilized proponents of synthetic phonics, including many parents throughout the country. Then, the publication of the book *Learning to Read: The Great Debate* (Chall, 1967) divided reading professionals into two camps, those advocating synthetic phonics and those advocating more holistic and analytic methods of phonics instruction. The First Grade Studies (Bond & Dykstra, 1967a, 1967b; reprinted in *Reading Research Quarterly*, 1997) attempted to answer the question once and for all. Guy Bond and Robert Dykstra, and their colleagues involved in the First

Grade Studies, concluded that no one method was so much more effective in all situations that it should be considered the one best method for teaching reading. Unfortunately, both sides interpreted the findings to support their positions on phonics. According to Bob Dykstra (Shearer, 2001), "Reading educators all over the country were telling their audiences that the most important conclusion of this research was that the teacher is the most important element in the instructional situation. Although this may well be true and is a 'feel good' thing to say, it was not a conclusion we reached, nor that the data support" (p. 2).

In response to perceived concerns about a lack of phonics instruction, some researchers during the 1960s and 1970s became very interested in examining the linguistic foundations of the reading process. From their work came new approaches including programmed reading with its sequential lessons in workbooks, cards, and worksheets (Sullivan & Buchanan, 1963), reading machines (e.g., the language master[3] and tachistoscope[4]), color-coded text, scripted teacher's guides (see Figure 1.9), and the Linguistic Approach, advocated by linguists interested in studying how "talk" is translated into reading (Fries, 1963). The intent of these methods and programs was to

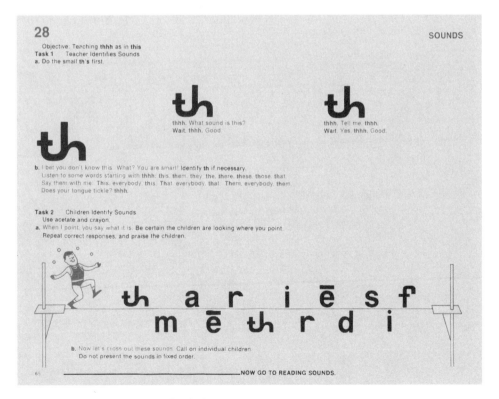

FIGURE 1.9   DISTAR Teacher's Script

(From S. Engelmann and E. C. Burner, *Distar Reading I, An Instructional System.* Copyright © 1969 by Science Research Associates. Reprinted with permission of McGraw-Hill Educators.)

provide beginning readers with consistency, explicit instruction, a great deal of practice in decoding, and the gradual introduction of texts that contained the specific linguistic elements that were being taught.

One of the most interesting experiments implemented during the 1960s and early 1970s was the Initial Teaching Alphabet (i/t/a) (Downing, 1962; Mazurkiewicz & Tanyzer, 1966). The i/t/a alphabet was originally called the Augmented Roman Alphabet, and it consisted of forty-four lowercase characters, twenty-four of them conventional letters. Each symbol in i/t/a, according to Sir James Pitman who created the alphabet, had one phonic meaning. For example, the two sounds of the *th* digraph, as in *the* (voiced) and in *thistle* (voiceless) had two distinctive symbols. The purpose of i/t/a was to provide children with a phonetically regular alphabet so that they could quickly learn to read i/t/a stories, with the goal of eventually transferring their developing reading skills to conventional English. Children's books were written with i/t/a (see Figure 1.10), and, not surprisingly, though the students learned to read these books, many had difficulty later when they attempted to read conventional texts.

During the decade of the 1960s, a social, political, cultural, and moral revolution was occurring outside the walls of schools. The Beatles changed the music, clothing, and culture of the students, the Vietnam War polarized the nation, marijuana and LSD began to show up in even the most rural schools, and television brought the Civil Rights

FIGURE 1.10   Initial Teaching Alphabet Text
(Reprinted from M. Miller, *The Trick.*)

Movement and "The War" into every home. University attendance exploded as large numbers of white students and a small, but increasing, number of students from various racial and ethnic groups took their seats as "first generation college students," many to avoid the draft. In general, the public schools seemed oblivious to these social and moral phenomena, continuing to ask the same pedagogical questions, independently of the context of the times.

As teachers began to place a greater emphasis on phonics and decoding, many found their students were not developing proficient comprehension. As with phonics, a discrete list of comprehension skills was identified and it was recommended that the skills be taught and that students practice them frequently through a variety of skills exercises (Clymer, 1968). Among these comprehension skills were: finding the main idea and supporting details, sequencing, drawing conclusions, making generalizations, comparing and contrasting, and identifying cause-and-effect relationships.

The primary instructional materials during the 1970s and 1980s were basal reading programs[5] and they included leveled readers, phonics activities, and a great deal of comprehension skill practice, usually found on the pages of the accompanying workbooks. The programs also included highly structured, detailed teacher's guides, with different lesson plans for each of the three instructional groups (high, average, low). The fallout from the political and cultural revolution of the earlier decade fostered an attitude of conservatism that was manifested in instructional materials designed for schools.

However, as with the other approaches and methods that had been used over the decades, some problems appeared. These included:

1. Because reading instruction took place in ability groups, there were built-in advantages for capable readers because they were exposed to far more vocabulary in the "high" group reading books than in the books assigned to the "low" groups. Over the years of elementary school, therefore, the "rich got richer, and the poor got poorer" (Stanovich, 1986).

2. The contrived texts, for the most part, contained stories (with very little informational text) that reflected little or no diversity in characters, families, and cultures.

3. The teacher's guides and workbooks included end-of-story questions and activities that kept students busy, but which simply tested, rather than taught, comprehension. Once again, the methods and materials for teaching fell into disfavor.

During the next two decades (1980s, 1990s), theorists and researchers from across the fields of psychology, linguistics, and education explored how readers think about text, how they make connections while they read, and how they ultimately construct meaning. Educators' conversations about reading methods and materials included references to schema formation, the influence on meaning-making of prior knowledge and experience (Anderson & Pearson, 1984); transactional theory, the view that meaning is constructed through an active interchange of ideas within a particular context, as with reader and text (Rosenblatt, 1978); and scaffolding, how learners benefit from the assistance of more experienced individuals, and how they eventually gain independence when that support is gradually lessened (Bruner, 1983; Vygotsky, 1978). Instead of focusing on the finite skills that readers develop, educators began talking about how to build students' backgrounds, promote concept formation, instill joy and delight in reading, and forge connections among the language processes of reading, writing, listening, and speaking.

Also during the early 1980s, computers began to be used in the schools, mostly for drill and practice, and for teaching students to learn to write basic computer programs. Remember, at that time, we actually believed that computer users would have to write their own programs! Not surprisingly, in the early stages of computer use, teachers lacked the time, training, and technical support to help students, and software was comparatively unsophisticated.

At this same time, linguistics and psychology were influencing instructional approaches as some researchers began to write about the reader more holistically (Calkins, 1983; Cambourne, 1984; Goodman, 1986). Drawing implications from sociolinguistics and psycholinguistics, as well as from research on the writing process, a professional movement and theoretical perspective evolved into what was eventually called "whole language" (Strickland, 1995). What made this movement different from others in the past is that the great majority of whole language proponents were classroom teachers. It is an amazing example of a grassroots movement. For about a ten-year period in the United States (mid-1980s to the mid-1990s), there was a decreased emphasis on teaching discrete skills, whether phonics/decoding or comprehension. The 1985 publication of *Becoming a Nation of Readers* (Anderson, Hiebert, Scott, & Wilkinson, 1985) supported this shift in pedagogy. Instructional materials for reading included literature with a wide variety of unadapted texts, stories, and books that were not contrived and that had not been controlled for vocabulary difficulty or readability.

As you might have guessed by now, once again reading approaches and materials came under intense scrutiny. This time, the changes were propelled by a number of factors, including:

1. The low reading performance of students as measured by standardized tests in some states where more holistic teaching approaches were used;
2. A series of federally funded research studies that revealed that, for most children, learning to read is not a "natural" process; that for most children, identifying, blending, and segmenting sounds in words appears to be an important predictor of eventual reading achievement; that these same children appear to benefit from explicit phonics instruction; that many children need practice in reading texts with a high percentage of decodable words; and that young children who have difficulty learning to read benefit from early, intensive reading intervention (Adams, 1990; National Reading Panel, 2000; Snow, Burns, & Griffin, 1998);
3. The huge influx of immigrant children in states such as California, Texas, and Florida whose home language was other than English.

These factors collectively had an enormous impact on reading instruction toward the end of the 1990s. In the next section, we look at what's to come in the twenty-first century.

TEACHING READING AT THE BEGINNING
OF THE TWENTY-FIRST CENTURY

Several very influential documents were published in the late 1990s and early 2000 that were widely disseminated not only to educators and administrators, but also to national and state legislators and other policymakers. These included substantial research syntheses of studies related to reading/language arts. The Report of the National Reading Panel (2000), the Report of the Committee on Reading Disabilities (Snow, Burns, & Griffin, 1998), and reports of the Center for the Improvement of Early Reading Achievement (CIERA) continue to have a powerful influence on the literacy research agenda for the decade of the 2000s. (Note that these documents are listed at the end of this chapter. We strongly encourage you to become familiar with them and other national reports as they are released over the next years.)

Major findings from these reports include:

- assessment and instruction are inextricably linked, and assessment must be viewed as a dynamic, ongoing process that leads to instructional decision making;
- most children need systematic and explicit instruction in decoding;
- fluency isn't sufficient for comprehension, but it is absolutely necessary for good comprehension;
- beginning readers need a variety of texts in order to make progress;
- explicit instruction in comprehension skills and strategies is needed for most children;
- writing, spelling, and reading are highly related, especially in the early stages of learning to read;
- children and adolescents need to spend more time reading and writing;
- children and adolescents should have many experiences with quality literature;
- motivation for reading can be enhanced and assessed;
- children not reaching benchmarks benefit from thirty minutes a day of intensive intervention in addition to regular classroom reading instruction;
- teachers should actively make connections between school and home literacy events.

Despite the fact that the federally funded reports, particularly that of the National Reading Panel (NRP), were embraced by legislators and the press, and they served as the catalyst for reform efforts throughout the country, such as Reading First, there were also thoughtful, scholarly, and highly critical responses to them (Cunningham, 2001; Purcell-Gates, 2000). These suggested that the National Reading Report had serious flaws primarily because the methods used by the Panel for selecting research studies to analyze were limited.

Cunningham (2001) concludes, "The U.S. Congress, the NICHD [an influential agency of the federal government], and the Secretary of Education convened the Panel and shaped its goals and operation. Does this mean the National Reading Panel was a bold attempt by powerful political forces to gain control of reading research? That will depend on whether persuasion or enforcement was the goal, and only time will tell"

(p. 335). The controversy surrounding the Report of the National Reading Panel and its subsequent influence on the No Child Left Behind legislation in 2002 illustrate why reading specialists must be independent, critical examiners of events, issues, and policies in literacy education.

Other Voices: Timothy Shanahan

The following piece was contributed by Tim Shanahan from the University of Chicago. A member of the National Reading Panel, Tim provides insight into the processes that guided the panel in deciding the kinds of studies included in the report.

Research-Based Practice

Policymakers increasingly demand that the schools use research as the basis of instructional practice in reading. They want teachers to use methods and materials proven to work, and they are wary of those who encourage schools to use practices based on theory or belief alone. Federal laws, such as the Reading Excellence Act and the Reading First provisions of the Elementary and Secondary Education Act, call for the application of research to the teaching of reading, as do many state laws.

There are several approaches to reading research, so which kinds of studies should be used as the basis of educational policy? More important than anything else, a study should be designed to answer the kind of question being asked. Most policy questions in instruction ask what works and those sorts of questions are best answered by experiments because experiments require teachers to adopt a method or practice to see whether this leads to subsequent learning advantages for children. Other research approaches may be valuable, but they can't answer these kinds of questions. These other studies either describe existing practice (so we can't be sure that other teachers could adopt these practices successfully) or they provide only indirect evidence (such as the fact that good readers might have some skill) to determine what we should teach.

The more children are to be affected by a policy, the more rigorous should be the standard of evidence. Experiments in which teachers try out the method under question are essential determiners of what works in reading. Policies and practices based on such evidence are more likely to lead to learning than those based upon less substantial proof.

Group Inquiry Activity   Based on what you've read in this chapter so far:

1. If you could ask Tim Shanahan only one question, what would it be?
2. If you could ask Jim Cunningham only one question, what would it be?

We encourage you to read both the Cunningham article and the NRP Report. Discuss your thoughts with other class members. Remember, there's a danger in forming opinions about such important issues without reading the original sources. We hope you will keep this advice in mind throughout your career as a responsible literacy professional.

Issues Warranting Increased Attention

Another area of literacy instruction that warrants increased attention in the next decade is how the home environment and early pre-K years impact a child's subsequent literacy development. Throughout the country, educators and policymakers are considering making preschool available for all children at little or no cost. Certainly, there is agreement in the field of reading that children who come from literate homes where hundreds or even thousands of stories have been read aloud to them generally have an easier time learning to read. As Elfrieda Hiebert (2001) says, "These are the children who don't have to depend on the school to teach them to read."

For these youngsters, many of whom have developed phonemic awareness and other emergent literacy skills prior to coming to school, the amount of explicit instruction needed for learning how to read may be considerably less than that needed for children who come from what many educators describe as *less-enriched* environments. But did you notice that *less-enriched* is in italics in the preceding sentence? We gave the phrase emphasis because we believe that what constitutes *enrichment* differs widely according to how children's experiences are situated. When we look within home cultures we find a variety of rich and complex literacies, many of which are not valued in school. That is, within a sociocultural perspective, context is (nearly) everything and we believe educators are only beginning to realize the impact of context and its power to drive effective literacy acquisition.

Among the forward-looking initiatives is the recent interest in adolescent and secondary school literacy programs and promising new programs of literacy intervention for these older students. Moreover, many literacy programs are striving to become more culturally responsive, recognizing and honoring the various literacies of the community. Given the changing demographics and increasingly diverse student populations, these philosophical shifts are imperative.

A recent emphasis on critical literacy has been spurred by the amount of information flooding into our homes and schools via the Internet. Educators are investigating ways to help students navigate complex media messages and investigate the origins, motives, values, and stances of those who produced the incoming messages (Schmidt & Pailliotet, 2001). Understanding the dynamics of how we link various forms of text with one another, with our experience, and with events in our world has captured the interest of literacy researchers in the last decade. Doug Hartman (1995) describes this interactive phenomenon as *intertextuality*, a merging of theories related to schema (Bartlett, 1932) and sociolinguistics (Vygotsky, 1978). Also of interest are aspects of Discourse Theory, such as students' use of language in rule-governed ways that vary widely according to context (Gee, 2001); Activity Theory (Bean, 2001) in which researchers are investigating how tools mediate internal and external literacy events, and Reader Response (Lewis, 2001) emphasizing the dynamic, highly personal interrelationship of reader and text.

The questions we are asking have never been more complex or difficult to investigate. These questions challenge all of us to think about literacy in new and expanded ways.

Author Connection: MaryEllen   I once had a student, Danny, who at thirteen read and wrote at about the first grade level. When I talked to him about his schooling experiences, I discovered that he had grown up as a "carny kid." With some further prodding, I learned that Danny's father worked for a traveling carnival, setting up and taking down the carnival rides, games, and booths that went to towns during the spring, summer, and fall months. His dad also "barked" for one of the carnival games; he was the "barker" who stood outside the booths and called people into them to play the various games. Danny was as worldly-wise as any kid I'd ever met. He'd traveled to small towns in nearly every state, and had met all types of "city people," as well as hobos and other transient carnival workers. He had never known his birth mother, but had dozens of surrogate mothers over the years. During his life, he had never lived in a house, only motels, and he had never attended the same school for more than four months (November—February). He had no school transcripts because they never caught up with him before he and his dad moved on.

Group Inquiry Activity   What does it mean for children's experiences to be *enriching*? In education, we usually describe "enriching preschool experiences" as those that prepare children "to do school." Yet, it's hard to argue that Danny's experiences in the carnival had not been enriching. With a small group, brainstorm all the "literacy experiences" Danny undoubtedly had as a child growing up within the context of a traveling carnival.

Now, look at each item on your list.

1. What, if any, school-related tasks would these literacy experiences prepare Danny for?
2. As teachers and reading specialists, how can we use whatever experiences children bring to the classroom to help them develop literacy?
3. And, while we're at it, what types of "literacy" are we trying to develop?

In subsequent chapters, you will see that students come from a variety of enriching environments; however, not all prepare them to be successful in school. Reading specialists have an obligation to provide teachers with an understanding of how these varied contexts influence and support literacy development. We must situate literacy instruction within a sociocultural perspective, one that acknowledges and celebrates the unique backgrounds from which we all come.

In the next section, we look at how reading specialists have fulfilled their roles over the years. We also discuss how reading specialists are increasingly viewed as the stewards of the literacy vision in elementary and secondary schools.

THE EVOLUTION OF THE READING SPECIALIST

In a textbook on the role of the administrator in reading programs, Carlson (1972) reported that, in 1969, the "U.S. Commissioner of Education, James E. Allen, Jr., felt duty-bound to proclaim that the right to read was 'as fundamental as the right to life, liberty, and the pursuit of happiness.' Commissioner Allen warned educators not to get bogged down in debate over 'methods of teaching reading, but to organize all possible resources toward eliminating reading deficiencies which exist among more than a quarter of our population . . .'" (p. 7).

Does this sound familiar? As you discovered in the previous sections, American educators have searched for over 200 years for approaches that will enable everyone to become readers. In the next section, we discuss how the role of the reading specialist evolved in the United States during the last half of the twentieth century.

The Reading Specialist: 1960–1990

The previous statements from Commissioner Allen in 1969 were made at the end of a decade in which the educational system of the United States underwent incredible change. From the launching of Russia's Sputnik to the landing of Americans on the moon, "more schools were built, more children educated, more teachers trained, more money was invested, and more innovations were attempted than in all of the previous decades of American education put together" (Carlson, 1972, p. 8). Federally funded Research and Development Centers and Regional Educational Laboratories brought together top academicians to coordinate programs of research, development, and dissemination related to reading and teacher preparation, as well as other areas. Title I programs for improving reading, Title II for improving library resources, and Title III of the Elementary and Secondary Education Act (ESEA) for fostering relationships between educational and community organizations, all had some degree of impact on the teaching of reading. Still, there were children who were not becoming proficient readers, and at the end of the 1960s, the Commissioner for Education sounded an alarm.

With the infusion of funds from Title I and other sources, such as the Miller-Unrah legislation in California, specially selected and sometimes specially trained reading teachers began to take on more responsibility for working with youngsters with reading problems, or, as they were often labeled at this time, "disabled," "retarded," or "handicapped" readers. Classroom teachers were assigned school and district responsibilities for reading and they had a variety of titles, such as reading specialist, reading resource teacher, reading consultant, reading supervisor, or reading coordinator.

Teachers holding these positions in the 1960s and 1970s had a variety of specific roles, including those identified by Robinson and Rauch (1965, p. 1): Resource person, adviser, inservice leader, investigator, diagnostician, instructor, and evaluator. Throughout the 1970s reading specialist positions funded by Title I or other state initiatives were common in most states. In some cases, a reading specialist had responsibilities for only one elementary or secondary school, while some specialists "traveled" from school to school. The primary focus of many reading specialists was on students, providing reading diagnosis and remediation in small groups in a pull-out program. This model was sometimes referred to as "the closet clinician model" because reading specialists provided instruction in all kinds of rooms, from classrooms to custodial closets. Wherever there was a place to teach, the reading specialist taught.

In the 1980s, changes in Title I required that reading specialists assume a variety of roles, but primarily they provided remedial instruction for students in pull-out programs. Five distinct roles for the reading specialist were listed in 1986 by the International Reading Association (IRA): diagnostic/remedial specialist; developmental reading/study skills specialist; reading consultant/reading resource teacher; reading coordinator/supervisor; and reading professor. However, by 1992, IRA identified only three primary responsibilities: teacher or clinician; consultant/coordinator; and teacher educator/researcher (Wepner & Seminoff, 1995).

Toward the end of the 1980s and into the 1990s, especially in states where there was economic recession, reading specialist positions were "down-sized" or completely eliminated. Students needing specialized assistance in reading were increasingly referred for special education services. Students who did not qualify for special education were left without extra assistance; those who were accepted were often taught by special educators with little advanced preparation in reading.

The Reading Specialist: 1990–2000

In 1995, the International Reading Association disseminated an issue paper titled *Who Is Teaching Our Children? Reading Instruction in the Information Age*. In this paper, IRA made a number of important recommendations, including the following (Quatroche, Bean, & Hamilton, 1998, p. 3):

- School boards should evaluate whether or not they have professionals with the strongest background in teaching reading; and
- Reading specialists need to be a part of every classroom where there are students needing help to learn to read.

However, Dick Allington and Shawn Walmsley (1995) suggested this was hardly the case. They reported that in the 1990s a large number of Title I programs throughout the country were using paraprofessional instructional assistants ("teachers' aides"), rather than certified reading teachers or specialists, to provide reading instruction to educationally disadvantaged students. This was also confirmed by a study commissioned by the International Reading Association (IRA; Long, 1995).

In 1996, the Executive Board of the IRA appointed a Commission on the Role of the Reading Specialist to investigate the roles, responsibilities, and working conditions of reading teachers identified as Title I Reading Teacher, reading specialist, and reading supervisor/coordinator (Quatroche, Bean, & Hamilton, 1998, p. 4). The Commission found, not surprisingly, that reading specialists' roles appear to depend on context: with whom the specialist works (classroom teachers with their own set of expectations) and the setting and location of their work (school/district; pull-out/in class).

The Commission also found there is sparse research on whether there is a direct link between the work of reading specialists and a school's reading achievement. A number of studies examined successful literacy intervention and developmental reading programs, and conclude that "programs with the strongest backgrounds in the teaching of reading have the highest rates. Therefore, it appears critical that professionals with extensive knowledge of reading instruction be part of every classroom where there are students who need help learning to read" (Quatroche, Bean, and Hamilton, 1998, p. 18).

In an extensive survey of reading specialists, the IRA Commission found that today's reading specialists' primary roles include instruction (in-class, pull-out, and supporting classroom testing); serving as a resource (providing materials, ideas, and support to teachers, special educators, and other allied professionals); and administration (activities such as documenting and monitoring performance of students and completing reports) (Bean, Cassidy, Grumet, Shelton, & Wallis, 2002, p. 736). A majority of the responding reading specialists indicated that they believe they have a responsibility not only for struggling readers, but also for school-wide literacy improvement for all students. They also reported that recent changes in their jobs included an increasing amount of paperwork, their serving as a resource to teachers, more planning with teachers, and providing more in-class instruction for students (p. 741).

The Reading Specialist: Into the New Millennium

During the late 1990s, as a result of flat and in some states decreased reading scores on the National Assessment of Educational Progress (NAEP), legislators came to realize what educators had suspected for some time: Many children and adolescents in the United States were not becoming proficient readers, those who could deal with the increasingly complex reading demands of a new century. As the new decade and century begin, reading specialists (now often called reading/language arts specialists or literacy specialists) are in increasing demand due in part to the No Child Left Behind legislation of 2002, and the Reading First Initiative. In several parts of the country university graduate programs in reading are now experiencing unprecedented growth, and graduates from these programs are finding an expanding job market. The IRA Standards for the Preparation of Reading Specialists (both IRA/NCATE) as well as most state standards for graduate programs in reading require that candidates have advanced study in the reading process, theory and research, assessment and diagnosis, intervention, curriculum, and instruction. Candidates must also have advanced study in the roles and responsibilities of the reading specialist, including coaching, mentoring, and serving as a resource; leadership; supervision; selection and evaluation of reading programs; and professional development. Also, increasingly, in addition to the previously cited responsibilities, often reading specialists are required to provide reading and language instruction for English language learners, as well as students receiving special education services.

Group Inquiry Activity   Think about the school in which you teach.

1. What do you see as the three most critical needs related to teaching reading/ language arts?
2. What could a reading specialist do to help alleviate these needs? Share your identified needs with a small group.
3. How many of the concerns are related or similar? Discuss what each of you has suggested that a reading specialist could do to help with these concerns. How could you get started?

REVISITING THE VIGNETTE

1. Reflect on Barbara Johnson's (the district reading specialist) dilemma that was described in the opening to this chapter. Are there any recommendations you would now modify based on what you learned in the chapter and through discussion with your peers?
2. Using what you have learned about the historical trends in reading instruction and the evolution of the roles of reading specialist, how could Barbara begin to bring some cohesiveness to her district's reading program? What steps should she take to begin this process?
3. How can she reconcile the differences between the methods promoted by the university and those used by classroom teachers?

POINTS TO REMEMBER

Since the inception of American schools, educators have debated the best approaches for teaching children to read, and teachers and children have used a wide variety of methods and materials for teaching reading. Early in the country's history, children of the elite were taught the alphabet and sound–symbol relationships, and they learned to read didactic texts. Later, analytic and synthetic phonics approaches were adopted, with ongoing debates as to the efficacy of each. Basal reading series were used in nearly every school in the country for many years, and teachers grouped students for instruction according to their abilities and reading levels. More holistic and integrated methods of teaching reading appeared in the 1980s and 1990s, though they had fallen into disfavor by the end of the twentieth century. Federally funded research and national panel recommendations that were controversial and critically reviewed urged more explicit teaching of phonemic awareness and phonics, as well as vocabulary and comprehension. There is now general agreement that reading is a complex process involving the integration and thoughtful application of a variety of skills and strategies within a variety of social, political, cultural, and educational contexts.

Reading specialists have been found in U.S. schools primarily during the last third of the twentieth century. Their responsibilities have varied over time, though most have revolved around assessing and teaching students with reading problems. At the beginning of the twenty-first century, the reading specialist's role has greatly expanded, and now it includes professional development, mentoring, implementing, monitoring and evaluating the effectiveness of school and district reading programs, supervision, curriculum design, and, of course, assessing and teaching students with reading problems.

PORTFOLIO PROJECTS

1. Interview a parent, grandparent, or other older person about how he or she learned to read. Ask about reading materials, instruction, or anything else that the person can remember about early literacy experiences. Share the responses during class.

2. Create a time line or other graphic organizer of the historical trends presented in this chapter. Relate them to current approaches and methods for teaching reading/language arts.

3. Create your own literacy history. Chronicle as many memories as you can about learning to read and write. Be sure to situate your experiences in pop culture and political/historical/social contexts. As you engage in this reflection, consider also your beliefs about students, teaching, and learning. What do you feel strongly about that's related to

teaching reading (Dillon, 2000)? How did your family and community beliefs about the definitions, uses, and the importance of literacy influence your development and beliefs? After you are finished, identify the communities and literacies present in your autobiography and compare them to those valued by schools. Write your literacy history or use another medium to convey your memories (such as create a picture book, poster, video, poem, etc.). Use the Literacy History Prompts in Appendix A (McLaughlin & Vogt, 1996) to jog your memories. Be sure to share your literacy history with others in your class; you'll be amazed at the power of this activity!

4. Personal Goal: Revisit the goal you set for yourself at the beginning of the chapter. Create a portfolio item that reflects what you have learned relative to your goal.

RECOMMENDED READINGS

Bean, R. M., Hamilton, R. L., and Quatroche, D. J. (2002). The role of the reading specialist: A review of research. *Reading Teacher, 55*(3), 282–294. This comprehensive review of the literature on the role of the reading specialist should be a must-read for all current and soon-to-be reading specialists. It further delineates the findings alluded to in this chapter.

Cunningham, J. W. (2001). The National Reading Panel report. *Reading Research Quarterly, 36*(3), 326–335. This is a thoughtful, comprehensive, and critical review of the Report of the National Reading Panel. Don't read the Panel report without also reading this insightful critique.

Hiebert, E. H., Pearson, P. D., Taylor, B. M., Richardson, V., & Paris, S. G.(1998). *Every child a reader.*

Ann Arbor, MI: Center for the Improvement of Early Reading Achievement (CIERA). The CIERA Web site has a number of interesting and helpful articles and references: www.CIERA.org.

Ruddell, M. R. (2001). *Teaching content reading and writing* (3rd ed.). New York: John Wiley & Sons. Chapter 1 presents a comprehensive historical overview of reading instruction in the United States.

Snow, C. E., Burns, M. S., & Griffin, P. G. (Eds.). (1998). *Preventing reading difficulties in young children.* Washington, DC: National Academy Press. This text explicates a number of research studies conducted during the 1990s. Explicit recommendations for reading and language arts instruction are included.

National Reading Panel. (2000). *Teaching children to read: An evidence-based assessment of the scientific research literature on reading and its implications for reading instruction.* Washington, DC: National Institute of Child Health and Human Development (NICHD). The Executive Summary of this report is brief and clearly written. The entire, lengthy text is available on the Web site for the National Reading Panel. Again, specific recommendations for instruction are included. Note that what constitutes "scientific research literature" as described in this report has been a controversial issue among reading scholars. This document is available at no cost at: http://www.nichd.nih.gov/publications/pubstitle.cfm.

NOTES

1. Phonics: A way of teaching reading and spelling that stresses symbol–sound relationships, used especially in beginning instruction (Harris & Hodges, 1995, p. 186).
2. Behaviorism: The view that psychological study should be limited to observable behavior (Harris & Hodges, 1995, p. 19).
3. Language Master: A recording machine that included cards with magnetic strips. Words and phrases were recorded on the cards. Students would slide the cards across the machine, say the words, and hear the recorded words.
4. Tachistoscope: Any mechanical device for the controlled and usually very brief exposure of visual materials, such as pictures, letters, numbers, words, phrases, and sentences (Harris & Hodges, 1995, p. 250).
5. Basal Reading Programs: A collection of student texts and workbooks, teacher's manuals, and supplementary materials for developmental reading and sometimes writing instruction, used chiefly in the elementary and middle school grades (Harris & Hodges, p. 18). The majority of instructional materials were leveled for 3 reading groups: below grade level, at grade level, and above grade level, and nearly all instruction took place within these three "ability" groups.

CHAPTER TWO

ESTABLISHING A LITERACY TEAM AND DEVELOPING A VISION STATEMENT

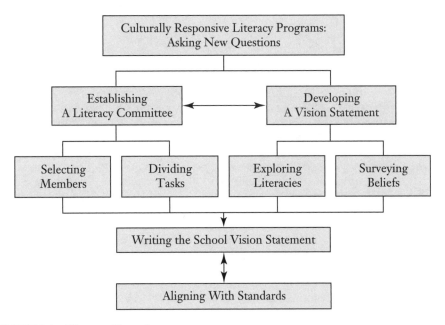

FIGURE 2.1 Chapter Overview

LEARNING GOALS

After reading, discussing, and engaging in activities related to this chapter, you will be able to:

1. develop a context-driven written vision statement that is consistent with district, state, and IRA/NCTE Reading/Language Arts Standards;

2. establish a collaborative literacy team and define the role of the team within the decision-making structures of the school and community;

3. **Personal Learning Goal:** In a three-minute brainstorming session, share what you know about developing a vision statement and establishing a literacy team. Write a goal or a question that reflects something you want to learn as we explore these topics. Share this with others in your group.

Vignette

Mark has been a fourth-grade teacher for seven years at a mid-sized (600 students), midwestern suburban elementary school. Recently, he completed a master's degree in reading, was hired as a reading specialist, and told by the principal that he was expected to "improve the reading program." Mark is a highly respected professional with excellent people skills.

Although the neighborhood was formerly one of economic privilege, it is now almost entirely comprised of white middle-class English-speaking families. Fewer than twenty African American students attend the school. However, within the last five years, a small but growing number of Hmong families have moved into an area bordering the city and the suburb. Approximately fifteen students in the elementary school speak Hmong as the primary language of their home. The largest reformed synagogue in the metropolitan area is two blocks from the school and approximately one out of five students are from homes in which Judaism is practiced to varying degrees. Most of these students attend Hebrew classes and participate in activities at the Jewish Community Center. The school schedules inservice and professional development for teachers on the High Holy Days.

Of the forty-four teachers at Cedar Park Elementary, Mark is one of two African American males. The son of a bus driver and a third-grade teacher, Mark was raised in a predominantly African American middle-class urban neighborhood adjacent to this suburb, and experienced the undercurrents of distrust and prejudice between the adjoining Jewish and African American communities as he was growing up.

District test scores are moderately above both state and national averages. Officially, the school has always used a commercial reading series, but, because scores are relatively high, many teachers just close the door and "do their own thing." Recently, the state has developed model academic standards for Reading/Language Arts. The State Department of Instruction has required each district to develop a written curriculum within the next two years and to specify the classroom practices that align with each standard. The principal has assigned Mark the job of writing and aligning curriculum and standards. These must reflect what students should know and be able to do, how they will demonstrate this knowledge and ability, and how well they must perform. The standards will also shape the way teachers must teach.

Thinking Point   Mark is at a loss as to where to begin "to improve the reading program." What are the first three things you suggest that Mark should do?

Expanding the Vignette: Exploring the Tensions

Mark distributes copies of the state standards for reading/language arts to all the teachers. The document is over forty pages long and contains lists of content proficiencies students should acquire by the end of fourth, eighth, and twelfth grades. Rather than help-

ing, the document has increased anxiety lev- *others. Until now that has been easy to do*
els. The fourth-grade teachers are particu- *because teachers have been able to imple-*
larly anxious because they notice gaps in the *ment their own visions. Mark is concerned*
knowledge of students depending on what *that the reading wars that have persisted*
was taught in previous grades and how it *for decades on a national level will now be*
was taught. Fortunately, these are faculty *fought in his school. He is definitely feeling*
members who seem to value the ideas of *overwhelmed.*

Thinking Points

1. What additional tensions and questions have you identified in the vignette?
2. What are some short-term suggestions you would give Mark?
3. What long-term measures should Mark consider?

Keep your answers to these questions in mind as you read. We will revisit the vignette at the end of this chapter.

CULTURALLY RESPONSIVE LITERACY PROGRAMS: ASKING NEW QUESTIONS

Mark's position as reading specialist forces him to examine the literacy program in his school in a new way, that is, systemically. Increased pressure from federal, state, and local governments related to standards and testing require districts to respond to demands for accountability. Because the overall economic, social, and cultural contexts of Mark's community reflect relative comfort, and because educational resources are adequate and test scores remain stable, little attention has been focused on establishing a cohesive, systematic schoolwide literacy program. Indeed, few teachers know how reading is being taught in the classroom next door, nor do they know much about their colleagues' beliefs about reading/language arts instruction.

We believe in the power of the past to inform the future. Therefore, in the previous chapter we provided a review of the evolution of the reading specialist. This is consistent with our sociocultural perspective because it seeks to situate the reading specialist in time and culture. In Chapter 2, we guide the reading specialist in creating a literacy team whose mission is improving the school's literacy program. Included are possible roles and responsibilities of the team and its members with emphasis on team building, collaborative problem solving, agency, and context. Two literacy cases are used to mediate understandings of the notions of "communities" and "literacies." The chapter concludes with a step-by-step, collaborative framework to identify core beliefs and develop a written vision statement.

Author Connection: Brenda   In my many years as an educator, I cannot count the number of times I heard a teacher say, "'I close my door and I do my own thing." I probably said it myself, especially when I began my career as a first-grade teacher in an urban Milwaukee school at the height of the Civil Rights movement. Of course, I was searching for that one right way to teach reading and I was pretty certain I was zeroing in on it. Do I still believe teachers should possess a high degree of agency over the ways they conduct literacy activities in their classrooms? Of course, I do; MaryEllen and I both do. But we also believe there are some fundamental understandings that must support the decisions teachers make. Although the social and cultural context of Mark's school setting is very different from that in which I first taught, the fundamental questions necessary to develop dynamic, effective, and socially responsive literacy programs are the same. What is literacy? What do we know about effective literacy instruction? What are the beliefs and cultural forces that shape the ways in which literacy is defined and used in and out of school within the various literacy "communities"? Who has agency in the decision-making processes?

It may seem to Mark that finding answers to these questions is a daunting task, and, indeed, it will require a substantial amount of work, especially if he reverts to traditional hierarchical leadership models. Mark will need to find new ways to think about these questions if he is to realize the hopes he has for success in his new role as reading specialist. In this chapter we will explore ways to define shared vision, the kind that supports the agency of teachers, parents, administrators, and students.

ESTABLISHING THE LITERACY TEAM

Why We Need a Literacy Team

Teamwork. It is evident in the heroic deeds of Red Cross volunteers working in teams to assist the victims of disasters. It is also evident in more humble feats, such as in the preparation of the fast-food cheeseburger, the result of a sophisticated ballet of teamwork. Yet, Gene Maeroff (1993), senior fellow at the Carnegie Institute for the Advancement of Teaching, points out that teamwork, for almost any purpose, is foreign to most teachers. Often the degree to which teachers are deemed successful is measured by how adept they are at working alone. In spite of years of discussion about cooperative learning, in which students are placed in groups and taught how to collaborate in their learning, Maeroff found that there is no corresponding move to encourage such collaboration among educators. They are expected to be neither leaders nor followers of other teachers. However, it is probably safe to assume that most people recognize the power of teamwork to solve both long- and short-term problems and bring about change. Richard Wellins and his colleagues found that teamwork resulted in increased knowledge and expertise, ownership, and empowerment for participants (Wellins, Byham, & Wilson, 1991). In Figure 2.2, we applied these assumptions to school literacy teams.

The Process of Forming a Literacy Team

Many of the books written about supervision and administration provide a wealth of information and advice about effective literacy team strategies (Radencich, 1995; Radencich, Beers, Schumm, 1993; Wepner, Feeley, & Strickland, 1995). However, little

---

Literacy teams capitalize on the following strengths of teachers:

Knowledge and Expertise
Teachers are closest to their work. They are experts with a great deal of individual and collective knowledge and experience in the teaching of literacy. They know best how to enhance and improve their jobs.

Ownership
Most teachers want to feel that they "own" their jobs. They consider themselves professionals, capable of making meaningful contributions to the literacy goals of their school and community.

Empowerment
The Literacy Team provides possibilities for empowerment not available to individual teachers. Teams are given authority for important decisions about the fundamental nature and direction of the literacy program. Traditionally, such authority has been the sole province of administrators.

FIGURE 2.2   The Value of Literacy Teams: Underlying Assumptions

guidance is given about whom to include as members of the literacy team. At first, this may appear to be an oversight. A more practical explanation is that, by necessity, the composition of a school or district literacy team is unique to its school and community context. Thus, universal directives are likely to be of little help. Perhaps a better approach is to examine the possible roles, personalities, and power positions of stakeholders as you consider team composition.

Possible Members of the Literacy Team

A school's literacy team is made up of a variety of stakeholders, often with seven to fifteen members (Patty, Maschoff, & Ransom, 1996). Usually, a team has representatives from several groups including students; administrators; reading specialists; teachers; other support personnel, such as psychologists, media specialists, and Title I teachers; parents; and community members.

Issues Surrounding Effective Literacy Team Building

Building a literacy team appears to be a relatively straightforward process: Assemble a dozen key participants, including the reading specialist and administrator; meet for a week in summer to define goals and responsibilities and formulate questions; plan the needs assessment process; and discuss the steps in creating and assessing a plan of action. Why then do we see so many team efforts fail to reach their goals? Gene Maeroff (1993) sees some elements present in effective teams that are missing in the usual school teams and committees. One is that an effective team understands how to *be* a team. What counts is that the team is honed into a unit that sees itself as a force for change.

> Driven by a common vision that has been fashioned through consensus, members of the team are to carry out their work in visible ways that implicitly invite colleagues to embrace the team's mission. The team is made up of surrogates for the entire faculty and community who learn an approach that they can impart to others (p. 514).

In order for the literacy team to begin its work, there are a number of important questions that need to be to asked and discussed with school and/or district leaders and administrators.

What Is the Administrative Support for the Mission of the Literacy Team?

- Will teachers have adequate release time for planning and implementation?
- If after-school or weekend meetings are scheduled, how will participants be compensated?
- Does the administration support the authority of the team to make the plans, decisions and solutions?
- Is there a possibility that services such as child care and transportation will be provided, if necessary, so that community members/parents can be included in collaborative activities?
- Or might the school hold meetings at times when community members/parents can attend, such as late in the day or even on a Saturday?

Are There Provisions for Training Teachers in Effective Collaboration?

- Is the collaborative model culturally responsive and consistent with discourse models of the school and of the various communities?
- What can be done to help facilitate individuals in the process?

What Measures Will Be Taken to Include All Voices?

- What is the power structure of the school and community?
- How can these powerful and influential agents be supported in adapting to a collaborative model of decision making?
- What can be done to help facilitate input by non-team members?
- Will meetings be open and welcoming to all interested individuals?
- Will each team member act as a liaison to a specific group?
- How will a core team of approximately six to twelve members be representative of the cross-section of stakeholders?
- Is there a system to replace members in staggered two- or three-year terms to ensure continuity?

How Will the Group Anticipate Problems and Adjust the Process?

- What are possible barriers related to people, resources, scheduling, attitudes, and training?

- For each, is a proactive plan in place?
- How will the schoolwide literacy plan be assessed, adjusted, and modified using a formative model for short- and long-term goals?

How Will the Team Disseminate Information on Programs, Assessments, Goals, and Outcomes to the Various Communities In and Out of the School?

- How will the team report its activities?
- What public relations tasks are important to include?
- How will assessments be shared?
- What are the expectations for interaction with the school board?

Undoubtedly, as you start this process, you and your team members will think of many more questions that need to be asked. However, by dealing with some of these up-front, the literacy team can avoid a number of roadblocks normally encountered in school literacy initiatives.

LITERACIES AND COMMUNITIES: ASKING NEW QUESTIONS

What are Literacy Communities?

In a complex social system such as a school or district, there are many subsystems, or communities. Researchers have framed the concept of community in a number of ways. Among them are *community* as "neighborhood" (Delgato-Gaitan, 1996), as "culture" or "ethnicity" (Cairney & Ruge, 1998), as "associations" (Saleebey, 1997), or as "circles of kinship or friendship" (Moll & Gonzales, 1994). In her definition of *community*, Elizabeth Moje (2000) adds circles of "position and power" to those of "kinship or friendship." Jim Gee (2001a, 2001b) refers to "affinity groups." Individuals may belong to a number of these communities, many of which overlap.

We have purposely defined the term *community* as loosely as possible so educators can explore the concept in multiple and perhaps even novel ways. Within these communities, language and literacy may be used, valued, and defined in unique or highly specific ways. Some are more obvious than others, such as signs and billboards written in languages other than English. Some stretch our notions of traditional forms of literacy. These might include graffiti, on-line 'zines, artwork, crafts, music, MTV, soap operas, cartoons, and logos on clothing. Others may involve values and the pragmatics of language, such as the way adults are addressed by children, the use of nonverbal signs and symbols to signify greeting, the way language is used in rites and ceremonies, or the emphasis on oral language over written language. Given the varied and complex ways in which humans construct meaning in social contexts, educators are moving beyond traditional text-based definitions of literacy to acknowledge that there are multiple literacies and multiple texts (Moje, Young, Readence, & Moore, 2000). The challenge is to find ways to bring these multiple literacies and texts into the service of school and community goals.

Which Literacies Do We Privilege? Two Case Studies

To illustrate the concepts of communities and literacies, consider these two cases (see Figure 2.3).

Case 1: Eric Torgerson

Eric Torgerson was raised in a small midwestern community with a strong Protestant Scandinavian heritage. Although a few of the older residents spoke a bit of Swedish or Norwegian, English was almost exclusively the language of the home and community. After attending the nearby Lutheran college, Eric chose teaching as his life's work. He has taught fifth grade for twenty-two years and has a master's degree in Elementary Education. His wife, Jan, is a nurse and their twin sons attend the local high school. Eric identifies with the community of teachers who are politically conservative, and he is on the bargaining committee for the local teachers' union. It is safe to say that many would characterize him as serious and hardworking. Eric's father was a gifted and respected secondary mathematics and physics teacher. His parents were strict, even by the standards of the community, and the children were not allowed to venture far from home. Music was central to the culture of the Torgerson home. All of Eric's siblings received musical training from their mother, a talented pianist, and two of the seven children became professional musicians with symphony orchestras. Like his siblings, Eric can play a variety of instruments: violin, piano, tuba, and recorder. Holidays often featured performances by the family orchestra. Education was also highly valued in Eric's home. The children were surrounded by print, including newspapers, magazines, and shelves of nonfiction and fiction, many of them part of the traditional Western literary "canon." Lively family debates about politics, religion, and philosophy were standard at dinnertime. Eric and his siblings were expected to know the issues of the day, and even the younger children were encouraged to

voice reasoned opinions. Eric has continued to engage in the activities he loved as a child. He plays the organ at church and meets weekly to jam with three other local jazz musicians. He has a strong commitment to civic duty and has served on the boards of the town library and historical society. His interest in the history of the area, particularly that of the St. Croix River around 1900, is reflected in the research and writing he continues to do. Eric remains an avid reader, devouring books about philosophy and politics. Eric's wife and sons share his love of music. The Torgerson traditions live on as a new generation of visitors are treated to informal concerts by the family quartet.

Case 2: Carmen Coballes-Vega

When she was six, Carmen Coballes-Vega moved with her family from rural Arecibo, Puerto Rico to the Lower East Side of Manhattan. Most of the adults there spoke Spanish or Italian, and their children were able to speak at least some English as well. Carmen's father worked as a courier for the New York Stock Exchange and her mother cared for children in their apartment. Carmen was the first member of her family to learn English. A neighbor showed her how to write her "full name" and helped her obtain a library card. Soon curiosity led her from the small nearby library to the medieval fortress on Fifty-Third Street. To get there, Carmen had to negotiate the subway system by herself. It was in this dusty old NYC library that Carmen Coballes became a lover of literacy, loading her arms with books and faithfully returning for more a week later. She describes a number of literacy experiences outside of those traditionally honored by the school: the beautiful ballads her father sang to her as he

---

FIGURE 2.3   Which Literacies Do We Privilege? Two Case Studies

strummed his guitar, the stories of her Puerto Rican family heritage and culture shared around the kitchen table, and the rhythms of language echoing from the porches and balconies at night. Carmen often served as translator for several generations of her family, carefully writing b-e-a-n-s on the shopping list as her grandmother said, "habichuelas," translating recipes into Spanish as her mother cooked, or helping much older siblings learn to read English. She was often asked to accompany elderly neighbors to the doctor where she learned the discourse of medicine, translating information about aches, pains, diabetes, and heart problems. It was Carmen who completed all of the forms needed by the family and acted as a liaison between her parents and the school. Carmen received scholarships to attend college and earned a Ph.D. in Education with a reading/linguistics emphasis. She is currently Dean of the College of Education at The University of Wisconsin-Oshkosh. She remains a lover of language, and recognizes the power associated with the ability to negotiate literacy tasks in the dominant culture. Her reading preferences lean strongly toward narrative and biography—books about people's lives. As an adult she continues to share her own stories not only with her children but also with colleagues, community organizations, inservice and professional groups, and, of course, with students in the College of Education.

Group Inquiry Activity   In groups of three or four:

1. List the literacies you can identify in Eric's home and community cultures.
2. List the literacies you can identify in Carmen's home and community cultures.
3. Put a check mark next to those that would be honored and included in school literacy activities.
4. Analyze the experiences of both and decide how these events relate to a social constructivist literacy perspective.
5. How would your group define *communities*?
6. How would your group define *literacies*?

As you compare the rich sociocultural contexts of *both* Carmen's and Eric's childhoods, think about whose literacies and culture are more highly honored in today's schools. What are the implications for the students and for the school? In many ways Eric's "communities" reflect the attitudes of the dominant midwestern culture with regard to the value and purposes of literacy. However, Kathy Au and Taffy Raphael (2000) would argue that many of Carmen's experiences are highly literate and accomplished, and that their applications may be even more advanced than some of those required in school. It is obvious that sociocultural dimensions within both families have had a profound effect on the identities of these individuals. Both share values with others in their various "communities." As a fifth-grade teacher, Eric's beliefs and values will be reflected in how he teaches and how he interacts with the culture of the school. Carmen's will be reflected in how she interacts with the culture of the university. Each parent, student, administrator, and teacher embodies the same sociocultural complexity. From a social constructivist perspective, literacy practices are imbedded in and defined by particular social contexts, and shaped by cultural values and local ideologies (Street, 1996). At the same time, these practices and beliefs define the culture of the school and the culture of the community. Thus, any of our initial questions about literacy can only be answered relative to the context of the communities in which they occur.

DEVELOPING A WRITTEN VISION STATEMENT

If you have ever been to a shopping mall you can relate to standing in front of one of those kiosks, squinting at the little red and green and blue boxes (the various shops and stores) and emitting a sigh of relief when at last your eyes land on the "YOU ARE HERE" arrow. A vision statement illuminates a path or direction for a district or school to follow. Our first task in creating a vision statement is much like that of the disoriented mall shopper. We need to find out *where we are* relative to literacy and literacy instruction, so that we can figure out *where we want to go* and *how best to get there*. The vision statement embodies a mission or vision inspired by belief, theory, and research; it has practical implications for transforming the literacy curriculum; and it includes long-term commitment to collaborative planning and problem solving. From the social constructivist perspective, educators will not only want to determine *where* they are, but also *who* they are.

The vision statement has four important purposes:

1. *It identifies beliefs and examines how they define literacy and literacy practice in various contexts.* Defining literacy has both political and moral implications. The way we define and teach often determines whom we invite into the literacy "club."

2. *It clarifies a general direction for change over time.* "If we're doing X now, but our goal is to do Y in two years, we need to do Z." The result of this kind of formative thinking is that it has the potential to simplify hundreds or even thousands of smaller decisions (Kotter, 1996).

3. *It motivates people to reorient their actions toward achieving the goal.* Even if they are forced out of their comfort zones, individuals guided by a vision statement may acknowledge that change is necessary and yield to the process, especially with support from colleagues. Many adults will admit that they were "dragged" into the computer age because their jobs required literacy in technology. Perhaps part of their resistance stemmed from the fear of moving out of their comfort zones rather than general resistance to new ideas.

4. *It coordinates the actions of different people in egalitarian ways.* A clear vision statement reduces confusion by helping people define and situate their actions. It fosters shared responsibility.

Often, vision statements are created at the district level. However, there are many situations in which it is appropriate to develop a vision statement for a single school. In districts where schools are afforded a high degree of autonomy or where schools are managed on site, a school-level vision statement is more suitable. This is also the case for charter schools, private schools, and magnet schools in large districts.

Whether a vision statement is designed for a school or a district, the process is much the same. As you read the steps, you may substitute *school* for *district* or vice versa to fit your context. In either case, we suggest you collect the data and complete the group tasks at the school level using the framework below. If the vision statement is developed at the district level, the reading specialist and the literacy team can collect information, pool the data, and coordinate the tasks in individual schools.

How Beliefs Shape Instructional Decisions

Why is it important for teachers to examine their individual and collective beliefs? Beliefs are powerful. Not only do individuals tend to hold onto beliefs, there is evidence that they also embrace their misconceptions with the same tenacity. Research on misconceptions in science and physics demonstrates that, even when presented with powerful text evidence to the contrary, students cling to their misconceptions (Alvermann, Smith, and Readence, 1995; Hynd, Qian, Ridgeway, & Pickle, 1991).

It is precisely this powerful connection between beliefs and practices that impels us to identify beliefs at the beginning of any investigation of school programs. With regard to literacy practice, a teacher's beliefs about how literacy is defined have an impact on all classroom literacy events. As Peter Mosenthal points out, we cannot answer the question, "What is reading?" without addressing the concomitant question, "What should the definition of *reading* be?" He cautions that "as soon as we introduce the notion of *should be* into the equation of defining *reading*, we move beyond a scientific approach to an agenda-setting and agenda-implementing approach for deciding reading's fate and future" (Cunningham, Many, Carver, Gunderson, & Mosenthal, 2000, p. 69). As teachers decide which beliefs to embrace, they also decide which to dismiss. Patricia Hinchey (2001) reminds educators that beliefs that are excluded have a powerful defining effect on literacy practice and on the culture of the school. She maintains that in addition to, "*What* is not there?" we should also ask, "*Who* is not there?" Whose voices and perspectives are missing? Shared vision requires agency of all teachers, even those who rarely share their opinions. Therefore, it is important to design collaborative inquiry in ways that not only honor, but also foster, multiple perspectives.

The Role of Dissension in Shared Vision Models.   We believe shared vision is not a coercive process. It does not mean everyone agrees on everything. Rather, in true collaboration, divergent perspectives are honored in that they inform, influence, and shape the thinking of the group. Dissension is necessary to the process of change and it goes beyond the concept of majority rule. It is a subtle process of socially negotiated decision making, and is more than simply giving lip service to the idea of listening to other voices. Groups committed to shared vision truly recognize how important and valuable divergent ideas are to moving the group's thinking forward, because dissenters often ask the questions the group should be asking.

The Four Tasks in Developing a Vision Statement

The quintessential question in the process of developing a vision for a school or district is to consider how various individuals will answer the question, "What is literacy?" Most educators are now comfortable with the idea expressed by Allen Luke and Peter Freebody (1999) that there is "no single, definitive, truthful, scientific, universally effective, or culturally appropriate way of teaching or even defining literacy" (p. 1). That said there *are* ideas about literacy practices on which the vast majority of educators can agree. The task is to identify a set of shared beliefs about literacy and to transform school practice in the service of those beliefs within specific contexts. See Figure 2.4 for an outline of the task progression for developing a strong vision statement. Each of the four tasks involves different groupings of individuals. For example, in Task One teachers work in their grade-level or subject area groups to complete surveys identifying the ways in which literacy is defined, used, and valued in the school and the various literacy communities. The completed surveys activate prior knowledge and begin the dialogue that will be expanded during the all-faculty workshop in which teachers complete Task Two, exploring ways to create culturally responsive classrooms. Task Three involves informal grade or content area groups working to identify beliefs; and Task Four involves the Literacy Team, collaborating to synthesize the information and create a draft of the Vision Statement.

Task One: Surveys are completed by teachers before the first faculty workshop   Several weeks before meeting with the faculty, distribute the following questions to various groups of teachers (such as grade-level or content area teachers who meet in weekly planning sessions). Request that they collaborate to create a list of responses to each question and return them to the reading specialist one week before the meeting. Encourage group

---

Task One: *Surveys are completed by teachers before the first faculty workshop.* Identify the ways literacy is defined, valued, and used in the school and in the various communities that surround the school.

Task Two: *All-staff workshop, with teachers working in collaborative groups.* List ways the school can incorporate the literacies students use outside of school to create a more effective and culturally responsive school literacy program.

Task Three: *Collaborative groups meet informally to complete survey.* Teachers complete surveys in collaborative groups to identify beliefs about literacy and classroom literacy practice.

Task Four: *Literacy team works to synthesize and share drafts with teachers.* Synthesize the information from Steps One through Three to create a written vision statement that reflects the sociocultural context of the school and community.

FIGURE 2.4   Creating a Shared-Vision Statement

members to consider both their personal responses and their systemic responses, reflecting perceptions relative to the school:

- How does this school define what it means for our students to be literate? How is literacy used in the school?
- What are the kinds of materials, objects, assignments, and literate activities that define school reading, writing, and language?
- What are our goals for our students?

Collect these lists before the meeting. Organize and classify the responses and share them in print or on overheads with the large group as a catalyst for further discussion and discovery at the next whole-group meeting.

Task Two: All-staff workshop with teachers working in collaborative groups   Open the next whole-group meeting by displaying the response patterns from the collaborative sessions and providing opportunities for discussion and group revision. Share "The Four Tasks for Creating a Shared-Vision Statement" and announce that the teachers will be focusing on Tasks One and Two. Because the notion of examining sociocultural contexts of literacy is new to many educators, it is probably wise to explain the idea of communities, perhaps using the examples presented earlier in this chapter. Group mapping is a powerful way to represent the complex, overlapping relationships among the communities identified. Note that the first set of questions in Task Two engages teachers in reflecting on the sociocultural forces that shaped their beliefs about literacy. Only then are they ready to examine the forces that define literacy in multiple contexts. Our experiences with teachers in brainstorming sessions have taught us the value of setting a specific time limit on each segment of the session. In fact, we suggest you estimate how long you think it will take and allocate one or two minutes less. By limiting the time and by signaling that time is running out, you will accomplish three important goals: (1) maintaining task focus; (2) projecting a professional image that signals the importance of the process; and (3) maximizing progress.

The questions for Task Two are:

- As an educator, what experiences, influences, cultural contexts, and communities shaped and continue to shape your beliefs, values, and interactions with your students?
- What are the various literacy communities within the neighborhoods served by the school or district?
- What is the role of literacy within each community our group identified? How are reading, writing, and language used within the communities and what is being read and written?
- How would you define the literacy goals of these communities?
- What are the areas of congruence between the literacy community of the school and the various literacy communities served by the school?

- What are the areas in which the definitions, uses, materials, and goals with regard to literacy differ?

As a culminating activity, compare the ways teachers defined *literacy*, and the uses and goals of literacy within the school community to those of the various literacy communities that were identified. Ask someone to record ideas as participants engage in informal discussion.

At the conclusion of the meeting, collect the group lists, maps, and notes and announce the next step in the process: using the insights from this meeting to explore common beliefs and to create a shared-vision statement. You will find that the items you collected create a rich and varied tapestry of interwoven values, beliefs, and practices about literacy. Because of the ability of visual representations to facilitate the rapid processing of large amounts of information, you might find a graphic organizer or grid useful as a tool for organizing and sharing. When the grid is complete, we recommend distributing it to the faculty and staff so that it can be refined, distributed, and used as teachers identify shared beliefs.

Task Three: Collaborative groups meet informally to complete survey   By this stage in the process, teachers have knowledge and process bases from which to draw. Once again, teachers work collaboratively to identify beliefs. One way that is particularly generative is to start by soliciting reaction to a simple, but powerful, belief statement written at the top of a sheet of paper, such as, "We believe all children can learn to read." Copies of the sheet can be distributed to various groups of teachers who discuss the belief (and perhaps reject it) and create their own statements which reflect a shared vision. Task Three questions include:

- How do you react to the following belief statement?
- What are some statements on which the majority of teachers might agree?
- What are the beliefs on which your group agrees?

Because teachers have told us they find it helpful to see examples of vision statements from various school districts while they are brainstorming their lists, we have included two in Appendix B. Later, the literacy team can use the lists to create the written vision statement.

Task Four: Literacy team works to synthesize and share drafts with teachers   The literacy team meets to examine the "belief lists" created by the teachers. Each member of the literacy team reads several statements aloud without attempting to classify them. The purpose is to get a feel for the kinds of statements made. The next step is to reread the statements and collaborate to create broad categories in which to organize them. Some examples of categories might include beliefs about integration of language processes; beliefs about grouping, beliefs about approaches; beliefs about the role of phonics. Each member examines all responses in one category and the team arranges sets of beliefs in a hierarchy starting with those most frequently stated. According to the reading specialists in our graduate classes in Wisconsin and California, strong patterns emerge and the process is not as difficult as one might guess. The following questions can be used in the process:

- What are the major themes or patterns of beliefs in the lists?
- How can these be converted to a cohesive, written set of statements that are goal-oriented, serve as a vision for the direction of the literacy program, and can be translated into action for the school or district?
- How will this vision statement be shared in ways that will foster participation by all stakeholders in the refining of the draft?

The literacy team lists the most frequently occurring beliefs and creates a written vision statement. Usually, a literacy team will identify anywhere from four to twelve core beliefs, such as "We believe in a balanced approach to literacy instruction combining skill development and language-rich activities." The belief statements frame choices about the curriculum, classroom organization, language events, staff development, and the nature of the texts, activities, and objects used. For example, the teachers who wrote this statement are unlikely to use heavily prescribed, commercially prepared, skills-based materials. We developed a sample belief chart (see Figure 2.5) that could be used

---

Belief: We believe in a balanced approach to literacy instruction combining skill development and language-rich activities:

Rationale/Research Support:
Pressley, M. (1998). *Elementary reading instruction that works: Why balanced literacy instruction makes more sense than whole language or phonics and skills.* New York: Guillford. The book advocates a balanced literacy approach in which emphasis is placed on word-level skills in the service of the development of comprehension.

Gambrell, L. B., & Asbury, E. (1999). Best practices for a balanced early literacy program. In L. B. Gambrell, L. M. Morrow, S. B. Neuman, & M. Pressley (1999). *Best Practices in Literacy Instruction.* "What we observed was a very balanced approach to literacy development with strategies that utilized an integrated language arts approach. The children learned through explicit instruction and by collaborative problem-solving situations" (p. 66).

Au, K. H. (2000). A multicultural perspective on policies for improving literacy achievement: Equity and excellence. In M. L. Kamil, P. B. Mosenthal, P. D. Pearson, & R. Barr (Eds.), *Handbook of reading research, Vol. III* (pp. 835–851). Mahwah, NJ: Erlbaum. This research synthesis includes the recommendation to provide students with authentic literacy activities *and* instruction in specific skills.

Allington, R. L. (2001). *What really matters for struggling readers: Designing research-based programs.* New York: Longman. Describes the effects of differences in instructional opportunities for proficient and struggling readers and advocates a shift to emphasize more reading and language-rich instruction for struggling readers.

FIGURE 2.5 Sample Belief Chart: Rationale and Implications

by the literacy team to examine each core belief according to its research base and to illustrate its impact on programs, professionals, practices, and resources.

The final task is to incorporate the list of statements into several paragraphs, forming the school or district's vision statement. Because all the information has been assembled, the task is relatively simple. One approach is to work with two or three literacy team volunteers to create a draft. The draft is then revised by the literacy team before the vision statement is distributed to administrators and then to the faculty for approval and final suggestions. When all revisions are complete, the vision statement should be presented at an official school board meeting, if possible, and it could be printed in the school newsletter or, in smaller communities, in the local newspaper. The vision statement then serves as the basis for the literacy program. All decisions about literacy curriculum, goal-setting, methods, programs, and assessments are guided by this vision. Thus, it is more than a simple statement of beliefs. As with all visions, it looks beyond the present toward what we see ourselves becoming.

ALIGNING BELIEFS WITH STANDARDS

The standards movement had its roots in the 1980s. It was born of the union of two concurrent initiatives; school restructuring and expanded assessment practices (Luis, 1997). It sounded innocuous enough, after all; who could have possibly been *against* having standards for their students? How then, did the baby become the behemoth? Sheila Valencia and Karen Wixson (2001) remind us about the original intent of standards-based reform:

- Standards-based reform is about creating a set of challenging performance standards and helping all students attain them within their local schools, regardless of ethnicity or socioeconomic factors.
- It includes assessments that can help all stakeholders, beginning with students, but including school personnel, parents, and community members, to monitor progress and provide assistance as needed.
- Some form of accountability has always been involved, although the role of high-stakes testing has been a continual source of controversy (Linn, 1993; Resnick & Resnick, 1985).
- When assessment is aligned with standards, accountability focuses on outcomes and adjustments in curriculum and resources can be devoted to helping students achieve those outcomes.

As Sheila Valencia and Karen Wixson (2001) point out, the National Council on Standards and Testing (1992) intended that schools would have the flexibility to make the kinds of instructional decisions and adjustments necessary to meet the standards in any way they chose. Certainly, responsible educators recognized that the kinds of integrated literate thinking and learning advocated by the standards would take time. What happened was that, as schools sought ways to raise test scores quickly in response to political scrutiny and misinterpretation, they began to look for the quick fix. As we know, the quickest fix is to "teach to the test" and to "teach the test." By going back to the original intent—that the standards are a middle ground, not so broadly interpreted that they lack direction, but not so prescriptive that they deconstruct meaningful literacy processes and practice—we will be able to achieve substantive reform.

Amy Gutmann (1999), who has written extensively on issues related to equity, ethnicity, and democracy in education, maintains there is a way to honor both the national vision and the local knowledge through the democratization of the schools. She and David Pearson (1998a, 1998b) advocate discussion and decision making at the local level by all stakeholders in the community, recognizing that agency is not the province of any one organization or person. We believe that a truly responsive literacy team can be the catalyst for this process by actively and systematically soliciting input from as wide a range of stakeholders as possible.

How then does a district align its vision with the International Reading Association (IRA) and National Council of Teachers of English (NCTE) *Standards for the English Language Arts* (1996), as well as state and local English/Language Arts standards? Unfortunately, the process is so complex, so context-specific, and so broadly interpreted, that it is beyond the scope of this book. However, we provide general guidelines about developing local standards documents and access to helpful resources throughout this chapter. Because we cannot provide examples from every state and because standards are state-specific, our examples are meant to give you some idea of how these documents look in the districts near both of us. They are not meant to serve as one-size-fits-all examples or to suggest that a Wisconsin or California document is the ideal one. Certainly, you will want to adapt or replace them with ones that match with your state standards and your own vision.

What Are the IRA/NCTE English/Language Arts Standards?

The IRA/NCTE *Standards for the English Language Arts* (IRA/NCTE, 1996) define what students should know about language and be able to do with language (p. 1). Definitions of *literacy* have expanded and the Standards reflect this. Literacy processes include not only reading and writing, but also, listening, speaking, viewing, and visually representing. The Standards document states:

> The ultimate purpose of these standards is to ensure that *all* students are offered the opportunities, the encouragement, and the vision to develop the language skills they need to pursue life's goals, including personal enrichment and participation as informed members of our society (p. 1).

Although the document lists twelve standards, IRA/NCTE stresses the importance of recognizing the interconnectedness of the standards, viewing them as a whole, and reading the entire sixty-nine-page explanation. The standards reflect the complexity of literacy processes. They advocate depth and breadth of reading and writing, requiring students to use flexible approaches to comprehend, produce, interpret, and evaluate texts, adjusting for both the nature of the text and for specific purposes of the literacy event. One of the standards that emphasizes writing states: "Students employ a wide range of strategies as they write and use different writing process elements appropriately to communicate with different audiences for a variety of purposes." Thus, the standards are written in such a way as to focus on what literate humans must be able to do if they are to participate fully in the range of life experiences.

You can find the IRA/NCTE Standards for the English Language Arts Summary, listing the twelve standards, at the IRA Web site: www.reading.org. The complete document can be purchased on-line through the IRA Bookstore at this site.

State Literacy Standards

You can obtain a copy of the literacy standards for your state by contacting your state's Department of Public Instruction (or Department of Education). In most cases, the document will be available on-line, and it is likely to be on file in your district office. The state education agency may also have complete sample standards reports from schools and districts that have already finished the process. Often, reading specialists from nearby districts are willing to share their written standards and act as cognitive coaches to other reading specialists. Even within states you will see many different models of local standards. We see this as desirable because we believe that it is important for local communities to contextualize the process.

You need to exercise caution when searching for Web-based standards information. Many sites have political or philosophical agendas. For example, a partnership between Achieve, Inc. and McREL, the Regional Educational Laboratory, has published a database containing standards from a majority of states that are aligned with McREL's *Content Knowledge: A Compendium of Standards and Benchmarks for K–12 Education*. It can be accessed at www.achieve.org. Because of the uniform format, a reader can compare specific standards, state-to-state. Although this may be helpful to you as you become familiar with standards in order to write them at the local level, we do not advocate any state-to-state comparison or evaluation such as McREL provides. First of all, standards are context-based and culturally situated, tailor-made to the school and community. In addition, as Sheila Valencia and Karen Wixson (2001) caution, the ranking or grading of state standards by organizations such as Achieve, a collaborative of governors and business interests, may be the next high-stakes activity in standards-based reform.

Often states will adopt a standard such as the following from the Wisconsin State Standards for Reading/Language Arts: "Students in Wisconsin will read and respond to a wide range of writing to build an understanding of written materials, of themselves, and of others." This is a broad K–12 goal. The job of the local school is to figure out from a developmental standpoint what a fifth-grade student, for example, should be able to do *now* if he or she is on track to be fully proficient in that standard by the end of Grade 8. Steps along the way become benchmarks, or interim goals.

Examine Figure 2.6. Notice that the Broad Content Standard is like an umbrella. It is broken down into substandards, which have different performance expectations at grades 4, 8, and 12. If you are a third-grade teacher, you know that by next year your

Content Standard: Students in Wisconsin will read and respond to a wide range of writing to build an understanding of written materials, of themselves, and of others.

Grade 4: Substandard A 4.1
Use effective reading strategies to achieve their purposes in reading.
- Use a variety of strategies and word recognition skills, including reading, finding context clues, applying their knowledge of letter-sound relationships, and analyzing word structures.
- Infer the meaning of unfamiliar words in the context of a passage, by examining known words, phrases, and structures.
- Demonstrate phonics knowledge by using letter/sound relationships as aids to pronouncing unfamiliar words and text.
- Comprehend reading by using strategies such as activating prior knowledge, establishing purpose, self-correcting and self-monitoring, rereading, making predictions, finding context clues, developing visual images, applying knowledge of text structures and adjusting reading rate according to purpose and difficulty.
- Read aloud with age-appropriate fluency, accuracy, and expression.
- Discern how written texts and accompanying illustrations connect to convey meaning.
- Identify and use organizational features of texts, such as headings, paragraphs, and format, to improve understanding.
- Identify a purpose for reading, such as gaining information, learning about a viewpoint, and appreciating literature.

Grade 8: Substandard A 8.1
Use effective reading strategies to achieve their purposes in reading.
- Use knowledge of sentence and word structure, word origins, visual images, and context clues to understand unfamiliar words and clarify passages of texts.
- Use knowledge of the visual features of text, such as headings and bold faced print, and structures of text such as chronology and cause-and-effect as aids to comprehension.
- Establish purposeful reading and writing habits by using texts to find information, gain understanding of diverse viewpoints, make decisions, and enjoy the experience of reading.
- Select, summarize, paraphrase, analyze, and evaluate, orally and in writing, passages of texts chosen for specific purposes.

Grade 12: Substandard A 12.1
Use effective reading strategies to achieve their purposes in reading.
- Apply sophisticated word meaning and word analysis strategies, such as knowledge of roots, cognates, suffixes, and prefixes to understand unfamiliar words.
- Gather information to help achieve understanding when the meaning of a text is unclear.
- Apply knowledge of expository structures, such as the deductive or inductive development of an argument, to the comprehension and evaluation of text.
- Identify propaganda techniques and faulty reasoning in texts.
- Explain and evaluate the influence of format on the readability and meaning of a text.
- Distinguish between fact and opinion in nonfiction texts.
- Consider the context of a work when determining the meaning of abbreviations and acronyms, as well as the technical, idiomatic, and figurative meanings of term.

FIGURE 2.6 Sample Content Standards

students will be expected to: *Use a variety of strategies and word-recognition skills, including reading, finding context clues, applying their knowledge of letter–sound relationships, and analyzing word structures*, the first performance listed under A 4.1. The fourth-grade standard becomes a target for grades kindergarten through three. The task is for teachers at each grade level to collaborate to write incremental steps or benchmarks that move students developmentally toward proficiency by grade four. Teachers in grades five to seven write incremental benchmarks aimed at the eighth-grade standards, and teachers in grades nine to eleven write incremental benchmarks aimed at the grade-twelve standards. If you have the responsibility to write standards for your district, or if you serve on a standards committee, you may find the following steps helpful:

- Write the standard or substandard.
- List performance expectations for each semester.
- Describe formal and informal assessments for the standard.
- Identify sample activities used to teach the strategy or skill.
- List the resources or tools used to mediate the learning activities.

As you examine your vision statement, the IRA/NCTE Standards and your state standards, you will arrive at a list of standards for your school or district. A useful organizing tool is a Standards-Based Curriculum Framework, such as the example in Figure 2.7, which is typical of one that aligns with state standards.

For each standard and substandard, the matrix contains the five steps previously mentioned. The sample matrix shows a GRADE THREE alignment with the *Wisconsin Reading/Language Arts Standards A.4.1.2. "Infer meaning of unfamiliar words in the context of a passage by examining known words, phrases, and structures."* This means that, although the children are in grade three, *by the end of fourth grade* the target is mastery of this context skill. Therefore, the goal at grade three may be development, rather than mastery.

However, for each semester, the third-grade teachers have indicated what the students should be able to do toward that goal. For example, in Grade 3—Semester 1, the *Performance Expectation* (in Column 2) is that students will be able to "Use inferring the meaning of unfamiliar words in the context of the passage with support." By Grade 3, semester 2, students are expected to "Apply all independently." Eleven *Sample Activities* (Column 4) are identified, such as "Use figurative language," "Storylords Strategies #2, 3, & 4," and "Ask a neighbor," to list a few. These are the day-to-day classroom activities that support the learning of the skill.

The last column identifies *Resources to Support Implementation*. Here the teachers have listed Spell Checker, Dictionary, and Thesaurus. You may notice that column three, *Assessment to Demonstrate Student Competency*, is blank. Teachers are working on the informal ways this will be tested, because the high-stakes test is given at grade four. The matrix actually has two columns under *Assessment to Demonstrate Student Competency*, one column for formal or standardized measures and one column for more authentic or performance measures. Notice that, at the bottom of the matrix (Figure 2.7), there is a series of codes to mark how often a concept will be tested the next year on the

Wisconsin Reading/Language Arts Standard A 4.1, Grade Three					
Complete Standard	Benchmark Expectations at Gr. 3	Assessments to Demonstrate Competency		Sample Activities and Strategies	Resources to Support Implementation
A 4.12 Infer the meaning of unfamiliar words in the context of a passage by examining known words, phrases, and structures	*First Semester* Infer the meaning of unfamiliar words in the context of a passage with support *Second Semester* Infer the meaning of unfamiliar words in the context of a paragraph independently	*Formal* WI Gr. 3 test	*Informal* IRI Teacher Notes Vocabulary Self-Selection	*All Year* Infer word meanings Bidirectional Second Language Development Group discussion of possible meanings Affixes, Synonyms, Antonyms, Homonyms, Homophones, Multiple Meanings, Figurative Language Expand/Enrich Personal Vocabulary Storylords Strategies #2, 3, and 4 Ask a neighbor, Read on, Context Clues	Spell Checker Dictionary Thesaurus Glossary
How often will this item be tested on the fourth grade mandated state test? 0 = Not tested ✓ = 1 to 2 items on test + = 3 to 4 items on test * = 5 or more items on test					

FIGURE 2.7   Standards-Based Curriculum Framework

fourth-grade test. For example, 0 = not tested at this time, ✓ = 1 to 2 items on the state test, + = 3 to 4 items on the state test, and H = 5 or more items on the test. Although the temptation is to teach to the test, the teacher may concentrate on covering the most tested areas and skip some of the least tested ones. This is where local beliefs and practices supercede state or national standards.

Reading specialist Deb Zarling and the literacy team in the Oshkosh Area School District have developed an assessment profile for each student reflecting progress for each standard (see Appendix C). The checklist covers the K–5 range and teachers record student progress on a quarterly basis. We purposely chose this fairly comprehensive checklist as an example for you. Again, we emphasize that you may wish to create a simpler model or adapt this to your local and state needs. The emphasis of this kind of assessment is less on skills and more on what students know and do. The same proficiencies are listed on each sheet, so teachers record levels of proficiency as they increase over several years. Thus, first-grade teachers focus on the desired outcomes over an extended period of time. The instrument is a wonderful tool for collaboration between the teacher and the reading specialist or grade-level colleagues. Most important is that the profile provides teachers with information they need to guide student progress toward the standards.

Obviously, this is an example of how one state has approached the writing of standards. Your state document may look very different. It is important to recognize that, as a reading specialist, you must be very familiar with your state curriculum standards, especially related to reading/language arts, and also with the IRA/NCTE Standards. It will be your responsibility to interpret these standards documents to teachers, parents, administrators, and other stakeholders. Therefore, understanding how standards are written, how they ostensibly lead to effective instruction, and how they relate to high-stakes testing is of the utmost importance for all reading specialists.

Authors' Connection: Brenda and MaryEllen   We would like to conclude this chapter with a discussion of the frequently heard remark, "I close my door and do my own thing." As benign as that remark seemed to us thirty years ago, we would no longer be able to say it from a culturally and morally responsible perspective. This is why. We agree with Patrick Shannon (1999), that when we remove ourselves from a reform or program or mandate, we merely give silent support to that policy or program or mandate, as well as a default value to our schools. When we remain silent in our agreement or disagreement, we unknowingly support the status quo. Chomsky (1999) calls this "consent without consent." This is a wake-up call for teachers and reading specialists to lend explicit resistance to policies that contradict respected research findings and the values and beliefs forged by the sociocultural contexts in which they live and teach.

REVISITING THE VIGNETTE

Now that you have completed the reading, discussion, and group activities in this chapter, how will you react to the thinking points below? Compare your suggestions to those you made earlier. How do the sociocultural dynamics of Mark's school and neighborhood influence how you answer these questions now?

1. What are the steps Mark should take to develop literacy standards?
2. What resources should he consult to assist him and his literacy team in developing the standards?
3. With whom should he and the literacy team share the school and district's vision statement?
4. Once the standards are developed, how should Mark use them to develop and implement curriculum and instruction that is congruent with the standards?

POINTS TO REMEMBER

All systematic and lasting change begins with a culturally responsive vision statement. In order to be effective, the vision statement must be grounded in the beliefs of all the stakeholders. Therefore, the establishment of a literacy team, composed in ways that represent as many voices as possible, requires a great deal of planning. In addition, the team must be structured to allow input from individuals who are not team members. We have seen the powerful influence of beliefs on teacher practice. Changes in teaching require a great deal of time and support because they reflect fundamental changes in beliefs that are resistant to change. Among the most important insights for adopting a culturally responsive curriculum is to recognize the multiple literacies and multiple communities. Teachers can then find ways to honor the various print and nonprint literacies found in and out of school and use them in ways that serve instructional goals. Establishing a literacy team that includes a wide range of voices promotes the ownership necessary for sustaining long-term change. Finally, we explored ways to align the school literacy goals and practices with state and IRA/NCTE Standards.

It is important to involve teachers in collaborative planning throughout the processes of identifying needs and beliefs, and planning curricular changes over two years. Insights into the specific contexts of the school and knowledge about effective instruction guide the literacy team in conducting a comprehensive needs assessment. The information from the needs assessment is then used to plan curriculum, modify instruction, establish formative assessments, and determine staff development and support for change.

PORTFOLIO PROJECTS

1. Interview a reading specialist. Ask the individual to describe the roles and responsibilities of the job. Create a matrix comparing the IRA roles of the reading specialist with the role of this individual. Write a brief summary of your findings including an explanation of how the sociocultural context of the school shapes the reading specialist's role.

2. Imagine you are asked to create a literacy team for your school or district. Describe how you will determine who will be included on the literacy team and provide your reasoning. Explain how the literacy team composition reflects context-specific needs.

3. Examine your district's and/or state's standards for the teaching of reading and language arts. Compare them to the IRA/NCTE Standards (available through IRA at www.reading.org). In what ways are they congruent? In what ways are they different? Discuss the benchmarks that could be established at varied grade levels for your school/district standards. How might these benchmarks be assessed?

4. Personal Goal: Revisit the goal you set for yourself at the beginning of the chapter. Create a portfolio item that reflects what you have learned relative to your goal.

RECOMMENDED READINGS

International Reading Association & National Council of Teachers of English. (1996). *Standards for the English Language Arts*. Newark, DE: International Reading Association; Urbana, IL: National Council of Teachers of English. This document includes a comprehensive explanation of the twelve IRA/NCTE standards. IRA and NCTE stress the importance of: recognizing the interconnectedness of the standards, viewing them as a whole, and reading the entire 69-page report.

Maeroff, G. I. (1993). Building teams to rebuild schools. *Phi Delta Kappan, 74*(7), 512–514. Maeroff provides the reader with step-by-step advice on team formation and long-term collaboration. The most helpful advice includes ways to overcome the pitfalls that lead to dysfunctional or ineffective teams.

Patty, D., Maschoff, J. D., & Ransom, P. (1985). *The reading resource handbook for school leaders*. Norwood, MA: Christopher-Gordon. This book is a highly practical systematic guide to team building and needs assessment.

Valencia, S. W., & Wixson, K. (2001). Inside English/language arts standards: What's in a grade? *Reading Research Quarterly, 36*(2), 202–217. These experts in assessment examine the tensions between the original intent of the standards and the ways the standards are implemented.

CHAPTER THREE

ASSESSING LITERACY NEEDS, ESTABLISHING GOALS, AND DEVELOPING A PLAN

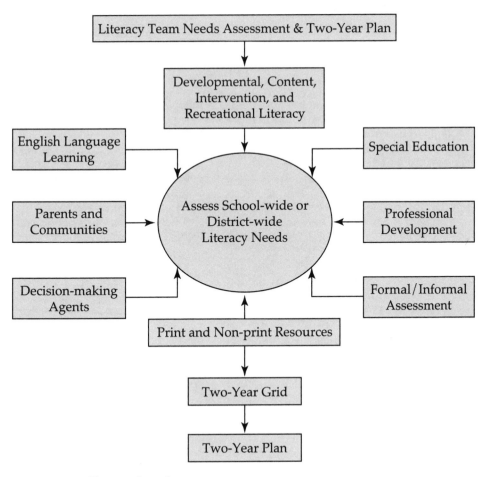

FIGURE 3.1   Chapter Overview

LEARNING GOALS

After reading, discussing, and engaging in activities related to this chapter, you will be able to:

1. design a systematic plan for assessing schoolwide and/or districtwide literacy needs, including a needs assessment survey;

2. organize and analyze information related to the following elements of the literacy program: demographics, literacy curriculum and instruction, developmental and content literacy, intervention, recreational literacy, assessment, support for English learners, special education, parent involvement, community involvement, professional development, and resources;

3. synthesize the information in a needs assessment summary;

4. collaborate with the literacy team, administrators, teachers, and parents to create a school or district two-year plan based on the needs assessment;

5. Personal Learning Goal: In a three-minute brainstorming session, share what you know about this topic. Write a goal or a question that reflects something you want to learn about the topic. Share this with others in your group.

Vignette

Janet Griffin has been hired as a school reading specialist in an urban K–6 elementary school in Southern California with a student population of 1100 students. Her principal is also new to the year-round school, and one third of the faculty members are in their first two years of teaching. Janet, who is in her early thirties, grew up in San Antonio with parents who encouraged her to explore a variety of cultural viewpoints and languages, and she is fluent in both English and Spanish. Seventy-two percent of the 1100 students in her school have been identified as Limited English Proficient (LEP). Of these, over half speak Spanish as the language of the home. Seven other languages are spoken by the remaining students, including Khmer, Chinese, Vietnamese, Cambodian, Farsi, Korean, and Hmong. Many of the students live in close-knit groups with others who share their ethnicity and home language. Nearly three quarters of the students in the school qualify for free or reduced lunch. There is a comprehensive ELD program to provide appropriate levels of in-class and pull-out support for the English language learners. Though almost half of the teachers speak at least some Spanish, all teachers struggle to find ways to deal with the language diversity within their classrooms.

Janet has been asked by the principal to coordinate the school's literacy program. The district's adopted reading series integrates the language arts and although the school selected a spelling program within the past year, most teachers aren't using it. Some of the teachers have complained that the reading series is too difficult and it is not meeting the needs of the children in this school.

Thinking Points

1. What is one question Janet should be asking the principal and one question she might ask the teachers as she begins her new job as a reading specialist?

2. What are the tensions and core issues that she must confront?

Expanding the Vignette: Exploring the Tensions

Three of the veteran teachers approach Janet with complaints about the new principal's unclear vision of the reading program. They strongly believe that the current program isn't meeting the needs of the students, and they want to enlist Janet's help in convincing the principal to let them design their own skills-based program with a synthetic phonics emphasis. Another group of teachers, mostly new to the classroom, want to design their own reading program based around literature themes, incorporating both the direct and indirect phonics approaches they learned in their university reading methods courses. Nearly everyone is confronting Janet with, "What these kids need is . . .," but when pressed for evidence no one can provide specific information. The new principal, wanting to establish a positive rapport with faculty but cognizant of state requirements regarding phonics instruction, is reluctant to take a firm position on either side of the issue, and has instructed Janet to negotiate the differences.

Thinking Points

1. What additional tensions and questions have you identified in the vignette?
2. What are some short-term suggestions you would give Janet? What immediate response could she give to the teachers who say, "These kids need . . ."
3. What long-term measures would you recommend to her?

ASSESSING THE SCHOOL LITERACY PROGRAM NEEDS

This vignette provides a realistic example of a good news/bad news scenario. Although Janet feels bombarded on all sides by teachers with differing agendas, the good news is that everyone involved appears to be focusing on the best interests and needs of the students. The bad news is that no one can provide meaningful evidence about what these needs are. Even so, a number of people Janet has encountered seem to have "all the answers."

Teachers make many assumptions about how reading and writing should be taught. These are based on their knowledge, beliefs, and experience as professionals and shaped by the contexts in which the teaching and learning occur. Indeed, in order to be effective agents for change, we need to have strongly reasoned convictions. As teachers we often deal in the commerce of answers; answers to administrators, answers to students, answers to parents. But we should never forget that, when we are at our best, we deal in questions.

In a "famous-last-words" story, the radical writer, poet, and feminist Gertrude Stein lay dying. Just at the moment when it appeared she would breathe her last, pondering the meaning of life she wondered aloud, "What is the answer?" When nothing came to her, she reportedly replied, "Well, in that case, what is the question?" (Sutherland, 1951, p. 207). Whether or not the story is true, we may apply this kind of thinking to arrive at the answer to what our students need. Rather than searching for answers, it will serve us better to figure out the relevant questions we should ask about our beliefs, practices, programs, resources, and, most of all, our students. In Chapter 2 we developed a vision statement and formed a literacy team. In this chapter we will use them to conduct a needs assessment and create a two-year plan for a school or district.

Designing a Needs Assessment

With renewed pressure for standards and the high-stakes assessments that accompany them, the temptation is for schools and districts to define needs in narrow ways, that is, in reaction to student test results. The needs assessment is one way to ensure you are meeting *actual* rather than perceived needs. It provides a starting point for planning and for informed decision making by all stakeholders.

A needs assessment is an evaluation in which information about the current status of the school literacy program is collected and examined. Its purpose is to document the probable needs for a program or service. The results of the needs assessment are used to determine priority goals, develop a long-term plan, and allocate funds and resources (Soriano, 1995).

Guiding the Inquiry.   A needs assessment is a substantial undertaking. It can involve the commitment of time and resources by many individuals. The process is most effective when it involves collaboration, and preplanning is essential. Together with your school literacy team, consider the following questions as you begin to design your needs assessment:

1. Decide what information you need to collect.
   - What do you want to know?
   - What questions do you want to answer?
   - Is there an element of the school's literacy program that needs greater attention than others? For example, if there is little or no consistency in reading instruction across grade levels and within grade levels, this may be an area of focus. Obviously, at this point in the process you're only hypothesizing because more information about the school's programmatic needs will come to the surface once you've gathered your data.
   - What will you do with the information? With whom will you share it—all stakeholders of the school or just the teachers and administrators? This is important to consider because your answer will affect the design of the needs assessment instrument.
2. Decide on the methods you will use to collect information.
   - How will the data be collected? Will you use a written survey? Interviews? Observations? Archival data (e.g., test scores, student records, district standards)? A combination of these?
   - Where are you likely to find the information you need? Who is likely to have access to specific pieces of information?
   - Who will collect the information?
   - What assessment or survey instruments will need to be developed? Who will develop them?
3. Organize and analyze the information.
   - How will you consolidate, chart, or report the information?

- How will you determine if any information is missing?
- How will you examine the various pieces of information in both macro and micro ways? That is, how will you determine what the big-picture ideas or themes are? These might include such items as books and resources or school-wide assessment. Microanalysis is important because it can yield information such as how particular assessments are used in some grade levels but not others, or how parent volunteers are very effectively used in some classrooms but not at all in others.
- How will you examine the connections among the pieces? For example, if students' spelling scores are weak, is there a relationship between the low scores and the fact that teachers may choose not to use the adopted spelling program? Or could these teachers have more effective spelling instruction than that found in the adopted spelling program? How will you scrutinize these types of relationships?
- How will you determine severity, special focus, or concentration (Center One, 1998)? That is, on a continuum how serious are some of the identified problems, concerns, or needs, and how will you know if you spot them?

Creating a School Profile.   "Who am I?" is one of those universal questions that has preoccupied both philosophers and those of us who are less lofty thinkers. When answering the question we might provide our name, age, date and place of birth, ethnicity, occupation, family roles, and physical characteristics—a snapshot of facts. This is the kind of information exchanged by people when they first meet. Although it does little to inform us of the character, needs, and desires of a person, it is our starting point in getting to know him or her. The question "Who are we?" is also the starting point for getting to know your school. As avant-garde writer and diarist Anaïs Nin once said, "We see things not as they are, but as we are."

The school profile contains basic descriptive data that will inform your inquiry into instructional needs and program planning. Because year-to-year data are easily compared, the profile can show trends in demographics and other data. You may already have a school profile written for accreditation if your state has such a periodic process. If not, then it is important to create one as you begin the needs assessment process. Your principal will be able to access much of this information; other data will be available at your district headquarters. The following kinds of data are typically found in school profiles:

- demographics of the district: location, population, socioeconomic level, ethnicity, stability of population, and recent trends;
- student demographics: number of students, ethnicity, percentage of English language learners and their levels of English proficiency, socioeconomic levels, percentage of students receiving free or reduced lunch, stability of student population, attendance rates, graduation rates, jobs, special needs instruction, and participation in school and community activities and programs;
- professional demographics of teachers, administrators, and support personnel: sociocultural characteristics, ethnicity, languages spoken, ratio of teachers to pupils, roles and levels of education, numbers of years of experience, degrees held,

special training or expertise in methods or programs, such as bilingual education, ESL/ELD, or Reading Recovery;

- parent, family, community members: family composition, students living with biological parents, multigenerational families, foster families, homeless families, skills, talents, interests, relationships with and involvement in the school, involvement in social services and community, and the degree to which business and community persons are involved with the school.

In creating the vision statement (see Chapter 2), teachers addressed issues of culture and community in subjective, global, and qualitative ways. By collecting quantitative data as well, such as those just suggested, a multidimensional description emerges that serves to inform the process of assessment and planning. Although these data are to be used for improving the literacy program, they can also be used as a basis for planning schoolwide reform.

Group Inquiry Activity   For this activity, do not sit with anyone from your school. By yourself:

1. Think of the demographic information you know about your school.
2. Examine the suggested list of data to be collected in the school profile.
3. For each point estimate what the data might be. (What percent of the students do you think receive free or reduced lunch, etc.?)

With others in your group:

1. Compare your "estimated" school profile with those from other schools.
2. How is your school profile like/unlike that of others?
3. Create a Venn diagram comparing and contrasting the school profiles.

How might these differences influence school literacy programs and practices?

Components of the Needs Assessment

What questions should we ask to guide the needs assessment inquiry process? The major questions or areas of inquiry are shown in Figure 3.2, the Components of the Needs Assessment. It is important to recognize that no "one-size-fits-all" set of questions, steps, or rubrics will be universally appropriate for all schools and districts.

Gathering Data.   The two groups of questions in Figure 3.2 provide areas of focus for data gathering. Each member of the literacy team can assume responsibility for one or more of the areas of inquiry. During team meetings, members can brainstorm about specific ways to gather information, such as surveying the staff. For example, the team members collecting data on content area literacy practices can submit questions they want teachers to answer; other Team members can do the same for their areas. Some team members may need help if they are having difficulty locating data. Those who

1. Demographics
   - What are the demographics of the school and community?

2. A Philosophy or Vision Statement
   - What is the District Philosophy Statement for Reading/Language Arts?

3. The Literacy Team Members
   - Who are the members of the Literacy Team?

4. Analysis of School Literacy Programs: The Needs Assessment Survey
   - What do each of the following components of the schoolwide literacy program look like? *Developmental, Content, Intervention,* and *Recreational*
   - What programs exist for *English Language Learners?*
   - How are the needs of *Special Education* students currently met?
   - How are *Parents* and *Communities* involved in literacy endeavors?

5. Resources
   - What are the print and nonprint resources in the media center and classrooms?
   - When, how, and where are technology resources used by students and teachers?
   - How are formal and informal assessments used to guide instruction?
   - Who are the agents in the leadership/decision-making processes?
   - Are financial resources and facilities adequate to meet instructional needs in literacy?
   - Are teachers included in decisions about systematic professional development?
   - How do teachers view their own professional development needs?
   - Who are all the stakeholders in this process (e.g., school psychologist, library/media, teachers, nurse, resource teachers, special education teachers)?
   - What is their involvement in the schoolwide literacy program?

6. Parent and Community Factors
   - How are parents and community members involved in literacy endeavors?

7. Analysis and Written Summary
   - How will the literacy team collect, organize, and synthesize information and list needs?
   - How will the needs be summarized and reported?

8. Using the Needs Assessment Summary
   - How will the Needs Assessment Summary be used to create a Two-Year Plan?

FIGURE 3.2   Components of the Needs Assessment

have relatively easy tasks such as collecting information about the media center can help those responsible for broad areas such as parent and community involvement. Some of these areas, such as developmental reading may be subdivided into more manageable pieces, such as the grades at which developmental reading is taught, methods and programs, materials, and technology. In this case, the reading specialist can focus team

Area of Inquiry	Who	Data Needed	Where?	By:	How Reported	Done 3
How is developmental literacy taught?	Mary S. Coord.	(See subtasks below)	(See subtasks below)	12/1	Synthesis of info below	
—grade levels of dev. rdg. instr.	Mary	Elem. MS, HS, Lit Classes	District office	10/1	Stats grid Overview Part of curriculum flow chart	
—method/ program	Martin	Amt integration Prog. used Strategies Spec. training Integ lang?	Curric. Guide Teacher survey Audit report Interv. w/Rdg. Spec.	11/1	List Chart by grade level Grid	
—materials	Martin	Amts, nature of, Integrated/skill based? Variety of perspectives, cultures/multi. literacies?	Tchr surveys Informal inspection MS/HS booklists Student samples Elem—H.S.	11/1	Lists by grade level Grid	
—technology in devel rdg	Don	Where/how used Software/forms/ Web/Internet Integrated w/ curric.	Interv w. tech coordinator Hardware software inventory Int. w/media Spec. Tchr survey K–12	10/1	Lists by grade level Grid	

FIGURE 3.3 Literacy Team Action Plan: Needs Assessment Data Collection

members and resources in formative ways during the process. Brief, frequent team meetings may be necessary during this time, and members who complete a task can help those with larger assignments.

Tasks can be organized in a simple matrix such as the one found in Figure 3.3. By adding all tasks to this matrix, the reading specialist and the literacy team will be able to assess progress and efficiently channel efforts.

Writing the Needs Assessment Survey. Begin by asking the various literacy team members to draft questions related to the areas for which they are gathering data. Keep in mind that teachers are very busy people, and you're more likely to receive completed surveys if they take only a few moments to finish. Typically, a Likert Scale works well with this type of survey. A Likert Scale is a five-point continuum with designations such as: 1 = Strongly Disagree; 2 = Disagree; 3 = Unsure; 4 = Agree; 5 = Strongly Agree. Participants are asked to circle a number on the continuum that best represents their feelings about each item. A disadvantage of using such a scale is that your respondents may rely too much on the mid-point of the continuum (number 3 on a 5-point scale), especially if they don't have strong feelings or if they're unsure about how to respond. Multiple-choice questions or statements can also yield good information, but this type of survey is more difficult to write because of the four or five possible answers that need to be constructed for each item. Open-ended items will give you a great deal of useful information, but teachers may be reluctant to take time to write out their responses. Therefore, we recommend the Likert Scale in combination with a few open-ended questions, as well as an area for comments.

Use broad categories for writing the statements to which respondents will reply. For example, on the Components of the Needs Assessment (see Figure 3.2), you will see some questions for the following two categories: Analysis of School Literacy Programs, and Resources. Use these categories and questions to guide the development of needs assessment statements for your own school's literacy program. We have provided sample items from a Needs Assessment Survey (see Figure 3.4). It includes Likert survey statements for the category of Instructional Practices: Developmental Reading.

Broadening the Lens. In spite of efforts to identify needs by inquiry into these components, there is a holistic element missing, a big-picture perspective. At least two questions are not answered in the Components of the Needs Assessment. The first is, "How effectively do the various components of the literacy program interrelate?" and "To what degree does the total program meet the needs of various communities?" Providing open-ended questions is one way to gather this type of information.

- What are the strengths of the literacy program in this school?
- What do we need to work on to make this a better program?
- What are some things that would be helpful to you in improving the literacy performance of your students?
- What are some suggestions for how best to meet your needs (materials, staff development, modeling, focused study groups, etc.)?
- Do you have any additional comments you would like to share with the literacy team?

Note that your entire survey could be adapted and distributed to parents, even translated into various home languages. One venue for gathering these data could be the school's PTO/PTA organization. Another approach is for team members to go into the community to meet with various small groups in focused discussion sessions during which the survey questions are asked. Team members can record ideas and opinions, remembering to be sensitive to various cultures and discourse practices when talking with parents and community groups. Interpreters, including some students, may be necessary. This is also an excellent way to involve student and parents as literacy team

Instructional Practices: Developmental Reading				
Strongly Agree		Unknown/ Unsure		Strongly Disagree
1	2	3	4	5

In our school, there is adequate consistency within grade levels in our developmental reading program; that is, teachers in the same grade are covering mostly the same reading/ language arts content using similar approaches.

1	2	3	4	5

In our school, there is adequate consistency across grade levels in our developmental reading program; that is, teachers across the grades are using similar teaching methods and approaches.

1	2	3	4	5

In our school, our school-wide developmental reading program is consistent with district standards for reading and language arts in the elementary grades.

1	2	3	4	5

The reading series we are currently using meets the literacy needs of most of the students in our school.

1	2	3	4	5

Most students are progressing satisfactorily in our school's developmental reading program.

1	2	3	4	5

I feel confident in my ability to provide the students in my classroom with an appropriate developmental reading program.

1	2	3	4	5

Comments about our developmental reading program:

FIGURE 3.4   Sample Items for a Needs Assessment Survey

members. Because students are the biggest stakeholders in the school's reading program, their voices are important to include in an assessment of school needs. An adapted survey could easily be distributed in classes, especially in the upper grades.

You may discover that parents and community members have misconceptions about what goes on in the school and limited access to relevant information. In fact, what you'll mostly be collecting are "impressions." These individuals are likely to base a number of their decisions on their own experiences in school, which may be based on a drill-and-skill model or on a culturally different educational system in another country.

This is a golden opportunity for two reasons. First, you will be able to assess how informed these stakeholders are. Such knowledge will help your team plan better ways to inform the community about the education program. Second, you will be able to disseminate information about the schools in a friendly, informal manner and directly address any misconceptions you encounter.

Professional Development. Another way to extend your data gathering is to include questions on the survey related to professional development. The purpose here is to determine teachers' needs and interests, and institute a comprehensive plan for updating and increasing teachers' knowledge and understandings of current literacy research and practice (for a complete discussion of professional development, see Chapter 11). You may find that the answers to some of these questions can be generated during individual teacher interviews or even group discussions during a staff meeting.

Among the questions you might ask are:

- Which literacy instructional practices and strategies work well for you?
- Which literacy instructional practices would you like to learn or improve?
- What additional training would you need to better assess the literacy levels of your students?
- For which three literacy instructional practices are you most interested in receiving support or training?
- What do you see as your strengths in teaching reading/language arts? Are there any demonstration lessons you could present to other teachers?
- What conferences, inservices, workshops, and reading council meetings have you attended in the past year?
- What's the most effective approach, method, or instructional strategy you've learned about in the past year? Have you tried it with your students? If so, how did it go?
- What new idea or instructional strategy have you tried that didn't work well with your students? Why do you think it didn't work? What would you recommend to make this idea/strategy more effective?

You can also focus your inquiry about professional development by listing a variety of topics and asking respondents to prioritize (such as top three) those that are of interest.

Before Distributing the Needs Assessment Survey. After you have determined all the questions for the survey, it's time to format the survey. Here are some hints we have found helpful:

- Include, at the top of the first page, an introductory note from you and the literacy team. In a sentence or two, explain the purpose of the needs assessment, when and where it should be returned (give a date), and your names or just "Literacy Team."
- Include a few lines for demographic information about the respondents such as their grade level; the years they've taught (group years for anonymity: 1–3, 4–6, etc.); additional literacy training they've had, and so on. This is important information when you begin examining responses.

- Use standard fonts, type sizes, and an easy-to-follow format. Remember that you want as many surveys returned as possible, so make them easy to complete.
- If you can accomplish your goal in a one- to two-page survey, that is ideal. The shorter the survey, the more likely it is to be completed. In any case, the entire survey should be no more than three pages. Watch for redundancy in your statements and questions—that will help in keeping down the number of pages.

A Needs Assessment Survey, created by one of our graduate students, is included in Appendix D. The teachers and administrators in her school completed it and, from the data she collected, she wrote a two-year plan. Note the reminder that the last important step to take before you make copies of the survey is to show it to your site administrator and get approval for distributing it to your teachers and other stakeholders. Hopefully, in true collaborative fashion, your principal and assistant principal have been involved in the process from the beginning. But, if they haven't, it's very important that they see and approve the instrument prior to its distribution to others.

Analyzing the Data. After you have collected all the data, on the survey calculate the percentages for each of the responses to the Likert Scale statements (see Figure 3.5). Note where there are strong or weak responses at either end of the continuum (see items 3, 4, 6, 7). You may also have items where responses are spread relatively evenly across the continuum, where some people may have strong feelings, but not all. What you're looking for are patterns across grade levels or within grade levels, or perhaps differences expressed by experienced versus beginning teachers, teachers versus other stakeholders, and so forth. In the example in Figure 3.5, which is an excerpt taken from an actual elementary school needs assessment survey, you readily see that the responding teachers, for the most part, are not satisfied with their present instructional materials and technology resources.

Next, read over all written comments and responses to the open-ended questions. Look for themes, areas of agreement or disagreement, and other ideas that can be clustered together. Are there contradictions between the Likert Scale responses and the written comments? Or does there appear to be general agreement and support across both sets of data? You may wish to code specific comments according to categories, such as Need for Professional Development, Instructional Approaches/Methods, Areas of Strength, Areas of Weakness, and so forth. You also may want to see if there are any missing pieces of information or if there are any new questions that need to be asked.

As you read, tabulate, and summarize, be sure you identify strengths before focusing on the needs. Undoubtedly, there are many aspects of your school's literacy program that are strong and deserve to be recognized as such. Teachers, parents, students, and administrators need to hear what they are. Your report should list them before you address needs. Only then should you move on to the next step and pinpoint your school's or district's literacy needs.

The process of categorizing needs is much the same as the process used to categorize beliefs. Strengths and needs are put into broad categories by the literacy team. Members in dyads or triads choose one of the needs and investigate it further. A needs organizer is a matrix or plan that can be used to organize the tasks. As you identity needs

Instructional Resources				
Strongly Agree		Unknown/ Unsure		Strongly Disagree
1	2	3	4	5

1. There are sufficient books in my classroom library.

1 = 0%	2 = 12%	3 = 19%	4 = 25%	5 = 44%

2. There are sufficient books for SSR (Self-Selected Reading).

1 = 0%	2 = 1%	3 = 31%	4 = 25%	5 = 43%

3. Our school-wide program supports SSR.

1 = 0%	2 = 0%	3 = 12%	4 = 19%	5 = 69%

4. Our Multi-Media Center is helpful for students.

1 = 1%	2 = 10%	3 = 25%	4 = 38%	5 = 26%

5. In the MMC and in our classrooms, students have access to appropriate technological resources (e.g., computers, listening centers, Internet access).

1 = 0%	2 = 0%	3 = 31%	4 = 31%	5 = 38%

6. I have the instructional materials I need for my developmental reading program (e.g., student anthologies, leveled readers, student practice books, transparencies, etc.).

1 = 0%	2 = 8%	3 = 4%	4 = 25%	5 = 63%

7. I have the instructional materials I need for providing in-class intervention for struggling readers and writers.

1 = 0%	2 = 1%	3 = 12%	4 = 31%	5 = 56%

FIGURE 3.5 Analyzing Data on the Likert Scale

you will complete a separate organizer for each. We provide an example of an Organizer for One Identified Need in Figure 3.6.

Disseminating the Results

When the needs have been analyzed and compiled, they are ready to be shared with stakeholders. This can be done by writing a narrative that summarizes the strengths and weaknesses of the current literacy program. If the document is to be read by a variety of constituents, it should be no more than three to four pages, and should include the categories identified in the Components of the Needs Assessment provided previously in the chapter (see Figure 3.2). These include the following:

1. Brief description of the district and school
2. A philosophy or vision statement

Middle School and Secondary/High School Content Area Literacy Program				
Strengths: ■ Students do well on knowledge-based items at all levels on state exams in Soc. Studies, Science, Mathematics, Language Arts ■ Teachers are presently beginning to use integrated content and process literacy instruction. ■ All stakeholders have demonstrated a commitment to literacy program improvement ■ The school has adequate resources to meet objectives of the vision statement. ■ Ongoing professional development continues to be a priority in the school.				
Identified Need	Team Member	Evidence of Need	New Questions	Additional Info/ Stakeholder Input
Content area literacy: integrated lang/arts needed at middle school & secondary, emphasizing concurrent content and process instruction.	John S.	9 teachers expressed need for help w/ C.A.R. Terra Nova Test scores drop steadily after gr. 4 through gr. 12 Incongruence between practice and belief statement #3 Observation reveals transmission model prevails	What do teachers want/need from rdg. spec. & team? (survey)	Teachers request: Professional devel. Release time to teach collaboratively Materials Univ. classes held at school Rdg. Spec/peer coaching Additional ideas: Distance ed. "study" groups
Final needs statement: Teachers in the middle school and secondary school need professional development and support to implement integrated content area literacy instruction into their teaching.				

FIGURE 3.6 **Example of Organizer for One Identified Need**

3. A description of the literacy team
4. Analysis of developmental, content area, recreational, intervention, English language learning, and special education programs
5. Resources
6. Parent and community factors
7. Analysis and written needs assessment summary
8. Using the needs assessment summary to create a two-year plan

Because the data are available should questions arise, the needs assessment summary need not address everything collected. Rather, it should highlight strengths and weaknesses in each category. For example, an analysis of findings related to Content Area Literacy in a schoolwide or district needs assessment report might state the following concerns:

> Content area teacher surveys reveal that current middle and high school literacy practices do not reflect the instructional guidelines in either the IRA Adolescent Literacy Policy Statement or the state standards, nor do they reflect the teachers' goals in the vision statement. The teachers and the reading specialist have identified the following as needs: support and staff development in instructional methods on integrating the languages arts, emphasizing both content and process, culturally responsive instructional practices, and inquiry-based learning. Scores on the Reading portion of the Eighth and Twelfth Grade Terra Nova state tests reveal a steady decline in percentile ranking from Fourth Grade test scores.

A completed needs assessment summary, written by another of our graduate students, is included in Appendix E.

With the writing of the needs assessment summary, a challenging part of the literacy team's written work is complete. Next, the two-year grid is developed from the information collected in the needs assessment survey, and the literacy team is now ready to engage in systematic long-term planning to achieve the school goals.

CREATING THE COMPREHENSIVE TWO-YEAR PLAN

With all the advances in technology, it may be a surprise to you that no one has ever been able to design a machine that can make a basket. Baskets are carefully planned, formed in ways true to their intended function and to the vision of the basket maker. There is a rhythm in the process of basketry, a flow that occurs between the soul and the fingers in that moment of perfect tension between weavers and spokes. The two-handled potato basket, dragged along the row while harvesting, is a wondrous amalgam of art and tool. When the harvest is done and the basket is pulled and stretched, it can be soaked in water and readjusted, true once more to the vision of its creator. Thus, even the most intricate basket, woven so precisely it can hold water, has all of the elements of any good plan. It begins with a vision and its form is determined by the needs that it will fill. Important, too, is that it can be adjusted again and again to realign with the original vision. The two-year plan has all of these dimensions, too.

What Is the Comprehensive Two-Year Plan?

A comprehensive two-year plan is a written document. It incorporates the components previously developed, including school and district demographics, a list of literacy team members, a description of current practices, a summary of the findings from the needs assessment, a proposal for professional development, and includes a two-year grid or schedule comprised of a step-by-step layout of activities over a two-year period that will move from each identified need to the intended goals or targets. Much of this information has already been gathered and written; now the task is to pull together the various pieces into a comprehensive whole. Earlier work by the teachers and the literacy team has already determined that the two-year grid and, consequently, the comprehensive two-year plan are aligned with the curriculum, the standards, and the vision statement. This plan is meant to be flexible; it is not an end in itself but, rather, the means for achieving improvement in the school literacy program.

Creating the two-year grid starts with the needs and identifies the people, resources, and professional development related to that need. As the leader of the literacy team, you, the reading specialist, will be primarily responsible for developing the two-year grid, but it is critical that you do this along with the members of the literacy team. The first step in this process can be facilitated through the development of a needs resource chart (see Figure 3.7).

As you review the needs resource chart, you might conclude that it seems like a plan for change. There are some important things to keep in mind about change. Examining the identified need, "Teachers in the secondary school need instruction and support to implement integrated content area literacy instruction into their teaching," leads to the realization that this is not the same as saying, "They need a set of encyclopedias in their rooms," or "They need to learn the Question-Answer-Relationship (QAR) Strategy." Meeting this need will require fundamental changes in teaching, and these changes in teaching take time because they can only happen after fundamental changes in beliefs have occurred. They happen incrementally, and they may require risk-taking and moving out of the comfort zone.

The list of possible actions (in the second column of Figure 3.7) contains nine different elements. Many will require sustained support, multiple professional development sessions over time, and numerous opportunities for teachers to experiment with new ideas in class. Consider the identified need of helping teachers incorporate integrated, interactive literacy activities in content areas. This endeavor will most likely take at least two years and perhaps more. In fact, effective teachers are never finished developing these skills.

You'll find it helpful if you, the literacy team, and an administrator look together at the list of identified needs and possible actions (see Figure 3.7), and ask the following questions:

- Which items are high priorities?
- Which items require long-term commitments?
- How much and what type of professional development will be required for each?
- Which may involve in-class demonstrations by the reading specialist?
- Which require release time for teachers?
- Which can be accomplished more quickly than others?

By dividing the two-year period into four semesters, you can spread the tasks involved over time. Many schools even create a three-year grid, and, depending on your identified needs, you may wish to explore this option.

Need Identified	Possible Actions	Resources Needed	People Involved
Teachers in the secondary school need education and support to implement integrated content area literacy instruction into their teaching.	Provide inservice on integrated L/A Model interactive strategies Series of inservices on inquiry-based learning Demonstrate subject specific strategies to dept. Staff development on incorporating literature into content classes Staff development culturally responsive teaching Create voluntary study groups Teachers attend workshops and present to peers Possible distance ed. or on-site professional development Univ. course	Multiple copies of Buehl's *Interactive Strategies* Copies of JAAL articles on interactive teaching, critical theory, reader response, multiple literacy, inquiry-based learning Copies of IRA Adolescent Literacy Position Statement Release time Literature sets for content classes	Administrators: Budget Concerns Teachers: Peer coaching, modeling, Attend wkshps & share Study groups Collaborative projects Co-teach workshops Reading Specialist: Professional Development/Staff development workshops Modeling Lessons Co-teaching Ordering materials Consulting w/ teachers Problem solving Literacy Team: Communicating w/ stakeholders Modeling, leading study groups, co-teaching, attending workshops, leading staff development

FIGURE 3.7 Needs Resource Chart

Scheduling Activities for the Two-Year Grid

For purposes of illustration, Figure 3.8 shows a partial Secondary School Two-Year Grid. As you create the two-year grid, consider the following suggestions:

- If there are short-term needs that are easily addressed, schedule them during the first semester.
- Save needs that can be met in approximately one full year for the second year.

Content Area Literacy	Year One	
	Fall	Spring
Need: (1) Students need integrated L/A instruction that presents content and process concurrently.	*Articles and Resources* IRA Adolescent Literacy Position Multiple Literacies Content-Specific Literacy Strategies JAAL Multiple copies of Buehl Strategies Bk	*Articles and Resources* JAAL Articles ROL Articles Technology strategies More interactive strategies Content-Specific Literacy Strategies Lang. Arts Journal
(2) Teachers in the secondary school need education and support to implement integrated content area literacy instruction into their teaching.	*Peer Support* Peers co-teach Teacher study groups Teacher modeling Form study groups *Rdg. Spec. support* Suggest resources Model or co-teach Share resources	*Peer Support* Technology sharing Peers co-teach Teacher study groups Teacher modeling Study groups *Rdg. Spec. support* Suggest resources Model or co-teach Share resources
Target: (1) Students will use integrated language strategies to demonstrate process and content knowledge in all classes.	*Staff Development* September: Two-day workshop Staff development on integrated L/A in content areas October: Half-day wksp Rdg. Spec. & teachers model strategies	*Staff Development* September: Two-day workshop Integrated learning Technology Cult. responsive teaching March: Half-day wksp Collaborative Prob/Solving Technology support Peer demonstration
(2) Secondary teachers will present content and process concurrently using integrated language processes in culturally responsive ways.	*Formative Eval:* Surveys Student work samples How well are we collaborating? *Adjust plan?	*Formative Eval:* Surveys Student work samples Informal tests? How well are we collaborating? *Adjust plan?

FIGURE 3.8   Secondary School Two-Year Grid

Year Two	
Fall	Spring
Articles and Resources	*Articles and Reosurces*
Multicultural literature	Using literature in content areas
Order book sets	Cultural responsive teaching
Inquiry Rdg/Writing	Vocabulary Self-Selection
Project-based learning	Multiple copies:
Technology sharing	Collaboration
Reader response	Peer talk
Peer Support	*Peer Support*
Peers co-teach	Peers co-teach
Technology sharing	Technology sharing
Teacher study groups	Teacher study groups
Teacher modeling	Teacher modeling
New study groups	Study groups
Rdg. Spec. support	*Rdg. Spec. support*
Suggest resources	Suggest resources
Model or co-teach	Model or co-teach
Share resources	Share resources
Staff Development	*Staff Development*
September:	September:
Two-day workshop	Two-day workshop
Inquiry Learning	(teacher identified additional support
Project-based learning	in previous topics)
October:	October:
Half-day wksp	Half-day wksp
Using Literature	Rdg. Spec. and teachers model
	strategies
*Possible distance ed. or on-site	
Univ. course	*Formative Eval:*
	Surveys
Formative Eval:	Student work samples
Surveys	Student/parent surveys
Student work samples	How well are we collaborating?
How well are we collaborating?	
	*Adjust/extend plan?
*Adjust plan?	*What is next goal?

- Begin working on the most ambitious need, the one requiring the greatest change, during the first semester.
- Approach these larger needs in four separate task blocks over the two years.
- Choose the second-biggest need and begin work on that one in the second semester.
- Find creative ways to have teachers act as mentors and coaches for each other.
- Troubleshoot with members of the literacy team about possible barriers to success and create proactive plans.
- Plan strategies you will use if you have to adjust the time line.
- Decide on staff development topics and schedule them over the two-year period (see Chapter 11 for information about professional development).
- Decide how you will evaluate and report incremental progress and successful goal achievement.

The two-year grid continues the process that started with the demographic description of your district and your vision statement. Because all the information has been gathered and decisions have been made, completing the grid is primarily a slot-filling exercise. The high school example in Figure 3.8 refines and translates the need identified in the Content Area Literacy program and expresses it in terms of both student and teacher needs: "Students need integrated language arts instruction that presents content and process concurrently," and "Teachers in the Secondary School need education and support to implement integrated content area literacy instruction into their teaching." Continuing down the first column, you'll notice that the identified needs are transformed into targets or goal statements that can be evaluated. The targets in column one of the sample two-year grid are: "Students will use integrated language strategies to demonstrate process and content knowledge in all classes," and "Secondary teachers will present content and process concurrently using integrated language processes in culturally responsive ways."

It is important to note that, although we have only provided two identified needs for the topic of content literacy, a typical two-year grid might include a number of other areas of need as well. This two-year grid is the culmination of our inquiry and the final piece needed for writing the comprehensive two-year plan.

A sample comprehensive two-year plan can be found in Appendix F. As an alternative to a two-year grid, a two-year schedule was written for this sample plan. Whether you choose to format the information in a two-year grid (as shown in Figure 3.8) or a two-year schedule (as shown in Appendix F), the intent is the same. What is important is that all critical information is included and that the plan is based on the assessed needs. (A thorough discussion of the professional development plan is provided in Chapter 11. It may be helpful to skim or scan this chapter as you prepare your two-year plan).

Evaluating the Progress of Targets and Goals

An evaluation component on the two-year grid suggests that the comprehensive two-year plan is a formative document. By this we mean that, at specifically designated points, progress toward the goal is evaluated and adjustments are made. Notice that, at the bottom of each column in Figure 3.8, there is a formative evaluation entry. These are designed to ask the questions, "How are we doing relative to our goal?" and "Do we need to adjust or add any elements to achieve our target by the end of two years?" For example, perhaps after the first semester you discover that content teachers are having a more difficult time than anticipated switching from a transmission model to one that is more integrated and interactive. The literacy team and a group of content area teachers might meet to brainstorm possible solutions, adjustments, and interventions that will support change. Maybe adjustment involves increasing the use of peer coaching or peer co-teaching at regularly scheduled intervals. Perhaps the reading specialist could implement weekly fifteen-minute mini-workshops on strategies. Whatever the adjustments, they are based on *recorded* evidence from informal surveys, observations, anecdotal records, and student project samples that reflect instruction and learning. There is no formal list or table of such evaluative procedures because they should reflect the unique contexts of the school and the instructional goals. In addition, evaluation should be heavily rooted in authenticity, using the daily events, activities, artifacts, and dialogues as bases for decisions (Valencia, Hiebert, & Afflerbach, 1994).

You have probably heard colleagues make comments like, "Wow—our reading program is awesome! The kids and I love it!" or "This spelling program is awful. The words are just too easy (or too hard). The parents don't like it at all." While these remarks certainly imply an evaluation of sorts, and they may represent anecdotal evidence, they also may not accurately portray what's really happening in the classroom. Glickman, Gordon, and Ross-Gordon (1998, p. 272), offer a tongue-in-cheek classification of five ways by which we may make judgments about literacy programs and approaches:

- Cosmetic method: You examine the program, and if it looks good, it is good.
- Cardiac method: No matter what the data say, you know in your heart that the program is a success.
- Colloquial method: After a brief meeting, preferably at a local watering hole, a group of project staff members (the literacy team perhaps?) concludes that success has been achieved. No one can refute a group decision!
- Curricular method: A successful program is one that can be installed with the least disruption of the ongoing school program.
- Computational method: If you have data, analyze them to death. Whatever the nature of the statistics, use the most sophisticated multivariate regression discontinuity procedures known to humans.

Obviously, we don't subscribe to any of these methods of evaluation, as tempting and ubiquitous as they may be. Instead, our recommendation is to encourage the literacy team to gather multidimensional evidence to see if what is being implemented is truly working. The United States Department of Education (as cited in Glickman, et al., 1998, p. 277) describes the types of evidence that are effective in attaining educational goals. As you read these generic recommendations, reflect on specific literacy-related artifacts you could collect for each type of evidence:

- Evidence demonstrating achievement/changes in knowledge and skills of students (performance assessments, test scores, structured observations of students' application of skills/strategies, content analyses of students' portfolios, projects, or products)
- Evidence demonstrating improvements in teachers' attitudes and behaviors (attitude assessments, surveys, interviews, structured observations, journals, logs, lesson plan books, self-reports, case studies)
- Evidence of improvements in students' attitudes and behaviors (review of school records, attitude assessments, case studies, structured interviews of students, parents, and teachers, journals, logs)

Ongoing Questions about the Process of Change

One of the important concepts related to effective elementary and secondary literacy instruction is the notion of concurrent teaching of content and process (Readence, Bean, & Baldwin, 2000). This is not only relevant to effective instruction, but it also has implications for needs assessments and two-year plans. While it is necessary to evaluate progress toward identified targets and goals, it is also important for the team to evaluate the processes of change. Regularly, we should be asking questions, such as:

- How are the stakeholders and the literacy team doing at acquiring collaborative skills?
- How are teachers doing with the change process?
- Who is taking ownership of the recommendations made in the two-year plan, including budget considerations?
- In addition to acting as a team, are we learning how to be a better team?

REVISITING THE VIGNETTE

Reflect back on the opening vignette and how Janet was being confronted by comments about the school's literacy program. Also, recall that her new principal was unclear about her vision for it. Now that you have knowledge about conducting a needs assessment and creating a two-year plan, discuss the following in a small group:

1. Identify the steps Janet can take to respond to the teachers' comments about "what these students really need."
2. What might Janet say to her principal and these teachers to get them involved in the process?
3. Reread the first paragraph of the vignette. Who would you recommend for Janet's literacy team? How might she actively involve such diverse stakeholders?
4. What, if anything, needs to be done differently in the needs assessment and two-year planning process to accommodate the needs of the English language learners in Janet's school?

POINTS TO REMEMBER

In this chapter we have examined the collaborative processes used in conducting an intensive examination of literacy programs, practices, resources, and stakeholders. This includes involving the literacy team in collecting, organizing, and analyzing data regarding the following: Instructional Practices (Developmental, Content, Intervention, and Recreational Literacy), and Resources, Assessment, and Services. Together, literacy team members collect data about each of the aspects of the school or district's reading/language arts program, using surveys, interviews, and observations. This information is used to acknowledge strengths and identify needs of the literacy program. Together the reading specialist and literacy team summarize the needs assessment information and complete a two-year grid. Based on this information, they then create a focused, formative, comprehensive two-year plan with targets and goals. All aspects of the plan are then evaluated in an ongoing, authentic, multidimensional, and collaborative process.

PORTFOLIO PROJECTS

1. Prepare an outline or narrative containing the specific arguments for engaging in a needs assessment and creating a comprehensive two-year plan. Write the two-page proposal for your principal or another administrator in your school or district.

2. Even though you may not have a literacy team in place yet at your school, create a needs assessment survey that you can pilot with either selected teachers or your entire faculty. Follow the procedures in this chapter for collecting and analyzing the data. Summarize your findings in a three- to five-page needs assessment summary. Remember to seek approval from your administrator prior to distributing any surveys to teachers.

3. Based on your needs assessment summary, create a two-year grid that reflects the needs you identified.

4. Incorporate the needs assessment summary and two-year grid into a comprehensive two-year plan suitable to submit to a principal, curriculum director, superintendent, or school board. Include a formative and summative plan for evaluating the school's progress in meeting the targeted goals.

5. Personal Goal: Revisit the goal you set for yourself at the beginning of the chapter. Create a portfolio item that reflects what you have learned relative to your goal.

RECOMMENDED READINGS

Erickson, L. G. (1995). *Supervision of literacy programs: Teachers as grass-roots change agents.* Boston: Allyn & Bacon. This is a practical, easy-to-read handbook that values teachers, collaboration, and teamwork. Erickson discusses how to facilitate change, while overcoming obstacles and con-

flicts. He states, "True learning involves changing not only how we think but also how we act" (p. xv).

Glickman, C. D., Gordon, S. P., & Ross-Gordon, J. M. (1998). *Supervision of instruction: A developmental approach* (4th ed.). Boston: Allyn & Bacon. This is a general text written for any type of supervisor or administrator. Included is a helpful chapter on Research and Evaluation Skills, with specific information on developing needs assessments and program evaluation tools.

Kapinus, B. A. (1995). Assessment of reading programs. In S. B. Wepner, J. T. Feeley, and D. S. Strickland (Eds.), *The administration and supervision of reading programs* (2nd ed.). Newark, DE: International Reading Association. In this chapter, Barb Kapinus provides an overview of large-scale assessments (such as NAEP), as well as district and schoolwide assessment recommendations. She encourages authenticity, increased involvement of teachers, collaboration, and acknowledgment of the complexity of the evaluation process.

CHAPTER FOUR

MATCHING CONTEXT TO STUDENTS: ASSESSMENT AS INQUIRY

LEARNING GOALS

After reading, discussing, and engaging in activities related to this chapter, you will be able to:

1. describe a model of contextualized assessment;

2. complete a Learner Assessment Profile (LAP);

3. design, implement, and evaluate a school and/or district assessment plan based on a vision statement, needs assessment data, and a two-year plan;

4. Personal Learning Goal: In a three-minute brainstorming session, share what you know about assessment and instruction. Write a goal or a question that reflects something you want to learn as we explore this topic. Share this with others in your group.

Vignette

Joan Forrester is the reading specialist at Crawford Middle School, and she has held this position for the past three years. The school is located in an urban district in a large western state. There are 1200 students in the school, and Joan is the only reading specialist. She is responsible for the school assessment/testing program, for coordinating both the developmental and remedial reading programs for the school, for providing demonstration lessons for teachers, and for teaching reading half-day to students who have been identified as performing below grade level. There are three other reading teachers who are certified in English and they teach in the reading program. Students who are reading at or above grade level are enrolled in "language arts block" classes taught by the English teachers. Those below grade level are enrolled in Reading POWER classes, formerly known as remedial reading.

Joan's school district requires annual standardized testing for all students. In addition, the districtwide literacy team, of which Joan is a member, has discussed at monthly meetings the need for more uniform assessments of students' literacy development. However, the process has stalled because of disagreements about the choice of assessments, time, and accountability. While the district literacy team agrees that standardized test scores provide little usable information for instructional planning, the team hasn't yet developed a more effective assessment system.

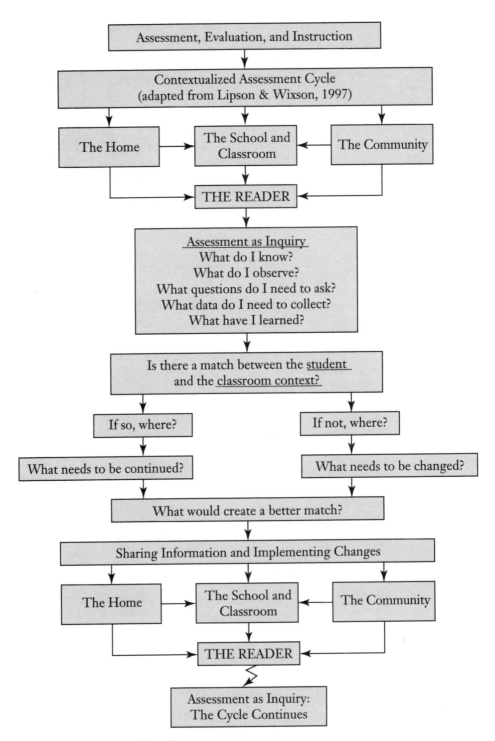

FIGURE 4.1   Chapter Overview

One of the newer reading teachers at Crawford Middle School is Elena Martinez. Elena is a conscientious teacher who is deeply concerned about her students' literacy development, but other than her secondary reading methods course she has had no additional preparation in reading/language arts. Elena is part of the school's literacy team, and was involved in writing a vision statement for Crawford's literacy program. She also helped Joan gather, tally, and analyze the survey data from the school needs assessment.

One Monday morning, Joan, the reading specialist, entered the teachers' lounge to pick up her mail. Before she made it to her box, Elena Martinez grabbed Joan and with some urgency whispered, "I just spoke with Jenny Stewart's dad and he's really worried that she's not progressing in reading as well as her twin sister, Emily. He brought in a copy of her standardized test scores and waved

them in front of my face! He was almost yelling at me. 'Look at these scores! Jenny is a sixth grader and this paper says she can only read at the fourth-grade level! Emily's scores say she's reading at the eighth-grade level. Why aren't you helping Jenny to read better?'"

Elena pleaded with Joan. "I really need your help to see if you think Jenny is having major problems with reading. I don't think she is because I often hear her read out loud. I just think her dad is overreacting to what I think are inaccurate test scores. I've done a few assessments with all my students, but I'm not sure what the results mean. I guess I need you to just tell me that I'm on the right track."

Joan picked up her mail, took a last sip of tepid coffee, and followed Elena to her classroom.

Thinking Points

1. What do you think the reading specialist, Joan Forrester, can do to help Elena?
2. What do you think her first steps should be?
3. What are some of the tensions that both Joan and Elena are faced with?

Expanding the Vignette: Exploring the Tensions

When Elena and Joan reached the classroom, a few students were standing outside in the hallway waiting for their teacher. Joan realized any further conversation with Elena was going to have to wait until after school, so they agreed to meet then. Joan asked Elena to put together some of Jenny's materials, including writing samples, her work folder, test scores, and so forth. She then comforted Elena with, "We'll figure this out,

Elena. I'll help you explain to Jenny's dad how she's doing in reading."

As Joan walked to her own classroom, she thought about how she was going to help Elena communicate to Jenny's dad about his daughter's reading progress. She also concluded that she, as the reading specialist, was going to have to do something about the lack of an effective, comprehensive, and consistent reading assessment program in her school.

Thinking Points

1. What additional tensions surfaced in the remainder of the vignette?
2. What are some short-term suggestions you would give Joan prior to her meeting in the afternoon with Elena?
3. What are some long-term measures that Joan should consider?

4. What are some proactive measures that a reading specialist could take to avoid confrontations with parents, such as the one Elena experienced with Jenny's father?

THE READING SPECIALIST'S ROLE IN ASSESSMENT

In nearly every school and district, a major responsibility of reading specialists is communicating to teachers, administrators, and parents the reading strengths and needs of students. This includes interpreting and explaining standardized test scores, and making recommendations about necessary instructional changes based on the scores. Especially in an age of accountability, when standardized test scores are increasingly used as a barometer of students' and teachers' successes, reading specialists also must be able to balance mandated standardized testing information with more authentic assessment findings. This involves assessing and reporting findings from a variety of individual assessments such as those dealing with alphabet knowledge, concepts about print, phonemic awareness, phonics, spelling, writing, vocabulary, and comprehension.

Obviously, effective assessment and instruction require knowledgeable, informed reading specialists. As we begin this chapter on the reading specialist's role in assessment, it's our expectation that you have most likely completed at least one, if not more, undergraduate and/or graduate courses in the assessment and instruction process. Therefore, we are not discussing here how to assess reading problems, nor will we be including or recommending particular assessment instruments. Rather, we've listed at the end of this chapter some titles of comprehensive texts on assessment that you may wish to review. If you have not had advanced preparation in assessment, then we recommend you try to get the "big picture" in the sections that follow. Think about how our view of the assessment process differs from what occurs in many school districts that subscribe to a "teach-em and test-'em" point of view. Also reflect on how this type of assessment fits with other recommendations about teaching reading that we've made up to this point.

In this chapter, we discuss assessment as a process in which learners' backgrounds (such as their homes, families, and prior experiences), communities (such as neighborhoods, cultures, and ethnic groups), and current instructional contexts (such as their classrooms and schools) are valued and understood for the roles they play in literacy development.

CONTEXTUALIZED ASSESSMENT

The process of implementing an effective school or district assessment system involves reading specialists and teachers who work together to understand and reflect on children's and adolescents' literacy development, as well as the home and educational contexts from which they have come and in which they currently reside. To accomplish this, we ask questions and gather information about learners' background experiences, their past instruction and approaches, outside communities to which they belong, their current classroom contexts, and how they perform while reading and writing. Because there are a wide variety of contributing factors that influence students' reading abilities, we must understand how these factors intersect, and then plan and implement appropriate instruction that is responsive to the demonstrated needs of the students.

Definitions of Assessment, Diagnosis, and Evaluation

Over the years, reading specialists have used the words *assessment, diagnosis,* and *evaluation* to describe the processes for determining students' reading strengths and needs. Let's examine each of the words as defined in the *Literacy Dictionary* (Harris & Hodges, 1995):

- Assessment: The act or process of gathering data in order to better understand the strengths and weaknesses of student learning, as by observation, testing, interviews, etc. (p. 12).
- Diagnosis: The act, process, or result of identifying the nature of a *disorder* or *disability* [our emphasis] through observation and examination. Technically, diagnosis means only the identification and labeling of a disorder. As the term is used in education, however, it often includes the planning of instruction and an assessment of the strengths and weaknesses of the student (p. 59).
- Evaluation: The judgment of performance as process or product of change. Evaluation is an attempt to understand a process that is sometimes guided by preset objectives but at other times involves objectives added during the evaluation process. Like assessment and testing, it entails collecting and weighing evidence for decision making (pp. 76–77).

As we discuss assessment practices for individual students, classrooms, schools and districts, it is important to understand the differences in the meanings of these words. At this point, we need to state up front that we have a difficult time with the term *diagnosis.* Although we were both schooled in the use of this term during our graduate preparation and have used it for years, we (along with many others) have come to view the word negatively when it is applied to reading. Why is this?

Think about the last time you visited the doctor when you were ill. What was the process you went through? Most likely it was something like this:

1. You checked into the medical facility.
2. You were led to an examination room where your *history* and vitals were taken.
3. The attending nurse and then the doctor questioned you about what your *problem* was.
4. The doctor *examined* you and gave you a *diagnosis.*
5. The doctor *prescribed* a medication for you and suggested that you *follow up* with a return visit in a particular amount of time.

6. You took the *prescription* to a pharmacy and it was filled.
7. You participated in a round of *treatment*.
8. You followed up (or didn't) with a visit back to your doctor.
9. Hopefully, eventually, you were *cured*.

Many of the italicized words or versions of them have been used in the field of reading for decades. As school and district reading specialists, we both took *histories*; we discussed students' reading *problems* or *disabilities*; we *examined*; we *diagnosed*; we *prescribed*; and we *treated*. In graduate school, we even did all this in a reading *clinic* during our *clinical* experience. Now, as you compare going to the doctor with teaching a child (or adolescent), where does this medical model break down? Can we prescribe medicines for our students? Are our students ill and should we be aiming for their cure?

The Difference Model

Martha Rapp Ruddell (2001) identifies three examples of the medical model that have been especially prevalent in reading education, special education, and compensatory programs, such as Title I. These include:

- Defect Model: Something is wrong with the child. The teacher's role is to find what it is and fix it.
- Deficit Model: Something is missing in the child's development. The teacher's role is to discover what's missing and teach it.
- Disruption Model: Some trauma is interfering with learning. The teacher's role is to remove or reduce the impact.

Notice how each of these implies the student *has* a problem or *is* a problem reader. Ruddell suggests that there is a more appropriate way of viewing student progress in reading and it doesn't deal with "problems" at all. It is called the

- Difference Model: There is a difference between a student's performance and expected achievement. The teacher's role is to locate the difference and adjust instruction and materials to achieve a closer match.

Note that this is not a medical model because there is no implied pathology; that is, there's nothing deemed *wrong* with the student. Additionally, where the previous medical models refer only to readers with problems, the Difference Model is appropriate for all learners for whom there is a mismatch with instruction. Also, here the onus is on the teacher or reading specialist whose role is to locate where the difference is and to make necessary adaptations in instruction to better meet the students' literacy needs.

Contextualized assessment lies within the Difference Model that has, at its center, the student. Marge Lipson and Karen Wixson (1997) suggest that "the notion of the proper match between student and circumstance is what we must grasp if we are to be effective evaluators and instructors . . . We must look at the individual in interaction with specific texts, tasks, and methods" (p. 58). We concur, and add that we also must look at the individual in interaction with his or her family, background, culture, language, life experiences, communities of involvement, and classroom contexts.

Contextualized assessment involves complex inquiry processes that acknowledge the factors that create the children and adolescents who are sitting in our classrooms. Evolved from an earlier diagnostic teaching process as conceived by Lipson and Wixson (1997), contextualized assessment is predicated on the belief that each student is an individual, and that one-size-for-all programs for assessment and instruction are antithetical to effective practice. This type of assessment involves gathering data from students' homes, communities, and classroom contexts, and leads to the planning and implementation of appropriate literacy instruction.

Within this view of assessment, it is not surprising that Jenny and Emily, the fraternal twins introduced in the vignette, are developing differently as readers and writers, even though they come from the same home, are the same age, and have had many of the same life experiences. Before assessing Jenny's reading and writing behaviors, however, Joan's first step in the contextualized assessment process is to gain a better understanding of the varied factors in Jenny's home that have influenced her reading development.

The Home

At this point in the assessment process, the reading specialist's job is to step back and collect clues. This includes information about the home environment and all other pertinent factors affecting school performance, including home language; the parents' educational levels; whether the family has remained intact; number and location of moves to new schools and communities; pertinent medical information; former schooling contexts and school records; current performance data and school records; interviews with parents or caregivers; and the student's interests and talents. The task is not to jump to conclusions, but rather just to record all the information you can gather. For example, it might be tempting to deduce, "She was premature. That must be it!" or "He was in four foster homes before grade three." Resist the temptation to solve the "mystery," and keep searching for other relevant information.

In Appendix G you will find a blank form we call the Learner Assessment Profile (LAP). Use it as you progress through the assessment-instruction process, and include all relevant background information. At the end of the chapter, you will find a completed LAP for Jenny, the middle school student introduced in the vignette.

Group Inquiry Activity

1. If you were Joan Forrester, the reading specialist, what would you do at this point to gather background information?
2. What information would you gather?
3. To whom would you talk?
4. What questions would you ask?
5. Where would you look for information?

Write down some ideas for gathering information about Jenny's background, family, and home contexts, and share them with group members during class.

The Community

In contextualized assessment, we take a broad view of what we mean by *community*. Within this context, community may refer to: (1) a language community (such as, all speak Vietnamese or another home language); (2) cultural community (such as, all are immigrants who arrived in America in the 1970s during the Vietnamese War, or any other cultural group); (3) socioeconomic community (any economic group—lower class, middle class, upper class, or anything in-between); (4) educational community (such as no high school; high school graduate; college graduate; graduate degrees); family community (all are related by blood, marriage, or adoption); interest community (all share a common interest, hobby, or other avocation); work community (all share the same vocation or workplace); religious community (all share the same faith); and so forth. While many, these may represent only a few of the communities to which *you* belong. Can you think of others?

Jim Gee (2001a) has identified four ways to view an individual's identity, or, as he says, "what it means to be a certain kind of person" (p. 100). For example, the same person might be identified as a left-handed, fraternal twin, who is a funny male teacher, who rides Harleys. Gee proposes that these identities function within particular contexts or across a set of different contexts. Thus, the first way to view our exemplar's identity is that he's a left-handed male twin. This, Gee suggests, is because of a force in nature—other identities resulting from a force in nature might include being a redhead, a female, gifted, artistic, tall or short, a breast cancer survivor, a recovering alcoholic, or an adult with Attention Deficit Disorder (ADD).

The person's second identity as teacher results from his position in an institution, in this case education. Holding positions as a judge, nurse, or newspaper reporter are other examples of positions authorized by institutions. The third identity of our male, twin teacher is that he's a funny person. Gee labels this as a discourse-identity, one in which individual traits become associated with people due to their interactions with others. A person is only funny when there's someone else who laughs; one isn't funny, or charismatic, or grouchy all by himself, but only in relationship to others.

The fourth way to view identity, according to Gee (2000a, 2000b) is by the various groups in which we choose to participate. In our example, the teacher owns a Harley motorcycle and belongs to a club of Harley riders. This is what Gee refers to as an "affinity group," because members share similar interests. Affinity group members may share little other than interests, and they may be dispersed across a great distance. "What people in the group share, and must share to constitute an affinity group, is allegiance to, access to, and participation in specific practices that provide each of the group's members the requisite experiences" (Gee, 2001a, p. 105).

Now, what do affinity groups, as well as the other ways of viewing identity, have to do with contextualized assessment? Communities, those groups that people choose to participate in, are similar to Gee's notions of affinity groups, and if we are to understand students' strengths and needs, we also need to be aware of their various communities, and, yes, identities. Now, we're not suggesting that you act as a nosy neighbor, poking around where you may not be appreciated. Rather, we think it's important to understand "where students come from." And this may include coming to an understanding of the multiple communities to which our students belong. This information is not hard to find; it can be attained through informal means such as interest inventories, reading logs, interviews, home visits, observations, and just through conversation.

Group Inquiry Activity

1. What types of questions might Elena and Joan want to ask in order to gather some information about the communities in which Jenny resides?
2. To whom should these questions be addressed?
3. How might this information shed light on Jenny as a learner?
4. Reflect on each of the four types of identities. How would you describe yourself? How would you describe the others in your discussion group? Is your description of yourself the same or different from the descriptions others hold? Why do you think this is so? What would you want others to know about you?

Share your questions and ideas with other group members.

The School and Classroom

In our desire to quickly determine students' literacy strengths and weaknesses, we frequently overlook two influential factors: the current classroom and school contexts. With contextualized assessment, it is of critical importance that we know what's going on in the regular classroom, especially as it relates to reading/language arts instruction. Additionally, we need to reflect on the school's vision, educational plans, standards, and provisions for meeting all students' literacy needs.

This oversight occurs when we view the learner as the sole source of difficulty. Other factors are missed, such as possible mismatches with instructional approaches, curriculum, materials, or grouping arrangements. But this is not a time to cast judgments about what's happening in the classroom—you're only gathering information at this point. If there's even a hint of disapproval about what you're observing when you go into teachers' classrooms, you'll lose an important data source about students' learning contexts. Teacher interviews, surveys, self-assessments, classroom observations, materials checklists, and conversations about literacy instruction all yield helpful information.

The Reader: Assessment as Inquiry

Now, we're ready to begin assessing the reader. Throughout this process, the following questions should guide our inquiry:

1. What do I know?
2. What do I observe?

3. What questions do I need to ask?
4. What data do I need to collect?
5. And . . . now, what have I learned?

As we have explored the student's background, learned about the various communities in which she participates, and developed insights about her present instructional context, we have begun to answer these questions. At this point, we also may have generated a few ideas about what might be preventing a student from making adequate progress. These insights and other relevant background information are recorded on the student's Learner Assessment Profile (LAP).

What comes next obviously depends on what we have learned up to this point about the focal student, as well as his or her age and grade level. We'll be gathering varied sources of information, including observational and interview data, findings from informal reading and writing assessments, and standardized norm-referenced tests. Also, before we begin the sit-down assessments, we recommend, if possible, that the student is "tailed." Kid-watching (Goodman, 1994) involves observing a student in a variety of different contexts, such as the lunchroom, playground, PE, and in the hallway with peers, and provides additional insights into how her behavior and motivation might differ throughout the day, depending on setting. Take notes during observations (record exactly what you're seeing, with no judgments or conclusions), and file them in a specially created assessment file for this student.

Note that, with contextualized assessment, it's perfectly appropriate to use any of the known, reliable assessment instruments that you have found to be helpful, such as phonemic awareness, phonics, and spelling surveys, retellings, and Informal Reading Inventories (IRI). Marge Lipson and Karen Wixson (1997) suggest that the assessment–instruction process is more of an art than a science. There are many decisions throughout the assessment process, and the complex interactions that exist between various factors that influence literacy development are never quite the same for any two students. Therefore, as a reading specialist you will need to have a variety of assessment instruments available to you and the teachers with whom you work.

When you have completed the assessments that you think will provide the information you need about the student's literacy skills and abilities, record the data on the Learner Assessment Profile. File the assessment protocols in the student's assessment folder. It's very important to keep all protocols, as you may need to refer to them or share them with the student, teachers, parents, or administrators.

Group Inquiry Activity   Share within your group the assessment instruments you have found to be especially helpful in providing useful information for planning literacy instruction.

1. Which of the assessment instruments have you administered in the past? Are there any that are new to you?
2. Have you analyzed assessment findings for each of them?
3. Would you be able to teach another person how to use each of them?

If you feel unsure about how to administer assessment instruments and analyze their findings, consult the list of sources at the end of this chapter for assistance.

Is There a Match between the Student and the Classroom Context?

This step in the contextualized assessment process, taken from Lipson and Wixson's (1997) diagnostic teaching model, requires that we step back from all the data we've collected and evaluate whether the instructional context is appropriate for the student's assessed strengths and needs. This allows us to ask and to begin answering the following questions:

1. If there is a match between the student's background, the instructional context, and the assessed strengths and needs, where is it? What needs to be continued?
2. If there is a mismatch between the student's background, the instructional context, and the assessed strengths and needs, where is it? What needs to be changed?

Group Inquiry Activity   For discussion purposes, take a look at Jenny's Learner Assessment Profile (LAP) at the end of this chapter. Review the background information that was gathered about her. What, if anything, is noteworthy in her background?

Notice that the assessment data suggest that Jenny is not a fluent reader of grade-level material. During her oral reading of the fourth-grade passage on the Johns Basic Reading Inventory, she read very slowly with many miscues. When Joan asked her to retell what she had just read, she was unable to do so, though she could answer comprehension questions when prompted. Also note that, while Jenny read aloud the third-grade passage, when asked to retell what she read, she was only able to recall a few details and missed the overall idea of the passage.

During Joan's observations in Elena Martinez's sixth-grade class, she noticed that the students were engaged in a whole-class reading of the novel, *Where the Red Fern Grows* (Rawls, 1961). While Jenny occasionally volunteered to read aloud from the book, she pulled back and participated very little during discussions, either with Elena or her peers. She appeared to follow and enjoy the story, but did not want to discuss it during class.

1. Based on the assessment information presented in Jenny's LAP, do you think there is a match or mismatch in the reading instruction that Elena is providing Jenny?
2. Why do you think so?
3. What are the areas of match?
4. What are the areas of mismatch?
5. What do you think might be interfering with Jenny's ability to successfully read grade-level materials?

Share your ideas with the others in your group.

What Would Create a Better Match?

Now, it's time to make some informed guesses as to the school and classroom contexts that might be more appropriate for Jenny. Within contextualized assessment, we may find we have a primary area of mismatch, or several areas, and it might be necessary to prioritize them by asking what is needed most. When you have generated a hunch, then consider how much control or influence is possible over what seems to be causing the mismatched area(s).

For example, based on the assessment data, it appears there is a mismatch between Jenny's needs and some of the reading instruction she's receiving. Her grade-level reading series has an anthology with wonderful fiction and nonfiction, and the novels that her teacher is reading aloud are compelling and appropriate for sixth graders. However, Jenny cannot read independently or even instructionally in either the anthology selections or the novels. She also regularly selects books that are too difficult for the daily silent reading activity. There appears, then, to be a rather serious mismatch between the texts that are provided for Jenny and the texts that she needs for reading instruction and practice.

You might also suspect that the whole-class literature discussions that Elena engages her students in may not be meeting Jenny's need for the explicit teaching and modeling of decoding and comprehension skills and strategies. Thus, we can predict that a better match for Jenny would include intensive instruction in decoding and comprehension skills and strategies, using texts that she can read, *in addition to* (not in place of) continued exposure to the grade-level vocabulary, concepts, and texts taught in the reading series. It might also help her access the grade-level anthology and novels if she has scaffolded support, such as can be provided in small groups with teacher-led reciprocal teaching (Palinscar & Brown, 1984).

At this point, it may be tempting to think, "Aha! We've got it!" But contextualized assessment involves more than a single solution or answer. Rather, there may be a number of ways to approach the mismatch found in Jenny's classroom literacy instruction. For example, Joan, the reading specialist, might offer to run a reciprocal teaching group in Elena's classroom so that students, including Jenny, could receive comprehension strategy instruction. Also, Joan might model the process for Elena so that Jenny's teacher could also work with a small group, teaching reciprocal teaching strategies. Or, Joan might see if Jenny could come into the reading specialist's classroom for some intensive group work with several other students needing similar help with decoding and comprehension. Or, a combination of these ideas might be feasible.

Sharing Information and Implementing Changes

With all the information gathered, it's time to complete the Learning Assessment Profile and share the results.

Group Inquiry Activity   In a small group, discuss the following questions:

1. Do you think that the completed Learner Assessment Profile should be shared with parents? If so, under what circumstances? If not, under what circumstances?

2. Do you think that the completed LAP should be shared with the classroom teacher? Why or why not?
3. Do you think that the completed LAP should be shared with the student? Why or why not? If your answer is yes, how might you do it in an individually responsive manner?
4. Do you think that the completed LAP should be shared with the principal? Why or why not? How about with other teachers (especially at the secondary level), or with other stakeholders, such as special education teachers?

How the LAP is written is important. If it's highly critical of the current classroom context or the home environment, you risk offending the teacher or the parents. Therefore, note that in the example of Jenny's LAP at the end of this chapter, information is provided in a factual way, without judgments or biases. We omitted wording that attributed blame, and stated recommendations in terms of what the teacher and reading specialist could do to learn about and then lessen the difference between Jenny's present and expected performance in reading. Writing the LAP takes practice; remember that the purpose of the contextualized assessment process is to ultimately achieve a closer match between Jenny's classroom context and her background and assessed needs.

Implementing Changes

As you begin to implement changes, you may feel unsure as to whether they're effectively lessening the difference between a student's assessed needs and the instruction the student is receiving, and you might wonder if other changes are warranted. For example, let's say that the reading specialist, Joan, decides to organize a reciprocal teaching group in Elena's classroom. She teaches the four reciprocal teaching strategies (predicting, questioning, clarifying, summarizing) to the entire class and then, while Elena works with the rest of the students, Joan pulls together six others, including Jenny, for small-group work. However, she soon realizes that, despite the small group environment, Jenny is still ill-at-ease and lacks confidence about participating. Joan, in consultation with Elena, decides that, in order to boost Jenny's confidence and participation, an even smaller group is needed. For the first two weeks of their work together, Joan works with Jenny and just two other children—and the book that they begin with is a high interest, low-vocabulary informational book about ballet, Jenny's first love. Bingo! A match is established and Jenny becomes involved. Joan suspects that other students can be added gradually to the group, and that other books of interest to Jenny and the group can eventually be selected.

Contextualized assessment suggests that, in our quest for a better instructional match, we need to try something different if our first idea isn't working. In other words, we need to search for a more appropriate context. In this case, changing the group size makes a difference in Jenny's participation. Joan also suggests that Elena incorporate more explicit instruction in comprehension strategies for all of her students, and she models how this can be done. Elena and Joan put up posters that list the comprehension strategies that good readers use, along with examples of students' think-alouds that are printed on the posters. Students make bookmarks with the comprehension strategies listed on them, and they are encouraged to talk about the kinds of connections they make while reading. All of these changes boost Jenny's confidence as she sees that all the students in her class need to learn comprehension strategies. Joan continues to work with Jenny on decoding and spelling in her own classroom, as well as in the small group with reciprocal teaching.

Gradually, Jenny begins to demonstrate that she's "getting it." She also begins to take a more active role in class discussions and, for the first time, she is able to verbally summarize what she reads, both from texts she reads at home (such as Web sites and magazine articles), and what she reads in school. When she writes her first research report, not surprisingly, the topic is ballet. During the oral presentation before her class, Jenny shares what she has learned with confidence.

It's important to remember that contextualized assessment and instruction involve a flexible approach to planning, and they require that the reading specialist have a repertoire of assessments, instructional strategies, and materials available for students and teachers. You will notice on the Learner Assessment Profile that there is room for you to record the student's projected learning outcomes and recommended instructional approaches, both those attempted and those that were found to be successful. And, don't forget to sign the LAP. As a professional, your signature demonstrates that you stand by your recommendations.

What Happens Now?

Again, it may be tempting at this point to think, "Ahhh . . . all's better now." However, if you review the Contextualized Assessment cycle in Figure 4.1 at the beginning of this chapter, you'll see that the procedures are ongoing and continuous, rather than linear. Assessment and teaching are recursive processes, as we reexamine, rethink, replan, reassess, and reteach, continually striving for closer instructional matches for all students.

There's one last caveat about this assessment process. Our expectation is not that you complete Learner Assessment Profiles for all students in your school, or even in your classroom. Not all students require this type of comprehensive assessment and subsequent instructional change. But, if you have students who are struggling, despite their intellectual, linguistic, or ability levels, they need (and deserve) appropriate literacy assessment and instruction. Contextualized assessment, situated in the Difference Model, can assist you and the teachers with whom you work in providing for these students.

IMPLICATIONS FOR DEVELOPING A SCHOOLWIDE ASSESSMENT PROGRAM

One of the most important tasks of the school's literacy team is to determine which assessment instruments will be used, by whom, for what students, at what grade levels, and at what intervals during the year. Increasingly, school districts are requiring that teachers collect assessment data, such as running records and fluency measures, and individual schools may have little flexibility about the assessment process. However, when the district requires assessments to be administered on a prescribed schedule, it is not unusual for teachers to complete these mandates and then file the results away until the next round of testing. Rather than viewing assessment as integral to instruction, they do what they're required to do, and don't use the rich assessment data to guide their decisions about literacy teaching. Part of this is because these teachers may not understand the relationship between assessment and instruction. They also may feel overwhelmed by the sheer number of students they have, all of whom have different needs and strengths that need to be addressed.

With a little adjustment, contextualized assessment can be implemented school-wide, and, of course, we believe that the reading specialist is the person to lead the effort. We have found that successful implementation of a schoolwide assessment–instruction model is much easier if you and the literacy team think about the following:

1. In Chapter 2, you learned how to examine your and your colleagues' beliefs about multiple literacies and the impact of a variety of factors on literacy development. Look closely at the culture of your school and at the cultural milieu of all of your students. What are their backgrounds? What is your community like? How would you describe the educational environment that your students are growing up in? Revisit your school's vision statement about literacy teaching and learning. Review the findings of your school's needs assessment. Just as you need to collect background information for assessing a student's strengths and needs, you also need to collect background about school and community strengths and needs.

2. Take a snapshot of the current literacy programs in your school, including materials, approaches, and interventions. Look at the developmental reading program and reflect on how well the adopted reading program and other instructional materials are meeting the literacy needs of your student population. Use the findings from your needs assessment survey to reflect on how teachers view the effectiveness of their reading programs. What are their needs? What are their wants? What do they see as program-matic strengths? What do they see as programmatic weaknesses? Go through the same process for any intervention or other literacy programs you have in place, including special education services and media/library resources and support.

3. Meet with the school's literacy team to review a variety of assessment instruments that are available and have been field-tested with a population similar to your school's. Examine what teachers are already using and discuss what works, what doesn't, and why. Think about how assessments should reflect district and state standards, as well as district benchmarks for performance.

4. Once the literacy team has reviewed the assessments and has recommendations ready to present to the faculty, plan for a retreat or faculty meeting with sufficient time to introduce, seek feedback, and explain the proposed assessment plan. In some cases, such a plan will require a vote of the faculty. Keep in mind that effective assessment requires knowledgeable teachers who understand the instruments and who buy into the process—they need to understand how assessment informs instruction, rather than see this as another set of mandates dumped from "on high." Practice sessions with the assessments, opportunities to share assessment findings with each other, and grade-level meetings to discuss effective instructional approaches are all very important to the process, and it's critical to let teachers know up front that they will have these opportunities to learn the process together.

5. In order for assessment to be viewed by teachers as useful rather than burdensome, provide a means of recording assessment data that doesn't require an inordinate amount of time. Some districts are providing electronic forms, while others rely on paper-and-pencil formats. We have included in Appendix H a Classroom Assessment Profile, a form that you might find useful. While the Learner Assessment Profile (Appendix G) is appropriate for an individual student, the Classroom Assessment Profile in Appendix H is designed to capture at-a-glance assessment information for an entire class.

6. It is up to the literacy team, with the reading specialist's guidance, to evaluate the effectiveness of the school's assessment plan. As with classroom assessment, schoolwide assessment must be monitored and changed if it's not working well. Talk to teachers and listen to what they say. Make changes based on their recommendations, if warranted. Most importantly, remember that, if the assessment process is viewed by your colleagues as just one more thing to do, rather than as an indispensable part of the instructional program in reading/language arts, they will ultimately either abandon the assessments or begrudgingly complete them . . . then file them away, never to be seen again.

IMPLICATIONS FOR DISTRICTWIDE ASSESSMENT PROGRAMS

The recommendations for developing a schoolwide assessment program are much the same as those for developing a district-level assessment program. If you are a reading coordinator or supervisor, you will still work closely with your district literacy team. Key decisions and recommendations will come from this committee, and, ideally, the Superintendent or your immediate supervisor will look to you for leadership in implementing an effective program of assessment. Again, vision statements, needs assessment results, and two-year plans will guide the development of your assessment system, as will the district and state content standards. Likewise, the multiple linguistic, cultural, educational, and socioeconomic communities represented in the district must be considered, so as to not privilege or disadvantage any group.

At the district level, the issue of standardized testing is usually paramount. Depending on your district and state, these tests may be perceived by some in the educational community as critical indicators of accountability that point to trends over time, by others as "necessary evils," and by still others as the bane of their existence; a cause of stress for students, parents, teachers, and administrators, alike. Regardless of your personal opinion about standardized tests, if you are in a district literacy position, you will almost certainly be required to fulfill a key role in implementing the district testing program. We hope you can have a long-term positive influence in shaping an assessment program that is responsive to the needs of the school and community as well as the students.

REVISITING THE VIGNETTE

Reflect on the next steps that Joan Forrester, Crawford Middle School's reading specialist, should take to establish a schoolwide assessment program that will foster more effective literacy instruction. In this vignette, Elena Martinez, Jenny's teacher, was very receptive to the reading specialist's suggestions and ideas. Consider a teacher you may know who would be less than receptive to a reading specialist's recommendations. How would you approach this person? What could you do to make this teacher more comfortable about having you in his or her classroom? What, if any, is the role of the literacy team in supporting teachers who are reluctant or resistant to change?

POINTS TO REMEMBER

Integral to effective literacy instruction is an equally effective assessment process. Assessment and instruction should be inextricably linked in a recursive, ongoing, and dynamic way. All of the factors that shape a child's literacy development are considered: background experiences; home environment; communities in which the student resides; previous educational experiences; the current classroom context; and the student's assessed literacy skills and abilities. Instruction is designed around assessment data, predicated on the belief that multiple data sources can lead to varied instructional approaches, materials, and methods designed to meet a student's assessed needs. Establishing the right match between the student's needs and appropriate literacy instruction is the ultimate goal of contextualized assessment. Schoolwide and district assessment programs can be designed around these basic principles. Because equity and access are inherent in this assessment model, it is especially congruent with a sociocultural perspective.

Remember, it is important to think about who needs what kind of information. The superintendent and school board will want broad comparative data. Parents often want to know how their child is doing relative to peers, and teachers need the kind of information that will determine their daily instructional decisions. High-stakes testing, in the form of standardized, norm-referenced tests, can be the cause of anxiety for students, parents, teachers, and administrators. However, we believe that we can use standardized test scores to inform us about longitudinal trends and global performance of students within schools and districts. Likewise, we encourage more authentic means of assessment for making instructional decisions related to reading/language arts. District reading specialists have the responsibility to inform, be informed, and work with all stakeholders in implementing and evaluating school and district assessment programs.

PORTFOLIO PROJECTS

1. Select two of your students who are at different levels of literacy development. Use contextualized assessment to locate matches and mismatches in their instructional programs. Complete a Learner Assessment Profile (LAP) for each student. At the end of the eight weeks, reflect on your instruction. Which aspects were especially appropriate for the students' needs? What would you change? How did the LAP help you in focusing on what needed to be changed? What will you do next to assist these students in overcoming their assessed reading difficulties?

2. Consider the assessment instruments that teachers are currently using in your school. If these are effective, adapt the Classroom Assessment Profile (Appendix H) for your own school's needs.

3. Even within a community of 50,000 or an area of a large city, the cultural community can vary greatly from school to school and neighborhood to neighborhood. Survey several schools in your district to determine the assessment instruments that are used. Is there consistency across the schools? Should there be consistency? What kinds of assessment results are being used by teachers to plan their literacy instruction? Check with your district's curriculum coordinator, reading coordinator, or supervisor of testing. See if you can discover how decisions have been made regarding the required assessments for your district. Who made the decisions? What test/assessments are required? What type of inservice do teachers receive about using these assessments to guide their instruction? What happens to all of the assessment findings? Is the process equitable for all students? Are any students disadvantaged by the process? How do you know? As the reading coordinator, what would you do to either improve the process if it's not working effectively, or sustain and maintain it, if it is?

4. Personal Goal: Revisit the objective you set for yourself at the beginning of the chapter. Create a portfolio item that reflects what you have learned relative to your objective.

RECOMMENDED READINGS

Johns, J. J. (1997). *Basic reading inventory*. Dubuque, IA: Kendall/Hunt. This is a widely used, comprehensive series of assessments. If you're starting out as a reading specialist, we recommend this group of assessments because you'll have a good variety of instruments for assessing word recognition, phonics, and comprehension—and there are multiple sets of leveled passages that can be used throughout the year.

International Reading Association. (1999). *High-stakes assessments in reading*. Newark, DE: Author. This is a position statement of IRA that includes a strong statement against high-stakes testing that compares students. It provides recommendations for what all stakeholders can do to use assessment appropriately to benefit learners.

Lipson, M., & Wixson, M. (2003). *Assessment and instruction of reading and writing disability* (3rd ed.). New York: Longman. This is a comprehensive text on assessment and instruction, intended for teachers and specialists. It includes a thorough discussion of how to select appropriate assessments, issues surrounding standardized testing, information about laws regulating special education, steps for creating detailed case studies based on assessment information, and much more.

U.S. Department of Education, International Reading Association, & HCI The Life Issues Publisher. (2000). *A practical guide to reading assessments*. Newark, DE: International Reading Association. This inexpensive guide to assessment includes the dimensions of reading as described in the document *Preventing Reading Difficulties in Young Children* (Snow, et al., 1998). Possible assessments for each dimension are described, with the targeted grade level, purpose, description of the assessment, why and when to use it, how to order it, administration requirements, and how to interpret results. This is an excellent resource for reading specialists.

FIGURE 4.2 Jenny's Learner Assessment Profile (LAP)[1]

Identifying Information		
Name **Jenny Stewart**[2] Date of Birth **2/18/89**		Date of Report **3/7/02**
Parents **Edward and Maria Stewart**		Phone **123-456-7890**
School **Crawford** Grade **6**		Teacher **Elena Martinez**

Background: Home and Community

Jenny Stewart was referred by her teacher and parents because her academic performance is 2–3 years below grade level. Her parents are concerned about Jenny's reading and they're considering hiring a tutor. Jenny has attended Crawford Elementary since first grade. During 4th grade, she received additional support in writing, three days/week. She lives with her mother, father, and fraternal twin sister, who achieves at or above grade level in all subject areas. Jenny's mother reports regular trips to the public library; Jenny also has a large library of books at home. Her favorite books are about ballerinas, ballet, and female athletes. She states she prefers having someone read aloud to her rather than reading to herself. Jenny identifies her father as someone who reads to her at home and states that she reads to her mother. Jenny and her sister are involved in Girl Scouts, their church youth group, and ballet. Jenny states that she wants to play soccer with her "best friend," Allison, in the YMCA youth league but she hasn't joined at this point. Her aspirations are to become a graphic artist like her mother. Jenny is of average height and weight for her age and is reported to have normal hearing, vision, no allergies, and she is currently not on any medication.

The School and Classroom

Jenny is in a heterogeneous sixth-grade classroom with 28 other students. Her teacher, Mrs. Martinez, is in her third year of teaching sixth grade. The student population includes four special education students, seven English language learners, and two children who are receiving special services for the gifted. The four special education children attend Reading POWER classes; Jenny does not. For her core reading instruction, Mrs. Martinez uses the district adopted reading series, *Literacy for All* (ABC Publishers). This integrated literature-based program includes spelling, grammar, and writing instruction; all literacy instruction is whole-class, and all students read the same core literature. Mrs. Martinez reads novels to her students, a chapter a day. All students have 20 minutes/day of DEAR (Drop Everything and Read). According to Mrs. Martinez, Jenny usually selects "very difficult books" for the DEAR time. Writing is taught in a workshop format once a week. A spelling list of 20 words from the reading series is provided all students each week, with a Friday test. The teacher reports that her literacy assessment consists of end-of-theme skills tests that are a part of the reading series. During four classroom observations of the language arts block, Jenny participated very little or not at all, often looking out the windows or playing with objects in her desk. Only when Mrs. Martinez asked

---

[1]Adapted from Lipson & Wixson, 1997, p. 464.

[2]This Learner Assessment Profile is based on an actual report completed by a recent graduate student in reading at CSULB. All identifying information for the student has been changed, and pseudonyms for the student, parents, and school are used here.

her direct questions, did she say anything. She was observed to volunteer once during around-the-room oral reading. During DEAR, she paged through picture books or magazines, seldom or never appearing to read any extended text.

Assessment Information		
Assessment	Date	Findings
Primary Spelling Inventory (Determines developmental spelling stage)[3]	2/20/02	Words correct: 8/25 Orthographic features: 44/60 Estimated stage: Within Word Pattern
Johns[4] Graded Word List (Leveled word recognition test)	2/20/02	Primer 19/20 Independent Grade 2 18/20 Instructional Grade 4 13/20 Frustration
Johns Basic Inventory (Child orally and silently reads leveled passages and answers comprehension questions)	2/25/02	Gr. 2 92 wpm 10/10 quest. Independent Gr. 3 70 wpm 7/10 quest. Instructional Gr. 4 50 wpm 8/10 quest. Instructional Gr. 5 42 wpm 6/10 quest. Frustration Silent reading of Gr. 4 (passage B): 7/10 ques.
Interest Inventory (Assesses interests and "favorites/least favorites")	2/26/02	Participates in ballet, soccer, and church activities; subscribes to *Teen People*; best friend: twin sister, Emily. Likes math, not reading; finds school "frustrating" but "fun"
Writing Sample	2/25/02	Completed approx. $\frac{1}{2}$ page on assigned topic of ballet; simple listing of reasons she likes ballet; multiple spelling errors; 2 sentence frags.; includes concluding sentence.
Standardized Test Scores: SAT9	4/01	Reading Vocabulary: Stanine 2 Reading Comprehension: Stanine 2 Total Reading: Stanine 2 Spelling: Stanine 3 Language Mechanics: Stanine 3 All stanines are below average

Analysis of Assessment

Interests: Jenny's favorite activity and where she exudes the most confidence is ballet; she has taken lessons since age 4. Her twin sister, Emily, also attends ballet lessons. Jenny wants to learn to play soccer. Her intense dislike of reading is readily expressed: "I hate it. Emily loves it. My dad doesn't think I'm a good reader. I guess I'm not."

Spelling: Jenny demonstrates mastery in initial/final consonants; has difficulty with short vowel sounds of *a, e,* and *o.* Demonstrates accuracy with some digraphs/blends, except for *ck, sn, ch,* and *ght* spellings. Writing sample also confirms difficulty with these sounds/patterns (misspelled *has* and *pet*). Confuses diphthongs *ou/ow.* Most spelling errors in Within Word Pattern stage.

[3] Primary Spelling Inventory: see Bear, Invernizzi, Templeton, & Johnston (2000).

[4] Johns graded word lists and leveled passages: Johns, J. J. (1997). Basic reading inventory. Dubuque, IA: Kendall/Hunt.

Reading: Errors on graded word list include short vowels, and vowel combinations (*ai, ea, a-e,* and *oa*). Word-by-word reading with finger pointing; long hesitations during oral reading of 3rd- and 4th-grade passages. When told pronunciation of unfamiliar words, quickly reads word in phrase with little attention to punctuation. Frequently looks to examiner for assistance and reinforcement; displays little confidence, especially in testing situation. Substitutes visually similar words (e.g., *frosty* for *forest*). Is hesitant to try any retellings (on 3rd-gr. passage provided few details, no overall main idea); requires prompted comprehension questions for all passages. Comprehends factual information well, despite frequent miscues and self-corrections. Fluency rates difficult to assess because Jenny stops and wants to discuss text—either with questions or text-to-self connections she's making. Doesn't appear to use strategies while reading; focuses almost exclusively on word-by-word reading. Was observed during class reading lesson often looking disengaged or confused by what Mrs. Martinez was teaching.

Match or Mismatch With Present Instructional Context

Matching Areas:
Jenny wants to select her own magazines and books for DEAR. She enjoys listening to Mrs. Martinez read aloud. She likes to write when she can write about topics that are familiar to her, such as ballet. The writing workshop format lends itself to the type of writing Jenny does best.

Areas of Mismatch:
There is a mismatch in the type of reading instruction Jenny is receiving and what she needs. The areas of mismatch include the following:

1. Texts: Grade-level texts for Jenny's reading instruction are too difficult and frustrating for her.
2. Nature of Instruction: Whole-class teaching is not meeting Jenny's assessed needs. It is too easy for her to become disengaged and uninvolved during reading instruction and discussions.
3. Spelling: Whole-class spelling instruction with the same weekly lists for all students is inappropriate to Jenny's assessed needs. The words are too difficult and she is not learning word structure and patterns.
4. Although Jenny participates in daily DEAR, she is selecting books that are too difficult. Frustration-level reading materials will not improve her reading.

What Might Achieve a Closer Instructional Match?[5]
We need to help Jenny develop confidence in and motivation to read. In order to accelerate her literacy development, we need to provide her with access to books that deal with topics she's interested in and wants to learn about (e.g., ballet and female athletes). We need to provide her with explicit and consistent instruction in reading in the following areas of assessed need: decoding strategies (including a review of orthographic patterns), comprehension skills, comprehension strategies, spelling, and writing instruction that focuses on varied genres. She will also benefit from fluency practice with instructional and independent level text. Most important, we need to continue to provide daily exposure to grade-level concepts, vocabulary, and text structures (such as she receives during work with the anthology and the teacher read-alouds), so that she can learn and practice reading skills and strategies in instructional level and independent level texts. We need to show her how to select appropriate and interesting texts for DEAR and at-home reading, and to monitor her text selection.

Recommendations
It is recommended that Jenny work with the reading specialist for a period (40 min.) each day from now until the end of the semester. In consultation with Mrs. Martinez, the instruction will take place

---

[5]Note how this section is written. Rather than saying, "Jenny needs . . . ," we're saying "We need to . . ." See the difference? The collective *we* is also intentional, implying "We're all in this together for Jenny's benefit."

in the reading specialist's classroom for four days/week. One day/week the reading specialist will work in Mrs. Martinez's room with a small group of children who are experiencing similar reading difficulties. It is important that Jenny continue to have exposure to and involvement with the grade-level core literature/reading instruction during the regular language arts block. Based on Jenny's assessment, the reading specialist will work on the following:

To Improve Spelling Knowledge:
- Work with word sorts and word hunts each week to reinforce short vowels, vowel combinations, and diphthongs. The patterns and contrasts will be based on Jenny's assessed level (Within Word Pattern);
- Use *Words Their Way* (Bear et al., 2000) games and activities for vowel mastery; slowly introduce sorts and activities from the Syllables/Affixes stage;
- Implement a word study notebook for recording patterns and new words found during word hunts and VSS (Vocabulary Self-Collection Strategy)[6];

To Improve Reading and Fluency:
- Comprehension skills and strategies[7] will be introduced, taught, and modeled daily with appropriately leveled text;
- Small-group instruction will facilitate literature discussion (reciprocal teaching) and comprehension development;
- Jenny will buddy-read familiar text with another child of like reading ability to build fluency; neurological impresse may be used between teacher/student if buddy reading isn't successful;
- Graphic organizers will be used to help Jenny organize information during reading;
- Both narrative and informational/expository texts at around the 4th–5th-grade level will be used for the small group instruction; gradually more difficult texts will be introduced as students, including Jenny, are able to read them;
- A variety of motivating and interesting narrative and informational texts at around the 3rd-grade level will be available for DEAR and at-home reading; gradually more difficult texts will be introduced; topics initially will focus on ballet and women's sports;
- Dictated group stories will be used for writing instruction and for fluency building;
- Time each week will be spent in the reading specialist's classroom reviewing and reinforcing grade-level concepts and vocabulary from the adopted reading series;
- Mrs. Martinez will, on a regular basis, flexibly group students for discussion circles related to the anthology selections.

Additional Comments

At this point, it is not recommended that Jenny receive formal tutoring outside of school. We encourage Mr. and Mrs. Stewart to continue to support and monitor Jenny's at-home reading and writing, and to assist her in making appropriate choices for her reading practice. We will implement this plan until the end of the semester and will meet to review Jenny's progress at that time. Mr. and Mrs. Stewart, Jenny, Mrs. Martinez, and I will attend that meeting.

Profile Prepared By   *Joan Forrester*   Date: 3/7/02

Reading Specialist, Crawford Middle School

---

[6]Vocabulary Self-Collection Strategy (VSS): Ruddell, M. R. (2001); Shearer, Ruddell, & Vogt (2001).

[7]Comprehension Strategies: See Harvey & Goudvis (2000); Keene & Zimmerman (1997); McLaughlin & Allen (2002).

Observations and Insights

3/25/02   After 2 weeks of small group work (6 students) in Mrs. M.'s room, Jenny is still reluctant to participate. When called upon, she responds but she won't volunteer information or engage in discussion. I think the group is too big; will halve it tomorrow and see what happens. J. F.

3/29/02   What a difference! I found several ballet books at the library and the 3 girls who are now in the reciprocal teaching group are avidly reading and talking about them. Jenny is gradually becoming more confident and involved . . . and because of her ballet background, she's even taking some leadership with the others. I think we're on to something here. . . . J.F.

4/3/03   Jenny's really enjoying VSS! I'm realizing that a key to her involvement is her having some control over what she's doing. She likes to select her own vocabulary words to add to her Word Study book—and not surprisingly, most have to do with ballet. Today, she brought in the word "tutu" and asked if I knew where the word came from. When I told her I didn't, she giggled and said, "It's French—and it may have come from baby talk for a person's bottom." At this point, the whole group cracked up . . . nothing like 6th-grade humor! J.F.

CHAPTER FIVE

ADAPTING INSTRUCTION TO LEARNERS' NEEDS: REFRAMING LITERACY INTERVENTION

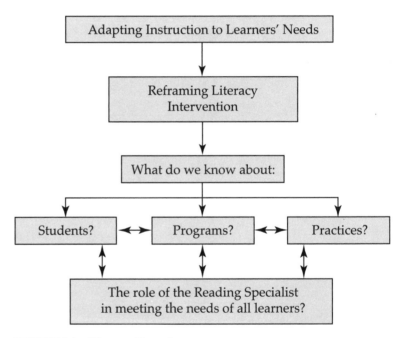

FIGURE 5.1   Chapter Overview

LEARNING GOALS

After reading, discussing, and engaging in activities related to this chapter, you will be able to:

1. design school or district programs for readers and writers who need additional support with literacy acquisition;

2. explain the role of the reading specialist in literacy intervention programs;

3. describe how former deficit models of remediation and "warehousing" can be socially, psychologically, and emotionally damaging to students;

4. Personal Learning Goal: In a three-minute brainstorming session, share what you know about effective literacy intervention. Write an objective or question that reflects something you want to learn as we explore these topics. Share this with others in your group.

Vignette

The sixth-hour bell rings and 2,200 students at Chicago's Boniface Middle School shuffle between classes. It's a hot September afternoon and students can hardly believe they've only been back in school for three weeks—it seems they never left. Several minutes later, as the bell rings to signal the start of the last period, Julio, a popular seventh grader who reads about two years below grade level, bursts into Liana Casals' Title I Reading classroom, obviously upset and on the verge of tears. Usually, Liana is standing near the door, greeting Julio and the other five students, two girls and three boys, in this literacy intervention class. Today, however, she is at her desk, using the few precious minutes to respond to a parent's E-mail message. As Julio slams his books on the desk and puts his head down on his arms, silence drops like a guillotine on his classmates and their teacher. Julio has always struggled with reading. With a mixture of anger, hurt, and embarrassment, he recounts that on his way to class three friends made fun of him because he had to go to the room where the "stupid kids go to read baby books." Liana notices the look on the faces of the other five students. They seem to share Julio's hurt and embarrassment, almost as if the words had been aimed at them.

Liana has been a Title I Reading Teacher for twelve years at Boniface. Approximately 40 percent of Boniface students are African American, another 20 percent are Hispanic English language learners, exhibiting various degrees of proficiency in both languages, and the remaining 40 percent are predominantly native English speakers. Although a smaller percentage of white children are in the Title I program, the ethnic mix of Liana's students reflects the diversity of the school and neighborhood. The area is one of poverty and many students struggle with reading and writing. Fortunately, Liana is knowledgeable about school-related literacy and various programs of effective intervention. Her Title I program has recently switched to a pull-out model. The goal is to provide intensive intervention, creating proficient readers and writers, and obviating the need for continued intervention. Liana has high standards, and she is well liked and trusted by her students, who receive one hour of small-group (six students) daily literacy instruction in place of the regular developmental reading class.

Both Liana and Julio's grandparents came from Mexico, and although both have been raised in a dominant English-speaking culture, Spanish is significant in the cultures of home and the immediate community. Liana and Julio consider themselves proficient bilingual speakers. Julio appears to have a sizeable English vocabulary and above average intelligence; all of his education has been in English.

Thinking Points

1. How might Liana react to Julio?
2. What would you suggest that she should do or say in response to his frustrations and concerns?

Expanding the Vignette: Exploring the Tensions

Liana has the next hour free and finds Tony, the reading specialist, in the copy room. She is upset by Julio's experience and confesses to Tony that she did not know what to say. Indeed, she has struggled with the issues of stigma and damage to self-esteem inherent in providing extra literacy help to struggling students ever since her first Title I assignment. Even though she speaks fluent Spanish, it has been two generations since her family left Mexico, and she feels out of touch with the lives of Spanish-speaking students who have recently moved to Chicago. Liana also admits she knows little about the home cultures of her African American students or her white students. She recounts to Tony that she did her best to reassure Julio he was definitely not "stupid" and he was fortunate to be getting extra help in reading in a supportive environment. However, Liana acknowledged that, even as she spoke, it was clear to her and to Julio that her words were of little help, no matter how noble her intentions. She wondered what she could do to help her students overcome the stigma of being singled out from their peers.

Thinking Points

1. What additional tensions and questions have you identified in the vignette?
2. How might Tony, the reading specialist, help Liana, the Title I teacher?
3. What long-term or periodic measures would you suggest to Tony or to Liana to deal with the issues you raised?
4. Is there anything proactive that could have been done to avoid this problem? Do you know of any fundamental systems or plans in your district that involve reading specialists and teachers that could alleviate or diminish the problem of students being singled out and labeled?

Keep your answers to these questions in mind as you read. We will revisit them at the end of the chapter.

PROVIDING AN APPROPRIATE LEARNING ENVIRONMENT

Liana's dilemma as described in the opening vignette is familiar to Title I and special education teachers, and to all who work with readers for whom literacy acquisition does not come easily. Caring professionals recognize the tension between providing the kind of support that is characteristic of intensive intervention and contributing to the diminished self-esteem that such differential treatment often evokes. While we recognize that being fully literate may not ensure access to a high-paying job and a happy life, we understand the high levels of literacy required for the average individual to get through a single day, and we want more for students than just survival. We want them to have full access to the job world, to the political process, to social inclusion, and to our institutions of higher education. We want individuals to be able to read, locate the information they need, receive pleasure from reading, and make personal connections. We also want to help them figure out how to use literacy in moral, legal, and ethical ways. We want it all for them.

Reading specialists' roles related to students who need additional support for literacy and language learning vary greatly from district to district. In this chapter, we examine a number of direct and indirect ways reading specialists interact with teachers and students in intervention programs. As you read, try to identify the complex factors, many of which are not directly related to instruction, that determine who receives services, who provides the instruction, how support is structured, and where that instruction takes place.

Three core beliefs drive our vision for this chapter and determine its composition:

1. Differences in literacy acquisition, use of language, and ethnicity can and do position students outside of the school culture. In addition to the ways ethnicity, language, and culture separate and sort learners, we suggest that failure to progress in sync with the school's developmental literacy clock (the defining characteristic of students referred for intervention) can also separate students from the dominant culture of school.

2. We can help all students increase literacy proficiency by changing what we do for individuals within groups. This does not imply that what schools teach is unimportant. Literacy as taught in schools today *is* valuable, crucial for survival. After all, our schools are enabling more students to achieve higher levels of literacy than ever before (Bracey, 1997). However, we can use and build on much of what we currently do right to reach greater numbers of learners who are marginalized despite our best efforts.

3. Rather than attributing blame, we suggest expanding definitions of literacy and classroom practice. Students who differ by virtue of literacy proficiency need something in addition to explicit instruction: they need *connection*. They need their teachers to show them how to bring their differing lived experiences and prior knowledge into the classroom, and how to use these to enhance learning. The teaching techniques involved are not difficult to master. The barriers lie in altering some fundamental beliefs that drive daily classroom events.

Marginalization can occur in many contexts with many different students—native English-speaking students who live in poverty, middle-class students who struggle to read and learn, and students whose language, ethnicity, or home culture differs from the majority—these are only a few examples. We do not suggest here that marginalization is the same in quality or degree for all students. To do so would trivialize the overt prejudices suffered by those who wear their differences in ways that society can readily recognize. However, the philosophical, political, and sociocultural issues related to power, identity, and voice are what thinkers like Paulo Freire (1970) would suggest unite these literacy learners.

As we discuss the programs designed to provide instructional support for various groups of students, it is important to keep in mind that groups are made up of individuals, and many individuals don't choose their group membership, especially some of the groups discussed in this chapter and the next. Also, many of these students have been labeled in some way, a practice that has changed little since the two of us began teaching in the public schools. There are no easy answers to some of the questions we (and hopefully, you) will raise—instead we address these big issues as opportunities for inquiry.

It is essential to apply our Difference Model from Chapter 4 to the intervention programs we address here. How we view our task—as *remediation* (a Deficit Model) or as *intervention* (a Difference Model)—will have a powerful influence on programmatic and instructional classroom practice. The intervention programs of today have the potential to be highly responsive to context, and a sociocultural perspective is especially suited to this discussion for two reasons: (1) The cultures of home, school and community have a profound effect on the way a child internalizes literacy events (Cummins, 1990); and (2) minority students are highly overrepresented in special education, Title I, and intervention programs (Allington & Walmsley, 1995; Cummins, 1984; Rodriguez, Prieto, & Rueda, 1984).

In this chapter, we examine the role of the reading specialist in intervention programs, K–12, and offer examples of in-class alternatives to pull-out programs. We discuss common factors among effective programs and explain how to adapt intervention in ways that are culturally responsive. In the last ten years we have learned much about how to bridge the cultures of home and school in ways that benefit every student in the classroom. We address both the promise these new insights have given us and the challenges that remain.

REFRAMING LITERACY INTERVENTION

The External Dimensions of Literacy Intervention

There are four dimensions that characterize the external structure of intervention within a school or district. These Four Aspects of the Literacy Intervention Framework are: (1) Program Models; (2) Literacy Intervention Personnel; (3) Student Selection Processes; and (4) Classroom Coordination (see Figure 5.2). While these elements have little to do with actual strategies, techniques, and classroom events, they define the framework that undergirds service to students and create a context based on the school's philosophy. When designing intervention, a common mistake is to overlook this supporting external structure and to focus instead on planning instructional events. With the Four Aspects Framework, we provide reading specialists, literacy team members, and administrators with an overview that defines the delivery model.

Exploring the Four Aspects Framework for Literacy Support Programs

Aspect One: Program Models   A number of factors determine whether we should provide help for struggling readers by using a pull-out or an in-class instructional model. For example, a very small rural district may have few students with similar needs, not enough to support hiring a specialist to teach them. In such schools, a portion of the reading specialist's day may be allocated to assuming the role of Title I reading teacher, either by assisting students and teachers within the classroom or by pulling students out for group instruction. In contrast, larger urban schools usually have sufficient numbers of students to group for pull-out or in-class support. In these large districts, reading

Program Models	Literacy Intervention Personnel

1. Pull-Out (Longitudinal)
 2. Pull-Out (Short-term, Intensive)
 3. Combination In-Class/Pull-Out
 4. In-class specialist models
 5. In-class specialist/teacher/
     paraprofessional models
 6. In-class teacher implemented models
 7. Supportive models/tutorials
	1. Literacy specialists with advanced
	     licensure (Reading Specialists, Title I)
	 2. Teachers provided with professional
	     development
	 3. Paraprofessionals with specialized
	     training
	 4. Peers, adults, parents, university
	     students, cross-aged tutors

Student Identification Process	Classroom Coordination
1. Formal test scores 2. Teacher/parent/self-referral 3. Formal/informal assessment 4. Surveys/student self-evaluation/ affective factors 5. Combination	1. Separate literacy curriculum 2. Supportive literacy cirriculum

FIGURE 5.2   The Four Aspects of Literacy Intervention Framework:
A Decision-Making Framework

specialists may support and coordinate the efforts of those who work with various groups of students.

Even though the typical Title I model is shifting toward in-class support many districts are experimenting with short-term, intensive pull-out programs designed to return students to the regular classroom in less than a year. Within a school, students who require high levels of support may be served in pull-out programs while others may receive an appropriate level of help within the classroom. Reading specialists may also coordinate systematic professional development to enable the classroom teacher to instruct these learners, or a reading specialist/Title I teacher may work with groups of students within classrooms. Ideally, support personnel and classroom teachers can maximize the number of children served through a shared-teaching model. Some schools include a tutorial program using paraprofessionals, parents, or other trained volunteers in supplementary (not primarily instructional) roles.

Aspect Two: Literacy Intervention Personnel   State licensure laws often shape a district!s decisions about who will serve literacy learners in need of additional support. Some states require every district to have a reading specialist with a master's degree. Most require Title I teachers to have a number of graduate level credits for a "Reading Teacher" license. However, as we saw in the first chapter, districts have a high degree of autonomy in how they interpret these state laws. Many programs train paraprofessionals to work in classrooms for reasons that have more to do with cost effectiveness than with sound pedagogy. Allington and Walmsley (1995) and the International Reading Association concur that in far too many districts, noncredentialed/licensed personnel (such as instructional assistants) are responsible for much of the instruction in Title I and other programs for struggling readers.

Aspect Three: Student Selection   Although Special Education and Title I programs have specific state and local parameters that govern student referral and qualification, there are compelling arguments to include a variety of other authentic, classroom-generated measures of student's reading and writing processes as well as products (Valencia, Hiebert, & Afflerbach, 1994). Such analyses as the Learner Assessment Plan (LAP) in Chapter 4 provide a rich corpus of information that can be used to assess perform-ance and inform instruction. As we already know, the terms we choose to describe our assessment are important. Based on the perspectives of Rhodes and Shanklin (1993), Joyce Many (2001) argues that it is essential for educators to understand the distinction between *assessment*, collecting and analyzing data that will inform instruc-tion, and *evaluation*, judgment of students' abilities according to some set criteria (see Chapter 4 for further discussion of this distinction). Among the collaborative roles advocated by Donna Ogle and Ellen Fogelberg (2001) is for reading specialists to support teachers in improving their observational techniques and authentic assessment procedures.

Aspect Four: Classroom Coordination   Intensive programs, either long- or short-term, described in Aspect One may end up supplanting instruction in the regular education classroom. However, when we consider inclusionary laws, research findings (and common sense), intervention programs are more likely to be successful when they serve students in ways that *support* rather than *supplant* regular reading instruction. Title I programs in particular are designed to maintain a supportive role, and funding is tied to adherence to Title I laws and policies.

District or building decisions about these four aspects determine when, where, and how reading specialists spend each day. Note that administrators may make these decisions without your input. An informal survey of our graduate students reveals that many districts do not have written descriptions for reading specialists' responsibilities. Complex issues related to available funds, teacher attitudes toward inclusion, and the district's philosophy about the importance of providing various kinds of additional literacy support, affect reading specialists' roles. If a systemic structure is in place, the reading specialist's task, as well as that of other stakeholders, is to examine what is known about the elements of effective programs at various levels, and investigate how to implement and alter them based on the school's context and students' needs. As we discuss current research on effective programs for elementary, middle school, and secondary readers, we encourage you to shift your focus from "What works?" to "What works, for whom, under what conditions?"

As you reflect on decisions you'll make for each of the four aspects in the intervention framework, note how much of the reading specialist's role is dependent on *context*. The most important decision that impacts your role is whether you'll work directly with students, act in a supportive role, or both. Your involvement in a district's intervention programs may include any or all of the following:

- serving as Title I or literacy intervention teacher in pull-out programs for the majority of the school day;
- acting as a liaison between such programs and regular education classrooms;

- working directly with students and teachers within classrooms, or spending a portion of the day in classroom settings and a portion in pull-out settings;
- serving as a consultant and resource to teachers in assessing, adapting, and planning instruction for individual students;
- providing sustained professional development, and assisting in forming focused study groups among teachers;
- modeling and co-teaching lessons on ways to modify and adapt effective strategies and practices for the specific contexts of the school and the classroom;
- coordinating services among all literacy-related special education and intervention programs;
- consulting with specialists and teachers as they adapt materials and classroom events to accommodate differences in learners;
- remaining informed about legislative issues, assuming an advocacy role, and disseminating current information and resources to teachers and parents.

Even in districts with well-defined position descriptions, it seems that the reading specialist can individualize the role. For example, if the job description states, "The reading specialist will serve as a resource to classroom teachers in planning appropriate instruction for individual students," this may be interpreted as forming study groups, providing materials, modeling strategies, promoting advocacy, or any number of specific activities. As we explore what we know about struggling readers and instructional practice in intervention, keep these possible roles in mind and try to imagine what you might do in your own context.

Early Intervention Program

In the last decades of the twentieth century, increased focus on early intervention resulted in a number of effective models aimed at helping beginning readers. Among them are Reading Recovery (Pinnell, Fried, & Estes, 1990); Early Intervention in Reading (EIR) (Taylor, Short, Shearer, & Frye, 1995); and Success for All (Slavin, Madden, Dole, & Wasik, 1996). These programs and the others like them are effective in increasing the literacy proficiency of young children. In addition, they serve to inform us about characteristics of successful intervention. We know that, in effective models:

- Reading for meaning is the primary consideration and fluency is among the major goals;
- Intervention is frequent, regular, and of sufficient duration;
- Instruction is fast-paced, using a variety of sequenced and selected texts and leveled books;
- Familiarity with print is gained through reading and writing;
- Intervention is coupled with sound first instruction (Pikulski, 1995).

The proliferation of these programs, designed primarily for first graders, became the basis for exploration of ways to help both younger and older students. Recently, Elfrieda Hiebert and Barbara Taylor (2000) shared their findings from a study of effective kindergarten intervention. They suggest that a solid foundation for reading can be established by:

- restructuring literacy activities for the whole class;
- defining the role of the teacher as supporting *individuals* through informal conversation in planned and skillful ways, rather than through one-to-one or pull-out programs;
- providing activities and experiences that involve foundational processes of reading and writing, overall literacy and book concepts, and phonemic awareness (Ayres, 1998; Durkin, 1974–1975; Hansen & Farrell, 1995; Phillips, Norris, & Mason, 1996).

Instruction resides in the focused engagement and planned feature discussions during book reading, poetry chanting, and other typical kindergarten activities. However, sustaining momentum in these language-rich kindergartens requires a reading specialist, teachers, and other school personnel who are committed to ongoing professional development (see Chapter 10).

Less formal measures aimed at helping kindergarteners who lack exposure to story reading attempt to recreate the lap-reading experience (Klesius & Griffith, 1996), the mutually rewarding, highly social, interactive, book-sharing scenario between child and parent. In this language-rich dyadic model, both parent and child interrupt the reading frequently to comment, point out features, ask questions, or make experiential connections (Dickinson & Smith, 1996; Teale & Martinez, 1996). These discussions become increasingly complex as the adult skillfully reduces the amount of scaffolding (Bruner, 1983) to reflect the child's growing knowledge of character, story elements, cause and effect, and other elements of comprehension (Snow & Goldfield, 1982). Margo Wood and Elizabeth Prata Salvetti (2001) found that carefully trained university volunteers in the America Reads Challenge and community volunteers were able to conduct high quality, focused, read-aloud discussions.

Isabel Beck and Margaret McKeown (2001) noticed that children often ignored text information and responded to questions about story content by focusing on pictures and background knowledge. They developed an approach to read-alouds called Text Talk, in which the teacher intersperses reading with open questions and discussion, and follows each story with explicit vocabulary instruction. Continued investigations such as these provide teachers, tutors, and caregivers with information about how to best support literacy awareness and development for these children.

While research and the resulting implementation of intervention programs in the 1980s and 1990s were occurring in elementary schools, little attention was focused on the development of similar intervention for older students. The good news is that researchers have recently devoted their efforts to creating programs to help struggling adolescent readers (Moore, Alvermann, & Hinchman, 2000). An added challenge for those developing adolescent literacy intervention programs is reversing the damage to self-esteem caused in part by the years these students spent comparing themselves to their peers (Colvin & Schlosser, 1997/1998).

Such a student is Eliza Nauman, the central character in Myla Goldberg's novel *Bee Season*. In this book, Eliza is the daughter of Rabbi Heimel Nawman, and the sister of brilliant Aaron Nawman. She is also a student in Ms. Bergermeyer's combination fourth/fifth-grade class. Eliza, along with everyone else in the school, is aware that this is the room to which all the "unimpressive fifth graders" have been assigned. In the last three years Eliza has come to realize she is among those "from whom great things are not expected." By this time she has grown accustomed to those posters of puppies and kittens clinging precariously to the ropes and ladders they are struggling to climb. Usually such posters include supposedly motivating captions, such as *Hang in there!* and *If at first you don't succeed. . . .* Because she is a C student, Eliza is among those who never win school contests, get chased by boys, or become Student of the Week. As a result, when the annual school spelling bee is announced, Eliza hopes the pain and humiliation will be mercifully terminated by swift defeat. "She has no reason to expect that this, her first spelling bee, will differ from the outcome of any other school event seemingly designed to confirm, display, or amplify her mediocrity" (p. 2).

Author Connection: Brenda As I read the passage in *Bee Season*, I thought about all the Elizas, both male and female, I came to know in my many years of working with readers "from whom great things were not expected." Most of these students did become competent and confident readers and writers, or at least adequate ones. In fact, many have completed degrees at universities and technical colleges. But I still worry about those whose literacy skills are marginal, the ones who "got away." How are they doing? Which doors are open to them and which doors are closed? As a teacher in a Learning Disabilities classroom, I cringed when I heard my students described as L.D.: "He's L.D." "She's L.D." Many days we set aside the mind-numbing timed tests and scripted materials, hallmarks of L.D. Programs in the 1970s and 1980s to talk about coping with the instructional isolation, insensitive comments from peers, and confusion about identity: "Am I my disability?" Some days, tacit knowledge of what reading should be led us, a teacher and her students, to put aside our remedial materials and simply read—for the whole hour—out of books we brought in: "You want to read this? I'll help." I remember my admiration for sixth grader, Robbie, as I watched him labor through an autobiography of Jackie Robinson, unable to believe the prejudice Robinson endured. When at long last he closed the book, he looked up and said, "This is the first book I ever finished!"

I recognize that some students need a great deal of support with literacy activities, but I am saddened about what we special educators and reading specialists didn't seem to know at the time: That literacy is socially situated; that students deserve to experience rich discourse models and a variety of challenging materials within the same settings as their peers; that they have a right to read books that reflect their own experiences; that by choosing different tools we can alter internal and external literacy events; and, especially, that these students are perfectly capable of making decisions about their instruction.

Struggling Older Readers, Adolescent Readers, Teacher Attitudes, and Practices

In a study of struggling middle-school readers, MaryEllen Vogt (1997) confirmed the insights of earlier investigators (Kos, 1991; Meek, 1983) who looked into the nature of struggling adolescent readers. These researchers agreed that:

- most had difficulty with reading since the beginning of their schooling;
- many adopted complex strategies to avoid situations in which they were required to read out loud, often acting out or withdrawing during literacy-related activities
- the majority had poor grades, low self-esteem, and little interest in school or extracurricular activities;
- although they had limited decoding skills, most could read one-syllable regular words but had difficulty with multisyllabic words and words with irregularities;
- by middle school, they had given up hope of ever improving their reading ability and openly proclaimed their distaste for reading (Shearer, Ruddell, & Vogt, 2001).

Keith Stanovich (1986) and MaryEllen Vogt (1989) also uncovered a number of disturbing incongruities between both preservice and inservice teachers' attitudes and practices relative to high and low achievers. When compared to opportunities given to their lower-achieving peers, higher-performing students:

- spent more classroom time engaged in silent rather than oral reading;
- were provided with more instructional time related to comprehension;
- were given more opportunities to engage in higher levels of thinking and strategic learning, and more independent research and synthesis projects;
- were asked questions requiring higher levels of thinking followed by more wait time;
- were provided with richer, comprehensive, grade-level texts and supplemental materials;
- were offered greater opportunities for leadership.

Such discrepant opportunities led Keith Stanovich to describe a phenomenon he called the "Matthew Effect," borrowed from the Book of Matthew. When it comes to literacy development, "The rich get richer, and the poor get poorer."

Group Inquiry Activity   With others in your group explore the following issues:

1. Using a brainstorming technique called the Whip, take turns as each person provides a response to the question, "What are some reasons all students do not achieve literacy proficiency in our schools?"
2. When all group members have contributed three ideas, discuss the responses and add to the list.

3. Develop a group reply to the following question: "Given unlimited resources and the necessary commitment, could we help all students reach their literacy potential?" Provide reasons for your answer.
4. Place an R before ideas expressed by your group that involve Readjustment of Instruction. Place an IE in front of ideas that would require Increased Expenditures.

Share your responses with others in the class.

Research-Based Assumptions That Inform Instructional Practice for Struggling Readers

As you read the following research-based assumptions, ask yourself if they apply exclusively to students who find learning to read and write difficult, or to students of all literacy and ability levels (see Figure 5.3). By examining how to apply each of them in specific contexts, reading specialists and literacy educators can design intervention programs that are both pedagogically sound and culturally responsive.

Consider, for example, how recent research findings acknowledge the primacy of the reader's role, and how they reflect an even greater emphasis on social negotiation of meaning, critical literacy skills, and issues of "choice and voice." Despite all the discouraging notions associated with struggling readers and classroom practice, recent

---

Students who read most read best.
  (Pressley, Wharton-McDonald, Block, Tracey, Books, Cronin, Nelson, & Woo, 2000; Taylor, Pearson, Clark, & Walpole, 2000).

Traditional ability grouping has been unsuccessful in meeting the academic and social needs of students who are not in the top group.
  (Allington, 2000; Allington & Walmsley, 1995; Vogt, 1989).

All students benefit from support and assistance from individuals with more experience.
  (Pearson & Fielding, 1991; Palinscar, 1986; Vygotsky, 1978).

There is no set of instructional techniques that is effective all of the time for all students.
  (Dykstra, 1978; Allington, 2000).

Literacy processes are interrelated and integrated.
  (Tierney & Shanahan, 1991).

Literacy learning requires social interaction and collaboration.
  (Rosenblatt, 1978; Vygotsky, 1986).

FIGURE 5.3   Research-Based Assumptions about Instruction for Struggling Readers

adolescent intervention programs (Colvin & Schlosser, 1997/1998; Shearer, Ruddell, & Vogt, 2001) echo the recurring themes of hope and promise identified by Gay Ivey (1999), When students are provided with materials that include an array of interests and levels of difficulty, they state that they like to read. When provided with opportunities to collaborate with peers, struggling readers enjoy social interaction and want to share their experiences. They are motivated by real purposes for reading, and they want to be and can become good readers (Ivey, 1999). These intervention models reflect a shift in the roles of teacher and student.

We invite you to share in some of the insights we gained during our intervention research in collaboration with our colleague, Martha Rapp Ruddell.

1. *Students benefit when strategic reasoning is supported through peer mediation and social negotiation.* The idea that effective instruction in strategic reasoning is helpful to reading-delayed youth and adolescents has been substantiated (Anderson, Chan, & Henne, 1995; Cooper, 1999; Palinscar & Brown, 1984). For example, incorporating reciprocal teaching in reading instruction with struggling readers enables students to build on their repertoire of strategies and to use those strategies in increasingly flexible ways (Palinscar & Brown, 1984; Vogt, 1998). This holds true for beginning readers as well (Pressley et al., 2000; Taylor, Graves, & van de Broek, 2000). In the reciprocal teaching model, students read passages paragraph by paragraph or in designated chunks. During reading, students support one another in learning and developing proficiency in four basic strategies associated with comprehension: predicting, questioning, clarifying word meanings and ideas, and summarizing. These processes often include writing. Gradually, the responsibility for instruction shifts to the students, with the teacher observing and providing needed guidance.

2. *Students benefit when the teacher's role is that of cognitive coach.* Leah McGee (1992) and her colleagues (McGee, Courtney, & Lomax, 1994) demonstrate how teachers can model, coach, and nudge students toward new perspectives and act as literacy "curators." Teachers can model how to use language and genre as tools to organize, question, explain, and connect the characters and events in literature to student beliefs and experiences. Such coaching may also assume more direct forms when necessary. For example, the teacher provides individualized guidance and feedback through modeling, coaching, and explaining if explicit instruction is necessary for a child or small group. During our middle-school study, we spent ten minutes of instructional time for several weeks teaching word-chunking, adopting the methods developed by Shefelbine (1995) and used in the Read-2-Succeed model (Vogt, 1998) to meet individual needs. As students gained insight into the unique processing of their peers, discussions became more interactive, more focused on strategy application, and involved much less teacher participation.

3. *Students benefit when they are encouraged to make strong personal connections with text through a variety of response modes.* Such connections can only be made when students use a number of language processes to interact with texts in which they see their own lived experience. For example, students should be encouraged to use writing *during* reading, such as writing questions, reactions, understandings, confusions, summaries, or vocabulary. Discussion as a mediating tool can broaden their perspectives and provide models of how others construct meaning and solve problems. Personal connections are also enhanced when students are able to exercise a degree of choice about what is read both within and outside of school.

4. *Students benefit from reading, responding to, and reproducing a variety of texts (including multiple media and other sign systems) in critical ways.* For example, students can discern how the choices made by the author, such as the words used and the genre of the piece, reveal the author's purpose. Students can analyze whose voice is included and address issues of gender and cultural bias. Even very young children can move beyond enjoying a story to create multiple meanings, construct critically social texts, and exhibit high degrees of critical literacy (Comber, 2001; Hanzl, 2001). Whether they are watching television, reading text, going to the movies, singing along with music videos, or engaging in Web-based activities, all students need to be taught to use analytic skills (Luke, 1999). Ladislaus Semali and Ann Watts-Pailliotet (1999) provide convincing arguments that the challenges of critically reading and writing across a variety of symbol systems, called "intermediality," present exciting possibilities for developing critical literacy skills.

5. *Students benefit from reading texts that include a wide range of difficulty.* While most early literacy programs stress the use of leveled texts (Allington, 2001; Clay, 1985; Taylor et al., 2000), in our intervention model for older readers we decided to include a variety of difficult pieces, such as stories by Edgar Allen Poe or readings from science and social studies. Our reasoning was that, if we were to successfully prepare students to deal with difficult narrative and expository text, hypermedia, and other complex discourse systems, instruction must include difficult (at or above grade-level) readings interspersed with easier shorter pieces. To our surprise we discovered that, by providing appropriate levels of scaffolding (and intensive instruction in how to read multisyllabic words), and then involving students in the selection of difficult pieces, they were willing and able to put forth the substantial effort necessary to read, discuss, comprehend, and write critically in response to extremely challenging text. Recently, we discovered that Paul van den Broek and Kathy Kremer (2000) also described successful comprehension instruction for struggling readers in which an entire class period was devoted to understanding a few paragraphs. This type of intensive discussion moves literacy learning for older struggling readers far beyond more transitional remediation approaches that focus on skills sheets and isolated phonics lessons. Rather, it has at its center our strongly held belief, "Just because they can't read, doesn't mean they can't think."

6. *Students benefit from socially situated language processes that invite awareness of the rules of discourse.* As students work together, whether in kindergarten or in high school, they can be supported to discover that literacy activity is socially situated (Rosenblatt, 1994; Vygotsky, 1978), and that the discourses and interactions within the activity reflect the context in rule-governed ways (Gee, 1990). For example, they learn that conversation in some school situations, such as teacher-centered discussion, may require students to raise their hands and wait to be called on before responding. In a different social context, such as group collaboration, other rules of discourse apply.

7. *Students benefit from selecting the words they want to study.* Allowing students to choose their own vocabulary and spelling words from anywhere, in or out of school, has a powerful and lasting impact on comprehension, word awareness, and facilitation of independent vocabulary acquisition (Ruddell & Shearer, in press). Our research using Vocabulary Self-Collection Strategy (VSS; Haggard, 1982) demonstrates that, when given the opportunity to select their own words, students will consistently choose important, challenging, interesting words. VSS journal entries reflect the personal connections and highly insightful strategies of these students. In addition, comparative test scores reveal that they will devote more effort to learning self-selected words than to the traditional commercial word lists imposed on them. Through social negotiation, employing a variety of strategies (which only sometimes includes referring to the dictionary), students not only learn words but also how to learn words (Haggard, 1982; Ruddell, 2001; Ruddell & Shearer, 1999; Ruddell & Shearer, 2002; Shearer, Ruddell, & Vogt, 2001). Consider, for example, the insight of students in a discussion about what makes a word a "good one" to bring into class. One student brought in the word *lacolith* and the following comments ensued:

> **Teacher:**   Given a scale of 1–5, how would you rate the word *lacolith*, with 1 being "useful" and 5 being "very useful"?
>
> **Student 1:**   I'd rate it a 3, because it's useful in class, but not so much in life.
>
> **Student 2:**   I disagree. How important a word is depends on a person's situation. Let's say you're a seismologist—then the word would be a 5, but if you're a banker, it's a 1.

8. *Students benefit from large amounts of in-class reading of connected texts, supported by additional recreational reading outside of school.* Of the forty-three minutes of instructional time, at least thirty-five minutes of class time in our middle school intervention program was spent reading connected discourse in its many forms. Students were also required to read for twenty minutes every evening from easy, enjoyable selections of their choosing, and to keep a reading log that required a full parental signature for each entry.

9. *Students benefit from and are capable of participating in goal setting and evaluation.* Informal conferences with students help them set goals and evaluate progress toward their goals. Jenny Watson Pearson and Carol Santa (1995) discovered that students are capable of investigating their own learning. Our own work with middle-school intervention confirms that goal-setting and evaluation are effective tools (Shearer et al., 2001). Including students in the decision-making process honors what they want to learn in addition to what a teacher might value. This is not only a form of critical thinking but also a vehicle through which students can internalize dimensions of identity and self-efficacy.

10. *Students benefit when they are able to build fluency through a number of collaborative and tutorial relationships that encourage rereading.* Cross-age and cross-grade partnerships between older and younger students are beneficial to everyone involved. Older students practice reading stories that they will later read to their younger Reading Buddies. In addition to motivating the older students to reread for fluency, there are obvious benefits related to self-esteem for those who find themselves in mentorship roles for the first time. Strategies like partner-reading or taping stories for other students also improve fluency. Additional fluency builders include Readers Theater, Echo Reading, and reading along with tapes. We discovered that, when students are provided with explicit instruction and modeling in effective group processes (Au, 1993) and given specific tasks and guidelines, reading class becomes what Patterson, Cotten, Pavonetti, Kimball-Lopez, & VanHorn (1998) describe as a complex adaptive system with shifting roles and stances that do not automatically include a teacher. "It is no surprise, given the litany of ways instruction is differentiated for high and low achieving students, that the majority of students in traditional remedial reading programs receive little opportunity for these kinds of interaction (Shearer et al., 2001).

Author Connection: Mary Ellen and Brenda   If you cover the title and first part of this chapter and read only the ten suggestions in the preceding section, you might surmise that we are discussing strategies to use with gifted students. In fact, we are, because we believed the students in our intervention program were capable of the same kinds of reasoning as their academically successful peers, and we treated them accordingly. Would you be surprised to discover that, among the seventeen struggling middle-school readers, who began the school year reading at least two years below grade level, the average gain in reading was over four years? As we developed our instructional approaches and conferred with Marty Ruddell, we decided that, from the first day of school, we would treat our students as if they were gifted. As the year progressed, they, too, came to see themselves that way. However, even we were skeptical about such huge gains, so we returned a year later to retest them to find out if those gains were real. The students had spent that following year back in regular classrooms, receiving no intervention. To our delight, we found that the gains these students worked so hard to achieve persisted. What we hadn't considered was the profound effect these seventeen individuals would have on our own growth as educators and researchers. We thank them for these lessons.

Alternatives to Pull-Out Models of Intervention

As schools seek alternatives to pull-out programs, a number of ways to structure intervention involve support within the regular education classroom. Many of these alternatives relate to one or more of the Four Aspects of the Literacy Intervention Framework. For example, among the most visible features of literacy intervention is the degree to which students are served in pull-out programs that separate them from their classmates, or provided with support in their classrooms. Whether students are formally identified as requiring special education, Title I support, or literacy intervention in school-designed programs, the trend is to provide such service in the regular education setting. The decision that must be made both programmatically and individually is: To what extent can we meet the literacy needs of this student in the regular classroom?

It is interesting to examine the early terminology of special education legislation as it signals the shift in our philosophical orientation to supporting students with special needs. Descriptors present in early legislation such as *handicapped* and *disabled* (PL 94-142, 1976) labeled and sorted students according to deficits. Although the current wording in our journals and scholarly writing appears to focus on individuals as readers and writers who struggle or readers and writers "at-risk," all of us who consider ourselves caring educators continue to grapple with any descriptions still present in legal discourse that have the effect of stratifying learners. As we abandon our deficit models in favor of ones that emphasize developmental support, we attempt to shift our characterization of these delivery models of instruction from compensatory to supportive, replacing the notion of remediation with intervention (Allington, 2001; Hiebeit & Taylor, 2000; McGill-Franzen, 2000).

As school reform measures increase the amount of in-class intervention in the schools, concomitant changes in the roles of classroom teachers, reading specialists, Title I teachers, and paraprofessionals are inherent. Donna Ogle and Ellen Fogelberg (2001) envision the role of the reading specialist as increasingly collaborative both with classroom teachers and with networks of reading specialists supporting one another in exploring and expanding the dimensions of inclusionary instruction. Such instruction not only enables strong connections with classroom programs (missing in pull-out programs), but also increases instructional minutes by obviating transitions between classrooms. Increased emphasis on student standards, assessment, and performance outcomes makes the need for collaboration among school-based professionals imperative (Ogle & Fogelberg, 2001). Adjustments that facilitate collaboration include:

- a shift in the typical spread of at-risk students so that teachers can group similar students with whom specialists can work. As a result, specialists will not be required to go into every classroom at every grade level. Note that we're not talking about long-term isolation or ability-grouping;
- careful consideration of the teachers in whose classrooms the children will be placed and with whom the specialist will work;
- support for staff development to help teachers in transforming their grouping practices and conditions;
- an administrative climate that sets the context of change and includes allocation of time, resources, positions, and materials to facilitate the changes;
- a commitment that instruction for struggling readers is provided by highly trained professionals. While we recognize that limited school resources compel districts to use paraprofessionals and volunteer tutors, such as Vista and AmeriCorps volunteers, the limited information on the effectiveness of variables associated with volunteer programs indicates a cautious approach by the schools (Klenk & Kibby, 2000).

In this chapter we explored some of the issues, techniques, insights, and programs that support readers who struggle with literacy acquisition. The proliferation of intervention programs for struggling readers in the last years of the twentieth century has contributed greatly to our understanding of how to facilitate that process. Intervention currently incorporates a rich variety of authentic texts, integrated processes, and socially constructed meanings. Students and teachers are beginning to share in instructional planning, goal-setting, and material selection. The efficacious reading specialist must possess high levels of expertise in intervention, systemic thinking, and the ability to sustain professional development and motivation.

As we explore these exciting new ideas, we must never forget that, just thirty years ago, some educators and researchers thought walking a balance beam was an effective way to retrain the brains of students who were classified as dyslexic, and that such a procedure would ultimately improve their reading. We also segregated and isolated students whose physical limitations served as labels and categories, thereby denying them an equitable and appropriate educational environment. Today, these notions are difficult to conceive, especially if you're a teacher who, as a child, grew up with all kinds of students in your schools and classrooms. These stark examples remind us that terms like *best practice* are fluid concepts and perhaps serve us in more restricted ways than we have imagined, as demonstrated in the following Other Voices segment.

Other Voices: Michael Nelipovich, Rh.D.

The following excerpts are from an interview with Michael Nelipovich, Rh.D., Director of the Wisconsin State Bureau for the Blind, in Milwaukee, Wisconsin, by Brenda Shearer. As a young child, growing up in Detroit in the fifties, Michael was diagnosed with choroidoremia, a rare, irreversible genetic disorder that results in blindness. He was the first to complete a doctorate in rehabilitation from Southern Illinois University. Michael's past and current presentation and publication agenda places him at the forefront in the study of substance abuse among adults with blindness or visual impairment. This is his story.

When I was five, I had the first symptom of the disease . . . night blindness, bumping into things in low light conditions. I had an uncle who was blind. I remember the ophthalmologist in Ann Arbor saying, "Someday you'll be almost totally blind, except for recognizing a light source." So, I began the slow forty-year process of losing my vision.

When the diagnosis was final, in about first or second grade, I was pulled out of regular school and put in special classes about three to four miles from home. A city bus picked me up. There was a bus driver and a matronly woman that kept the kids in line. When we got to school, the majority of kids entered the front, but my bus pulled up to the back door. We had to walk down a long sidewalk. There were kids with orthopedic disabilities and all sorts of impairments. All I knew was that the weird kids were on my bus and I just had a little problem seeing at night. I was confused.

The standard program in the fifties was "Sight Saving Classes." We had millions of fluorescent light bulbs in the ceiling, terrible for creating glare, and thick glasses.

The desks were elevated and angled so we were closer to the books. In later elementary, we had the homeroom concept: go to classes—get assignments—go back to the Sight Saving Classroom with the blazing lights—then walk back to class. I'd be told, "Come back in fifteen minutes and we'll discuss your assignment." Often, when I'd get back, I'd interrupt the class because they'd already started. That or I'd bump into things, and there was no way I was anonymous. I lost my anonymity. No one ever talked to me about going blind—how I felt or what I needed. There was no discussion of emotions or feelings at home, and I didn't have time to talk to anyone at school. So, I was extremely uptight emotionally.

When I left White Elementary for Burrows Junior High, I had to take two city buses. I remember my mom bought me a long three-quarter-length coat with a hood, and I'd carry my books and wait for the bus. Because it was out of my neighborhood, I had NO friends—kids I saw at school were not my friends. I would contribute in junior high, speak if asked a question. I was a good student. (I skipped a grade in elementary; I was double promoted.) Gym was especially bad. I HAD to participate, but I couldn't see the ball. When it came time to go to high school, I had to attend the one high school in Detroit that had a Sight Saving classroom way off in a different neighborhood. I still never really understood what was happening—high school *defining* me by my disability. I did take Drivers Ed, and went to the prom. Eventually I even had a driver's license for about three years.

Finally, I changed schools. There was this technical high school for good students way downtown and I wanted to go there. I majored in electrical studies, learning to wire houses. I had to work in the dark—lots of movement in potentially dangerous areas—lots of algebra and advanced math, and lots of boardwork which, of course, I couldn't see. I was on probation by the end of the first year. So I transferred again, this time to a high school in my neighborhood—a typical Detroit high school—about 80 percent of the students were African American. It was a pretty feisty environment. I found I was a better student than most of my classmates and I got by and fit in by wisecracking. When I was a senior, my study hall counselor, with my mother's intervention, got me hooked up with the state Agency for the Blind to put me on the path to go to college, which I did.

Reading! I never read for pleasure. I remember going to the library and checking out books, but I barely started them. Most people remember a favorite childhood book, but I didn't have one. I used to bring a chair into the bathroom whenever I had to read. It had the best lighting, but as a kid I never figured out why I did that! Reading was a pain in the neck. It gave me headaches. To pass a course I'd read the material once and try to understand it fully, because it was so much work to read it again! When someone would talk about skimming or rereading something to understand it, I couldn't imagine why *anyone* would want to put themselves through that much pain.

Most of the time, teachers would feel sorry for me. They'd skip past me to avoid putting me on the spot. I wish there had been a grown-up along the way to take the time to listen—to ask me what I needed! Did I really understand the subject matter? Nobody ever did; not teachers, not family. I grew up in a silo—grew up feeling different and weird. So all those years—from second grade to graduate school—school taught me to be isolated, taught me I was NOT a mainstream kid, taught me I was different. And I didn't understand. "Why?"

Group Inquiry Activity As you can see from the interview with Michael, school has a powerful effect in defining who we are, how we are valued, and, ultimately, how we define ourselves.

1. What might Michael's teachers have done to make his schooling more meaningful and appropriate?
2. What might a reading specialist have done to help him find a way to enjoy literature and "good books"?
3. How could you assist a teacher in learning how to provide Michael with appropriate literacy instruction?

Share your responses with others in your group and class.

LITERACY AND PROGRAMMING CONSIDERATIONS FOR STUDENTS WITH PHYSICAL LIMITATIONS

As we discuss this topic we again must navigate the landmines of deficit labels such as the term *disability*. Literacy programming for students with physical differences depends on the specific type and extent of the physical challenges. For example, a student with restricted mobility may not need any special assistance during literacy events. On the other hand, visual or hearing differences may be severe enough to extend beyond the expertise of the reading specialist and require a portion of a child's instruction from other highly trained professionals. Such professionals might also act in a supportive or consultative role to classroom teachers, helping them adapt instruction to student needs. However, two problems persist that create powerful barriers for these students: *warehousing* and *response to disability*.

Warehousing is a term that describes what happens to students with disabilities when they are placed in regular classrooms, yet spend most of their day "outside of the educational loop." When their teachers are not adequately trained to help them, these students may not benefit from inclusion because they receive so little assistance in learning. The second barrier is that even preschool children's affective responses toward other people have been shown to reflect a global preference for those who are "like me" (Derman-Sparks, 1989).

Fortunately, both problems can be addressed by committed educators. Reading specialists must see that awareness of these issues is inextricable from process and practice, and professional development efforts that assist teachers in learning how to fulfill the spirit of full inclusion are warranted. In addition, teachers can directly acknowledge and address the issues of disability in the same way they acknowledge differences in race and skin color. By positively acknowledging young children's skin color and other physical attributes, teachers contribute to children's development of a positive sense of identity (Boutte, La Point, & Davis, 1993; Derman-Sparks, 1989).

The CORE Concept in Our Consideration of Differences among Students

When considering how to deal with classroom issues of ethnicity, culture, gender, sexual orientation, disabilities, and other differences among human beings, we cannot emphasize this point enough: *Teachers MUST create an environment that ensures that all children see people from their identity group reflected positively in the instructional materials, pictures, books, and videos used in the classroom and throughout the school* (Boutte & McCormick, 1992). As Derman-Sparks (1989) observes, "We see the world in terms of ourselves" (p. 13). Therefore, treating all children the *same* may translate into treating everyone as white or male, or heterosexual, or Western or without physical barriers or without language differences. Denying children's unique identities, and the reality of biases, are still powerful forces in our society.

An endless media barrage, critical of the reading performance of our nation's children and the adequacy of the schools to produce literate citizens, would lead us to believe that reading scores are in serious decline. However, according to Berliner and Biddle (1995) what has passed as fact is largely a "manufactured crisis." Contrary to public perception, most recent international comparisons indicate that children in the United States read as well or better than children of the same ages around the world (Elley, 1992). In addition, at all grade levels, children today outperform children from earlier eras of North American schooling (Bracey, 1997). However, Dick Allington (2001) points out that, within these indicators, there are several disturbing trends. It appears that U.S. schools currently work better for children from certain kinds of homes. Students from homes in which parents have lower levels of education and family income continue to perform below those from families with higher education and income levels. Children from minority families also perform less well than those from majority families.

We have long believed that a fully literate citizenry will solve our social and economic ills, when in fact evidence is indicating that race and ethnicity may have an even stronger influence on vocational opportunities, income, and power (Dudley-Marling & Murphy, 1997; Gee, 1990). However, as Deborah Dillon (2000) reminds us, there is a moral dimension to our teaching. We will fulfill that obligation only when we come to grips with and find solutions to issues of hegemony, voice, identity, and equity.

REVISITING THE VIGNETTE

1. What advice do you have for Liana as she prepares to respond to Julio the next day?

2. What can the reading specialist do to help Liana, her students, and the teachers with these issues?
3. What are some obstacles that will continue to challenge teachers who work with struggling literacy learners or those who differ from the dominant culture?

POINTS TO REMEMBER

The issues in this chapter are among the most difficult ones with which we deal as literacy educators. We have examined what we know about readers and writers who struggle, and we know that their difficulties have powerful effects on self-esteem and motivation. Moreover, we see that even well-intentioned teachers unconsciously differentiate in their treatment of high- and low-achieving students. However, we have also seen how new ways of integrating literacies into instruction and including these students in rich socially mediated contexts may enhance their access to literacy.

In the second part of this chapter we addressed differences in physical ability. The issues addressed are similar to those found in considerations of gender, sexual orientation, and other classifications by which our society labels and sorts individuals. The primary themes of the chapter are culturally responsive teaching and bridging instruction between home and community. We believe there is a moral aspect to education that drives us to find better ways to deal with power, access, voice, and culture.

PORTFOLIO PROJECTS

1. In your role as reading specialist, create a brochure for classroom teachers with suggestions for helping struggling readers experience success with content area texts and media.

2. Draw three parallel time lines: one with your reading/writing/literacy development (events, books, assignments, etc.); one with the historical/political/local/world events of the times; and one with the cultural/social/media elements (favorite TV shows, sports, musicians, magazines, hobbies, videos, etc.) of the times. Where are points of intersection? Where are points of divergence? What do you think accounts for each?

3. Create a portfolio item that reflects your learning relative to the goal you set for yourself.

RECOMMENDED READINGS

Allington, R. (2001). *What really matters for struggling readers: Designing research-based programs.* New York: Addison Wesley Longman. Allington's book synthesizes a wide range of research related to struggling readers. He adopts a provocative stance and dispenses advice for educators, administrators, and all those who work with readers and writers who struggle.

Dillon, D. (2000). *Kids Insight: Reconsidering how to meet the literacy needs of all students.* Newark, DE: International Reading Association. Deborah Dillon's book addresses moral, philosophical, cultural, and pedagogical issues and ties them to classroom practice. This would be an excellent book to use in teacher study groups.

Roller, C. M. (1998). *So . . . What's a tutor to do?* Newark, DE: International Reading Association. Cathy Roller draws on her years of clinical expertise and experience working with struggling readers to create this practical and valuable tool for literacy tutors.

Taylor, B. M., Graves, M. F., & van den Broek, P. (Eds.). (2000). *Reading for meaning: Fostering comprehension in the middle grades.* This book contains a wealth of information on reading and literacy practices and processes. Especially relevant is the chapter by van den Broek and Kremer on comprehension.

CHAPTER SIX

ADDRESSING ISSUES
OF CULTURE AND LANGUAGE

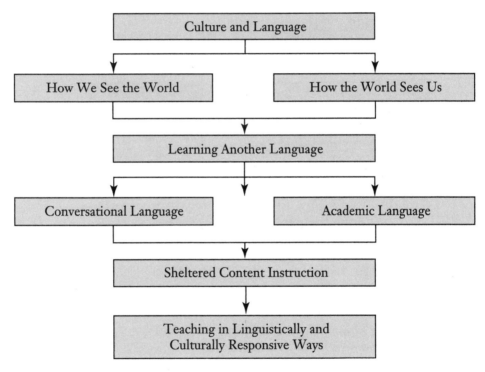

FIGURE 6.1 Chapter Overview

LEARNING GOALS

After reading, discussing, and engaging in activities related to this chapter, you will be able to:

1. discuss the role of culture in students' language and literacy acquisition;

2. analyze the appropriateness of language and literacy programs for English language learners;

3. explain the role of the reading specialist in supporting students who are English language learners;

4. Personal Learning Goal: In a three-minute brainstorming session, share what you know about effective literacy intervention for English language learners. Write an objective or question that reflects something you want to learn as we explore these topics. Share this with others in your group.

Vignette

Susan Weiss, the reading specialist at Thomas Jefferson Elementary School, straightened up her desk in preparation for the arrival of Felipe Rodriguez, the district bilingual coordinator. Susan had asked Felipe for help in providing more appropriate instruction for the growing number of English learners at Jefferson after she had observed a recent reading lesson in a third-grade classroom. During that particular whole-class lesson, one boy, Jose, who had recently arrived in the United States from Mexico and who had very little English proficiency, sat in the corner of the room with crayons and a coloring book.

For the entire lesson, he sat and colored while the other children participated in a shared reading experience with the teacher. When asked why Jose was coloring while the others were involved in the story, the teacher responded with some exasperation: "Jose can't speak any English! How do you expect him to participate in reading lessons? Besides, this was a story about pioneer days in the West. He wouldn't know anything about that, so I just thought it was better to have him do something he could be successful with. He didn't seem to mind, and anyway, it wasn't that long that he was coloring."

Thinking Points

1. What are the issues, so far, in this vignette?
2. How might Susan, the reading specialist, approach this teacher about appropriate assessment and instruction for her new student, Jose?

Expanding the Vignette: Exploring the Tensions

The relatively rapid growth in the number of English language learners (ELL's) had taken Susan's school district by surprise, primarily because to this point, the rural Arkansas community had very few students whose home languages were other than English. Instead, former "language issues" were related to Ebonics, the dialect spoken by the large African American population.

Susan glanced over the questions she was prepared to ask Felipe. These included the following:

1. What does research say about how to effectively teach students acquiring English?
2. What can teachers do to help ELL's learn content when they cannot read the textbook?
3. How can we tell whether an ELL student has a reading problem or is he just having trouble with English?

Thinking Points

1. Do you know the percentage of English language learners in your school? In your district?
2. Do you know how many and what languages are spoken by the students in your school? Your district?

ISSUES OF CULTURE

The word *culture* is one we frequently encounter in a number of contexts. Because it appears in the title of this chapter, it would seem reasonable to define it as we begin our inquiry into the topic. Unfortunately, just as there is no single definition of reading, so, too, is there no single definition of *culture* on which individuals can agree. Kathy Au (2000) describes culture as a collection of values, beliefs, and standards that guide individuals' thoughts, feelings, and behaviors in various social settings. We find her definition of culture, with its emphasis on the things people *do*, rather than on a set of static or descriptive criteria, extremely useful from the perspective of context. Shirley Brice Heath (1982) indicates that students come to school from various cultural and social backgrounds and that these factors manifest themselves in different "ways of taking" from books and using language. Figure 6.2 shows how the NEA/CRUE and Family–School Partnership illustrate culture.

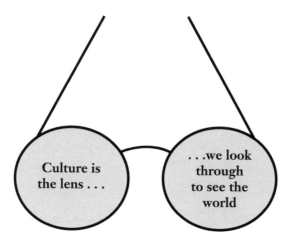

FIGURE 6.2   What Is Culture?

Language is among the primary markers through which human beings express culture. Kathy Au (2000) and Deborah Dillon (2000) make the following observations about culture:

Culture is complex and socially constructed through interactions with others.

- It is constructed as members of the group share common understandings.
- Culture is further shaped and influenced by forces within the broader sociopolitical contexts.
- Culture is constantly changing.
- Culture is intimately linked to the purposes for which language is valued and used.
- Understanding the dimensions of culture, how it is constituted, and its influence on individual students and groups is integral to providing culturally responsive instruction.

Nieto (1999) noted that students arrive at school with "cultural capital" or ways of knowing that are culturally based. Heath (1982) was among the first to discover what others (Au, 2000; Dillon, 2000) have confirmed: The more closely the child's "ways of knowing" match what is considered valuable within the culture of the school, the more likely the child is to benefit from school literacy instruction. Thus, learning is thought to be heavily influenced by social "contexts." Most reading educators think of "context" as a comprehension element of text in which words and ideas are situated. However, in our discussion of culture, when we use the term *context*, such as *context of the learning*, *context of community*, or *social context*, we mean not only the physical setting but also the political, sociological, and psychological spheres that influence our thoughts and behaviors.

As we've mentioned before, sometimes the cultural capital and background experiences a child brings to school are not honored. Similar to providing inequitable differential instruction to high- and low-achieving students, some teachers engage in similar discriminatory practices with students outside of the dominant culture. We can begin to explore culture by examining our own cultural backgrounds and beliefs as learners and teachers. Deborah Dillon (2000) and others (McLaughlin & Vogt, 1996) recommend that all educators and preservice teachers write literacy autobiographies to explore the factors that have shaped their attitudes, beliefs, and abilities related to literacy, and we've encouraged you to do the same (see Appendix A for the Literacy History Prompts).

Learning about the Cultures of Our Students to Understand Their Literacies

Luis Moll (1998) advocates that teachers discover their students' cultural identities by going beyond the school walls and into the community to see the bodies of knowledge of the home and community, how members of families (households) share information in networks, and how they engage in *activity* within various social contexts. By examining their worlds through the lens of multiple literacies, as discussed in Chapter 2 and throughout this book, you will begin to find ways to connect the experiences of the student to the content and goals of the school culture.

School Values and Emphasis	Cultural Values and Emphasis

The School may emphasize:
  Competition
  Individual responsibility
  Teacher-controlled lesson
	Native American/Native Alaskan cultures may value:
	  Cooperation
	  Group learning
	  Shared responsibility
	    (Ladsen-Billings, 1996)

Some schools may emphasize:
  Eye contact with adults
  Answering quickly, raising hand to show that you know the answer
  Downcast eyes signal guilt
	Some Native American cultures may emphasize:
	  Averting eyes when adults speak
	  Waiting to answer indicates to the inquirer that the question deserves careful thought
	  Downcast eyes signal you are listening
	    (Diaz-Rico & Reed, 1995)

Some schools may emphasize:
  Traditional story structure
  Beginning, middle, and end
	The Arapaho may emphasize:
	  Meandering story structure
	  Stories with no formal ending
	    (Delpit, 1995)

FIGURE 6.3 Examples of Differences in School and Cultural Values

Some aspects of culture and language can have a significant impact on how a student responds to classroom discussion and activity. Lily Wong-Fillmore (1991) discovered that incongruities between students and school cultures can lead teachers to make erroneous judgments about students' knowledge, motivation, and learning. To illustrate the point, we will provide three examples. As you read them, consider how the narrowly constrained and traditional school notions of discourse, literacy, response, and problem solving have the potential to marginalize those who are unlike their peers with regard to culture (see Figure 6.3).

Each of these beliefs and values shapes classroom interaction. It is easy to see the potential for misunderstanding resulting from a culturally static interpretation on the part of a teacher, who might attribute a student's lack of eye contact to guilt or lack of quick response to lack of understanding. The student might also misunderstand and have little idea what the expectations are. However, it is *very important* that we not stereotype cultural mores and make assumptions that all persons who reside in a particular culture share the same values or beliefs. The notion of identity, "Who am I?" is always socially constructed and unique.

MODELS OF SUPPORT FOR ENGLISH LANGUAGE LEARNERS

In this section, we analyze programs for English language learners, in particular sheltered instruction and issues related to inclusion. We honor the complex, overlapping issues, such as linguistics, identity, literacies, discourse, and power, and the important role of the reading specialist in programs for supporting English learners and their teachers.

Have you ever heard stories about Native American children or other limited-English-speaking children who were punished for speaking their home or heritage language? While this seldom (if ever) happens today, there are many reasons children feel pressure to speak only English at school, the most powerful of which is that English may be the only language spoken that is understood by the majority. Further, parents and teachers often feel that the sooner a child learns English, the better able the child will be to benefit from school instruction (Wong-Fillmore, 1991).

Yet, becoming an English (or any other language, for that matter) learner is not an easy task. Many students acquire a functional level of English that allows them to communicate with their peers in about two years. However, it takes about five to seven years to acquire *academic language*, which is necessary for meeting the demands of school (Cummins, 1979; Wolfe, 1992). Just learning "new words" isn't enough; there are content concepts, procedural steps, and vocabulary that need to be understood before content can be mastered. Students who can already read and write well in their primary language have an easier time adjusting to school where a new language is spoken—much of what they know can be transferred to the new language system. However, these English language learners still need effective and productive instruction and interaction. Much of what ELL's need depends on their stages of English proficiency. The several stages have been defined as follows (Au, Garcia, Goldenberg, & Vogt, 2002, pp. 8–9):

- Beginning/Preproduction: Students at the Beginning/Preproduction stage may comprehend limited amounts of English instruction, such as simple repeated sentences, but will rely on visual and other clues to understanding. They can be expected to respond not only verbally, but by pointing, gesturing, and by imitating sounds and actions. Students will follow shared readings and will rely on illustrations and graphic clues to attach meaning to printed material. Students may illustrate characters, objects, and actions to convey meaning.
- Early Production/Speech Emergent: Students at the Early Production/Speech Emergent stage are actively developing receptive vocabulary, but are ready to voluntarily produce one- and two-word answers, short phrases, or short sentences, and can recite and repeat poems, songs, and chants. They can also retell simple stories using pictures and objects, and can engage in dialogues, interviews, or role plays. They comprehend simple passages and can follow text during group reading. They can use simple sentences and details in their writing, write from dictation, and write using a variety of genres.
- Intermediate/Advanced: Students at the Intermediate/Advanced stage continue to build receptive vocabulary, but are able to respond to prompts and questions in more extended form. They speak fluently in conversations and group discussions, and appropriately use English idioms. These students may engage in independent reading according to their level of oral fluency and prior experiences with print. They are able to write in greater detail, in a wide variety of genres, and for a wide variety of purposes, including creative and analytical writing.

Group Inquiry Activity Reflect on when you learned a language, whether in childhood, in high school, or college. In a group, discuss your responses to the following questions:

1. In the early stages of learning the language, how did you feel?
2. When you were required to respond orally in the new language to the teacher's questions, how did you feel? What did you do?
3. At what point in the language acquisition process did you begin to gain confidence in speaking?
4. After two years of formal study, how well prepared were you to learn content material (such as math or chemistry) in your new language?
5. What are the implications of your group's responses for teaching English language learners?

In rural areas with small numbers of English language learners (ELL's), assisting students who need support for learning English may fall to the reading specialist or Title I teacher, whether or not this person is educationally prepared to assist these students. In sizeable urban communities with large numbers of English learners, classroom teachers may have 80 to 90 percent (or more) of their students whose home language is other than English. In these schools, there may or may not be bilingual bicultural specialists to help children learn English, and the reading specialist may be involved in assisting teachers. Many of the decisions about how best to facilitate instruction for students with diverse language backgrounds depend on a number of factors that are unique to the school and community context.

In many American classrooms, two common models of English language learning are found: bilingual education and ESL (English as a Second Language) pull-out programs (Dillon, 2000). In bilingual programs, students are taught most of their academic subjects in their primary languages while they are developing proficiency in English. An ESL transitional model that is found in some states is the 50-50 model. It promotes bidirectional bilingual language learning. This means that the school offers an integrated bilingual setting to both native English speakers and students with limited English proficiency (LEP). The group stays together for all instruction, during which equal amounts of time are allocated for instruction in the two languages. Teachers in these programs are also bilingual, bi-literate, and can teach in two languages. Typically, in the United States half of the instruction is in English and half is in Spanish, because the largest number of ELL's are Spanish-speaking (Padilla et al., 1991). Benefits for students in these programs are that they acquire proficiency in two languages and develop a deep appreciation of and sensitivity to other cultures (Thomas & Collier, 1997/1998). This model is most suitable where there are large numbers of students who speak the same minority language and all teachers are bilingual (Dillon, 2000).

Some pull-out programs for ELL's have not proven to be successful because they have treated English learners as remedial learners, have marginalized their culture, and have separated them from their classmates. Language learning in these programs has been decontextualized or is less related to authentic social settings and purposes. These models commonly exist in schools where there are smaller numbers of ELL's or students who speak a number of different languages, thus precluding the implementation of the 50-50 model.

At the time of this writing, bilingual education (where students receive content instruction in their home language) is under attack in a number of states. For example, in both California and Arizona, voters' referendums require most instruction to be provided in English, unless parents seek waivers. This trend is spreading to other states, as well. The results remain to be seen, but early data from California seem to indicate, somewhat surprisingly, that with intensive English instructional support (English Language Development) and sheltered content instruction, many of the children formerly educated in bilingual classrooms are doing well. However, there is still a great disparity between the academic achievement (as measured by standardized tests) of English language learners and their native English-speaking peers.

A number of educators (Echevarria & Graves, 1998; Echevarria, Vogt, & Short; 2000; Guzman, 1986; Krashen, 1998; Ruddell, 2000) suggest that, as English learners develop proficiency in English, they must be provided with content instruction that enables them to reach grade-level standards. The approach, Sheltered Instruction (SI) or Specially Designed Academic Instruction in English (SDAIE), uses English as the medium for providing content area instruction while emphasizing the development of English proficiency. This integration of language acquisition and subject matter learning honors the notion that language is acquired in meaningful contexts (Krashen, 1985). It provides comprehensible input about content concepts and fosters connections with students' experiences and prior knowledge (Cummins, 1984; Echevarria, Vogt, & Short, 2000). Sheltered instruction stresses the development of students' English proficiency, content knowledge, cognitive and academic skill development, and reasoning—all required for learning in content areas.

The Sheltered Instruction Observation Protocol (SIOP) (Echevarria, Vogt, & Short, 2000) was designed to assist teachers, supervisors, peer coaches, and others in creating and evaluating sheltered content lessons. Among the SIOP components for the effective instruction of English learners are the following:

1. clearly defined content and language objectives that are reflected in lesson planning, lesson delivery, and assessment of student knowledge and application;
2. appropriate age and grade-level content reflected in lesson planning and delivery;
3. supplementary materials (e.g., photos, illustrations, graphs, models, demonstrations) used to a high degree;
4. adaptation of content (e.g., texts, assignments) for levels of students' English proficiency (Note that this does not mean changing content standards—rather, this may involve adapting texts and providing alternate means of accessing the content);
5. meaningful activities (e.g., authentic reading/writing; hands-on application opportunities) integrated throughout the lesson;
6. concepts specifically linked to students' backgrounds and prior experiences and to past learning;

7. key vocabulary emphasized (e.g., introduced, written, highlighted), reviewed, and assessed;
8. speech appropriate for students' English proficiency levels (e.g., slower rate, clear enunciation; simple sentence structure for beginners; varied response expectations);
9. clear explanations of academic tasks (such as what it means to "share with your partner," "discuss," "list," "summarize," etc.);
10. a variety of techniques used to make content clear (modeling, visuals, hands-on activities, gestures, pantomime, demonstrations, etc);
11. ample opportunities to use cognitive, metacognitive, and affective strategies;
12. consistent use of scaffolding techniques;
13. a variety of question types, including higher order, with sufficient wait-time after questioning, and multiple ways of responding to questions, such as group response;
14. frequent opportunities for teacher–student and student–student interactions;
15. grouping configurations that support language and content objectives (not just whole class);
16. ample opportunities to clarify concepts in the L1 (primary language), if possible;
17. appropriate pacing of content delivery depending on students' language proficiency;
18. regular feedback provided to students on their output (e.g., language, content, work);
19. assessment conducted on students' comprehension and learning throughout the lesson and at its conclusion (e.g., spot-checking, group response).

These indicators have been summarized from a list of thirty that are part of the Sheltered Instruction Observation Protocol (SIOP). By teaching language arts, math, science, social studies, and other content subjects using these techniques, students are afforded a much greater opportunity to function in the mainstream (Ramos-Ocasio, 1985). Although we are limited in our ability to provide in-depth information on sheltered literacy instruction in this book, we encourage you to refer to the texts listed at the end of this chapter for more information about sheltered instruction.

In addition to sheltering content for ELLs, it's important to remember that:

- participation in some programs designed for English learners may result, not in bilingualism, but in subtractive bilingualism, or loss of the child's primary language (Wong-Fillmore, 1991);
- children who are forced to give up their primary language and adjust to an English-only environment may not only lose their primary language, but may not learn the second language well (Wong-Fillmore, 1991);
- when children lose their primary language relationships with parents, grandparents, and others in the culture, they may also have difficulties with identity issues; there may be additional emotional, social, and cognitive developmental consequences for these children (Cummins, 1981);

- when children are able to use the complex and rich understanding of their primary language in their instruction, they are able to transfer these skills to a new language (Wolfe, 1992).

The Issue of Dialect and Its Implications for Culturally Responsive Classrooms

While the needs of English language learners has been an area of study and focus for the past decade, there has been less discussion about teaching students with dialect differences. Most everyone has a dialect, a variety of language, usually regional or social, that is distinguishable from others in pronunciation, vocabulary, and grammar. Teachers sometimes feel it's their job to reinforce conventional English and discourage nonstandard dialects. It's undeniable that some people *do* privilege certain dialects, such as a Boston accent over, perhaps, a Mississippi accent, and there may be some children who suffer because of a teacher's lack of understanding of dialects. For these teachers, there may be misunderstandings about the differences between dialect, and "bad" or "poor" grammar, "inappropriate" language, "ignorant" speech, or "improper" ways of communicating. In fact, Wolfram (1991) points out there is no evidence that language variation, such as pronouncing *with* as "wif" or saying, "She didn't pay no attention" instead of "She didn't pay any attention," interferes in any way with understanding or learning. The National Council of Teachers of English (NCTE), took a strong position in 1974 affirming students' rights to the patterns and variations of their nurture, and championing their rights to their own, identity, voice, and style (pp. 2–3). You might remember the Ebonics controversy in Oakland, California in the late 1990s in which there were heated discussions about whether students had the right to use Ebonics (an African American dialect) in schools, whether Ebonics should be taught, or whether the schools had the right to actively discourage students' use of the dialect. Because of these ongoing arguments, we urge that such issues remain a source of thoughtful and enlightened conversation among literacy educators.

The Role of the Reading Specialist in Supporting Programs for English Language Learners

In larger school districts, it is unlikely that reading specialists will be required to develop ESL/ELD or bilingual programs, though they may be expected to assist in creating and implementing effective sheltered content classes. Further, since English learners can have difficulty learning to read in either or both of the L1 and L2, it is essential that reading specialists have understandings of first and second language and literacy acquisition. In smaller districts, when a single non-English-speaking family relocates to the community, it is often the reading specialist who is assigned to work with the children. Because of the wide variety of students' home languages, teachers and reading specialists may lack knowledge of the language and culture of these students. Therefore, an understanding of sheltered content instruction is important for these teachers.

It is also necessary for reading specialists to work with teachers, administrators, special educators, and bilingual specialists to properly assess the language proficiency and literacy acquisition of English learners. All too often ELL's are referred and admitted to special education programs because of reading and language difficulties. The reading specialist needs to be able to ascertain whether a student has a true reading problem or whether the difficulty he or she is experiencing in the classroom is due to his or her level of English language proficiency. This isn't always easy to determine; therefore, it's important to work together to plan the most appropriate placement for these youngsters.

Reading specialists also can (perhaps must) play a major role in helping teachers learn how to provide appropriate sheltered content instruction for ELL's, who may have difficulty accessing grade-level vocabulary, content, texts, and concepts. Also, as you review the indicators previously listed for effective sheltered instruction (see the SIOP), keep in mind that most of these also are very effective techniques for working with struggling readers. However, many teachers don't know of them and you can assist in modeling through demonstration effective sheltering techniques.

Helping Children Use Language to Communicate, Interpret, and Organize Their World

What follows are some additional ideas about how to provide a learning environment in schools that honors and values the linguistic and cultural diversity that we all share.

- Educators can create an environment that values the language and culture of the child's home. They can encourage children to use their first languages, while supporting their acquisition of English, and they can help students explore and value their rich literacy autobiographies.
- If qualified minority-language speakers are not available, collaboration with parents and linguistically diverse members of the communities can provide opportunities for children to use their language and to validate its importance.
- Because strong family/school partnerships provide cultural continuity, parents can be encouraged to talk to their children and share oral and written stories in the home language. They can be encouraged to share these stories and cultural artifacts with the child's class.
- Gestures, actions, pictures, manipulatives, and other mediating tools are all ways for the teacher to enhance communication (Okagaki and Sternberg, 1993). Classroom signs and directions on the wall can incorporate students' languages. English-only teachers and classmates can value and support an English learner's language and culture by learning common phrases and expressions in the student's home language.
- Teachers and students can be encouraged to view different styles of discourse and regional dialect as additions to the richness and diversity of the classroom.
- Just as Carmen (see Chapter 2) translated within her Puerto-Rican community, students can use translation in the classroom to enhance literacy.

- Developing students' critical literacy strategies will enable them to analyze how cultural images are presented within and across literacies and symbol systems (intertextuality, intermediality).
- Drawing specific attention to the rich metaphorical, poetic, and often lyrical languages and styles and dialects of other cultures might do much to enhance the linguistic repertoire of all Americans.
- Provide students of various ethnic and cultural backgrounds with multiple opportunities to see their lives, beliefs, experiences, and appearances represented in school settings and instructional materials.
- Multicultural literature can help all students (and their teachers) understand and appreciate multiple perspectives including non-Western views of the world (Bean, 2001).

As much as we educators want to provide for all students' language and literacy needs, this is not an easy task for many teachers, primarily because most represent the majority culture, both linguistically and culturally. As Patty Schmidt points out in Other Voices, students in undergraduate and graduate education programs and teachers in all parts of the United States are from predominantly white, middle-class cultures. She provides a model for helping prepare educators to support learning in culturally diverse classrooms.

Other Voices: Patricia Ruggiano Schmidt

Dr. Patty Schmidt, who teaches in the Education Department of LeMoyne College in Syracuse, New York, has written and published a number of books and articles on facilitating culturally responsive connections among teachers, parents, communities, and learners. Preliminary studies implementing her ABC's of Cultural Understanding and Communication *demonstrate its promise for changing teacher education in substantive ways.*

ABCs of Cultural Understanding and Communication

Research and practice demonstrate that strong home–school connections not only help students make sense of the school curriculum, but also promote literacy development (Au, 1993; Heath, 1983; Schmidt, 2000). However, for several reasons, in recent years home–school connections have become a significant challenge. First, as our school population has become increasingly diverse, both culturally and ethnically, our teaching population has consistently originated from European American, suburban experiences. Typically, educators describe themselves as white and middle class and often add during discussions about diversity, "I'm an American; I don't have a culture" (Florio-Ruane, 1994; Schmidt, 1999). Second, many present and future teachers have not had sustained relationships with people from different ethnic, cultural, and lower socioeconomic backgrounds, so much of their knowledge about diversity has been influenced by media stereotypes (Tatum, 1997). Third, school curricula, methods, and materials usually reflect only European American or white culture and ignore the backgrounds and experiences of students and families from lower socioeconomic levels and differing ethnic and cultural backgrounds (Nieto, 1996; Purcell-Gates, 1993; Walker-Dalhouse & Dalhouse, 2001). Fourth, many teacher education programs do not adequately prepare educators for making strong home–school connections (Lalik & Hinchman, 2001). Consequently, this disconnect has become a national problem, the impact of which has been linked to poor literacy development and extremely high dropout rates among students from urban poverty areas (Banks, 1994; Edwards, Pleasants, & Franklin, 1999; Schmidt, 1998b).

As a teacher educator, I searched for ways to prepare present and future teachers for the diversity in their classrooms. I discovered that the most successful programs are those that incorporate authentic encounters with people from different backgrounds and experiences while learning content related to racism, sexism, and classicism (Cochran-Smith, 1995; Willis & Meacham, 1997). Furthermore, these programs often claim that teacher self-knowledge may be the first consideration when attempting to help teachers understand diverse groups of students (Britzman, 1986).

Considering all of the above factors, I designed and developed the model known as *ABC's of Cultural Understanding and Communication*. It is a process based on the premise that knowing oneself is basic to the understanding of others. K–12 present and future teachers who experience the process often begin to successfully connect home and school for literacy learning (Leftwich, 2001; Schmidt, 2001; Xu, 2000). The model's five-step process is supported by previous research and is briefly explained in the following paragraphs.

Step 1: Autobiography—Know thyself. First, each teacher writes an autobiography that includes key life events related to education, family, religious tradition, recreation, victories, defeats, and so on. This helps to build awareness of personal beliefs and attitudes that form the traditions and values of cultural autobiographies (Banks, 1994). Because it is well documented that writing is linked to knowledge of self within a social context (Yinger, 1985), writing one's life story seems to construct connections with universal human tenets and serves to lessen negative notions about different groups of people (Progoff, 1975). The autobiography experience sets the stage for the second step, learning about the lives of culturally different people.

Step 2: Biography. After several in-depth, audiotaped, unstructured or semistructured interviews of a person who is culturally different, each teacher constructs a biography from key events in that person's life. This helps teachers begin to develop the cultural sensitivity necessary to analyze similarities and differences in the two life stories (Schmidt, 1998a, 1998b, 2000; Spindler & Spindler, 1987).

Step 3: Cross-cultural analysis and appreciation of differences. For the third step in the process, each teacher studies the autobiography and biography and charts a list of similarities and differences, which leads to the fourth step.

Step 4: Self-analysis of differences. Self-analysis of differences is a key component of the process. The teacher carefully examines the chart that lists similarities and differences and writes an in-depth self-analysis of cultural differences, explaining the reasons for any personal discomforts and/or positive affects. Through this process teachers begin to acquire insights about others and sense their own ethnocentricity (Spindler & Spindler, 1987).

Step 5: Home–School Connection Plans for Literacy Development. After experiencing the previous steps in the process, K–12 teachers design year-long plans for connecting home and school for children's reading, writing, listening, and speaking development based on numerous modifications of the ABC's Model for their own classrooms and schools. They see ways to develop collaborative relationships with families in an atmosphere of mutual respect, so students gain the most from their education (Derman-Sparks & ABC Task Force, 1989, 1992; McCaleb, 1994).

Just as many researchers have discovered, families have a wealth of knowledge to share that helps the teachers develop relevant literacy lessons and motivate children's literacy learning (Edwards, Pleasants, & Franklin, 1999; Faltis, 1993; McCaleb, 1994; Schmidt, 1999). *The ABC's of Cultural Understanding and Communication* helps teachers learn about family and community values and shows them how to value what communities and families know. The results are clear—the boundaries are blurred between home and school in an atmosphere of collaboration and learning.

Group Inquiry Activity Because so many teachers come from white middle-class backgrounds (even those who teach in culturally diverse settings), many have never been challenged to consider the implications of their own ethnicity. Whether or not your childhood included culturally diverse experiences, we ask that you consider the following questions:

1. In what ways is it disadvantageous to grow up in a majority culture?
2. Are there advantages?
3. What are the implications for *teachers* of being raised in such a context?
4. What are the implications for students of these teachers, and how does the degree of diversity in the school affect your answer to this question?

In a fascinating article by Althier Lazar (2001), the author describes her research on preparing white preservice teachers for urban classrooms. Her conclusions are cautious ones. Lazar found that, for the most part, her students worked hard to become aware of their own "whiteness" and cultural privilege. They did in fact increase their recognition of biases in the structure and classroom events within urban schools. The study contradicts the conclusion drawn by Haberman (1996) that European Americans may not be the best choice as teachers for diversity. However, in spite of the intense focus on understanding these cultural dynamics, a small number of preservice teachers persisted in their biased assumptions about children's ability and language and a few remained insecure about teaching in urban schools. Lazar concludes we have a long way to go in understanding the complexities involved in the processes of preparing such teachers to work in urban settings. Clearly this interesting line of inquiry and the questions that Patty Schmidt poses have great potential to inform all of us.

Linguistically and Culturally Responsive Instruction

We would like to add a few caveats about culturally responsive instruction. First, as Kathy Au (2000) suggests, no matter how much the idea (culturally responsive instruction) seems to make sense pedagogically, we have yet to see a body of research to support its efficacy. Second, we want to caution educators to beware of superficial attempts to respond to language and culture, such as celebrating "heroes and holidays" or other single events where foods, crafts, clothing, or aspects of language and culture are placed in the forefront briefly. We suggest that these measures must be coupled with rich classroom experience; that teachers and reading specialists find ways to incorporate values, literature, beliefs, and images in their instruction; and that activities allow connections that defy the common stereotypes. We urge you to consider using the suggestions of Ann Watts-Paillotet (2000) and David O' Brien (2001) by providing avenues for expression that allow *all* students, not only those with limited English language proficiency, to express their knowledge through art, music, or intermediality.

The role of the reading specialist is to provide teachers with support, guidance, ideas, and models of instructional practice that respond to language and culture in a variety of ways. Culturally responsive instruction does not imply abandoning or lowering our goals, expectations, or standards, for such a stance is inherently discriminatory. Rather, like all good instruction, it makes full use of all the resources available to meet the existing goals. We would argue that a student's background knowledge and experience and culture and values are important resources on which connections to new content knowledge can be based. If we are to use the "cultural capital" (values, behaviors, experiences, tastes, perspectives) children bring to school as Au (2000) and Nieto (1999) suggest, we will have to find ways to help students make personal connections between the worlds of their school and community.

REVISITING THE VIGNETTE

It seems Susan Weiss, Jefferson Elementary School's reading specialist, is not particularly knowledgeable about the instructional needs of English language learners in her school, and she's wise to collaborate with her district's bilingual coordinator as a start. If she is expected to serve as a resource in her school, obviously she'll need to do some reading about current, accepted approaches for teaching ELL's. She also might want to spend time teaching a small group of English language learners while implementing sheltered instruction techniques and approaches, so that she'll be credible when she works with other teachers. She might want to form a study group with colleagues in order to learn more about how to plan appropriately for students with linguistic and cultural differences that may make it challenging for them to be successful in the majority culture. Asking for help, and not feeling inadequate when her school experiences a rapid increase in the number of English learners, is an important step for Susan to take. These students deserve the best Susan and her fellow teachers can offer them, and her willingness to learn, practice, and adapt her teaching are all important to their eventual mastery of English.

POINTS TO REMEMBER

Culture is not an easy concept to define, but it is something through which all humans make sense of our world. Recognizing and valuing students' cultural differences entails more than a "heroes and holidays" approach. Rather, teachers and specialists should view culture as a changing phenomenon that is always contextually based. That is, depending on a certain context, we may find ourselves in a particular culture, and it may be related to our family, linguistic, educational, ethnic, or socioeconomic group. Research shows that, while we may learn a conversational level of a new language in about two years, it may take five to seven years to learn the academic language necessary for success in school. In order to support English language learners as they learn a new language, sheltered content instructional approaches and techniques are recommended.

PORTFOLIO PROJECTS

1. Create a collage on a poster or chart paper. Use photos, illustrations, magazine pictures, graphics, and text (words or phrases) that celebrate your "culture." Culture here may relate to a number of groups, such as language, ethnicity, family, heritage, socioeconomics, education, or however else you define yourself. Describe, explain, and celebrate your poster with others.

2. Create a linguistic family tree, going back as far as you can to explore and define your linguistic heritage and culture. How many languages can you identify that have been spoken by your near and distant relatives? How have these language and cultural groups defined who you are today?

3. Design, teach, and evaluate a sheltered instruction lesson. Videotape yourself as you're teaching, and determine how well you provided access to grade-level concepts, content, and vocabulary. Reflect on your teaching and what you can do to provide a linguistically and culturally responsive environment for all learners.

RECOMMENDED READINGS

Diaz-Rico, L. T, & Weed, K. Z. (1995). *The crosscultural, language, and academic development handbook: A complete K–12 reference guide*. Boston: Allyn & Bacon. These authors have assembled an enormous amount of information and created a comprehensive overview of academic programs and practices in language and culture. It is an excellent reference guide.

Echevarria, J., & Graves, A. (1998). *Sheltered content instruction: Teaching English language learners with diverse abilities*. Boston: Allyn & Bacon. This text explains in detail the needs of English learners and builds a strong rationale for providing appro-priate instruction based on individual students' needs. Sheltered content instruction is described and a variety of instructional techniques are explained.

Echevarria, J., Vogt, M. E., & Vogt, K. D. (2000). *Making content comprehensible for English language learners: The SIOP Model*. Boston: Allyn & Bacon. This book describes in detail how to plan, teach, and evaluate sheltered content lessons. It contains the Sheltered Instruction Observation Protocol (SIOP), an instrument that guides lesson planning, lesson delivery, and lesson evaluation.

PART II

THE READING SPECIALIST: RESOURCE TEACHER AND CURRICULUM DEVELOPER

CHAPTER SEVEN

IMPLEMENTING A READING/LANGUAGE ARTS PROGRAM IN THE ELEMENTARY SCHOOL

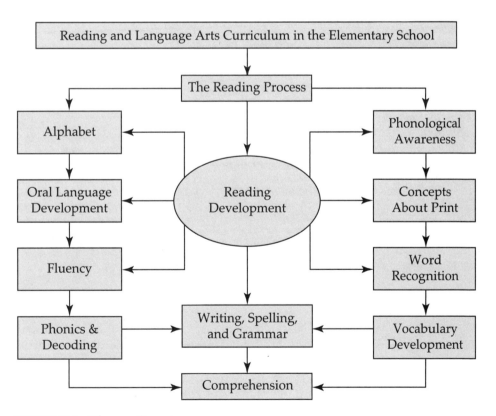

FIGURE 7.1 Chapter Overview

LEARNING GOALS

After reading, discussing, and engaging in activities related to this chapter, you will be able to:

1. provide an overview of the reading process;
2. describe a standards-based elementary school curriculum in reading and language arts;
4. work with students, parents, teachers, and administrators in implementing and sustaining an effective elementary literacy program;
5. Personal Learning Goal: In a three-minute brainstorming session, share what you know about effective elementary literacy programs. Write a goal or a question that reflects something you want to learn as we explore this topic. Share it with the members of your group.

Vignette

It is the beginning of a new school year, and Claudio Martelli has just been hired in his first position as a reading specialist at Lincoln Elementary School in the southwestern United States. The school is comprised predominantly of Hispanic students (85%), with African American (8%), Caucasian (4%), and Southeast Asian children (3%) making up the rest of the 480 students. The school operates year-round with four different tracks; one of the tracks (approximately 120 students and four to five teachers) is on vacation at any given time.

Claudio has been hired on a ten-month contract, and will be working with all four tracks in grades kindergarten through fifth. There are a variety of reading programs in place at Lincoln, including bilingual,[1] transitional bilingual,[2] sheltered instruction (SI),[3]

special education, and English mainstream instruction. This school also has a large number of first-year teachers in the primary grades.

The principal has several specific jobs in mind for the reading specialist. The school's reading scores are down and the principal feels it is part of the reading specialist's responsibility to work to improve them. Also, Claudio is expected to focus his efforts on assisting the first-year teachers with their language arts program, as well as developing strategies to improve reading across the grade levels, particularly with the English learners. Although Claudio will oblige his principal by assisting the new teachers, he is also eager to help struggling readers in all grades to improve their reading.

Thinking Points

1. What are some of the tensions that Claudio faces as he begins his new job?
2. What are the first three things you think he should attend to?

Expanding the Vignette: Exploring the Tensions

One of the first steps Claudio took was to distribute an introductory newsletter to all

teachers on the staff. He also invited the first-year teachers to join him each week for a one-hour meeting related to reading/language arts, and stated that these meetings would focus on the following topics: assessment, management, instructional strategies, and guided reading. Most of the new teachers, though feeling overwhelmed by the onset of the school year, appeared to welcome the new reading specialist's offer of assistance.

Marcia Wilson, one of the first-year teachers, recently entered teaching as a second career. She secured her position with an emergency teaching certificate due to a shortage of teachers in the district. As such, she is required to begin taking six units of methodology courses at the nearby university. Even though Marcia has not had formal teacher preparation, she appears to be quite confident and attributes this to volunteering in her children's classrooms and teaching Sunday school for a number of years. Marcia is assigned to a third-grade mixed class of twenty-four students, most of whom are intermediate speakers of English, with a few transitional English speakers. She is teaching in a portable classroom behind the main school building, and has few opportunities to observe and talk with the other teachers.

Within the first few weeks of school, Marcia noticed that one of her students, Visal, was having difficulty with reading and writing—he seemed to be significantly behind his peers. Visal, eight years old and the middle child of five in his family, speaks only Cambodian at home. He speaks English only during school time. He has attended Lincoln since kindergarten and has always been in bilingual and transitional classes. Because of

her concerns about Visal's literacy development, Marcia asked Claudio to stop by her classroom to see if he had any suggestions for how she might better meet the child's needs.

Responding to Marcia's request for help with Visal, Claudio reviewed the boy's cumulative file, noting his previous standardized test scores, as well as former teachers' written comments. He then scheduled an observation in Marcia's third-grade classroom during the reading/language arts block. He noted that she taught reading as a whole class endeavor, with the same literature anthology used for all students. Similarly, skill and strategy lessons were taught whole-class, and from the daily schedule posted on the white board, it appeared there was no scheduled time for a teacher read-aloud or self-selected reading by students. Perhaps most important, Claudio observed that Visal was unengaged during the reading lesson, and at times, he appeared confused.

Claudio decided that he also needed to visit some other classrooms, particularly those of the first-year students. What he found was a wide variety of approaches and reading materials that teachers were using, along with inconsistencies in the amount and quality of available reading materials. As Claudio ventured into the classrooms of the more experienced teachers, he realized that there, too, was a great assortment of methods and materials that the teachers were using for their individual reading programs. He decided that he also needed to informally visit some other classrooms, particularly those of the first-year teachers.

Thinking Points

1. Identify what you think are the three major tensions Claudio is confronting. Of the three, which should be of the highest priority?
2. What short-term actions should Claudio take to assist Marcia Wilson and the other teachers?

3. What long-term actions should Claudio consider to meet the principal's charge to raise test scores?

THE READING AND LANGUAGE ARTS CURRICULUM IN THE ELEMENTARY SCHOOL

Before we can make recommendations to Claudio about how to implement a balanced, comprehensive reading program in his school, let's examine the reading process, especially for beginning and developing readers. In doing so, we can begin to identify the critical literacy elements that must be present in every primary (K–2) and intermediate (3–5) classroom and how to adapt them in culturally responsive ways.

The Reading Process

Over the past thirty years, researchers have investigated the interrelatedness and reciprocity of the language processes. They have examined the social nature of language and literacy and how active young children develop their literacy competencies in a variety of speech communities (Heath, 1983; Heath, 1995; Moll, 1994). We know with certainty that language and literacy development do not occur in a vacuum, but through multiple and varied interactions with other human beings. Louise Wilkinson and Elaine Silliman (2000) situate the following assumptions about literacy learning within a social constructivist perspective:

1. Literacy learning is a social activity—interpersonal behaviors, both observed and enacted in the classroom, are the basis for new conceptual understandings in cognition and communication.
2. Literacy learning is integrated—strong interrelationships exist between oral and written language learning.
3. Literacy learning requires active student engagement in classroom activities and interaction—engaged students are motivated for literacy learning and have the best chance of achieving full communicative competence across the broad spectrum of language and literacy skills (pp. 337–338).

When they enter school, children have a fundamental system of oral communication, and, as they develop as learners, their system is enriched, enhanced, and expanded due to their interactions with those around them. One aspect of oral communication is what is required for success in school. "[Students] must know with whom, when and where they can speak and act, and they must provide speech and behavior that are appropriate for given classroom situations. Students must also be able to relate behavior, both academic and social, to varying classroom situations by interpreting implicit classroom rules" (Mehan, 1979, p. 133).

As with oral communication, literacy learning is also highly contextualized. In effective instruction, what children learn about literacy is situated in relevant, meaningful experiences that help them transfer their new learning to other settings, such as their homes and communities. In the sections that follow, we provide a brief overview of how readers develop proficiency and what they need to know and be able to do while reading. It is beyond the scope of this book to go into great detail about complex literacy processes and development; therefore, if you desire more information, we refer you to the recommended readings at the end of this chapter and others throughout the book.

Reading Development.   In order to understand how beginning readers learn to read, and to better understand why some children have difficulty, researchers have investigated what it is that successful beginning, developing, and proficient readers do. They have examined the relationship between oral language development and beginning reading, how children acquire understandings about the alphabet, concepts of print, sound–symbol relationships, and how comprehension is fostered. Some researchers have described reading acquisition through developmental continua for oral language, reading, and writing. For example, Jeanne Chall (1983) suggests that a developing reader moves through a series of stages, each of which builds on the one that comes before. Linnea Ehri (1994) describes word-reading development as falling into three phases; these emerged as an organizational construct from the results of many studies she conducted and reviewed. Researchers and educators who believe in a stage theory of literacy acquisition might ask, "In what stage of reading and writing development is this child? How can I help him or her to move to the next stage (or phase)?"

Other researchers' current explanations of the reading process and literacy development suggest that children might not progress through a series of stages, or exhibit characteristics of particular phases when they are learning to read and write. Rather, these researchers (see Dyson, 1993, 1994; Sulzby, 1994; Yaden, Rowe, & MacGillivray, 2000) propose that the unique perspectives, experiences, oral language competencies, and backgrounds of each individual child are more likely to provide information about how each acquires literacy. Because literacy activity is socially situated (Luke, 1994), the question these educators might ask is, "In what unique ways does this child engage in language-related tasks and interactions? How can I use this information to provide appropriate literacy instruction for him or her?"

Though some reading experts decry any notion of reading stages or phases, we find it helpful to view reading development along a loosely woven continuum, believing all children can become proficient readers given appropriate instruction and practice. These phases are fluid and within them readers are viewed as individuals. How they approach and understand texts is largely influenced by how a text is situated within their experiences, purposes for reading, familiarity with the topic, and motivation. This holds true for all readers, beginning, developing, or fluent.

Foundations for Learning to Read.   Recent research has informed us about the importance of providing foundations that enable beginning readers to make sufficient progress in learning to read and write. As we briefly discuss each of these, reflect on the implications for an elementary school's reading program. Think about the reading materials, methods, approaches, and supplemental resources that need to be in place in order for teachers to successfully teach children to read and write.

Oral Language Development. As young children begin to explore and develop language, they are also establishing an important foundation for subsequent reading proficiency. They hear words and sentences, realize how language is used, and develop understanding about the phonological structure of English long before they come to school. They also develop understanding about how the world works through interactions with a wide variety of texts, including images, words, forms, shapes, and whatever they use to textualize[4] their world (Wade & Moje, 2000). We need to examine what these texts are in order to use the multiple literacies of the home and the community to enhance school literacy acquisition.

For example, perhaps you have heard a young child say something like, "My mom *goed* home" or "I *sleeped* at Grandma's house" or "My mom *telled* me that story already!" These oral language patterns tell us about young children's (and some English language learners') developing understandings of English morphology, syntax, and text structure. If students are frequently corrected (or perhaps chastised) for these types of oral language "errors," this may have an impact on their self-esteem and subsequent language production. Besides, these language structures aren't really errors. Instead, the children are overgeneralizing from known linguistic patterns to those they are creating in their speech. Instead of correcting, we encourage children to experiment with language so they may begin to internalize and adopt flexibly the uses of conventional English as they learn the various contexts for particular speech acts (such as the classroom, church, or the supper table).

Thus the notion of "correct" English has given way to the appropriateness of a particular discourse form as a reflection of its context. Certainly, we want children to know conventional English forms, and it is important for them to acquire the language of the dominant culture in which they live, primarily because it's easier to participate as a citizen with full rights. However, we also recognize that using conventional English (or any other discourse model) has implications about what the accepted form of speaking implies, including the speaker's stance, voice, and perspective.

Frequent read-alouds from children's literature, nursery rhymes, and songs all help develop oral language fluency, and they assist children in understanding how the language works in a variety of contexts. Those who have not had this language stimulation during their preschool years will need to have many opportunities to engage in talk, language play, and discussions about reading once they reach school and these opportunities need to expand as they develop as readers. Research clearly reveals that children's oral language facility serves as an important building block for later reading development (Hiebert, Pearson, Taylor, Richardson, & Paris, 1998).

Knowledge of Letter Names and Concepts about Print. A strong correlation exists between children's knowledge of letter names and their success as beginning and developing readers (Snow, Burns, & Griffin, 1998). Adams (1990) found, in her comprehensive review of research on beginning reading, that "letter naming facility continued to show itself as a superlative predictor of reading achievement even through the seventh grade" (p. 62). However, just knowing letter names does not guarantee later reading proficiency; the relationship between letter-name knowledge and reading achievement is more complex than simple causality.

The names of most letters offer clues to the sounds they represent and children who can accurately name them begin to develop understandings of letter–sound associations. The understanding that letters represent the sounds of spoken and written English is often referred to as the "alphabetic principle." Again, young children who have heard many stories, poems, and books read aloud tend to internalize this principle almost automatically. However, others, who do not come to school with these experiences, may need more explicit teaching in learning how letters and sounds are related.

As young children listen to, play with, and look at many stories and books, they begin to develop an understanding about print concepts (Clay, 1985), which include:

1. Directionality: In English, print runs left-to-right and top-to-bottom. We read from the front of the book to the back.
2. Meaning: Print carries the meaning in books, not the illustrations.
3. Speech-to-print match: One spoken word matches one written word.
4. Spacing: Printed words have spaces before and after them.
5. Book concepts: Books have authors, illustrators, titles, beginnings and endings.
6. Sentences: Sentences begin and end with capitalization and punctuation.

Other concepts about print are related to book handling and story structure (how stories "work"). Clay (1991) suggests that we also should assess children's understandings about words, such as: letters and letter combinations create words with spaces between them; words and spaces can form sentences; and words have first and last letters. For children who arrive at school with little book experience, these print concepts must be taught and reinforced through the oral and shared reading of many big books,[5] little books, and stories.

Phonological and Phonemic Awareness.   "Phonological awareness, simply stated, is an awareness of the phonological segments in speech—the segments that are more or less represented by an alphabetic orthography. This awareness develops gradually over time and has a causal reciprocal relationship to reading (Blachman, 2000, p. 483). Occasionally, phonological awareness is referred to more broadly as a reader's discernment of the units that comprise oral language, including words, syllables, onset and rime, and phonemes. Instruction in phonemic awareness includes focusing children's attention on manipulating phonemes in spoken syllables and words (National Reading Panel, 2000; Yopp, 1992).

As children develop phonemic awareness, they recognize that a word has a sequence of sounds that can be blended, segmented, and rhymed. Phonemic awareness has been found to be a very strong predictor of later reading achievement, and children who demonstrate phonemic awareness in the beginning stages of learning to read are less likely to develop later reading problems (Blachman, 2000; Goswami, 2000; National Reading Panel, 2000; Snow et al., 1998; Wilkinson & Silliman, 2000). As with oral language development, children who have been exposed to word play, nursery rhymes, and hundreds of stories may arrive at school already phonemically aware. However, it is unmistakable that other children may need explicit instruction in identifying, counting, rhyming, blending, and segmenting the sounds in words. It is also clear that phonemic awareness and learning to read are mutually supportive. While phonemic awareness enhances the process of learning to read, learning to read also strengthens phonemic awareness.

Phonics. "Phonics is the relationship between the letters in written words and the sounds in spoken words. The letter–sound relationships of phonics are a set of visual directions—a map, if you will—telling readers how to pronounce words they have never seen before" (Fox, 2000, p. 3). That phonics knowledge is a precursor and strong predictor of reading proficiency is a fact no longer argued in the research literature (National Reading Panel, 2000; Wilkinson & Silliman, 2000).

Benita Blachman (2000) states that, despite evidence that children can develop phonological awareness and phonics knowledge outside of the context of literacy instruction, "there is considerable evidence that this instruction is enhanced when the connections to print are made explicit" (p. 487). That is, we can help children learn how to apply the alphabetic principle to the English writing system. We are teaching phonics when we demonstrate that the letter *m* represents the first sounds heard in the words *monkey, milk,* and *Mike*. We are also teaching phonics when we are helping children compare and contrast the sounds represented by words such as *mad/made* and *fin/fine* (Bear, Invernizzi, Templeton, & Johnston, 2000; Fox, 2000).

Michael Pressley (2000) suggests that there is increasing evidence that "skilled decoders do not sound out letter by letter when they encounter an unfamiliar word, but rather recognize common letter chunks, such as the recurring blends (e.g., *sh-, br-*), prefixes, suffixes, Latin and Greek root words, and rimes (e.g., *-ight, -on, -ime, -ake*) of the language" (p. 546). This ability to recognize these chunks is seen in many pre-schoolers and young readers who are just beginning to decode.[6] Once the chunk is learned and recognized, it can be used by analogy to read new words.

While some teachers may think that teaching children to decode through analogy is a new concept, it is not. In Figure 7.2 you see a lesson and illustration taken from a phonics book titled *A Peep into Fairyland,* published in 1927! Notice the blackboard example of the onset rime/phonogram (Moore & Wilson, 1927, p. 113).

One last point about phonics. A valid criticism leveled at the whole-language movement was that children were being taught to rely too much on context and picture cues, and too little on phonics when decoding unknown words. What is clear in the research is that struggling readers appear to rely more on context clues than do proficient readers (Snow, Burns, & Griffin, 1998), in part because they have ill-developed decoding skills. Therefore, we advocate focusing children's attention on phonics in the beginning stages of learning to read, while helping them to use context and other clues such as pictures, to support and confirm. At the same time, we strongly urge the reading of good literature to assist children in understanding *why* they are learning all about sound–symbol relationships.

Group Inquiry Activity   In groups, discuss the following questions.

1. Why do you think the issue of teaching phonics is such a political and emotional issue for so many people?

FIGURE 7.2   Onsets and Rimes from
Peep into Fairland: **1927**

(From M. Moore & H. B. Wilson. (1927). *A Peep into Fairland: A Child's Book of Phonic Games, First Grade.* D. C. Heath.)

2. Because it is viewed with such controversy, what specifically can reading specialists do to clarify issues surrounding phonics instruction?
3. How can you inform the public and policymakers, including boards of education, about appropriate and effective phonics instruction?
4. What *specifically* can you do to impress on parents, administrators, and policymakers that reading is a complex process, not just a matter of teaching students to "bark at print"? This question is so important because it has to do with methods, approaches, reading resources (such as workbooks vs. good literature), teacher preparation, and professional development.

Discuss your answers to these questions with others in the class.

Instant Word Recognition.   Even though about 84 percent of English words are phonetically regular (Blevins, 1998), there are a large number of words that students must read that cannot be "sounded out" by using phonics. Therefore, beginning readers must also develop a large repertoire of words they can read instantly. The sight words that children must learn to read rapidly and accurately include words such as *the, of, who, you,* and *was.* High frequency words are those that are most often used in texts written for children. Adams (1990) reports that approximately 90 percent of words found in children's and adults' reading books consist of 5000 common words (p. 184). Cooper and Pikulski (2000) state that approximately 300 words represent about 65 percent of words in texts, and only 500 words account for 90 percent of the running words in children's texts (p. 18). Instant recognition of these high frequency words is a characteristic of skillful beginning and developing readers.

Fluency. *Fluency* is defined as the "freedom from word identification problems that might hinder comprehension in silent reading, or in the expression of ideas in oral reading, or automaticity" (Harris & Hodges, 1995, p. 16). Fluent readers are able to read with speed, expression, and accuracy, and fluency is considered to be a critical factor in effective reading comprehension (National Reading Panel, 2000). Fluency is closely related to *automaticity*, described as accurate and quick word identification, a reading skill discussed in the research literature for decades (LaBerge & Samuels, 1974). Fluent readers not only automatically read words, but can also *control* their reading; that is, they read with purpose and accuracy, and can devote attention to constructing meaning rather than figuring out words.

Fluency instruction and practice have been somewhat overlooked in schools, and they are sometimes misinterpreted by children as engaging in a "race to the finish." However, in practice, fluency appears to develop best through guided repeated reading, which involves students orally reading familiar passages with explicit feedback from the teacher. Independent silent reading also appears to be related to fluency, and researchers concur that those students who engage frequently in independent silent reading often appear to be the most fluent readers. Although a causal relationship between independent silent reading and fluency has not been conclusively established (National Reading Panel, 2000), teachers are nonetheless urged to assess, encourage, and model independent, self-selected reading by children.

Vocabulary Development. Research evidence suggests that there are strong relationships among the following factors (Snow et al., 1998):

- a reader's background knowledge and vocabulary development
- vocabulary knowledge and reading comprehension
- the amount of reading one does and vocabulary development

That is, children develop vocabulary through reading; reading enhances children's vocabulary development and background knowledge; and vocabulary knowledge contributes to reading comprehension. For beginning readers, each new day brings opportunities to expand their conceptual understanding and vocabulary development. Listening to stories, discussing and sharing, writing, playing with words, listening and creating poems, singing, and observing life all provide opportunities for vocabulary growth. Bill Nagy (1988) suggests that this type of vocabulary development occurs incidentally, and that literally thousands of new vocabulary words are learned this way. J. David Cooper (2000) states that, while the research on the powerful influence of wide reading on vocabulary development is compelling, "some students under some circumstances may profit from the direct teaching of vocabulary . . . [even though] direct teaching is not as powerful in achieving overall growth in vocabulary and comprehension as is wide reading" (p. 229).

It is important to recognize that vocabulary instruction has two goals. The first is acquisition of new meanings; for example, a teacher may preteach vocabulary to facilitate learning in a science lesson. However, many teachers forget the second aim of vocabulary instruction, which is to help students acquire strategies for independent vocabulary acquisition. Camille Blachowicz and Peter Fisher (2002) concur and add that research studies suggest four main principles to guide vocabulary instruction (p. 504):

1. Students should be active in developing their understanding of words and ways to learn them.
2. Students should personalize word learning.
3. Students should be immersed in words.
4. Students should build on multiple sources of information to learn words through repeated exposures.

In keeping with these principles, many teachers have adopted the Vocabulary Self-Collection Strategy (VSS) (Haggard, 1982; 1986; Ruddell, 2001; Shearer, Ruddell, & Vogt, 2001). This approach encourages students to select words from anywhere (their reading, TV, music, interests, or from school) that are important to them, and to incorporate these words in class spelling and vocabulary lists. VSS has been shown to be highly effective in increasing motivation, awareness, and independent vocabulary acquisition (Ruddell & Shearer, in press).

For English language learners, vocabulary development is obviously crucial. It appears that reading skills transfer from the first (L1) to the second language (L2) only after a level of proficiency in the L2 oral language has been achieved. Additionally, it's been estimated that, in order for English learners to understand about 85 percent of most texts, they need to know about 2000 high frequency words (Blachowitz & Fisher, 2002, p. 514). For these students there exists a paradox: less frequent words that need to be learned are usually only encountered in reading, but the English learners don't know enough words to be able to read well. As with phonics teaching, there is some disagreement among researchers as to how much direct versus indirect teaching is most effective for English learners. From our experience and research, contextualizing vocabulary and encouraging English learners to learn words through VSS are both effective approaches.

It has been estimated that students need to learn approximately 3000 words per year if they are to complete high school with an adequate vocabulary (Beck & Mc-Keown, 2001), and evidence clearly suggests that teachers must utilize both incidental and direct methods for reaching this goal. We also know there is a strong correlation between vocabulary knowledge and comprehension, but we have little understanding of the exact nature of the interaction. Any number of variables impinge on our understandings of the links between vocabulary and comprehension, and serve both to obscure that understanding and emphasize the complexity of the relationship itself (Ruddell, 2001).

Comprehension. Dolores Durkin (1978), in her very influential study of reading instruction in American schools, found that despite all the skills work, teachers weren't teaching reading as much as *talking* about it (such as explaining how long vowels work). She also confirmed that, although we were providing students with mounds of reading comprehension exercises, the majority of time devoted to comprehension was spent with teachers *testing* not teaching (such as "read the passage and answer the questions"). Durkin referred to these ineffective practices as "mentioning and interrogating."

R. C. Anderson (1984) suggested that comprehension requires readers to make connections between their prior knowledge and experience and the text being read. This led researchers to investigate how proficient readers think and process information during reading. For twenty years, 1980–2000, comprehension research examined a variety of factors impacting reading proficiency, including vocabulary development, fluency, prior knowledge, and text structure (Vogt & Verga, 1998). A primary focus was on comprehension as a thinking process, as researchers examined the strategies that successful readers use to construct meaning from text (Dole, Brown, & Trathen, 1996; Dole, Duffy, Roehler, & Pearson, 1991). They described the use of these strategies in terms of metacognitive awareness in which readers analyze and purposefully select tools to assist them in constructing meaning. Dermody and Speaker (1995) characterized metacognition in reading as:

1. matching thinking and problem-solving strategies to particular learning situations;
2. identifying important points in a message;
3. clarifying purposes for reading;
4. monitoring one's own comprehension through self-questioning;
5. taking corrective action if comprehension fails.

Several comprehension strategies have been reported as especially important to teach. These include: prediction, generating questions, determining importance, drawing inferences, and self-monitoring (Dole, Duffy, Roehler, & Pearson, 1991). Other researchers have suggested that imagery, story-grammars, question-answering, and prior knowledge activation are also critical (Pressley, Johnson, Symons, McGoldrick, & Kurita, 1989). When strategies are taught, modeled, reinforced, and practiced with sufficient scaffolded support, it appears that students' comprehension is considerably improved (for a thorough review, see Pressley, 2000; Pressley & Woloshyn, 1995).

Questions about strategy instruction still exist primarily related to which strategies should be taught and whether some readers benefit more than others from explicit strategy instruction (Dole, Brown, & Trathen, 1996). The National Reading Panel (2000) suggests, "the rationale for the explicit teaching of comprehension skills is that comprehension can be improved by teaching students to use specific cognitive strategies or to reason strategically when they encounter barriers to understanding what they are reading. Readers acquire these strategies informally to some extent, but explicit or formal instruction in the application of comprehension strategies has been shown to be highly effective in enhancing understanding" (p. 14).

Michael Pressley (2000) suggests that teachers should focus attention on two other aspects of comprehension instruction, in addition to the metacognitive strategies. He states that research indicates that instruction aimed at improving comprehension should also be focused on developing word-level competencies (defined as decoding) and building background knowledge, so that children can make personal connections with what they're reading. He makes the following recommendations regarding comprehension instruction (pp. 551–556):

1. teach decoding skills;
2. teach students to use semantic context clues to evaluate whether decodings are accurate;
3. teach vocabulary meanings;
4. encourage extensive reading;
5. encourage students to ask themselves why the ideas related in a text make sense;
6. teach self-regulated use of comprehension strategies.

Pressley concludes by suggesting that, though many teachers would say they are already incorporating these suggestions into their teaching, in reality, with the exception of (4), they're not. "Comprehension instruction in elementary schools seems not to be what it could be. A reasonable hypothesis is that if elementary reading instruction were to be transformed so that children were taught [these] skills and [this] knowledge, children's comprehension would be better. This is a hypothesis worth testing in the immediate future" (p. 557).

Group Inquiry Activity

1. Why do you think comprehension instruction has been perceived as so difficult to teach?
2. Why do you think that, as children move into grades 4, 5, and 6, many who have not had reading problems before begin to develop them?
3. Claude Goldenberg (1993) has found that, when students participate in instructional conversations (a scaffolded instructional model in which teachers use techniques to elicit students' responses and engage them in discussion), comprehension improves. Why do you think this occurs? What is the role of discussion and conversation in a balanced literacy program?
4. What can a reading specialist do to help teachers become more effective in teaching comprehension?

Writing, Spelling, and Grammar.   Whereas there may be a lack of agreement among researchers about whether reading development can be characterized through stages or phases, there is little disagreement about characterizing spelling as a developmental process (Templeton & Morris, 2000). For beginning readers, there appear to be very close relationships among reading, writing, and spelling, and young children should be encouraged to use their knowledge and understandings of phoneme–grapheme relationships (sound–symbol) when they write. This is often referred to as "invented" or "temporary" spelling.

Because spelling is a developmental process, logic tells us that individual children will develop at different rates; therefore, spelling instruction should accommodate these differences (Templeton & Morris, 2000). For older and developing readers, spelling instruction that emphasizes an inductive or an exploratory approach is most effective, especially when students are working at their own appropriate developmental level. This type of approach encourages analysis of words and learning new words through analogy (see Bear et al., 2000). For struggling spellers, however, it appears that a more deductive, systematic, and direct approach is more beneficial. The emphasis for older students should be on the interrelatedness of spelling, phonics, morphology (word structure), and vocabulary (Templeton & Morris, 2000).

Research strongly discourages teaching grammar as isolated exercises or as a subject separate from the other language arts. Writers Workshop, a popular and effective way to integrate the writing process, spelling, and grammar, continues to be recommended (Hiebert et al., 1998).

Texts for Reading Instruction.   The texts that are used in teaching reading are almost as controversial as the type and amount of phonics instruction that is included. Recall the variety of texts that have been used over the years discussed in Chapter 1. Clearly, this has been a topic of debate for decades, but current research offers some guidelines for selecting appropriate texts. (Note that a more complete discussion of how to evaluate and select reading texts and other resources is found in Chapter 9).

We know that beginning readers benefit from texts that encourage them to use and practice their developing decoding skills. "If the phonics information taught in lessons does not connect to the words in the books that children read, it is unlikely that children will integrate the new information into their word recognition strategies . . . children benefit from exposure to many books rather than a handful of books which they memorize" (Hiebert et al., 1998, Topic 4, p. 3).

Clearly, young children also need frequent, daily exposure and interaction with meaningful texts, such as picture books, informational articles, poetry, narrative stories, nursery rhymes, chants, and songs. Older students need to read and be exposed to quality fiction, nonfiction, informational texts, and a variety of genres, such as drama and poetry. All students need daily opportunities for self-selected reading in appropriately leveled texts in order to practice developing skills and strategies.

REVISITING THE VIGNETTE

You may recall from the vignette that opened this chapter that the reading specialist, Claudio, completed a series of observations in the classes of his teachers in order to get an idea of how each was implementing literacy instruction. He also distributed a needs assessment and compiled the results, which he shared with his staff and administrators. From this assessment, he learned that many of the teachers, new and experienced alike, had only surface understandings of the reading process. He therefore requested of his principal fifteen minutes at the beginning of each monthly staff meeting to review and talk about the various elements of a comprehensive, balanced reading program. He was able to purchase several copies of professional texts and documents that were made available to his teachers on a check-out basis. Together, the teachers reviewed these materials and established a list of areas they felt were those where weaknesses in their programs existed.

Another concern that surfaced was the teachers' feelings of inadequacy in teaching reading to English language learners. Claudio requested the assistance of his district's ELD (English Language Development) specialist who agreed to present an inservice related to sheltered instruction and English language development. Claudio followed up throughout the year with additional support and assistance, observations, and conferences, especially with the beginning teachers. Marcia Wilson, the new, but older teacher who at first had experienced such confidence, came to understand that she had a great deal to learn. As she took her methods courses and relaxed a bit in her management style, she experimented with and eventually adopted a variety of grouping strategies, texts, and approaches, and she more appropriately provided instruction for her English language learners. Assessment began to serve as the springboard for her instructional decisions. Her end-of-year assessments yielded literacy and language growth for nearly all of her students. Also, as the year was concluding, Marcia expressed her gratitude to Claudio for his assistance, support, and patience.

POINTS TO REMEMBER

Reading involves complex processes that require a purposeful reader to integrate a variety of skills and strategies, flexibly and critically, to construct meaning in specific contexts with a variety of texts, print and nonprint. Beginning readers and writers develop understandings about the alphabetic principle, phonological awareness, and concepts about print. Fluency, rapid and accurate decoding, is gained through reading manageable texts and through exposure to rich literature. It appears clear that children benefit from experimenting and approximating while they write and spell (invented spelling). While there is some disagreement in the field about precise stages or even the notion of developmental phases of reading, it can be helpful to assess and be attentive to how children gain proficiency. Vocabulary development and spelling are enhanced through both direct and indirect approaches to teaching. Grammar can be taught through teacher and peer discussions about students' writing, as well as more explicit means. Comprehension instruction involves explicit and implicit instruction in decoding skills, background building, and metacognitive strategies.

An important responsibility of the reading specialist is to assist teachers in developing deep understandings about the reading process, assessment, approaches to teaching reading, appropriate grouping configurations, and the special needs of English language learners. Information about what teachers know about reading can be gained through needs assessment and observation.

PORTFOLIO PROJECTS

1. As a school reading specialist, how could you communicate to your principal those elements of your school's reading program that need improvement? What might you say if the needs have been identified based on observations of new and experienced teachers? What is your responsibility to the teachers related to confidentiality? How can you communicate what you perceive as the school's literacy needs without jeopardizing your relationship with the teachers in your school? For your portfolio, create a plan for observing teachers, discussing findings with them, and then reporting the results to your principal.

2. Personal Goal: Revisit the goal you set for yourself at the beginning of the chapter. Create a portfolio item that reflects what you have learned relative to your goal.

RECOMMENDED READINGS

Bear, D., Templeton, S., Invernizzi, M., & Johnston, F. (2000). *Words their way: Word study for phonics, vocabulary, and spelling* (2nd ed.). Upper Saddle River, NJ: Merrill/Prentice-Hall. This book is one of our favorites for learning about children's writing, spelling, and reading development. The authors clearly explain the links between early reading and writing, and provide a wealth of hands-on, meaningful activities for word study. It's a must for every reading specialist's library.

Blachowicz, C., & Fisher, P. J. (2002). *Teaching vocabulary in all classrooms* (2nd ed.). Upper Saddle River, NJ: Merrill Prentice Hall. The authors establish a foundation for effective vocabulary instruction with four guidelines. In subsequent chapters, they present a compendium of instructional strategies for teaching vocabulary in context, in content areas, through literature, and to children with special needs.

Cooper, J. D. (2000). *Literacy: Helping children construct meaning* (4th ed.). Boston: Houghton Mifflin. J. David Cooper's newest edition of his reading methods textbook includes a balanced approach for teaching reading and language arts. All of the elements of the reading process are discussed, with sample lessons and recommended instructional strategies for each.

Echevarria, J., & Graves, A. (1998). *Sheltered content instruction: Teaching English language learners with diverse abilities.* Boston: Allyn & Bacon. This book defines and describes sheltered instruction for English learners. In these classrooms, teachers speak in English, teach grade-level concepts and content, but provide access to the content through sheltering methods.

Kamil, M. L., Mosenthal, P. B., Pearson, P. D., & Barr, R. (Eds.). (2000). *Handbook of reading research, Volume 3.* Mahwah, NJ: Erlbaum. This is a comprehensive volume of chapters on all aspects of literacy written by well-known and respected experts in the field, representing a variety of viewpoints and perspectives. We highly recommend it.

NOTES

1. Bilingual programs: School instruction using two languages, generally a native language of the student and a second language (Echevarria, Vogt, & Short, 2000, p. 197). In most bilingual programs, most of the instruction is in the student's home language, with additional English language development.

2. Transitional bilingual: Some instruction may still be in the student's home language, but as students transition to English, increasingly English is the language of instruction.

3. Sheltered instruction: An approach to teaching that extends the time students have for receiving English language support while they learn content subjects. SI classrooms, which may include a mix of native English speakers and English language learners (ELLs), or only ELLs, integrate language and content while infusing so-

ciocultural awareness. Teachers scaffold instruction to aid student comprehension of content topics (Echevarria, Vogt, & Short, p. 200).

4. Texts: Here we're using a broad sense of the word *text*, moving beyond words on a page. Instead, we're referring to texts as "organized networks that people generate or use to make meaning either for themselves or for others" (Wade & Moje, 2000, p. 610).

5. Big books: An enlarged version of a beginning reading book, usually illustrated and with very large type, generally used by a group of students to read together and learn about concepts of print and various reading strategies (Harris & Hodges, p. 18).

6. Decode: To analyze spoken or graphic symbols of a familiar language to ascertain their intended meaning (Harris & Hodges, 1995, p. 55).

CHAPTER EIGHT

MEETING THE LITERACY NEEDS OF ADOLESCENT LEARNERS

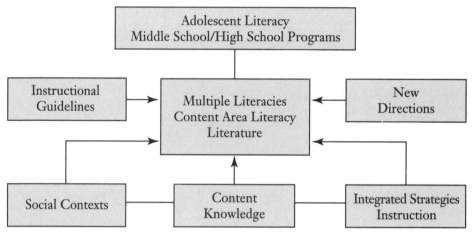

FIGURE 8.1 Chapter Overview

LEARNING GOALS

After reading, discussing, and engaging in activities related to this chapter, you will be able to:

1. explain the underlying theory of adolescent literacy and its implications for classroom practice;

2. redefine content area literacy and instruction in response to new theories about literacy and to the changing demands of society;

3. explore ways to meet the diverse needs of all adolescent learners;

4. analyze middle school and secondary programs and support schools and teachers as they implement culturally responsive, standards-aligned curricula;

5. Personal Learning Goal: In a three-minute brainstorming session, share what you know about literacy programs in middle and secondary schools. Write an objective or question that reflects something you want to learn as we explore this topic. Share this with others in your group.

Vignette

Judy and her literacy team have just completed their needs assessment for the Timber Valley School District in rural West Virginia. As the new reading specialist in this small community, Judy is anxious to begin on the right foot and project an image that she is here to serve teachers. The superintendent and principals of the three schools (elementary, middle, and secondary) agree that Judy's job will be to assess, improve, and oversee the literacy curriculum and serve as a resource to teachers rather than work directly with intervention or Title I students on a daily basis. The teachers in each building have an afternoon teachers' workshop every month, a two-and-one-half-hour block of time devoted to professional development. At the first meeting Judy introduced herself, shared her job description, and emphasized some of the services she could provide. Generally, the reception Judy has received from teachers in all three buildings has been favorable. She recognizes how fortunate she is to be in a district that is willing to employ a full-time reading specialist in a resource role.

As Judy and the literacy team examine the newly completed needs assessment, they discover that students at the secondary level are receiving little or no strategic literacy instruction in the content areas. They also note that scores on the mandated tests in all areas show a general decline from those at the elementary and middle school levels. As Judy walks down the hall at Timber Valley High School and peers into classrooms, she observes teacher after teacher at the front of the room lecturing students in the traditional transmission model. She is convinced that students aren't being provided with the opportunities for thinking and problem solving that are necessary to succeed in life, much less improve their test scores. From her limited contact with these teachers, she is convinced that, if they only knew a better way to approach their teaching, they would be willing and eager to change. Judy is excited because she has a wealth of materials to share. This is one problem she can fix.

Thinking Points

1. What is your first reaction to Judy's situation?
2. What would you recommend to Judy as a start?

Expanding the Vignette: Exploring the Tensions

Judy meets with the secondary principal and explains her plan to create a set of resources for all content areas. She spends many hours preparing a binder of dozens of interactive teaching strategies such as K-W-L, Semantic

Feature Analysis, I-Charts, Text Frames, and Analogy Graphic Organizers. She creates instructions for each strategy and includes content area examples. The binders are comprehensive, attractive, and user-friendly.

Judy puts one in every teacher's mailbox in the high school. She includes a letter explaining how teachers can adapt their lessons to include these strategies and that she is available to help. Several weeks pass. A few teachers mention the binders and thank Judy, but she sees no evidence that even a single teacher is using the resource she has created. Whenever she tries to engage teachers in conversations about the binders, they say they intend to use them, but haven't gotten around to it yet. Judy is confused and a bit hurt.

Thinking Points

1. What additional tensions and questions have you identified in the vignette?
2. Why aren't teachers using these great ideas?
3. What are some short-term and long-term measures Judy could take?
4. What might Judy have done differently to bring about the changes she and the team see as necessary?

THE NEEDS OF ADOLESCENT LITERACY LEARNERS

Author Connection: Brenda   This vignette is adapted from one developed by Kristin Anklam and Deb Rupnow, two graduate students in my Administration and Supervision class. It is particularly powerful in that it illustrates one of the most common and frustrating problems a reading specialist encounters. What do you do when you are convinced you have the solution to a problem? How do you cope when you know that if you could just get (fill-in-the-name) to do (fill-in-the-teaching-practice) a big problem would be solved? This vignette generated a great deal of emotionally charged discussion in our class because it tapped into the very heart of the change process. In order for people to change behavior, they must change internally. They must change what they believe. In effect, they must change who they are. The binder was such a wonderful resource, but it was presented in such a way that it was doomed to fail in its goal of changing classroom practice. In fact, our class began to characterize all such ideas, ones that were ambitious and well meaning, but doomed to failure as "bad binders." The metaphor of a bad binder has come to mean more than just a folder. The gesture made by Judy failed to bind individuals together in a common goal, it failed to bind the teachers in a community of learners, and it failed to bind the reading specialist in one-to-one relationships with teachers. As we think about the challenges of transforming literacy programs in middle and secondary schools, the bad binder metaphor will be useful. Keep it in mind as you read this chapter. Perhaps you will find a number of ideas to help Judy and her reading specialist colleagues when we revisit the vignette.

Beliefs and Practices of Content Area Teachers

When students emerge from our universities, ready to begin careers as content area teachers, their beliefs reflect a strong commitment to interactive teaching and hands-on, activity-based literacy and content instruction. Why then, when we visit their classrooms a year or two later, do we find some of them using highly traditional teaching models? How can they possibly revert to the transmission model of teaching that is the antithesis of their stated beliefs? After all, haven't we been focused on content area literacy since the 1970s, when the movement to incorporate reading instruction into content teaching started to gain momentum? Perhaps one of the problems was and is that the momentum never came from content teachers but from university professors, administrators, and reading specialists. Marty Ruddell describes those early days when the remedy was to bring in a professor for an all-day inservice for middle and secondary teachers to convince them of their responsibilities and to model the strategies that would incorporate reading into their content teaching. She states, "I have faced many a tight-lipped, arms-crossed faculty under those circumstances, and I'm not alone in that experience. The success of these efforts varied widely (just as it does today)" (Ruddell, 2000, p. 10). Indeed, when we teach undergraduate content area literacy courses, we see many future subject area teachers enter our classes with the same enthusiasm they take to the dentist's office. Our course in reading is required or there is no way they would be there because, "Hey, I'm not a reading teacher, I'm a Science (or P.E. or music, or whatever) teacher." As literacy professors we assure them of the primacy of their subject areas and by the end of the semester many recognize that literacy can support and enhance content learning. In his contribution to our Other Voices feature, Tom Bean explores this tension between teacher beliefs and practice and poses questions that will guide our thinking and our discussion of this issue.

Other Voices: Tom Bean

The following discussion piece was contributed by Tom Bean, Professor in the College of Education at the University of Nevada, Las Vegas. Tom is among the most prolific writers and researchers in Secondary and Content Area Literacy. As a member of the Adolescent Literacy Commission of the International Reading Association, he is among the authors of IRA's Position Statement on Adolescent Literacy. His co-authored Content Area Literacy *textbook is in its seventh edition. As you read this piece, reflect on your answers to Tom's questions and share them in groups with class members.*

Tensions between Content Area Teachers' Beliefs and Practices

A fairly extensive body of research now documents the powerful sway of content teachers' own experiences as students on their subsequent classroom instruction. Moreover, content teachers' literacy autobiographies, interviews, and classroom observations show that experienced content teachers, with a history of learning textbook content in a rote memorization fashion, also tend to teach by covering their content texts without much regard for critical thinking and critical literacy. Despite all the advances in content area teaching strategies, many teachers opt to use the transmission-of-information approach to content instruction that maximizes teacher control and places learners in a passive stance.

Content teachers take required content area reading courses in most universities around the country as part of their preservice teacher preparation. Indeed, in a number of studies, content teachers espoused a student-centered, constructivist philosophy of teaching, but when they were observed in field experiences these beliefs were not apparent in practice. Rather, content teachers stayed very close to low-level text concepts and factual assessment.

In addition to the shallow coverage of content, the growing distance between school-based learning and the funds of knowledge students bring from their respective communities looms as another area of tension in classrooms. Most students have specialized knowledge about television, films, music, cars, advertising, and popular culture. However, teachers' discipline subcultures in math, history, science, and English often prevent this outside-of-school knowledge from being included in classroom units and lessons.

A number of reading specialists find themselves in the pivotal and difficult role of a school Learning Strategist (or some related title). They are responsible for assisting content teachers with struggling readers, as well as offering extra assistance and metacognitive study skills instruction.

Group Inquiry Activity As you reflect on Tom Bean's description of many secondary content classes, discuss the following questions with others in your group:

1. Think about your own experiences as a student in science, math, history, and English classes. Do you agree or disagree that there is a problem, even today, with a transmission model of content instruction?
2. Why might university content area classes have so little impact and influence in reducing the didactic, transmission style of teaching we've all experienced?
3. Do you feel that it is best to continue the separation between school-based content and out-of-school content? Why or why not?
4. If content teachers are firmly rooted in their lifelong beliefs about covering content, how can the reading specialist have any impact in a middle or secondary school? What would you do in this role?

We suggest there may be some compelling reasons why new teachers are not incorporating content literacy strategies in their teaching. David O'Brien and Roger Stewart (1992) offer insights into resistance to content area reading that are tied to the culture of the school. Like Judy in the vignette, most reading specialists and professors believe these teachers misunderstand the ways content area reading can "improve their teaching." Thus, these well-meaning educators have been trying to "fix" the attitudes of content teachers. When we examine the culture of the schools, we find that there are responsible and effective teachers who choose not to incorporate more reading into their teaching. Some cite the poor quality of materials available in traditional texts (O'Brien & Stewart, 1992). Additionally, in some content areas, reading may be seen as a second-rate approach to hands-on learning (Schallert and Roser, 1989).

If we approach adolescent literacy practices from a sociocultural perspective, we must reorient our ideas about how best to assist content teachers in achieving their goals. We suggest that reading specialists consider the following questions before they attempt to change the practices of middle and secondary teachers:

- What is the culture of the school—the culture of students' and teachers' worlds, the structure of the school and curriculum, and the pressure to cover content and conform to imposed institutional goals?
- Should all teachers be teachers of reading, or, as Cochran-Smith & Lytle (1990) wonder, are only some teachers with certain teaching styles capable of teaching content through reading? Are there some teachers whose effective pedagogical styles may not be compatible with our literacy emphasis?

We propose that reading specialists carefully consider the overall culture of the school, the cultures within certain domains or content areas, and the pedagogical styles of individual teachers when they consider how to approach program planning.

Adolescent Literacy

Within the last decade there has been a noticeable increase in the use of the term *adolescent literacy* to describe reading and writing programs at the middle school and high school levels. The term reflects more than a simple combining of programs. It signifies a philosophical shift, precipitated by what we know about the nature of adolescent learners, their needs, and the ways in which literacy is acquired. Moje, Young, Readence, and Moore (2000) argue that the term *secondary literacy* evokes images of the old reading labs. We both remember the speed-reading machines and isolated study skills classes that characterized such programs in the 1960s and 1970s. In addition, Moje et al. maintain that "content area literacy" has come to be associated exclusively with school-based, subject area reading and writing. It encompasses both secondary and content area literacy, and greatly expands the ways in which literacy is defined and taught in middle and secondary schools.

Adolescent literacy replaces the notion that literacy after elementary school means content area literacy. We have been led to believe that in the lower grades we "learn to read" and in the upper grades we "read to learn." Educators now recognize that literacy learning is a lifelong endeavor. Even as adults we are constantly learning to read and reading to learn. For example, let's say you want to set up a revocable living trust. You buy the software and proceed to follow the steps. However, negotiating the language of legal documents is no small task. It takes you awhile to get comfortable with this discourse model, but after you read awhile, you fall into the rhythm of the language and adjust to its patterns. Thus, you are learning to read while you are reading to learn. Teachers who recognize how essential it is for students to adjust their reading strategies to the specific content learning task are much more likely to teach content and process concurrently.

The Forces Driving Change in Literacy Instruction for Adolescents

Standards in language arts, social studies, mathematics, and science have helped teachers acknowledge the necessity of developing the literacy skills of adolescents in the service of subject area learning. Educators are beginning to question whether incorporating traditional literacy skills in content area instruction is enough. For example, Bean (2001) maintains that content area literacy has moved well beyond defining literacy as being able to read and write in the content areas. He argues that "the real problem in content area literacy is being able to discern whether the multitude of text information we can download or locate in our libraries is worthwhile" (p. 1).

Response to pressure for more rigorous content area standards, mandated testing, and calls for accountability are among the forces that are driving districts to rethink their middle and secondary school literacy programs. We would argue that these districts are adapting instruction in fundamentally reactionary ways; there are more compelling reasons to transform our literacy curricula. These reasons have to do with recent insights into how knowledge is constructed, how literacy is defined, and how instruction is provided in increasingly diverse classroom settings. The following constructs, when applied to classroom activities, reflect a sociocultural perspective in which learning is shaped through the social interactions of individuals and the context in which the events are situated. Recently, educators are finding ways to address significant moral, social, and political aspects of learning including identity, voice, hegemony, agency, and efficacy.

Identity.   Who I think I am and who I think you are has a tremendous influence on how I frame my interactions with you. In fact, as we interact, we both redefine our identities through our social interactions. We often hear people say that they don't so much write what they think but to find out what they think. Activities that challenge students to express opinions and beliefs enhance their identity formation. Teachers can foster a sense of identity in their students by engaging them in interactions in which they see themselves and their experiences, challenging them to make connections with characters, situations, and beliefs. Using young adult literature is one way to accomplish these goals. It is especially important for students whose backgrounds differ from that of the dominant culture to see themselves represented in text.

Consider the following class discussion of the book *Catcher in the Rye* in a racially and ethnically diverse high school literature class. This 1950s J. D. Salinger novel about Holden Caulfield, a white upper-middle-class male, explores the alienation he experiences in adolescence. Lucas, an African American male, Tina, a white female, and Martin, a Mexican American male, make highly personal and vastly different connections with the main character.

> **Lucas:**   I know just how he feels—uh—like when you just get so fed up, you know, and think, I'm quittin' this. The best way to get back is not to do somethin' bad—but to just not do what they want. Like Holden, you just don't do it. There!

Tina: (Sarcastically) I didn't like Holden. What do I care about some rich white guy and his little problems? I want his money. That's what I want. I'll trade.

Martin: I liked him. I mean, he may be rich and that part, but he . . . I mean, everybody has the feelings like Holden.

Martin and Lucas identify strongly with Holden, while Tina finds she has little in common with him. Although the most positive aspects of identity formation occur when students find common ground with a character or situation, allowing Tina to voice her negative feelings actually forces her to define herself as well. Although no book will resonate emotionally for all students in a class, Tina does have a need to read about characters with whom she can identify, and we hope the varied reading assignments will offer her that opportunity.

The selection of this book is an interesting one. Although *Catcher in the Rye* continues to be a commonly used novel in secondary literature classes, the book may or may not provide a great deal of connection for many students in today's increasingly diverse classrooms. The danger, of course, is to ignore all the old standard pieces and use only multicultural/multiethnic selections. We believe works such as *Catcher in the Rye* can provide the basis for discussion and comparison with multicultural literature. For example, Tomas Torres, the main character in J. C. George's *Shark Beneath the Reef*, struggles with identity, life goals, and alienation. The realities of the adolescent worlds of Holden and Tomas are very different, as are the stories themselves. However, they provide opportunities for intertextual contrast and comparison. We agree with Heriberto Godina (1996) that integrating powerful, socially themed multicultural literature with selections from the traditional adolescent canon can be a catalyst for critical thinking about values and identity.

A conscious effort by teachers to include literature that reflects a variety of cultures, values, and perspectives is essential, but does not go far enough. We need to reorder classroom discussions and events to explore issues of identity. We need to explicitly demonstrate how students can use multicultural literature to examine their own cultures and identities through activities such as writing parallel biographies (theirs and a character's), creating Venn Diagrams, completing character maps, journaling, and, most of all, engaging in critical and frank group discussion.

Voice.   In this classroom, all three students have a voice. It would certainly appear that the teacher respects their opinions and promotes frank discussion. Imagine how different the interaction might have been had the teacher begun by saying, "Let's talk about Holden. All of you will recognize and relate to his feelings." Is there a chance that Tina would be less likely to voice her opinion if she knew what her teacher wanted her to feel and say? Tina might well have allowed Lucas and Martin to do the talking and remained silent—invisible. As educators it is imperative that we ask ourselves, "Whose voice is missing?" (Hinchey, 2001). This question certainly applies to class discussion, but it also relates to text material and whose voice is heard and whose is missing in the material we assign.

Hegemony.   Hegemony relates to the idea of power relationships in our social inter-actions in various contexts. For example, in a traditional content area classroom we often find a teacher at the front of the class with students raising their hands and taking turns answering. Often the teacher will validate the answer by saying, "Very good" or nodding her head in assent. The discourse in this setting follows a strict set of rules that provide little opportunity for free exchange of ideas. Moreover, these students are unlikely to have much, if any, say in the instructional methods or materials used. New perspectives on adolescent literacy promote a more hegemonic environment where students' ideas are integral to the decision-making processes.

Agency.   Closely related to the notion of hegemony is the notion of agency. In the classroom, agency pertains to individuals' autonomy to choose their actions toward self-determined goals. Historically, students have not been afforded this opportunity. We are all familiar with the traditional social studies assignment requiring students to write a paper on a teacher-selected topic, such as "Describe the rights and freedoms of contemporary U.S. women." Instead, the teacher might seek ways to transfer ownership of the writing to the students by providing the broad topic of rights and freedoms, but allowing them to work in groups to develop their own related question and then choose the role, audience, and format that will shape the inquiry. When a group of eighth-grade students were given just such an opportunity, they chose to investigate sexual harassment and to present their information in the form of a play. Although it was creative and motivating, it was highly substantive as well, incorporating all of the information a reader would encounter in a traditional paper (Shearer, 2000). In order to complete their inquiry project, these students had to transform the information to fit their format rather than merely lifting the information from one source and delivering it in much the same form in a paper.

Efficacy.   When individuals are efficacious, they are successful in achieving their goals and they are confident in their abilities to meet future goals. In order to become this kind of adult, they need the literacy skills that will be required for their jobs, but they also need to be able to make the kinds of decisions and evaluations necessary to function in a complex world. The efficacious adult has an internal locus of control. As professors we see a number of undergraduates who live below the poverty line. However, their life outlook is very different from those who are trapped in the cycle of poverty with few skills and fewer job opportunities. These university students believe, "Tomorrow will be a better day, because I have the skills and opportunities I need and my hard work will enable me to achieve my goal to be a teacher." When students are engaged in projects in which they have to use content area knowledge to solve real problems, they begin to see themselves as efficacious. For example, in a science class, the teacher showed student pairs how to conduct computer-simulated experiments in electrophoresis to run genetic tests for gene markers of breast cancer, Huntington's Chorea, and Alzheimer's Disease. Many students chose certain simulations because they knew of individuals with a particular disorder. In order to run the experiment, a number of fairly complex literacies were needed. When students engage in this kind of learning perhaps they will be more likely to think education pertains to what they can *do* as well as to what they *know*. As educators, we believe that students must leave our institutions equipped to increase their own literacy abilities in response to the rapidly changing world they will encounter as they live and work. We also believe they need to be confident they possess the literacy, problem-solving, and decision-making tools to be efficacious in life and work.

These new notions about student and teacher roles will require nothing short of a revolution in the way we envision the adolescent classrooms of the future. We are reading a great deal about these issues in current practitioner journals and it is apparent teachers are experimenting with them. However, we must keep the nature of the change process in mind and recognize that it will take time before these beliefs and theories will translate to substantive changes in pedagogy.

Building on What We Know about Sound Practice

When we hear the expression "new literacies," it is important to know that we are not abandoning "old literacies." That is, the cognitive strategies needed to read informational text in academic settings remain important to students' success. Our students *must* be taught how to summarize, how to recognize text structure, how to give weight to important ideas, and how to become facile in using the myriad of strategies traditionally taught in university content area literacy courses. In this section we focus on traditional instruction. However, throughout this chapter we will explore ways in which newer theories shape and extend perspectives, discussion, social interaction, classroom events, and the tools of instruction. Although we are unable to include in-depth strategy descriptions in this chapter, we provide an overview of traditional strategy instruction as well as direct you to a number of resources. If it has been a while since you took a course in content area literacy, a trip to your nearest university bookstore or library will provide you with a current edition of such a textbook. We have included several content area texts in our Recommended Readings at the end of this chapter.

Prereading Strategies.   Most *before reading/writing* instructional strategies are designed to help students think metacognitively about their prior knowledge. The strategies enable students to tap into their schema—the network of knowledge stored and organized in their brain. Not only must readers, writers, and speakers determine what they know about a topic, but also be able to infer which aspects of that knowledge are going to be relevant to a particular lesson. Students have to access knowledge about content, texts, discourses, and procedures. When they use various brainstorming techniques to generate, refine, and clarify lists of what they know, they construct a "collective prior knowledge" that can be brought to the literacy task. Teachers use any number of strategies involving previewing text. These involve: locating headings and turning them into sentences or questions to guide the reading; examining the visuals in a text, such as its graphs, charts, and pictures and using those to predict or inform; discussing, classifying, and connecting vocabulary terms; and engaging in brainstorming, predicting, or questioning.

During Reading Strategies.   Most teachers regard the strategies used *during reading* as those that help students monitor their comprehension and adjust their reading and other language processes in flexible and purposeful ways. These strategic processes are regulated by students' knowledge, their purposes for reading, the demands of the text, and the context in which the literacy activities occur. Newer ways of describing regulating factors indicate that beliefs, values, culture, and ability to make connections also play powerful roles in constructing meaning during literacy events. Strategies typically involve confirming earlier predictions, summarizing, searching for answers to questions, realizing where and how these answers are found, using a variety of means to access unknown concepts or vocabulary, adjusting rate, setting and monitoring progress toward goals, self-questioning, evaluating, recognizing and responding to text structure, and adjusting hypotheses. Teachers might use think-alouds, text structure frames, mapping, response or learning journals, or study guides. Many adopt an apprenticeship framework for their instruction in which they think out loud to model processes, then scaffold the use of strategies as students move toward independence. Methods such as Reciprocal Questioning (Manzo, 1969), Question and Answer Response (Raphael, 1984), Directed Reading–Thinking Activity (DR-TA) (Stauffer, 1969), and Survey, Question, Read, Recite, Review (SQ3R) (Robinson, 1946) are among the best known of this type of strategy. Increasingly, maps and frames designed to correspond to text structures, such as compare–contrast, opinion–proof, time-ordered sequence, simple listing, or other ways to visually organize and display information are evident in content area classrooms. Teacher-prepared study guides can serve to focus students on salient features and information in the text.

In the last quarter century, university content area classes promoted the idea of using text-based reading and writing across the curriculum. However, advances in technology have rendered this notion limited. Recently, teachers have begun to recognize the multiple forms of text, including sign systems, hypertext, overlapping media forms, and superimposed messages. These novel ways of defining text have driven research in the new literacies. Reading the world has never been more complex and educators are seeking new ways to apply theory to instructional practice.

Post-Reading Strategies.   The traditional view of *after reading* strategies is that they help students organize and retain information. Indeed, strategies such as Donna Ogle's (1986) (Know–Want to Know–Learned (K-W-L) help students work through text and recognize and record ideas. Many of the same text frames and study guides used during reading are also appropriate to use after reading as organizers. Again, the biggest determiners of strategy selection are students' prior knowledge, the nature of the text, and the goals of the reader/writer.

Writing is particularly well suited for use as a culminating activity because it promotes synthesis, generalizing, connecting, and evaluating. As students work collaboratively to develop inquiry questions and organize the information on grids or Inquiry Charts (I-Charts) (Hoffman, 1992), they have opportunities to engage in critical literacy, asking the kinds of questions that guide such a perspective. In addition, the inquiry *becomes* a curriculum (Harste, 1994) a way of using discourse, a type of genre.

An Instructional Framework for Prereading, during Reading, and after Reading.
An instructional framework for teaching students how to interact with informational

and expository texts incorporates all of the reading phases. Designed loosely on SQ3R, this process has been found to improve students' comprehension and engagement with text. It also promotes comprehension strategy use, and research findings indicate that it transfers to the reading of other kinds of expository texts. The framework is titled SQP2RS and it includes five steps: Survey, Question, Predict, Read, Respond, Summarize (for a detailed discussion, see Vogt, 2000). In the beginning stages of using SQP2RS, the teacher models and guides students through each of the steps. It is intended that students work with partners and small groups throughout the SQP2RS lesson. Vocabulary Self-Collection (VSS) (Haggard, 1982) can be infused into the instructional framework when students select vocabulary that is important to the study of the respective topic. This occurs during and immediately following the reading step. SQP2RS has been found to be an especially effective means of assisting struggling readers in accessing the content found in informational texts. Though highly structured, the process enables students to gain enough information to be able to engage in other kinds of critical, reflective, and meaningful activities.

NEW PERSPECTIVES ON LITERACY

The most fundamental determinant of how we teach literacy is how we define it. In the previous section, we have seen that academic literacy is often narrowly defined, honoring reading, writing, and speaking in traditional text-based forms. Not only do these academic literacies fail to include computer, visual, graphic, and scientific literacies, Donna Alvermann (2001) argues that they also ignore the fact that "different texts and social contexts (reading for whom, with what purpose) require different reading skills" (p. 5). Other researchers concur (Barton, Hamilton & Ivanic, 2000; Gee, 1996; Street, 1996). Instead of thinking in terms of literacy, it is more helpful for the reading specialist and all educators to think in terms of *literacies*. Instead of asking what a text means, perhaps we might more accurately ask how a text has come to have a particular meaning and not another (Alvermann, 2001).

Luke and Freebody (1999) remind us that texts are not fixed entities. Rather, their meanings are fluid and constructed over time. When we read history textbooks from the early 1900s, we find many excerpts that would seem racist or sexist in contemporary U.S. society, but were considered acceptable at the time. The words are the same. Time and cultural context alter our construction of meaning and, in effect, alter the text.

Ways That Adolescents Acquire Literacy Skills

Alvermann (2001) points out the importance of recognizing that, when students use reading and writing, they do so in specific places and times within the broader practices of the society in which they live. For example, reading a history assignment may be seen as part of the students' broader educational process in the same way that studying for the drivers' exam is part of the societal goal of being able to drive a car to work. Students bring their lived experience and their multiple literacies with them when they come to school. As we saw in the rich literacies of Carmen Coballes-Vega, described in Chapter

2, many of these home literacies are as complex or more complex than those traditionally found in school (Au & Raphael, 2000). Effective instruction builds on these informal literacies in addition to traditional school-based literacies. Experts in adolescent literacy (Ruddell, 2001) use the term *connectedness*, linking new information to personal experience, when they describe essential elements for construction of meaning during reading.

WHAT ADOLESCENT LEARNERS NEED

Adolescents Need Instruction in Literacy Strategies

Among the recommendations of the Commission on Adolescent Literacy of the International Reading Association (Moore, Bean, Birdyshaw, & Rycik, 1999) is to provide adolescents with instruction that not only builds the skills but also the desire to read increasingly complex materials. The commission describes the role of teachers as models who provide explicit instruction in strategies across the curriculum and who understand the complexity of the reading processes of their students. They provide students with maps, text frames, and interactive literacy experiences. A health/P.E. teacher might use K-W-L (Ogle, 1986) to explore the students' knowledge and misconceptions as they begin a unit on sexually transmitted diseases. Among the differences in the way the strategies are taught relative to new theories is that students are encouraged to use their knowledge, values, and questions critically, and to search for ways to make connections, not only with their own experiences, but also with those of their peers. This socially mediated literacy across media, genres, cultural systems, and affinity groups requires new methods of preparing students to read.

Adolescents Need to Develop Critical Media Literacy Skills to Understand Increasingly Complex Information Sources

Adolescents are bombarded by media images. Consider the nightly news. The talking heads of ten years ago have been replaced by shrunken heads, encased in logos, text boxes, moving text banners along the bottom of the screen, montages, and music. It is not unusual to have five messages competing simultaneously for the viewer's attention. You may only have tuned in to receive one of the messages, but you get them all. Technology such as the World Wide Web, E-mail, fax, and electronic messaging devices are increasingly intrusive and limit our selection processes. Many of these messages attempt to manipulate what adolescents buy, what they wear, and how they think. It is small wonder that critical literacy, the ability to get under the surface of messages to understand their purpose and how they attempt to achieve that purpose is such a dominant theme in adolescent literacy practitioner journals. Ladi Semali and Ann Pailliotet (1999) call this "deep viewing."

As an example, think of the media coverage in the weeks following the destruction of the World Trade Center. We saw images manipulated for a variety of purposes, many to evoke patriotism (as defined in many ways), to incite us to anger or hatred (images of Osama bin Laden as the devil) or images meant to inspire and soothe (people helping people). Many of us were inundated with E-mail messages that had passed from person to person. In many of these E-mails, it was impossible to discern the source, the original author. Who decided what images we saw? How were those images manipulated and edited? Whose voice was missing? What were the words and devices used? How could a different word, image, background have changed the message?

Group Inquiry Activity   Turn on any of the all-news networks, such as CNN:

1. For a five-minute period, record in your journal the multiple images and messages you see.
2. What are the relationships among the messages that appear simultaneously?
3. Is there a single coherent message or theme or are these parallel messages?
4. Who decided and what is the stance of those who decided what you will see and hear? What is the author's intention and what are the techniques used to meet those ends? What are the values? How do they compare to yours?
5. Are there messages that command more attention than others for you? What factors determine your focus?
6. Bring these notes to class and discuss them with your small group and with the class.

In your small group, write a single paragraph explaining what you learned from this project. Select one member of your group to read this paragraph to the class.

Adolescent Readers Need to Read and Understand a Number of Symbol Systems

They will need to be able to reproduce these forms as well. Creating Web pages, sending E-mails, writing poetry, manipulating digital images, recording ideas in a journal, and creating hypertext are a few of the skills needed to be fully literate in today's world. From a critical literacy perspective, genre itself is a form of social practice, a situated literacy, that can signal the author's stance (Gee, 2001a).

Ladislaus Semali and Ann Watts-Pailliotet (1999) examined the complexities involved as students navigate hypermedia, the links readers make spontaneously between computer windows and the mix of media texts, often with great facility. In this process, the clicks of the mouse create a text-from-texts as the sequence and forms of media place the reader in the position of reader and author. The interaction of the pieces is not cumulative. Rather, when you see three images and spoken words simultaneously on CNN, they create a whole that is different from its parts. Ann Watts-Pailliotet (2000) calls this "intermediality." Again, Donna Alvermanm (2001) raises some questions about whether hypertext media are privileged over linear print text in allowing multiple interpretations. She ponders the consequences of this privileging as well as which students benefit and which do not. Jim Cunningham (2000) asks whether, in the near future, we are going to identify another area of "learning disability" to describe the student who is capable of navigating print text, but unable to navigate hyperlinks. Don

Leu (2000b) reminds us that it may be a while before we will know the answers to some of these questions because schools are only beginning to include the new technologies in their curricula.

Adolescents Need to Develop Strategies That Enable Them to Be Independent Learners

We cannot imagine the literacy demands the world will make on our students as they face the next fifty years of their lives and careers. Such a world will most certainly require our students to be self-teaching lifelong learners. In order to accomplish this, teachers in every subject area will have to teach content and process concurrently, as John Readence, Tom Bean, and Scott Baldwin (2001) advocate. Increasingly we will see strategies such as Vocabulary Self-Collection (Ruddell & Shearer, 2002, see Chapter 5) that enable students to make connections between their lived experience and the goals of school while increasing the student's ability to teach themselves.

We have thoroughly addressed the notion that literacy and learning are socially constructed (Rosenblatt, 1978; Vygotsky, 1978) and this is particularly important for adolescents who are addressing issues of identity, power, and efficacy. Tom Bean (2001) maintains that students use tools such as language and physical artifacts to mediate learning in object-oriented, rule-governed ways that alter both internal and external elements of the reader's world.

CHARACTERISTICS OF EFFECTIVE ADOLESCENT LITERACY PROGRAMS

In this and preceding chapters we explored a number of research-based assumptions about effective and responsive literacy instruction. We also examined elements specifically related to the nature and needs of adolescent learners. From the insights of others and our years of classroom experience working with competent and struggling adolescents, we offer the following suggestions for effective adolescent literacy programs (see Figure 8.2). They can be used as a checklist by the reading specialist, administrators, and the literacy team for designing effective middle school literacy programs.

The Role of the Reading Specialist in Shaping Adolescent Literacy Programs

If we embrace the broader definition of literacies, acknowledge the ever-expanding literacy demands of the workplace, and honor the increasingly diverse nature of the society in which we live, we must change the way we structure school literacy programs and instruction.

From a social constructivist perspective, literacy practices are embedded in and defined by particular social contexts, and shaped by cultural values and local ideologies (Street, 1996). At the same time, these practices and beliefs define the culture of the

**Questions to Guide Planning/Evaluation of Middle
and Secondary Literacy Programs**

- To what extent do content area teachers use interactive literacy processes to enhance content area instruction?
- Are students provided with sustained reading and writing opportunities with a variety of challenging and motivating texts, and are they guided in strategies aimed at helping them reproduce these texts?
- Does instruction build on the students' knowledge and uses of language to enhance literacy growth and content knowledge acquisition?
- Are literacy processes modeled as well as taught explicitly?
- Are multiple forms of text used to investigate content topics (intertextuality)?
- What are the beliefs and attitudes of content area teachers relative to incorporating language processes in instruction?
- How do various individuals define literacy?
- Do teachers recognize the role of self-efficacy and engagement in shaping the motivation and confidence students bring to their content area classes?
- Are culturally responsive classroom activities consistently imbedded in daily classroom events?
- Are students taught to read critically across genres and across texts?
- Are students taught how to navigate Internet and hypermedia sources in critical and responsible ways?
- Are teachers provided with support (materials, time, professional development opportunities) for improving and enhancing their pedagogical skills?
- Are the best and most highly trained professionals assisting those students who struggle with literacy acquisition?
- Are English language learners provided with appropriate levels of support and opportunities to use both languages in meaningful ways while learning content?
- Is the reading specialist provided opportunities to collaborate with content teachers in modeling and co-teaching lessons incorporating the new literacies?
- Is assessment in literacy consistent with the school instructional models as well as the goals of the school, the communities, and the parents?
- To what extent are students involved in setting their own literacy goals, planning ways to meet those goals, and assessing their progress toward their goals?

FIGURE 8.2 Planning and Evaluating Adolescent Literacy Programs

school and the culture of the community. Thus, any of our initial questions about literacy can only be answered relative to the context of the communities in which they occur.

We believe that limiting the role of the reading specialist only to working with readers who need additional support is a shortsighted decision. In certain parts of the country, increasingly, full-time reading specialists are being hired at the middle school and secondary levels. In these positions, the reading specialist might:

- serve as a resource to content classroom teachers, suggesting new strategies one-by-one and co-teaching lessons with content area teachers;

- help teachers rewrite lessons that incorporate interactive literacy strategies to enhance the learning of content;
- support teachers' efforts to include the literacies of the students' homes and communities to achieve school goals and increase learning;
- help teachers collaborate across content areas to encourage multiple perspective taking and intertextuality;
- provide sustained opportunities for reading, writing, and learning through tool-mediated group activities;
- seek information on teachers' needs and interests in topics for professional development and plan effective inservice;
- disseminate carefully selected articles and information to individuals as well as to all teachers;
- coordinate standardized and informal assessment and help teachers develop assessment skills;
- demonstrate how many of the research-based group and interactive strategies can respond to the needs of English language learners and struggling readers within the regular content area classroom;
- explore the literacies of home and community and help develop culturally responsive curricula;
- help develop programs for struggling readers and assist those that teach them;
- promote literacy within the community and serve as a literacy advocate;
- serve as a role model of professionalism and assist teachers in conducting classroom research;
- assume a proactive role in helping like-minded teachers form study groups;
- assist content teachers in adopting textbooks and selecting materials for teaching;
- assist the school counselor in order to better match the literacy demands of jobs with training and educational advice;
- assist teachers and administrators in securing outside funding for literacy initiatives and endeavors;
- match student volunteers with cross-age collaborations and literacy-related programs in other schools;
- help teachers locate or procure non-Western literature and text that reflects other perspectives and demonstrate how these materials can be used in content classrooms.

One of the most effective ways to inform teachers about how you can help them is to provide them with the following Middle/Secondary School Teacher Resource Request Form a few weeks into the first semester. The form (see Figure 8.3) is designed to help teachers identify possible service they had not considered. When Brenda used similar checklists in her recent year as a reading specialist, she heard many positive comments about the list and was surprised at its ability to generate dialogue and contact from teachers who had not previously approached her for help.

The reading specialist has the opportunity to be a powerful force for change in the secondary and middle schools. However, our experience in working with content area teachers has given us insight on how to proceed as this role is assumed. As we have seen, there are a number of reasons that the enthusiastic and sincere efforts of reading

Teacher's Name _____ Grade _____ Room # _____

Planning Times: _____ Ext. # _____

Dear Faculty,

I am trying to determine how I can better serve the school as your Reading Resource Specialist. Below is a list of services that I can offer you. Please check those that interest you and place the sheet in my mailbox when complete. I can provide articles or information on any of these topics. If I know your areas of interest, whenever I read something about that topic, I will share it with you. Some of these involve *very* new concepts and techniques. *Undoubtedly some will be unfamiliar. Please circle any unfamiliar terms* and I will provide a brief overview in your mailbox or talk to you.

____ Model specific learning strategies, such as vocabulary, test taking, questioning techniques, etc. Specify _____

____ Make presentations to your class on specific strategies. Specify: _____

____ Co-teach lessons. Specify _____

____ Evaluate textual materials with you/find and adapt material for a specific student

____ Assist in incorporating intertextuality into content instruction

____ Help with/demonstrate culturally responsive teaching and materials

____ Determine the reading ability of students

____ Demonstrate or help with collaborative grouping

____ Assist in implementing social constructivist group discussion strategies

____ Co-teach/demonstrate integrated content/process literacy strategies

____ Demonstrate current Reader Response strategies

____ Assist with a variety of appropriate strategies for English Language Learners

____ Help incorporate a wide variety of nontraditional literacies

____ Help with critical, effective Internet use and intermediality

____ Help with activity-mediated teaching

____ Locate information/journal articles on a specific topic. Specify: _____

____ Demonstrate/help implement Vocabulary Self-Collection Strategies (VSS)

____ Provide assistance for incorporating adolescent literature in content instruction

____ Help locate multicultural literature for content areas

____ Facilitate critical literacy instruction

____ Arrange for visits from people outside the school

____ Read aloud to your content area class (I love to do this.)

____ Facilitate inquiry writing/project-based learning

____ Help with instructional planning for specific lessons or help locate books

____ Provide staff development to assist you in recertification or research

____ Other: _____

Thank you. I look forward to hearing from you. My extension is # 7777.

Sincerely,

Reading Specialist

FIGURE 8.3   Middle School/Secondary School Teacher Resource Request Form

specialists often meet with so much resistance. The most common mistake is the one made by Judy (with her bad binder) in our vignette. Now, imagine another scenario:

Judy, the new reading specialist, surveys the content classroom teachers in her high school about their classroom literacy practices and their needs, and discovers that their need to meet content standards has opened them to suggestions. Judy looks at the curriculum and the unit plans of the teachers. One-by-one she finds an appropriate strategy. If she recognizes a small number of receptive teachers with a common interest, she might meet with them, demonstrate the technique, and offer to teach with them or cover their classes while they team with each other to try the strategy. She approaches more reticent teachers one-by-one, saying, "I have a strategy that I think you'd really like. I'd like to try it with your students; perhaps we could try it together or I could demonstrate it for you. It fits perfectly with your lesson on (fill-in-the-blank)."

Judy spends her first semester making these connections. Meanwhile, she becomes an astute observer of the beliefs, practices, and culture of the school and of the teachers. She makes sure everyone understands her role and that she is visible as she works side-by-side with teachers and students. During this semester, she puts together a literacy team, surveys teachers, explores the literacy communities in and out of school, and conducts a needs assessment. Only then does she begin the process of putting together a

systematic plan for gradual change that is responsive to the needs of the school and the teachers. She is careful to begin only one major strategy per semester. Judy's first project is carefully chosen. Although she is interested in several large reforms, such as assisting content teachers in the use of interactive strategies, beginning an intervention program for struggling readers, and incorporating more writing into content area instruction, she thinks about which of these three goals is the least threatening and implements that one first. She also considers for whom the strategies are appropriate and tries to determine if there are teachers for whom it is not.

In this case, she devotes most of her energies to developing the intervention program. Her approach pleases many of the teachers who have no idea how to help struggling students. One of the components of the intervention is support for content teachers. At the end of the first year, she has established herself as hardworking and supportive. Now she is ready to begin the kinds of changes that require teachers to "buy in." She is ready to begin working on those interactive instructional strategies. However, she will introduce strategies gradually, one at a time. Of course, she'd like the reform to happen more quickly, but that is not the nature of true transformation.

This process takes a great deal of time, and it can be frustrating, but we assure you that your efforts will result in the kind of trust-building necessary for lasting and substantive change. If you establish your credibility by working alongside teachers, you will avoid the "Do as I say" reputation so often associated with reading specialists. In our enthusiasm to help teachers and children it is easy to forget to ask teachers what they might want from us as reading specialists. We developed the Middle/Secondary Teacher Resource Request Form to achieve several goals. It establishes an attitude that you are responsive to teachers and willing to listen before you set an agenda. It helps teachers understand your job description, and the things you are able to do for them. It will help you understand the teachers' needs and their approaches to classroom instruction.

REVISITING THE VIGNETTE

Now that we've investigated some possible roles of the reading specialist and examined a number of difficulties encountered by them in secondary and middle schools, you probably have a number of ideas for Judy.

1. What advice do you have for Judy that might be more effective?
2. What was it about the binder, a wonderful resource, that produced such disappointing results for Judy and the teachers?

POINTS TO REMEMBER

Over the past decade, the emphasis of literacy learning in the secondary schools has moved away from "reading in the content areas" and notions of "every teacher is a reading teacher" to viewing content learning through a much broader lens. Although teachers are still encouraged to use a variety of approaches and activities, and to move away from the "sage on the stage" transmission model, the focus isn't so much on the activities as it is on investigating multiple texts, multiple literacies, and multiple perspectives. When secondary teachers adopt a critical literacy perspective, they may focus as much on the "why" as they do the "what." Why is this (whatever we're studying) important and relevant? Who made the decision that it is? If we deem it's important, then why should we think it's important for all learners? Someone made the decision to include this topic in our textbook—who was it? And why did that person include this here? Who would disagree and why would they do so?

If today's adolescents are going to be able to participate in the society of their future, they need to be taught to ask these questions—and then seek answers to them from multiple sources. These are the new literacies of our secondary schools.

PORTFOLIO PROJECTS

1. Role-play in your small group. One of you will be Judy and the others will be content area teachers. Explore the tensions from the vignette. First approach the teachers as Judy did initially. Then replay the scene incorporating a strategy you think might be more effective. Share your insights or reproduce your role-playing with the whole class. If you choose this as a portfolio item, you may videotape the session and critique the interactions.

2. Interview a secondary-level reading specialist. How does the person's job description

address the new literacies and align with content standards? Map this information in any way that you choose.

3. Take a traditional lesson in a subject area and transform it to incorporate one of the following: activity theory, intertextuality, or critical literacy. Regardless of your choice, make sure you include concurrent content and process instruction.

4. Choose a controversial subject in a content area (such as abortion in health, evolution in biology, pornography in art, etc.). Ex-

plore six Web sites related to the topic and engage in a critical media analysis of each addressing, Whose voice is it? Why was it written? What was used to accomplish the goal? What are the surface and subsurface messages? What are the values? How do they match my values? What might I do to produce my own message?

5. Revisit the objective you set for yourself at the beginning of the chapter. Create a portfolio item that reflects what you have learned relative to your objectives.

RECOMMENDED READINGS

Alvermann, D. (2001). *Effective literacy instruction for adolescents.* Executive summary and paper commissioned by the National Reading Conference. Available at: www.nrc.oakland.edu/documents/2001/alverwhite.PDF. This white paper contains the most current overview of contemporary issues and theories related to effective literacy study for adolescents. It is a must for reading specialists working in middle and secondary schools.

Bean, T. W. (2001). An update on reading in the content areas: Social constructivist dimensions. *Reading Online.* On-line journal of the International Reading Association. Available at: http://www.readingonline.org/research/bean.html. This on-line article updates the chapter that appeared in *The Handbook of Reading Research.* It provides an excellent up-to-date overview of current and future directions in content area literacy.

Buehl, D. (2001). *Classroom strategies for interactive learning* (2nd ed.). Newark, DE: International Reading Association. This interactive resource collection of content area strategies reflects the latest pedagogy, applying sound theory in adolescent learning.

Cunningham, J. W., Many, J. E., Carver, R. P., Gunderson, L., & Mosenthal, P. B. (2000). Snippets: How will literacy be defined? *Reading Research Quarterly, 35*(1), 64–71. Thoughtful and insightful discussion about the direction of literacy and classroom practice. This entire issue of *RRQ* is worth reading.

Fehring, H., & Green, P. (Eds.). (2001). *Critical literacy: A collection of articles from the Australian Literacy Educators' Association.* Newark, DE: International Reading Association. This collection of articles will provide you with a framework for understanding critical literacy.

McLaughlin, M., & Allen, M. B. (2002). *Guided comprehension: A teaching model for grades 3–8.* Newark, DE: International Reading Association. Though intended for teachers of grades 3–8, you'll find many of the instructional strategies are also appropriate for high school students. There are organizers, lesson ideas, and easy-to-follow directions for implementing a comprehensive model of comprehension.

McLaughlin, M., & Vogt, M. E. (2000). *Creativity and innovation in content area teaching.* Norwood, MA: Christopher-Gordon. Interactive, creative teaching practices reflecting the latest theoretical directions in content area literacy.

Ruddell, M. R. (2001). *Teaching content reading and writing* (3rd ed.). New York: John Wiley. This is a comprehensive resource for all content area teachers. It includes a wide variety of innovative and culturally responsive strategies.

Semali, L., & Pailliotet, A.W. (1999). *Intermediality.* Boulder, CO: Westview. An invaluable resource to guide your thinking about text, messages, and the interaction among elements of media.

Zeichner, K. M., & Liston, D. P. (1996). *Reflective teaching: An introduction to the social conditions of schooling.* Mahwah, NJ: Erlbaum. This hands-on resource contains numerous strategies for content area learning.

CHAPTER NINE

SELECTING AND EVALUATING INSTRUCTIONAL MATERIALS AND TECHNOLOGY RESOURCES

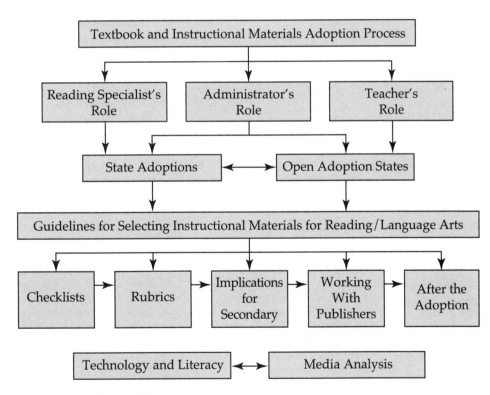

FIGURE 9.1 Chapter Overview

LEARNING GOALS

After reading, discussing, and engaging in activities related to this chapter, you will be able to:

1. describe the role of instructional materials in teaching reading/language arts;

2. position trade books, literature-based series, basals, informational texts, and supplemental resources within an effective reading/language arts instructional program;

3. prepare guidelines for the selection of instructional materials for a reading/language arts program, using research and district, state, and national reading/language arts standards;

4. serve as a member or chair of a school's or district's reading/language arts adoption committee;

5. work with teachers on how to use instructional materials appropriately and effectively, including technology, for teaching reading/language arts;

6. Personal Learning Goal: In a three-minute brainstorming session, share what you know about selecting and evaluating instructional materials. Write a goal or a question that reflects something you want to learn as we explore these topics. Share this with others in your group.

Vignette

Huong Nguyen, the district reading specialist in Butterfield School District, is heading out the door of her office when the phone rings. Reluctantly, because she's already running late, she lifts the receiver and identifies herself. The speaker on the other end of the line does likewise: "Hi Mrs. Nguyen. This is Sam Dowell, the sales representative for ABC Publishing Company. I'm in the area and wondered if I could drop by your office for a few minutes to show you some new reading materials." Because the ABC resources generally comply with her district's standards, Huong makes an appointment for the next day and rushes off to a meeting with a group of teachers and reading specialists from the sixteen elementary schools in the district.

The purpose of the meeting is to begin the process of adopting a new reading series for grades K–8. As chair of the committee, Huong realizes she's embarking on a very important activity, perhaps one of the most critical that she oversees. The current reading series that has been in place for the past six years has not been very well received by

some teachers and administrators, and reading scores have stagnated in some schools while they've dropped in others. At the time of the last adoption, however, there was great enthusiasm about the prospective new program. Teachers embraced its beautiful books, the many supplemental resources, the stories and other reading texts, and the apparent ease with which they could follow the teacher's guide. However, implementing the program was a nightmare; materials were late to arrive, incomplete orders were received, promises of professional development were ignored, the sales representative left the company soon after the adoption, and the string of replacement sales reps who had been in and out of the schools had not been helpful. To top things off, it quickly became apparent that despite spending hundreds of thousands of dollars, the reading series' scope and sequence was incompatible with the new district standards and teachers found the many components unmanageable. As Huong contemplated the forthcoming meeting about the next adoption, she winced.

Thinking Points   It's important as a reading specialist that you know how your own school and district adopt instructional materials, and that you recognize what you value when you select the materials you use to teach. How many of these questions can you answer?

1. What is the textbook adoption process in your own school district?
2. Is your state on a cyclical adoption or do the school districts in the state have the option of adopting materials whenever they wish?
3. Does your entire district adopt one set of reading materials or can each school's staff choose any materials they like?
4. In the past, how have you made decisions about the instructional materials you have used to teach reading and language arts?

Expanding the Vignette: Exploring the Tensions

As Huong enters the meeting room at the district office, she overhears the following comments from the teachers who are awaiting her arrival:

"I don't see why we need a new series. I like the one we have now! The stories are still good and kids like them."

"I can't wait to get the new series! I really don't like the stories in the one we have, and I'm tired of the activities in the teacher's guide."

"Did you hear that XYZ School District got a whole bunch of free paperback books when they adopted the Reading for Life series? We need to look at it and see if we can also get those books!"

"I don't even use a reading series, so I don't care so much about it. It's the new teachers who need a series, not experienced ones like us."

Huong fully realizes that the teachers and specialists in the room have strong feelings about the adoption of reading instructional materials. She also knows that, for this to be a successful process, she's going to need to tread softly and bring the divergent views of the committee members together so that, whatever decision they make, teachers and administrators will be satisfied with it. The district administration, in particular the superintendent, will also be closely watching the process, and she realizes that the broad spectrum of constituents who care deeply about the reading series adoption includes parents and, of course, the school board. Huong distributes the agenda to the reading adoption committee, takes a deep breath, and calls the meeting to order.

Thinking Points

1. What are the tensions that Huong is facing as she begins the textbook adoption process?
2. What are some short-term suggestions you would give Huong? What should she do first?
3. What long-term measures should she consider?

4. As a district reading specialist/supervisor, what should be Huong's relationship with the various publishers' sales representatives?
5. What are some proactive measures a reading specialist could take to avoid tensions related to the adoption of instructional materials?

THE TEXTBOOK AND INSTRUCTIONAL MATERIALS ADOPTION PROCESS

Did you know that in 1985 it was reported that 95 percent of teacher decisions are governed by the textbooks they are using (Radencich, 1995, p. 42)? And, did you know that about 90 percent of American schools use a commercial reading series for teaching reading (Feeley & Rhodes, 1995, p. 116)? As a reading specialist, you will (or should) have a major responsibility for assisting teachers in your school and district to select the best instructional materials that are available. This may involve serving as a leader in your school when reading instructional materials are being selected by individual teachers. Or, as the chair of your school's literacy team, you may be asked (or required) to coordinate your school's selection or adoption of a reading series or program. Some of you may also serve at some point in your career as your district's reading supervisor or coordinator. As such, you most likely will have as a major responsibility for the oversight of the periodic adoption and purchase of your district's reading programs.

The level of your involvement in the adoption of instructional materials may vary greatly from school to school, district to district, and state to state. In some schools and districts, the reading specialist serves as the chair of the adoption committee and coordinates the entire process. In others, committees are chaired by curriculum coordinators or other administrators, such as principals. In still others, a chair may be elected from an eclectic group made up of parents, teachers, administrators, support personnel, and the school site reading specialists share an equal role with other teachers.

Whatever the assigned position, reading specialists *must* take a leadership role during the adoption of reading series or programs as well as other instructional materials. Reading specialists are the ones in the school and district who have a thorough understanding of the reading process, who know the district reading/language arts standards, who should be able to sort through the "sparkle and glamour" of packaging and promotional pieces, and ultimately get to the heart of what's there: the philosophy, scope and sequence,[1] content, and instructional approach recommended for using the materials. Therefore, our purpose in writing this chapter is to assist you in this process by increasing your awareness of what to look for as you review instructional resources. Further, we discuss how to work with publishers' sales representatives, the textbook adoption committee, and the administrators who have to pay the bills and report the test scores. Because Huong is the person in charge of her district's textbook adoption, her anxiety as described in the vignette is understandable—this is one of the most difficult, emotional, and important responsibilities of reading specialists and district reading supervisors.

A note before we begin. What follows is a description of the textbook adoption process and the reading specialist's role in participating and coordinating it. Some of you may be in districts where no commercial reading program is used, and/or your personal belief system is such that you do not support the use of commercial reading instructional materials. While we personally endorse the use of great literature in every classroom, we also acknowledge that commercial reading programs serve the purpose of assisting teachers with planning, offering a wealth of instructional activities and strategies, and providing consistency and support for district standards and frameworks. Also, those of you teaching in Reading First schools and districts most likely adopted a commercial program as part of your grant writing process.

Therefore, in this chapter we're not focusing on how to select award-winning literature, including trade books, for the purpose of instruction or classroom libraries. We encourage you to contact the International Reading Association for their annual Children's Choices selections of excellent literature (www.reading.org), as well as other award-winning collections such as the Newbury and Caldecott winners. At the same time, we're not suggesting that basal or literature-based reading series constitute a school's or district's instructional *program*. Rather, basal and literature-based reading series are instructional resources and, as such, reading specialists much be knowledge-able about them and take leadership in their evaluation, selection, and implementation.

State Adoptions

As this book is being written, there are currently seventeen states that engage in what has come to be known as "state adoptions." These states include: Alabama, Arkansas, California, Florida, Georgia, Indiana, Kentucky, Louisiana, Mississippi, New Mexico, North Carolina, Oklahoma, Oregon, South Carolina, Tennessee, Texas, and West Virginia. State adoptions generally occur for a particular subject area on a regular cycle, such as every seven years. The process differs somewhat from state to state, but typically the state legislature allocates funding for instructional materials based on the adoption cycle. School district committees then review, pilot,[2] and purchase materials for the respective subject area during the allocated period of time.

Not surprisingly, in large states such as Texas, California, and Florida, textbook purchases represent millions of dollars and some publishers create special programs specifically for these states according to their particular content standards. Because of the amount of money involved, most states have very stringent rules and regulations that govern the adoption process. It is very important if you are the chair of an adoption process or committee, or simply a committee member, that you are fully aware of the regulations that govern your state and district adoption process.

Open Adoption States

The other states not listed as adoption states are considered open territories. That means that individual districts within these states may adopt reading/language arts (or other subject area) materials on cycles that they determine based on state funding allocations. Most school districts and states still have some sort of adoption cycle (generally six to ten years) for subject areas but there is little uniformity in the process across the state and from district to district. When instructional funds are released, districts and schools make decisions about purchases. Typically, there are committees that make these decisions, and piloting of the materials occurs widely. In some districts, instead of a committee decision, materials are selected through an all-teacher vote. As with state adoptions, there are differences in how much access to teachers and reading committees the publishers have—this again is in reaction to past practices that many deemed unethical or inappropriate.

In the next section, Dr. Deb Carr, a reading supervisor and curriculum coordinator from Pennsylvania, an open territory, shares her thoughts on the adoption process and budgeting for instructional materials.

Other Voices: Dr. Deb Carr

Dr. Deb Carr is the Reading Supervisor and Curriculum Coordinator for the Hazleton Area School District, Hazleton, Pennsylvania. She is a former secondary reading teacher and reading specialist. In addition to her full-time position in the school district, she also teaches part-time in the reading specialist/MA program at Kings College, Wilkes-Barre, PA. She is a district-level educator who advocates for literacy in everything she does.

In our district, we run a reading adoption for a *program*, not specifically for supplemental materials. There is a committee that reviews all of the existing programs and then decides which will be piloted. There are many discussions about which books to pilot based on the needs of the students and the teachers, and the piloting can take from three to six months. The piloting process has changed in recent years because most publishers are requesting districts to purchase the workbooks for the pilot classrooms. In the past, all pilot materials were provided to the district at no cost, but now it has gotten very expensive. Of course, during the piloting period the teachers divide themselves among the two to three pilots and settle into their own camps. Discussions about the different reading programs happen throughout the adoption process. In actuality, these are ongoing in the sense that I am facilitating information so that the people on the adoption committee and in the classrooms have the background knowledge to make the decision—a decision based on sound research practices rather than the color of the pages in the teacher's edition. I see too many supervisors trying to step back from that process—however, I think you still need to be the "guide on the side."

As school districts scramble to do more with less, this process of selecting reading materials becomes even more critical. Each new government report or research review reveals the need for new (or even old) materials to meet students' needs. Regardless of the currently embraced reading philosophy, there are realistic costs involved in providing reading teachers with what they need.

Understanding the budget process is integral to planning the implementation of these new initiatives. This planning needs to take place anywhere from two to six years ahead of the purchase of new reading materials. In an adoption year—the year the business office sets aside more than the residual costs[3] for a program—it is important to identify materials for the immediate adoption year, but also materials for where students and staff need to be in, say, six years. These funds must be placed in appropriate budget categories for revenues and for expenditures. You can see that coordinating the purchase of materials can be a complicated, multifaceted, and ongoing process.

The results of the adoption process really represent what your district believes about reading instruction. I don't mean that you have to select a camp, but you ought to be reviewing the available programs as much as the teachers and asking the hard questions to get them to look beyond the glitz. Your questions should lead the teachers to what they should be looking for. I find walking through an entire lesson in the program—start to finish—gives me a flavor. Does it take fourteen worksheet pages before you get to the meat of the lesson? I find it ridiculous when I hear some supervisors say they have had a "blind adoption." This means that the teachers don't know what publishing company they are reviewing. These days you are adopting a publishing house as well as a text. The staff development they provide and the reputation of that firm is at the heart of the program. Does the publisher stand behind its work and its authors, or is it just trying to kick out an old program for another state adoption?

Too often, teachers spend their own money for materials for their classroom. This happens when funds are not available, when teachers are looking for creative extensions to themes, or even when the teachers have not embraced the district's philosophy and purchase materials to match their own personal beliefs or biases. There are serious instructional issues when the adopted core materials are being ignored, and when teachers plan theme extension projects that last for months. On the other hand, the standards movement has put teachers on the verge of worksheet-and-computer-program mania in search of the quick fix to demonstrate the mastering of standards. There are worksheets and computer programs to track every skill and strategy under the sun. Regardless of the promise of tracking standards' benchmarks, the quality of materials needs to be maintained. Are worksheets—paper or electronic—needed to demonstrate the achievement of standards? District leadership needs to establish a balance and to develop guidelines for the implementation of teacher purchased or donated materials.

Group Inquiry Activity   Now that you've read Dr. Carr's Other Voices piece, do a Think-Pair-Share (think alone, share with a partner, and then the class) with the following questions:

1. As you were reading Dr. Carr's thoughts about the adoption process, what additional tensions did you identify that a reading specialist and reading supervisor must deal with?
2. What do you see as the major issues surrounding the adoption of reading instructional materials and a reading program?
3. What do you see as the primary responsibilities of the school-site reading specialist?
4. What do you see as the primary responsibilities of the district-level reading supervisor or curriculum coordinator?

GUIDELINES FOR SELECTING INSTRUCTIONAL MATERIALS FOR READING AND LANGUAGE ARTS

Recall that, in the vignette, you saw that Huong Nguyen, the district reading specialist, had created a committee to oversee the adoption process. Obviously, the size of your district will dictate the size of the reading committee, as will the scope of the adoption (Elementary/Secondary/K–12), but we recommend that, for management purposes, the committee consist of approximately fifteen to twenty people. Obviously, the more knowledgeable the people on the committee, the more wisely they will make decisions. However, as Dr. Carr pointed out, it will be necessary for you as a reading specialist and/or supervisor to provide background information and recent research articles in order to make sure everyone is working from a similar perspective and knowledge base. In addition, think about the discussions among teachers that Dr. Carr mentioned. These planned opportunities should be about recent research, district and state content standards, the state framework or curriculum guide, school and district philosophies about teaching reading, and the guidelines for making adoption decisions. In order to have as diverse a membership as possible, there are specific people who should be included on the district reading committee that will be in charge of making recommendations about reading instructional materials. As you build your committee, try to find a balance of people from each of the following categories: Reading specialists, teachers, principals, special education teachers, librarians or media specialists, ESL/bilingual teachers, resource teachers, technology specialists, parents, university professors of education, and student representatives, especially for secondary adoptions.

Once you have selected the committee, meet together as early in the process as possible. In state adoptions, the reading programs are generally available for review during the school year preceding the time of decision and purchase. Therefore, you may need to organize your committee about two years before the actual adoption year. This is especially important if you're going to set up pilot classrooms. Spend early meetings (once a month or so) discussing the research, your reading/language arts standards, and setting up your guidelines for adoption. Create a sequence of procedures, objectives, and tasks with doable dates for completion. Be sure to communicate this calendar to site and district administrators and other constituents involved in the adoption process. Include in the calendar dates and times for publisher presentations of the new materials, and when publishers should be notified of the procedures and guidelines they should follow during these important presentations. Remember to include specific time designations for these presentations—all publishers should have an equal amount of time to make their pitches.

Note that, in many states publishers receive very specific criteria for the instructional materials they will submit to the state, and in order to be "listed," the publishers must comply exactly with these criteria. These guidelines for publishers should be readily available from your state departments of education, and we urge you to review them carefully, especially if you're coordinating the adoption process for your district. We've often heard teachers complain about something that they've found in their reading series, and then on closer inspection we discover that the publishers were required by the state to include what the teachers were complaining about! If the reading committee understands clearly these requirements, you then can dig into other issues that warrant a closer inspection.

Creating Guidelines for the School or District Adoption

The next step in the process is to coordinate the writing of the guidelines that your committee (and perhaps other teachers and administrators in individual schools) will use to adopt the instructional materials.[4] Whether you are coordinating a schoolwide adoption or districtwide adoption, it is still necessary to know what you're looking for when you review all the submitted materials.

Earlier in the chapter, we referred to moving beyond the "sparkle and glamour" found in many reading series, and Dr. Carr referred to the same issue as "glitz." Even though the reading programs and materials may look similar, it's very important to look beyond the glitz and freebies, and determine whether the materials are really appropriate for your students, the district and school reading philosophy, current research, and your schools' assessed needs. A simple "flip test" through the instructional materials, a cursory glance, is clearly not enough (Radencich, 1995). Therefore, we recommend that you ask the following questions as you create adoption guidelines and make initial screenings of materials published for the teaching of reading and language arts.

1. What would an ideal set of reading/language arts instructional materials look like?
   - What's in a "must" category (e.g., a research-based foundation for the program, student anthologies with classic, contemporary, and multicultural literature, leveled reading books for beginning reading instruction, assessments, an easy-to-follow instructional sequence in the teacher's guide)?
   - What's in the "in our dreams" category (that is, the supplemental offerings that are considered "add-ons")?
2. How does the scope and sequence of this program/series, grade level by grade level, stack up to your district and state standards?
   - Reading First legislation requires explicit instruction, practice, and assessment in phonemic awareness, phonics, fluency, vocabulary, and comprehension. How comprehensive is the program for each of these areas, across all grade levels?
   - Are skills just introduced and taught once, or do you see that they are reviewed and assessed in a spiral fashion throughout the lessons, themes, and grade levels?
   - Does there appear to be a logical organization or scheme for the skills and strategies that are taught? If so, what is it?
3. If the publishers make claims about the effectiveness of their products in promotional materials, what kind of research evidence is available to support these contentions?
   - Is there a scientific research document from the publisher that serves as the foundation for the program/series? Is it readily available?

- Is there written evidence that the materials have been field-tested with real teachers and real students? If so, what did the field-testing demonstrate? Where did it take place? What were the results?

4. Who are the authors of the series or program?
   - Are they established educators and researchers?
   - What has been their role in the development of the program?
   - Do they represent diverse perspectives and backgrounds?
   - What is their philosophy about the reading process and instruction and is it evident in the materials?

5. If we follow a lesson from beginning to end, how much explicit instruction and modeling are included?
   - How much student practice is recommended?
   - How much silent "worksheet" work is included and recommended?
   - What is the balance between explicit instruction by the teacher and at-seat independent work by the student?

6. How many opportunities do students have to actually read and write about authentic topics (not just fill-in-the-blank activities)?
   - If the program claims to be "integrated," how are the language arts (e.g., spelling, writing, and grammar) taught, modeled, assessed, and practiced?

7. What provisions are included for English language learners (ELL's)?
   - Are students provided with appropriate instruction of grade-level concepts and vocabulary?
   - Are the supportive activities meaningful?
   - Do they provide access to the same content as the English-only students are receiving?
   - Is there an obvious attempt to scaffold reading instruction for ELL's?
   - Is English proficiency being taught and reinforced, as well as literacy skills?
   - Are the ELL recommendations more substantive than just one to two sentence cursory suggestions?

8. What are the expectations of the materials regarding what children and adolescents know and can do?
   - Are these appropriate to your school community?
   - What are the social skills and values being taught, modeled, and reinforced through the instructional plan and the literature?
   - Are they appropriate for your school, district, and community context?
   - Are the stories and other literature pieces representative of the students who will be reading them? That is, will the students "see themselves" in the various texts they're reading and contexts they're reading about?
   - Does the literature represent a variety of perspectives and views so that children/adolescents will have the opportunity to expand their own thinking? These questions are critical to investigate, especially if you value a sociocultural perspective. Keep in mind that in some conservative communities there are those who believe that schools should not be involved in discussions about values, ethics, and social contexts—they believe discussions about these should be left to the family. What we're advocating here is that you include in your

review and evaluation of reading resources and programs careful attention to the literature selections and instructional recommendations in terms of the values, perspectives, biases, and contexts that are included. Then you'll be ready when the questions about them come your way.

9. Are the narrative, informational, expository texts, and poetry all well represented?
   - Is there a variety of text structures and genres?
   - Is there a wide enough variety of reading levels represented in the texts so that students of all reading abilities can have access to independent and instructional materials?

10. Are the provisions for struggling readers and accelerated readers appropriate and doable?
    - That is, will teachers be able to include additional instruction and experiences for students within the daily instructional plan?
    - Is careful attention paid throughout the program to motivating all learners?

11. Is the instructional plan "sound"?
    - That is, does it activate, utilize, and develop students' background knowledge and experience?
    - Is there a balance of explicit instruction, indirect or implicit teaching,[5] and multiple opportunities for students to practice and apply what they have learned?

12. Is the instructional plan appropriate for a variety of teachers' skills, experience, and abilities?
    - Will all teachers find something they can use—whether beginning or experienced?
    - Will beginning teachers have enough structure and support to be successful with the program?
    - Is the plan easy to follow, comprehensive, and well designed?
    - Will experienced teachers find the instructional plans helpful, but not overly prescriptive?

13. In the instructional plan, are learning goals and objectives clearly stated and then assessed?
    - Does the plan ensure that students have exposure to, instruction in, practice with, and eventual mastery of the respective objectives and standards?

14. Do supplemental materials, such as workbooks, transparencies, and blackline masters support and extend instruction, while providing opportunities for meaningful independent practice?
    - Or are they "fillers" intended to just keep kids busy?

15. Which of the supplemental materials are truly "supplemental" and which are really "necessary" for the program to run smoothly?
    - If you don't purchase the supplemental materials, what will be omitted instructionally? This is where you may need to go back and compare your "ideal" list to your "in our dreams" list of program components from question (1).

16. Are the pacing suggestions appropriate for your student population?
    - If not, is there a way to slow down or speed up the instruction without incurring additional, time-consuming work for the teacher?

17. Are there extra handbooks or other resources that contain important instructional lesson plans for students needing additional support?
    - For accelerated learners?
    - For English language learners?
    - What is in these handbooks? How will they be used?
    - What will happen to these students if the handbooks are overlooked by teachers or not purchased by the district?
18. What is the role of assessment?
    - Is it integrated throughout the program?
    - Is it viewed as an ongoing process?
    - What skills are tested?
    - What is the format of the assessments and other tests?
    - Are there performance assessments as well as other formats that are reflective of standardized tests?
    - What is the balance of assessment formats?
19. Is there an appropriate balance between the number of pages of skills work, workbook pages, and so forth, and more authentic opportunities to respond to text?
    - Look beyond the labels. That is, most publishers will use similar labels, such as "intervention," "scaffolded instruction," or "integration." Take a closer look at the actual instruction, rather than just accepting the label at face value.
20. Is the teacher encouraged to use a variety of grouping configurations throughout the week's plans?
    - Do students have opportunities to engage in meaningful activities with partners? Small groups? The whole class?

Group Inquiry Activity   Bring to class a student anthology and a teacher's guide from the series or program you are currently using in your school. If you teach in a middle or high school, bring the current literature textbook that is being used. If you don't have access to a reading series or literature textbook, select a content area textbook appropriate for a particular grade level. In other words, bring something students are expected to read!

1. Divide into groups with like materials and focus on the questions that are asked in #8 from the previous list.
2. Take a critical literacy stance as you carefully look at the various texts. Begin by selecting an informational or expository text. From what and perhaps whose perspective is the text written? Does the author appear to have an "agenda?" If so, what is it?
3. What words does the author use to persuade or cajole the readers to buy into a perspective or agenda? Look carefully at particular words and phrases, such as *we* (who is the "we"?); *you* (who is the collective or individual "you"?); *our* (whose "our"?); "It will be beneficial . . ." (for whom? according to whom?).
4. Divide a piece of paper into three columns:
    - perspective (whose?)

- agenda (what?)
- proof (words or phrases that the author uses).

As an example, critical literacy theorist, Alan Luke, demonstrated at an IRA conference in 2000 an Australian social science textbook. The selection Alan chose was a discussion about land in Australia that some people wanted to keep undeveloped, while others (the developers) wanted it to be used for commercial purposes. Even though the chapter was supposedly an objective account, on careful examination it was clear that the author shared the developer's perspective. For example, an author could use phrases such as "a left-wing group," "environmentalists," "radical," "anti-development" to describe those opposing development. Those promoting development could be described as "pro-community," "pro-family," or "community-oriented." While these examples may seem obvious, others may be much more subtle. Look through your materials and see what you can discover! Share your findings with others in the class.

From Guidelines to Checklist

Once you have discussed and reached consensus on the answers to the twenty sets of questions we posed, the next step in this process is to develop a checklist for the guidelines that you and others involved in the selection and/or adoption process will use. We can't do this for you because only you and the other stakeholders know your district's and schools' needs. You know the context in which your community resides, and you know local politics, values, and issues that need to be considered. So, bite the bullet and draw up a checklist; then have it reviewed and approved by others on your district reading committee. Obviously, the district administration may wish to provide input, as well as members of the school board, if this is something they see as under their purview. Be ready to make a presentation to the board, and have your research foundations, state and district standards, and other rationale for the guidelines and checklist available for their review. Remember that the districtwide adoption of instructional materials should be a schoolwide and districtwide team effort.

Creating a Rubric

When the guidelines and checklist have been approved, the next step is to develop a uniform rubric that can be used by all reviewers. This could be an evaluative rubric, such as "Excellent, Good, Average, Poor, Very Poor," or you can create a rubric based on how frequently various items on the checklist are found through the program: "Consistently, Occasionally, Sometimes, Seldom, Never." Obviously, there are a variety of rubrics that can be used while evaluating the materials and some may be more closely linked to the particular indicators you're reviewing. Whichever you end up using, it's important that all reviewers and evaluators have training in what the rubric means, what each of the indicators looks like in the materials, and how you know an indicator when you see it. This training and several "practice runs" with discussion among members of the reading committee will result in a more reliable and effective evaluation process. Remember, you're looking for *excellence* overall as well as congruence with standards and ease-of-use by teachers.

Implications of Adoptions for Middle and High School Literacy Programs

Basically, all of the suggestions we have previously made regarding the evaluation and selection of reading materials apply equally to elementary and secondary schools. The twenty guidelines and their questions should also be asked when reviewing literature anthologies, intervention materials, and books for independent reading in grades six to twelve.

However, there are some additional guidelines that need to be considered when selecting reading instructional materials for adolescents. The central issue concerns readability,[6] the ease or difficulty of the texts that are selected. As students get older and gain in reading ability, the span in their reading levels also increases. Laura Robb (2000b) suggests the need for a variety of books at students' instructional levels. She states that, for adolescents, "friendly, readable texts can lead to a pleasurable reading experience because the learner comprehends and becomes involved . . . involvement in and comprehension of nonfiction texts increase when these books contain many stories and vignettes" (p. 22).

Chris Tovani (2000) adds that older secondary students need to be exposed and have access to books that are "important" to them, books that have personal meaning and value. She describes what she calls "fake reading," so commonly seen in secondary classrooms. This phenomenon manifests itself in book reports given on books never read, skimmed *Cliffs Notes*, and a general avoidance of all or nearly all reading. Therefore, we strongly recommend that students be involved in the selection of the materials they'll be reading. Invite one or two middle and secondary students to serve on the reading committee that will be reviewing the instructional materials. Give them a voice in the process!

WORKING WITH PUBLISHERS AND SALES REPRESENTATIVES

During a textbook adoption process, whether statewide or school-by-school, you will be working with representatives from publishers. They can help facilitate the process for you by providing samples of instructional materials, offering inservice on how the materials should be used, and assistance with ordering, reordering, and keeping track of what you have ordered and received. Here are some hints for forging a professional and satisfying relationship with publisher's representatives.

1. We encourage you from the start to maintain a strictly professional relationship with publishing companies, and that you view offers of free materials, resources, and other perks with a healthy skepticism. Keep in mind that all instructional materials and services cost money . . . even what appears to be "free." Usually the costs of the freebies are absorbed into the cost of the books, services, and other materials, so accept these accordingly.

2. Did you know that publishers' representatives are nearly all former teachers, principals, reading specialists, and/or district curriculum resource people? They're knowledgeable, they care about children and adolescents, and they (nearly all) deserve to be treated with respect. The reason we mention this is because publisher's sales representatives and consultants don't like to be called "vendors" or "bookmen." Because most are men and women with years of teaching experience, we need to view them as members of the educational team.

3. Consider providing sales representatives with the names of the reading committee and the planning periods or the best time to call. Also, provide the name and means of contact for the district- or school-level coordinator of the adoption.

4. If you accept an invitation to a function, please show up or at least let the sales representative know if you're unable to attend. The representatives must pay for these events out of their annual budgets, and wasted money must be made up someplace . . . most often in the costs of instructional materials. Also, remember what your mama said . . . when you attend a publisher's function or receive some samples or other materials, a thank-you note is always appropriate and appreciated.

5. All sales representatives have sales quotas and limits. As honorable as most of them are, there are a few out there who do not have teachers' and children's best interests at heart. Maintain an informed stance about what is absolutely necessary to buy, and what is not. Look at the unit pricing of all items, and stick to your budget. Think of all the "stuff" that ends up in book rooms and on teachers' shelves—materials that were purchased but not used. At the same time, don't overlook purchasing necessary support materials and supplemental teaching handbooks and student books. Too often, these are considered to be "ancillaries," nice but not necessary. Carefully review all components of the reading series; know what the products are, what they're intended to do, and what they're called. Sometimes these materials are integral to the instructional program, so check them out carefully, and be wise about the resources you order.

6. Maintain thorough written records of all of your dealings with publishers, including appointments, materials ordered, and materials received. Also, keep track of commitments they make, such as offers of professional development, consultant time, expected dates of delivery, and so forth. Ask for a professional development proposal in writing.

7. Some school districts have very strict rules about what you can and cannot accept from a publisher's representative. Be sure to review your district policies and act accordingly.

8. Remember that one of the very best places to review instructional materials is at your state reading association conference and at the annual regional and national IRA conventions. Joining the associations and attending the conferences is an important responsibility of school-site and district reading specialists and supervisors.

AFTER THE ADOPTION: IMPLEMENTATION

Once your district has selected a particular reading series, you have really just begun the adoption process. Too often, we have experienced or observed districts that spend tens of thousands of dollars on the adoption of reading instructional materials only to have them delivered to schools and teachers without any assistance in how they should be used. So, it's of critical importance that all teachers are provided with ongoing support for using the new materials. Keep in mind that reading specialists must receive inservice about the reading series in order to be able to help teachers, answer questions, and provide support, even if they will not be teaching the program themselves. Teachers need the opportunity to provide feedback about what's working with students and what's not. Ask them what materials they are actually using and which they have decided are irrelevant or unnecessary. In other words, meet with lead teachers and reading specialists from each school and debrief them about the reading program on a regular basis.

Districtwide, ongoing monitoring of the implementation process is also necessary and highly recommended. Some districts remove all vestiges of the former reading series or program from teacher's classrooms so that only the newer materials are being used. We have mixed feelings about this practice because (1) it devalues teachers and their ability to make decisions about the most appropriate materials for their students; and (2) often, the older reading program materials, especially the anthologies and student readers, can be used to provide additional independent reading resources. For example, cut up the outdated student books and save the best stories, poems, and informational texts. Add a tagboard cover and title, and you now have some "books" on various reading levels (from the different grade levels) to add to classroom libraries.

If you have individual teachers who resist changing to the new program and methods, approach them individually, provide them with support such as demonstration lessons and professional development, and then encourage them to move into the new materials as they reach a level of comfort. We're not suggesting that teachers just hang onto their "old ways" if they don't want to move into the new reading series and materials; rather, we're just acknowledging the fact that we don't all learn and change at the same rate.

TECHNOLOGY AND LITERACY

Technology resources for schools are changing so rapidly that it's very difficult to make recommendations about their selection and use that remain current. Don Leu (2000a) suggests that "if there is one thing that is certain in these uncertain times, it is that the technologies of information and communication will regularly and repeatedly change, constantly redefining what it means to be literate" (p. 183). He goes on to report that the National Center for Education Statistics reported that in 1998 51 percent of K–12 classrooms in public schools in the United States had at least one computer connected to the Internet (p. 184). Seventy-seven percent of classrooms had at least one computer connected to the Internet in 2000 (National Center for Education Statistics, 2001), and it was estimated that in 2002 nearly all U.S. classrooms would have access to an Internet connection. This remarkable growth in the availability of technology has changed and continues to change our very definitions of literacy and literacy learning (Leu, 2000b).

Kamil, Intrator, and Kim (2000) suggest that educators increasingly will be pressured to implement technology in literacy teaching and learning because of the public demand for it even though there is a paucity of related research that demonstrates how technology impacts literacy development. However, there are some promising findings about technology and the areas of writing and composition, hypermedia, multimedia, work with special populations, motivation, and collaboration (Kamil et al., 2000). These researchers suggest that "we view the research on . . . technologies and literacy as a tapestry under construction. The warp and woof of the fabric have not yet entirely come together. Rather, we have bits and pieces of an overall design" (p. 783).

Many younger teachers have never known life without computers while more experienced teachers have had a steep learning curve in order to keep up with their students. In virtually every state where publishers submit reading instructional materials, they must include a provision for technology resources, yet it is difficult to discern how effective these materials are in improving students' reading and writing abilities. There are also numerous Websites that offer teachers instructional ideas, resources, themes, units, and lessons. We recommend that you and your colleagues utilize district technology personnel to assist in reviewing and evaluating available software, and we strongly encourage you to learn about district policies and guidelines for protecting children from inappropriate Web sites. Two Web sites dedicated to protecting children and youth are www.SafeKids.com and www.SafeTeens.Com. These sites include articles, guidelines for parents, parent and family newsletters, technology resources, and directions for accessing search engines that are filtered or limited to sites that contain only appropriate materials.

It is also incumbent on reading specialists and school literacy team members to maintain a healthy skepticism about what's on the Web because, as with other print resources, just because it's there doesn't mean it's effective for developing students' literacy. An important responsibility of the literacy team is to become as knowledgeable as possible about what technology resources are available and then to assist teachers and parents in critically evaluating the Web sites and software prior to their use with children.

Some major publishers have created helpful Web sites that are open to all teachers, such as Houghton Mifflin's www.eduplace.com and Scholastic's www.scholastic.com. The International Reading Association has a wonderful on-line journal, *Reading Online*, that has a variety of links to articles about using technology in the classroom, Web sites, software resources, issues of access and ethics, and research. The journal can be accessed at no charge through the IRA Web site, www.reading.org.

The United States Department of Education Web site also has informative links and sites that we recommend:

- The Office of Educational Technology: This site includes evaluation and assessment resources, including evaluation tools; information about distance learning;

the digital divide ("haves and have-nots"); conference white papers, and information about Internet safety. It has a wealth of information for schools and districts.

- The Planning and Evaluation Service (PES) at the U.S. Department of Education evaluates the effectiveness of federal educational technology programs.

In our university classrooms and during inservices and workshops that we provide, we're frequently asked to comment on particular technology programs and software. Again, because what is available changes so quickly and it's impossible to be able to review all resources, we're reluctant to make specific recommendations. However, we urge reading specialists to consider the following when working with students and teachers:

1. Remember that literacy learning is a socially constructed process that occurs in interaction with texts, authors, and in collaboration with other people. There are some widely used computer-based reading programs that are supposedly "interactive" because they include leveled stories and books that students read at their own pace, along with comprehension questions to which the students respond. While some children find these books on the computer very engaging, the reading and subsequent responding activities are completed by the student independently. The student reads the stories or books alone, answers questions alone, and earns points alone. For some students who enjoy this solitary activity, these supplemental programs may be okay on an occasional basis. But, all students in grades K–8 need regular opportunities for "community reading" (where the entire class shares a story or book together) and "just-right" reading (where the teacher provides direct and indirect teaching of reading skills and strategies) (Paratore, 2000). It's important to help teachers, especially those who are new to the field, understand this very important point. Computer-based reading materials that youngsters engage in independently may be appropriate for "on my own reading," but they're not a substitute for literacy instruction.

2. There are a number of other software programs that are specifically related to reading and literacy, such as those that "diagnose," create lesson plans, help teachers organize assessment data, and "teach" phonics. For any of these, we urge caution. While some may be helpful and appropriate, others may be bordering on harmful, wasting valuable instructional time for the participating student. Some are created for students with learning disabilities and have a solid research foundation, while others are simply commercial programs with little or no research support. The reading specialist's role is to assist teachers in sorting all this out, and that takes time to investigate claims and read the research. Certainly, if you are responsible for allocating instructional funds and recommending materials, you must review and understand the materials that are available for purchase.

3. Electronic journals (e-journals) are an effective way of incorporating reading, writing, and E-mail into classroom literacy activities. They build community as students and teacher E-mail back and forth to each other, and they allow for a different level of personal communication between student and teacher, rather than the brief editorial comments students usually find on their work. E-journals also permit instant messaging, something older students may already be familiar with, but their messages at home don't usually relate to school-related topics and projects. E-journals connect students and encourage reflection and discussion about what they're learning (Vogt & Vogt, 1999).

4. Students' research projects take on new form when they're electronically created and presented. Karlin LaPorta, a fourth-grade teacher in Downey, California, and her fourth-grade teammates teach their students how to use PowerPoint, access the Web for their research topics, clip art, and other graphics, and make oral presentations that are professional and engaging. Most of these children are English learners, and these opportunities not only develop background and content knowledge, but they also improve their English proficiency.

In 2001, the International Reading Association Executive Board approved a position paper on the role of technology in the classroom. The full text is available through the IRA Web site (www.reading.org). An executive summary is presented in the section that follows.

Integrating Literacy and Technology Into the Curriculum

The Internet and other forms of information and communication technology (ICT) such as word processors, Web editors, presentation software, and E-mail are regularly redefining the nature of literacy. To become fully literate in today's world, students must become proficient in the new literacies of ICT. Therefore, literacy educators have a responsibility to effectively integrate these technologies into the literacy curriculum in order to prepare students for the literacy future they deserve.

The International Reading Association believes that much can be done to support students in developing the new literacies that will be required in their future. We believe that students have the right to

- teachers who are skilled in the effective use of ICT for teaching and learning
- a literacy curriculum that integrates the new literacies of ICT into instructional programs
- instruction that develops the critical literacies essential to effective information use
- assessment practices in literacy that include reading on the Internet and writing using word-processing software
- opportunities to learn safe and responsible use of information and communication technologies
- equal access to ICT

THE MEDIA AND A SOCIOCULTURAL PERSPECTIVE

The events of September 11, 2001 will be forever etched on the consciousness of the children and adults who witnessed, either in person or via the media, the terrorist attacks on the United States at the World Trade Center and the Pentagon. In the days following the tragedy, the National Reading Conference listserv included many suggestions about what resources teachers could use to assist children in coping with the media images they had seen, either in print, on the Web, or on television. Most of the recommendations that came from literacy experts around the globe were picture books and other pieces of literature that could be used for bibliotherapy.[7] Colin Harrison, while of course supporting the use of literature, also suggested another way we could help students try to understand what they were seeing and experiencing. With his permission, we include Colin's E-mail message dated Thursday, September 13, 2001, as one of our "Other Voices" contributors.

Other Voices: Dr. Colin Harrison

Dr. Colin Harrison is the Director of Research and Professor of Literacy Studies in Education, School of Education, at the University of Nottingham, United Kingdom. He is a former President of the United Kingdom Reading Association, and served on the International Reading Association's Family Literacy Commission (1994–1999).

One perspective which has not been mentioned thus far in the discussion of texts around which to focus conversations which might have the potential to help young people to come to terms with the terrible events of Tuesday (September 11) and its aftermath is that of media studies.

Clearly, to even make this suggestion is to risk offending many people, since to begin any sort of analysis of the visual and media texts would, for most groups, be felt to be inappropriate at this time. But, I would wish to align myself with those who argue that currently (in what we are pleased to call the developed world), it is through these visual and multimedia texts (especially newspapers, TV, and, increasingly, the Web) that we learn, and learn to form our opinions and beliefs.

The results of undertaking even a very limited analysis of what is presented to us by the media is nearly always problematic, and difficult for a teacher to handle. Yet, how much more difficult would it be to engage in a critical literacy discussion of how TV and other media have mediated our understanding, our representations, and our views . . . first of what happened, and second, of how we understand what happened, and third, of how we behave in the light of what happened, individually and collectively. Right now, it is the time for care, for hugs, and for helping kids to feel less afraid. But maybe later, when it's time to ask the questions about how we try to understand, teachers (and they will need to be very sensitive and perhaps brave teachers) will think about adopting a media studies approach. Media analysis begins with simple questions:

- What did we see?
- Why were we shown this?
- What were some of the effects of its being shown this way?
- What might have been some of the effects of its being done differently?

These questions can apply just as much to a family video of a wedding as to real-time TV coverage of a catastrophe. But (unless the teacher takes a very strong editorial line), such analyses tend to lead inevitably to one thing—to students gaining a thoughtful, critical, and better-informed personal understanding of the events that occurred. They also gain understanding of the ways in which it is impossible to represent "reality" without an editorial bias—and this leads to a more informed understanding of how meaning is made for us in our world by the media, and ultimately to an awareness that we can play an active part in constructing meaning for ourselves.

In the past two days (which seem like years—and I'm acutely aware that I am not an American, and come as a guest when I visit your country), adults and children in England have seen some terrible scenes repeated and repeated, and used as a visual backdrop to talking-head interviews. Someone decided to do this. Someone decided to show images of people in some communities in the world celebrating the tragedy with laughter and delight. Someone decided that we should see an interview with two New Yorkers who were looking for a lost loved one, but who said to the microphone, "Why are we hated this much?" How might people's feelings be different if they had—or had not—seen one or more of these images?

I cannot say, but I do feel that media analysis can help students to make personal sense of the world, as they reflect on what they have witnessed in the media, and on how those images were gathered, edited, juxtaposed, and broadcast.

Group Inquiry Activity   Ann Pailliotet (1998) calls on teachers to engage their students in the "deep viewing" necessary to investigate both the surface message as well as the underlying values, beliefs, and purposes of those who produce media. Over the next week, be especially aware of how major news events are provided to the public through various media sources. Keep track of the headlines, articles, TV reports, and broadcast and print images that you see on TV, in the newspaper, in magazines, and so forth.

1. What types of texts are being used?
2. How are they being used?
3. What is their intent (such as to invoke patriotism, anger, laughter, sadness, thoughtfulness)?
4. Who made the decisions to air, broadcast, and/or print them?
5. How did they make you feel?
6. What did you learn from them?

Bring your notes, reflections, and insights to class. Share them with others. What are the implications for teaching children and adolescents about their world?

REVISITING THE VIGNETTE

At the end of the first year of her work with the district reading committee, Huong Nguyen felt satisfaction that a great deal had been accomplished. Together, they had reviewed reading/language arts research, internalized the state and district content standards, and generated a checklist with rubrics that they would all use the following year when it was time to review various publishers' instructional materials. They had drafted a time line, scheduled publishers to present their materials, and organized subcommittees to review different components of the programs. Further, they had agreed that, by the beginning of the spring semester, piloting of the top three reading programs would be in place in six schools. The pilot teachers and procedures for the pilots would be finalized in the fall. The final decision about the adoption would be made by April 15 of the following year. As Huong reviewed the plans, and reflected on the year's work, she remembered her earlier concerns and fears. There was still a great deal to do, but the foundations for the adoption had been established thoughtfully and carefully. They were on their way.

POINTS TO REMEMBER

School-site reading specialists and district reading supervisors must be directly involved in decisions related to the adoption of reading/language arts instructional materials. They should facilitate the formation of a district-level reading committee made up of representatives from the literacy teams of all of the district's schools. Based on district and state guidelines, policies, and recommendations relative to the adoption of reading series/programs, they should work with the reading committee to develop evaluation guidelines based on standards and school/community needs. The next steps are to create a checklist and establish rubrics to be used during the review of the instructional materials. Throughout the adoption, it is important to foster and create professional relationships with publishers' sales representatives and consultants. Following the adoption, it is important to assist teachers in implementing the new program. This is facilitated through demonstration lessons, inservice, and ongoing monitoring and review of the school-site and district reading programs.

It appears that technology will increasingly define what literacy is and what it means to be literate. Because technology changes at such a rapid rate, reading specialists are encouraged to work with school and district technology resource people to select and evaluate resources for classroom use. District guidelines and policies for providing a safe environment for children must be developed and followed. Media analysis is a powerful way to help children and adults understand events that unfold around them that impact their lives.

PORTFOLIO PROJECTS

1. Investigate your district's textbook adoption process. Who currently makes adoptions about the literacy-related instructional materials? What, if any, is the role of teachers, administrators, students, reading specialists, media specialists, and other stakeholders in the selection and evaluation process? Write a proposal for your school or district on how to improve the adoption process.

2. Examine either an elementary reading program or a secondary English or literature program. Using the recommendations for balanced elementary reading programs (Chapter 7) or secondary literacy programs (Chapter 8), determine the extent to which the program you're reviewing is research-based and instructionally sound. What are the strengths of the program? Its

weaknesses? How well would the teachers in your school and/or district be able to implement the program? What types of assistance and professional support might they need?

3. Using the elementary or secondary reading/literacy program from (2) and your district and state literacy standards, compare and contrast the skills, strategies, and content of the commercial program to the

standards. In which areas is there congruence? In which areas are there problems? If you adopted this program, are there any areas that would need to be supplemented with additional resources? If so, what would you recommend?

4. Personal Goal: Revisit the objective you set for yourself at the beginning of the chapter. Create a portfolio item that reflects what you have learned relative to your objective.

RECOMMENDED READINGS

Burniske, R. W. (2000). *Literacy in the cyberage: Composing ourselves online*. Published by SkyLight Professional Development. Distributed by the International Reading Association. This book describes nine interrelated literacies, each of which focuses on an on-line communication skill. Included are Web sites, case studies, teaching tips, definitions, and examples of student writing.

Kapitzke, C. (2001). Information literacy: The changing library. *Journal of Adolescent & Adult Literacy, 44*(5), 450–456. This article describes the changes that are taking place in libraries as new technologies transform information access. "Cybraries," electronic "portals" to information service, exist at universities in Australia and elsewhere, and provide access to vast amounts and types of information from anywhere in the world. Implications for developing students' information literacy are included.

Myers, J., & Beach, R. (2001). Hypermedia authoring as critical literacy. *Journal of Adolescent & Adult*

Literacy, 44(6), 538–546. This is a helpful, practical, and very interesting article about how hypermedia foster literacy. Examples from a ninth-grade classroom model how students used videoclips, music, and still images to construct critical responses to literature.

Osborn, J., Stahl, S., & Stein, M. (1997). *Teachers' guidelines for evaluating commercial phonics packages*. Newark, DE: International Reading Association. This inexpensive publication is intended to assist educators and others in evaluating phonics programs. The recommendations are based on phonics research and an analysis of twenty commercial phonics programs.

Wepner, S. B., Valmont, W. J., & Thurlow, R. (2000). *Linking literacy and technology: A guide for K–8 classrooms*. Newark, DE: International Reading Association. This book is based on the premise that instruction drives technology, and it shows teachers and specialists how to use technology to enrich and support the literacy curriculum.

NOTES

1. Scope and sequence: A curriculum plan, usually in chart form, in which a range of instructional objectives, skills, etc., is organized according to the successive levels at which they are taught (Harris & Hodges, 1995, p. 227). Basal reading series generally include a scope and sequence for each grade level. These should be studied carefully when the instructional materials are being reviewed and evaluated.

2. Piloting instructional materials: Publishers provide district teachers with instructional materials

that are used with students over a particular time period, such as six months, a semester, or even a full school year. After the piloting period, the participating teachers review the quality of the materials, how the students responded and performed with them, and then they make recommendations about adopting or not adopting the products for the entire district. In most cases, reading specialists are very involved in the piloting process by teaching with the pilot materials and/or assisting teachers in implementing them.

3. Residual costs: These are the ongoing costs of additional and/or replacement materials in "off" years, when there is no official adoption. Such things as replacing consumable workbooks and worn anthologies, buying additional teachers' guides, and so forth, are considered to be residual costs.

4. Please note that it is beyond the scope of this book to provide you with detailed information about the budget process for purchasing school and/or district instructional materials. Check with your district's purchasing department, and, of course, your site and district administrators for more information about the purchasing process in your district.

5. Indirect or implicit teaching: This refers to those "teachable moments" when you can reinforce a skill, strategy, or concept without an explicitly presented mini-lesson or other directed teaching lesson.

6. Readability: Many variables in text may contribute to readability, including format, typography, content, literary form and style, vocabulary difficulty, sentence complexity, concept load or density, cohesiveness, and so on. Many variables within the reader also contribute, including motivation, abilities, background knowledge, and interests (Harris & Hodges, 1995, p. 203).

7. Bibliotherapy: The use of selected writings to help the reader grow in self-awareness or solve personal problems (Harris & Hodges, 1995, p. 19).

PART III

THE READING SPECIALIST: COACH, SUPERVISOR, AND PROFESSIONAL DEVELOPER

CHAPTER TEN

SERVING AS PEER PARTNER, COGNITIVE COACH, AND SUPERVISOR

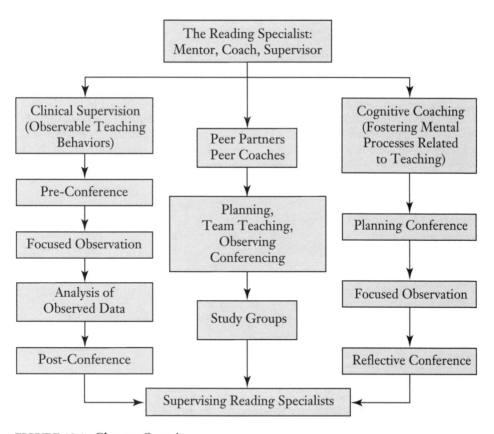

FIGURE 10.1   Chapter Overview

LEARNING GOALS

After reading, discussing, and engaging in activities related to this chapter, you will be able to:

1. define and describe cognitive coaching;
2. effectively serve as a cognitive coach for beginning and experienced teachers;
3. define and describe the role of a reading supervisor at the district level;
4. prepare for the role of reading supervisor at the district level.

Vignette

When hired for the position of reading specialist at Jefferson Elementary School, Caitlin Howard assumed that the majority of her day would be spent teaching children, especially those with reading problems. However, Caitlin's principal, Ed Tagliano, had recently attended an administrator's conference and returned home committed to having his school's reading specialist very involved in coaching the four new teachers at Jefferson. As the only reading specialist, Caitlin is worried about how she will be able to do this in addition to her teaching responsibilities. Jefferson Elementary, located in a rural area of the northeast, has 320 children and fourteen teachers, in addition to the reading specialist and special education teacher. Because of the size of the school, the principal is the only on-site administrator. Caitlin, with her MA in reading education and her advanced reading certification, has had little specific preparation in administration and management, and is understandably leery of becoming a "supervisor" for the teachers with whom she's already established a good working relationship.

Her concern about this newly assigned role grows when the principal asks Caitlin to observe one of the new teachers, Alex. The previous week, Ed had spent an hour during the reading/language arts block in Alex's first-grade classroom. To Caitlin, he expressed concerns about Alex's reading approach and suggested that she "get in there as soon as possible and see what Alex is doing with those kids." Caitlin trusts Ed's opinion and his knowledge of curriculum, including reading. She also knows he wouldn't ask her to observe Alex if he didn't have a well-founded concern.

Thinking Points

1. What can you identify as the primary tension in this vignette?
2. What do you think that Caitlin should do at this point?
3. How should Caitlin respond to Ed, her principal?
4. How might she approach Alex, the new teacher?

Expanding the Vignette: Exploring the Tensions

Obviously, Caitlin must respond to her principal's request, not only because he's her administrator, but also because he's an excellent principal who cares deeply about the children and teachers in his school. However, her instincts and experience tell her that she needs to tread softly with Alex for the following reasons: (1) He's a new teacher who needs support, assistance, and encouragement, rather than criticism at this point in his career; and (2) Her relationships with the other teachers, whether beginning or experienced, may hinge on how she establishes this new coaching and mentoring role. She remembers that Alison, a seasoned veteran, is also the school's representative on the council for the local teachers' union. Caitlin wonders if it's even legal for her to go in and observe Alex in the role of "coach" or "mentor."

Caitlin asks Alex if she can come into his classroom the following day to observe a first grader who Alex has referred for special education services due to the child's difficulties with beginning reading. She also tells Alex that she'd like to see how he as a new teacher is getting along, and asks if she can stay and observe during the reading/language arts block. Alex seems comfortable with Caitlin's request, agrees to the observation, and describes some of his reasons for referring the child. The reading specialist takes some notes, and the two agree on the time for the visit the following day.

When Caitlin arrives in Alex's first-grade classroom the next morning, the first things she notices is that several of the children are out of their desks, noisily playing on the floor, while he is trying to conduct a lesson with six children over at his small-group table. The child she has agreed to observe is in Alex's small group, so she pulls up a first-grade chair, pulls her knees up under her chin, and watches the lesson, frequently glancing at the other children in the room who are increasingly distracting.

Alex is attempting to teach a phonics lesson, and the six children at his table each have a large white piece of construction paper

on the table in front of them. Alex draws a large "A" on his own paper, and then asks each child to write with a crayon the first letter of his or her name on the construction paper. With varying degrees of skill, the children complete the task. Included in the group are children named Jaime (pronounced hī-mē) and Yolanda. Jaime is the focus child Caitlin is observing for purposes of the special education referral.

After the children have drawn their letters, Alex asks each child to draw pictures all around the piece of construction paper that represent "happy words" that begin with the letter of his or her first name. For a moment, Caitlin is afraid that she hasn't heard Alex correctly, but when she sees the blank expressions on the children's faces, she realizes with some concern that she has. To his credit, Alex models the task for the children: "See, the first letter of my name is an A. Some happy words that start with A are (and he draws a picture of mountains as he says the word) Alaska, because I visited Alaska once and it is a beautiful state, and apple, because it's red and is a healthy fruit."

While the children's blank stares continue, Caitlin frantically tries to think of "happy words" that begin with C: candy? Cindy? (her sister), cuddle? How would I draw that? At this point, Caitlin looks up and it becomes painfully obvious that Jaime and Yolanda are going to have a major problem with this lesson. The other children are also perplexed about what they're supposed to do. In desperation, Alex grabs off of his bookshelf an alphabet picture book so the children can at least find some pictures that start with the first letters of their names. One of the children pats Yolanda's arm and quietly says, "Don't worry, Yolanda. Just draw a lemon. It's yellow and yellow starts with a Y."

Thinking Points   This is an actual scenario that I (MaryEllen) encountered a few years ago when I was observing a new teacher in a first-grade classroom. While the teacher's name and other identifying characteristics have been changed, the lesson plan has not been changed.

1. Identify additional tensions that have arisen in this vignette.
2. What are the problems with Alex's phonics lesson? How might you discuss them with him?
3. From a sociocultural perspective, what should Caitlin set out to learn about Alex? Why is this information important to her coaching and mentoring relationship with him?
4. What do you think Caitlin should do at this point? How should she proceed with Alex?
5. What, if anything should she report to the principal, Ed Tagliano?

We'd love to tell you that I was able to make this teaching experience all better for the children in that first-grade classroom and for the new teacher who struggled through an impossible and poorly planned lesson. But, the reality was that positive changes don't happen overnight. As a reading specialist, you will find that one of your most challenging roles will be that of coach and mentor. What makes these roles so challenging is that reading specialists are not really administrators, yet we are required in many cases to work with teachers in what seems like a quasi-administrative role. This challenging rung on the educational ladder has been somewhat difficult to define.

SCHOOL AND DISTRICT ROLES OF READING SPECIALISTS

It is helpful to begin our exploration by distinguishing between school-site and district-level reading specialist positions (see Figures 10.2 and 10.3). The titles and job descriptions for these will undoubtedly vary from district to district and state to state, but, in most places in the United States, there are positions that resemble the following:

- School-Site Reading Specialist: Primary responsibility is the instruction of children with reading problems; as the only reading specialist in the school, is involved in curriculum design, planning, and implementation; reports to the building principal.
- School-Site Reading Specialist: Works as member of a team, alongside other reading specialists and support personnel (including the special education teacher, counselor, speech therapist, etc.); reports either to the principal or other administrator who oversees the work of the school's support personnel.
- School-Site Reading Specialist: Primary responsibility is serving as a "literacy coach," especially for new teachers and during the implementation of a new reading series or program; answers to the principal, but may report to a supervisor or administrator at the district or county level.

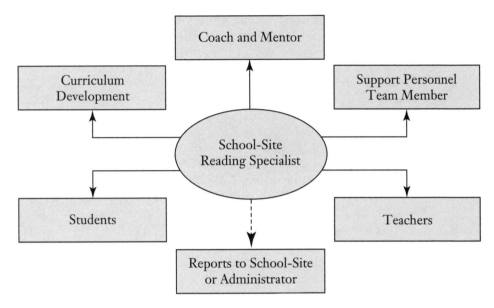

FIGURE 10.2 **School-Site Reading Specialist**

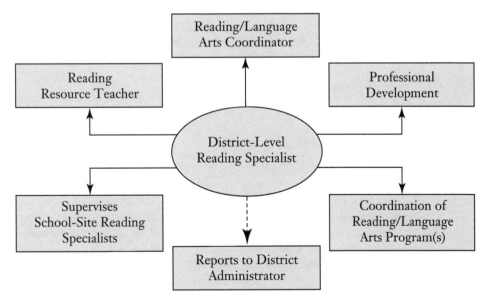

FIGURE 10.3 **District Level Reading Specialist**

- District-Level Reading Specialist: Works as a reading resource teacher, with responsibilities for working with a variety of schools and staffs on implementation of effective literacy teaching practices and materials; reports to the assistant superintendent for curriculum, or a curriculum director, or reading supervisor, or perhaps the superintendent.
- District-Level Reading Specialist: Supervises the work of school-site reading specialists (but does not engage in formal evaluation procedures); reports to the curriculum or reading director, assistant superintendent, or superintendent;
- District-Level Director of Reading or Reading Supervisor: Is responsible for all reading/language arts instructional programs; oversees the adoption of instructional materials; supervises and formally evaluates all district reading specialists and related personnel; reports to an assistant superintendent or superintendent.

As you review these reading specialist descriptions, you'll notice that only the last involves the direct supervision of personnel. Depending on your state and district certification procedures, people who assume this position may be required to hold an administrative credential or certificate in addition to advanced certification in reading, especially if the position involves writing formal evaluations that determine the hiring and retention of personnel. If you eventually intend to work at the district level, we recommend that you pursue advanced administrative certification so that you will have the preparation you need to serve in this type of district-level position.

If you serve as a school-site reading specialist or district reading resource teacher, your relationship with the teachers with whom you work will be different from that of "supervisor." Rather than *evaluating* the performance of personnel, your role may resemble that of a peer partner, mentor, or cognitive coach—one who models, guides, and assists others in becoming capable, confident, and expert teachers of reading. In the next sections, we will discuss several models of teacher support, including clinical supervision, peer teaching and coaching, and cognitive coaching.

THE READING SPECIALIST AS COACH

Clinical Supervision

Prior to the late 1960s, teacher supervision and evaluation were the province of an administrator who entered the classroom as an expert, briefly observed a lesson, and told the teacher what worked well, what did not, and what should be changed about the observed lesson. If a post-lesson conference occurred, most of the talking was done by the administrator who offered solutions to problems that had been observed. Usually, a written evaluation form was completed, signed by both the teacher and supervisor, and placed in the teacher's personnel file, never to be viewed again.

Morris Cogan, Robert Goldhammer, and their colleagues at Harvard believed this to be an ineffective way to evaluate teaching performance and developed an alternative model called Clinical Supervision (Cogan, 1973; Glickman, Gordon, and Ross-Gordon, 1998; Goldhammer, 1969). They suggested that the supervisory process should foster collegiality between the teacher and supervisor with each respecting the contributions of the other. Instead of functioning as a top-down process (from evaluator to teacher), the intended goal of clinical supervision is "to cultivate the teacher's self-appraisal, self-direction, and self-supervision" (Costa & Garmston, 1994, p. 15). This process of self-reflection is accomplished through a cyclical process:

- preconference with teacher;
- observation of classroom;
- analyzing and interpreting observation and determining conference approach;
- postconference with teacher;
- critique of previous four steps (Glickman et al., 1998, p. 298).

The conference approaches referred to in the third step of the process include directive controlling (supervisor tells teacher what to do); directive informational (supervisor offers information for teacher to consider); collaborative informational (supervisor shares information with teacher for both of them to consider); collaborative controlling (there's a guise of involvement—the supervisor makes teacher believe he or she shared in decision); nondirective informational (supervisor actively listens to teacher's information); and nondirective controlling (supervisor manipulates teacher to think he or she is making own decisions). The supervisor's role is to choose "the best entry-level supervisory approach and [foster] teacher development while gradually increasing teacher choice and decision making responsibility" (Glickman et al., 1998, p. 199).

The supervisor's role during clinical supervision is to assist the teacher in recognizing and reflecting on the overt teaching behaviors observed by the supervisor. As a model, clinical supervision is predicated on two principles: (1) Teaching is a collection of observable behaviors; and (2) Teaching can be improved by understanding, controlling, changing, and modifying these behaviors. Throughout the 1970s and 1980s, clinical supervision reigned as the accepted model of teacher supervision and evaluation. Although the power structure was inherently unequal, when it was implemented as designed the teacher evaluation process fostered collaborative and reflective classroom practices.

Author Connection: MaryEllen You may have noted this phrase in the last sentence of the preceding paragraph: ". . . and when it [clinical supervision] was implemented as designed, the teacher evaluation process fostered collaborative and reflective classroom practices." As a teacher, you may have benefited from an effective process of teacher evaluation. On the other hand, you may have been subjected to a process that not only did nothing to foster collegiality, but was inequitable and, at times, punitive.

In one middle school where I taught, the principal never once observed my teaching—and I taught in this school for five years. The assistant principal observed me once each year for about twenty-five minutes. There was no preconference or discussion of what I'd planned for the observed lesson and no follow-up conference, yet the administrators stated they were "doing" clinical supervision. After the scheduled observation, I simply received a memo that the evaluation form was ready for my signature in the office. I stopped by the principal's secretary's desk and signed it, and that was my teaching evaluation for the year. Some of you may now be thinking, "Yep, that's what I'm familiar with," while others of you may be gasping, "You've got to be kidding!"

We mention this because a model is only a theoretical construct until it is put into practice. A supervisor can say, "I use clinical supervision (or cognitive coaching, for that matter), but unless the tenets of the model are followed carefully, then what is done in the name of the model can become an aberration. As you reflect on clinical supervision, and then read about peer teaching and coaching in the next section, compare and contrast the essential elements in each. Do you think that clinical supervision is an appropriate model for school-site reading specialists? Are there any aspects of the model that may be problematic for you?

Group Inquiry Activity   With the others in your group, share the teacher evaluation processes in which you have engaged.

1. Which of these would you agree have been successful and effective ways to help you reflect on your own teaching?
2. Which have promoted thoughtful analyses of teaching practices?
3. Which focus not just on the teacher but also on the learners?
4. Which do little to promote reflection and modifications in your teaching?
5. Create a "wish list" of observation and/or evaluation practices that might be helpful to you in improving your own teaching.

Peer Partners and Peer Coaches

According to Garth Boomer (1992), one important role of the teacher is to assist children and adolescents in negotiating the curriculum. Together, the teacher and students engage in discussion, inquiry, modeling, and mediation about learning, and in the process students arrive at new understandings (Goldenberg, 1993). We believe this negotiation process is equally important for teachers, especially those who are new to a school. Laura Robb (2000a) describes a peer partner as "an experienced, nurturing teacher with strong communication and teaching skills who has earned the respect of colleagues" (p. 53). In this role, a reading specialist can assist beginning teachers and others new to the school in "negotiating" their way through the myriad responsibilities and tasks of teachers, from figuring out grading practices and policies to understanding the particular culture of a school.

Peer partnerships do not have to involve only reading specialists. Of course, experienced teachers can partner effectively with beginning or other new teachers. What reading specialists bring to peer partnerships, however, are expertise, ideas, and instructional approaches for teaching reading and language arts. Helping a new teacher, whether beginning or experienced, become acclimated to the school's various literacy programs, including intervention, supplemental materials, and family resources, can be of great value. For example, if a new teacher arrives without knowledge of or experience with the school or district's adopted reading series, the reading specialist can walk her through the program, describe the philosophy and research foundation for it, share lesson ideas and activities, provide demonstration lessons, and/or help with assessment and placement of students in the program. Meeting frequently, lending an empathetic (and perhaps sympathetic) ear, providing modeling and assistance, sharing ideas and methods, loaning books and resources—all of these can make a first-year experience more meaningful, productive, and satisfying. Also, keep in mind that experienced teachers who are new to a school have much to offer such as ideas, resources, and effective approaches. In a peer partnership, the give-and-take is more on an equal footing, and each partner can be of assistance to the other.

Collaborating with an expert, especially in a risk-free, nonevaluative environment, can be enriching for both the reading specialist and teacher, whether beginning or experienced. Think of the times you have had the opportunity to work with someone with more experience and knowledge than you have. If this person is offering freely of his or her wisdom and expertise, with nothing particular asked in return, you may have viewed this expert as a mentor, guide, or coach. If you are still teaching children or adolescents, your day-to-day encounters with students may help you better understand what classroom teachers are experiencing regarding schedules, interruptions, and the life of the classroom. An effective coach not only understands these realities of teaching, but also is willing to accept a teacher where he or she is, build a trusting relationship, and help the teacher explore new avenues.

Peer coaching has been likened to an art. Knowing how to interact with another teacher—when to question, model, coax, prod, and gently nudge—requires sensitivity and caring. It is obvious that a coach never launches into what went wrong with a lesson, but begins a post-observation conversation with questions such as, "What do you think worked well?" and "Do you have any questions about anything that happened during the lesson?" "Is there something you'd like me to address?" Because establishing trust is critical to the coaching relationship, it's very difficult to be a coach who is also a supervisor responsible for formal teacher evaluation. Rather, a coach is most effective when he or she a good listener and responds in ways that are nonjudgmental and nonthreatening. Answering questions honestly, responding to concerns quickly, sharing classroom stories, celebrating progress and successes, and making time for the teachers you are coaching, all help to build trust and reinforce a positive coaching relationship.

Prior to beginning a peer coaching relationship (or program), determine a clear purpose and goals. It will be helpful to consider the following questions posed by Glickman et al., (1998, p. 304):

1. Is the goal [of peer coaching] a question of peer assistance (reciprocal interactions of equals) or is it a matter of hierarchical, one-way assistance (a better trained or more experienced teacher helping less well-trained or less experienced teachers)?

2. Who is the recipient of assistance? Should a teacher who is the observer take from the observation some ideas to use, or should the teacher who is the observed take from the observation some actions to use?

3. Will the observations and feedback focus on common instructional skills that each teacher is attempting to learn and implement, or will the observations and feedback focus on the teacher's own idiosyncratic concern with his or her teaching?

4. Should the observations and feedback focus on the teacher's teaching or on individual students' behaviors?

5. Is the goal of coaching to be greater awareness and more reflective decision making, or is it to implement particular teaching skills?

Answers to these questions frame the relationship between the coach and the coached, and describe how each will relate to the other. We believe it's important for the teachers with whom you are establishing a coaching relationship to clearly understand what each of your roles involves. This clarification may prevent future misunderstandings about the expectations for the peer coaching relationship that each of you hold.

Among the suggestions Laura Robb (2000a) offers coaches are the following (p. 75):

- After a teacher accepts an invitation for you to visit her classroom, negotiate several long blocks of time during which you can observe. While visiting, circulate, participate, and support students.
- Schedule conference times when they're most convenient for the teacher you're going to visit.
- Plan lessons with the teacher before you observe, model, or team-teach.
- Offer choices. Does the teacher want to practice with you first, and then teach? Does the teacher want you to model the lesson or team-teach? If you're teaming, determine beforehand the parameters of jumping in, interrupting each other, and offering questions or suggestions.
- Ask the teacher to stay in the room and take notes if you're going to model an instructional approach or method.
- Accept the teacher where he is and gently move him forward. Build on what he does well, stress the positive, and still offer suggestions for growth.
- Help the teacher become reflective and self-evaluative.
- Honor the teacher with notes, phone calls, emails, and verbal acknowledgements of the positive changes you're observing.

We firmly believe you must maintain total confidentiality about anything you see in another teacher's classroom. If you disclose the events you observed to other faculty or an administrator, you will lose trust that has been established.

Group Inquiry Activity Recall that Ed Tagliano, the principal in the opening vignette, asked that Caitlin Howard, the reading specialist, observe and assist Alex, the new teacher. In a group, discuss the following questions and then share your responses with others in the class:

1. What questions should Caitlin have asked Alex prior to her observation? What might have prevented the problems that Alex had while teaching?
2. After observing Alex's phonics lesson, what could Caitlin say during a post-observation conference with him? Be very specific about how she might begin the conference. You may wish to role-play this scenario with group members.
3. Because the principal knew that Caitlin was observing Alex, he expected a report on what she had seen in his classroom. How do you think Caitlin should respond to Ed's questions about Alex's teaching?
4. If a reading specialist is expected by an administrator to serve as a mentor or coach, how should the parameters be established? What proactive steps might you take in discussing your role?

In the next section, we contrast peer coaching with cognitive coaching, a research-based model also used by supervisors and administrators. Though many of the elements of cognitive coaching are similar to the description of partnering and coaching that you have just read, you will also see some differences, primarily in how tightly the cognitive coaching model is structured.

Cognitive Coaching

Art Costa and Robert Garmston (1994, 2002) suggest that cognitive coaching is built on a foundation of clinical supervision, with two important differences. First, while clinical supervision focuses on observable behaviors that, with reflection and modification, may lead to improved teaching, cognitive coaching has as its focus a teacher's inner thought processes and intellectual functions, the consequence of which are the observable, overt teaching behaviors. Second, these observed teaching behaviors are changed when the teacher's inner and invisible cognitive behaviors are altered and rearranged. In other words, cognitive coaching is about enhancing "another person's perceptions, decisions, and intellectual functions" (1994, p. 2). The three primary goals in cognitive coaching are:

1. establishing and maintaining trust;
2. facilitating mutual learning;
3. enhancing growth toward holonomy.[1] (Think: "I am autonomous in my own classroom but my successes are interdependent with my students' and colleagues' successes. We're individuals, but we are all in this together and must work together as a team.")

Like clinical supervision, cognitive coaching is built around a planning conference, observation, and a reflective post-conference. With cognitive coaching, what occurs in each of these is of critical importance.

The Planning Conference.   During this phase in the cognitive coaching cycle, the coach mediates by clarifying lesson goals and objectives, anticipates teaching strategies and decisions, determines evidence of student achievement, and identifies the coach's data-gathering focus and procedures (Costa & Garmston, 1994, p. 18). The teacher and coach can discuss the context of the lesson, any anticipated problems, or questions the teacher may have. This is the phase where trust is established and the teacher can verbally rehearse the various lesson steps and procedures. An effective cognitive coach may ask questions such as "How will you know your approach (or strategy or method) is working?" or "How will you know when it's time to move into the next planned activity?" The planning conference also establishes some factors to consider during the reflective post-conference. The coach and teacher decide on the data that will be collected by the coach, so that the observation is framed not by what *happened*, but in terms of what were the teacher's *intentions* for the lesson. The planning conference also enables and encourages the teacher to think about his or her objective, plans, and means for assessing student achievement of goals. This process leads to self-coaching, in which the teacher asks questions such as, "What's my plan? What are my objectives? How will I know students are learning?" (Costa & Garmston, 1994, p. 20).

Observing the Lesson.   During this phase, the purpose is to shed light on the teacher as teacher–researcher, while the coach's role is that of data collector, observing and recording data based on the planning preconference during which specific lesson goals and objectives were agreed on. Note that the cognitive coach is nonjudgmental during the observation, and he or she is simply recording data as it is observed. For example, the teacher may have expressed concerns about students' on-task behaviors during times in the lesson when the teacher provides explanations and directions. Therefore, the coach may complete an on-task chart, recording every minute or so which children are on-task and which are not. This task analysis chart can then be studied to see if patterns emerge. Likewise, perhaps the teacher has expressed concerns about some students who don't participate actively during lessons. The coach could watch for teacher-to-student interaction patterns to determine if the teacher is focusing on and interacting more with some students than others. What's important is that the area of focus is predetermined and agreed on by the teacher and cognitive coach. This avoids a "scattershot" observational technique in which the observer just writes down everything that he or she sees. This type of recording can be overwhelming to the observed teacher because there is so little focus.

Reflecting Conference.   The purpose of this last phase in the cycle is for the teacher to reflect on the lesson goals and objectives and consider the extent to which he or she believes they were accomplished. Whereas it is advised that the planning conference take place just prior to the actual lesson, Costa and Garmston recommend that there be some time for consideration after the lesson and before the reflective conference. This allows the cognitive coach to organize and analyze the data and the teacher to think about the lesson while jotting notes for discussion with the coach. During the reflective conference, the coach encourages the teacher to describe his or her perceptions of the lesson, contemplate specific incidents or events that went well or that were troublesome, and reflect on what could be changed if the lesson were taught again.

For example, the teacher may notice on the interaction chart completed by the coach that she is only engaging with students who sit toward the front of the classroom. Interactions with these students are frequent, while those students who are sitting in the back of the room engage infrequently with the teacher. This discovery could lead to a discussion of how to organize student desks to better increase interactions, or the teacher may decide to teach from various places in the classroom, not just in the front. Through questioning and discussion, the teacher and coach can generate some ideas for alleviating the observed problem.

As you think about these three phases of cognitive coaching, do you see how simple, but potentially delicate, this coaching/mentoring role is for the reading specialist? Rather than evaluating or criticizing a teacher's lesson, your task is to hold up a thoughtful mirror through which a teacher might see a reflection of his or her teaching, relationships with students, lesson organization, and nonverbal modes of communication (such as facial expressions, position of hands, and stance). The reading specialist can also provide advice and assistance about how to plan appropriate literacy instruction based on assessments. She can guide a teacher in the selection and use of reading materials and provide feedback (if solicited) on how children are functioning in literature discussion circles. In all, during cognitive coaching, anything that is mutually agreed on can be the focus of observation, reflection, and discussion.

Cognitive coaching requires sensitivity and the ability to hold information in the strictest confidence. A positive working relationship can be established by learning how to offer constructive suggestions, understanding a teacher's belief system, and respecting differing viewpoints. This is not to imply, however, that your role as coach is only to accept everything that a teacher says and does. Part of the skill of an effective coach is to question in such a way as to promote and stimulate the teacher's thinking, one of the major goals of cognitive coaching. Some examples of desired mental processes and the questions that might produce them are suggested in Figure 10.4.

Please note that these questions are intended only as examples, and, as Costa and Garmston (1994) state, "they are not meant to be prescriptive or complete. Their intent is to engage, mediate, and thereby enhance the cognitive functions of teaching" (p. 225).

Dealing with Negative People and Learning from Your Mistakes

We both have experienced coaching and supervising successes, and what might be considered occasional failures, especially when we didn't listen well enough or when we tried to be too directive in our feedback. There have been times when we have coached teachers who have been resistant to reflection, analysis, and what we considered to be supportive comments. Nevertheless, we believe that cognitive coaching and all it entails represents an effective way to work with teachers, and we encourage you to try out your coaching skills with peers who welcome your observations and conversations about their teaching.

Planning Conference	
If the desired thought process in the teacher is to:	Then the coach might ask:
State the purpose of the lesson.	"What is your lesson going to be about today?"
Translate the purposes of the lesson into descriptions of desirable and observable student behavior.	"As you see the lesson unfolding, what will students be doing?"
Envision teaching strategies and behaviors to facilitate students' performance of desired behaviors.	"As you envision this lesson, what do you see yourself doing to produce those student outcomes?"
Describe the sequences in which the lesson will occur.	"What will you be doing first? Next? Last? How will you close the lesson?"
Anticipate the duration of activities.	"As you envision the opening of the lesson, how long do you anticipate that will take?"
Formulate procedures for assessing outcomes.	"What will you see students doing or hear them saying that will indicate to you that your lesson is successful?"
Monitor their own behavior during the lesson.	"What will you look for in students' reactions to know if your directions are understood?"
Describe the role of the observer.	"What will you want me to look for and give you feedback about while I am in your classroom?"
Reflecting Conference	
Express feelings about the lesson.	"As you reflect back on the lesson, how do you feel it went?"
Recall student behaviors observed during the lesson to support those feelings.	"What did you see students doing (or hear them say) that made you feel that way?"
Compare student behavior performed with student behavior observed.	"How did what you observe compare with what you planned?"
Make inferences about the achievement of the purposes of the lesson.	"As you reflect on the goals for this lesson, what can you say about your students' achievement of them?"
Become aware and monitor one's own thinking during the lesson.	"What were you thinking or what did you observe that made you change your plan while you were teaching?"

FIGURE 10.4 Examples of Questioning during Cognitive Coaching

(Costa & Garmston, 1994, pp. 222–225)

Reflecting Conference (continued)	
Analyze why the student behaviors were or were not achieved.	"What hunches do you have to explain why some students performed as you had hoped while others did not?
Draw causal relationships.	"Why did you do (or not do) to produce the results you wanted?"
Synthesize meaning from analysis of the lesson.	"As you reflect on this discussion, what big ideas or insights are you discovering?"
Self-prescribe alternative teaching strategies, behaviors, or conditions.	"As you plan future lessons, what ideas have you developed that might be carried to the next lesson or other lessons?"
Give feedback about the effects of this coaching session and the coach's conferencing skills.	"As you think back over our conversation, what has this coaching session done for you? What is it that I did (or didn't do)? What assisted you? What could I do differently in future coaching sessions?

There may be times when you're faced with a teacher who is so resistant and uncompromising that discontinuing the coaching relationship is the only viable decision you can make. If this happens, discuss it professionally and sensitively with your supervisor. To preserve confidentiality, avoid discussing directly what you've seen or heard. Rather, let your supervisor know that, despite your best efforts, the two of you have not been able to maintain a productive coaching relationship. If pressed for more details, try to set a time for a conference between you, the teacher, and the administrator so that all of you can discuss the issues in an open and honest manner.

SUPERVISING READING SPECIALISTS

If you're working as a district-level reading specialist or supervisor, most of what we have written here is equally relevant. We advocate a cognitive coaching model, in which you have a planning conference prior to observing a reading specialist at his or her school site, observe and collect data, followed by a reflective conference, in which you openly and supportively discuss the reading specialist's lesson. Note that this model works equally well if you are observing a small-group intervention lesson, a demonstration lesson, or even an inservice presentation by the reading specialist. If you learn as much as you can about the goals and objectives, about the context for the lesson or presentation, and about any concerns that the reading specialist may have prior to your observation, you will be much better able to assist, guide, facilitate reflection, and bring about positive changes in the work of the person you are coaching.

STUDY GROUPS

Within a single day, teachers must make hundreds, perhaps thousands, of decisions. Decision making requires three abilities according to Wasserman, as cited in Robb (2000a, p. 81):

1. the ability to observe students, then compare observations to similar and different situations and theoretical knowledge;
2. the ability to analyze the data collected from observations by selecting key points;
3. the ability to interpret these points by forming hypotheses or hunches that lead to informed action.

An on-site study group can be organized to meet weekly or monthly to help teachers make decisions about issues related to teaching and learning. The purpose of the study groups is to read research articles, study theoretical perspectives, and work together as teacher researchers to observe student behaviors within the context of topics that are mutually explored. The study groups can meet as grade-level groups, small groups within a school's faculty, or groups that are comprised of teachers and specialists from throughout the district (Robb, 2000a). Reading specialists can play a key role in organizing and facilitating the study groups by soliciting interest in particular topics, providing access to journal articles and books, and working with the teachers to negotiate topics, the curriculum, and the roles of the participants.

Generally, study groups involve those who are willing to set aside the time and then follow through with the mutually agreed-on agenda. The group establishes a purpose, such as deciding how to effectively and flexibly group students for literacy instruction. A couple of volunteers research the books that are available on the topic, and study group members select one to begin their reading. They purchase multiple copies using a small grant from their school's PTO (Parent–Teacher Organization), determine discussion responsibilities, and set a time line for their meetings. They also establish a loose set of "ground rules" for their study group, such as committing to read the agreed-on chapters, promising to show up for scheduled discussion meetings, and deciding who brings the always-necessary refreshments. As with any group, study groups create their own culture, and when ground rules are established and agreed-on early in the process, it is more likely that the study group will reach its goals.

We've included study groups in this chapter because, while coaching several teachers in the same school (or reading specialists in the district), you might find some common issues that would work well for study group topics. We recommend that you take a shared ownership approach to the study group process. The group belongs to everyone involved, and we recommend that your group rotate the role of facilitator, and that you share as a colleague (not an expert) in discussions. In some groups a volunteer takes notes or keeps minutes of the group's activities; however, we have participated in groups where individuals kept journals and shared them during sessions. If you haven't participated in a study group at your school, we encourage you to do so. It can be an immensely rewarding experience.

REVISITING THE VIGNETTE

By now, you probably have realized that the reading specialist, Caitlin Howard, was put in a very difficult position by her principal, Ed Tagliano. However, it wasn't really the principal's fault because he was looking to the reading specialist to work with Alex, the new teacher. Prior to the next observation of Alex, Caitlin, having learned about cognitive coaching and armed with some questions to stimulate Alex's thinking processes about teaching, will schedule a planning conference. She will assist Alex in carefully thinking about the lesson he will be teaching, and will help him focus on his students' learning goals. Rather than trying to watch everything that he is doing, she will focus her observation on a mutually agreed-on area of need. Caitlin feels confident that, with her supportive assistance, Alex will continue to grow as a teacher while, at the same time, she will grow in her ability to serve as his peer coach.

POINTS TO REMEMBER

Traditionally, teacher supervision and evaluation have been the purview of the school-site and district administrators. Clinical supervision, a research-based model designed to assist teachers in improving their practice by focusing on observable and measurable teacher behaviors, has been widely used for over twenty years. The model consists of a preconference, observation, analysis of observation data to determine an appropriate approach in working with the teacher, and a post-observation conference. More recent developments in effecting teacher change include peer coaching, in which teachers assist each other in reflecting on their practices in order to improve their teaching.

Cognitive coaching, another recent research-based model, extends clinical supervision by focusing on teaching as a thinking process. The cognitive coach assists the teacher's reflection about his or her teaching during a planning conference that is followed by an observation during which the coach focuses on mutually agreed-on aspects of the lesson. During the reflective conference, the cognitive coach, through questions designed to elicit thoughtful responses about practice, guides the teacher in making decisions about future lessons and students' achievement of particular learning goals.

Study groups, formed to investigate particular issues, theories, methods, or research, can be facilitated in the beginning stages by a reading specialist who assists in finding resources and identifying topics for discussion. The ultimate goal is for teachers to work together to solve common problems through their shared reading and research.

PORTFOLIO PROJECTS

1. Identify a teacher in your school who would be willing to serve as a peer partner or as a teacher with whom you could practice your cognitive coaching skills. If possible, arrange to observe the teacher and work on a mutually identified area of concern or need. Follow through with the procedural phases of cognitive coaching. Keep a journal

of your experiences, reflecting on what worked well, what needs improvement, and the implications for your position as a reading specialist.

2. Investigate your school district's preferred method for evaluating teacher perform-

ance. Is it a research-based method? Is it aligned with the forms that have been approved (by the teachers' union and school board) for teacher evaluation? How congruent is the method with cognitive coaching?

RECOMMENDED READINGS

Costa, A. L., & Garmston, R. J. (2002). *Cognitive coaching: A foundation for Renaissance Schools* (2nd ed.). Norwood, MA: Christopher-Gordon. In this new edition, you see how teachers' individual and collective capacities for continuing self-improvement are strengthened over time through cognitive coaching. This book includes a description of skills, protocols, guidance, research, and resources to use when implementing cognitive coaching in school settings.

Friend, M., & Cook, L. (1992). *Interactions: Collaboration skills for school professionals.* White Plains, NY: Longman. Though intended for special educators, this book offers good information about developing effective collaboration, communication, conflict resolution, and active listening skills. The focus is on creating productive working relationships with parents, teachers, special educators, and related service providers.

Glatthorn, A. A. (1997). *Differentiated supervision* (2nd ed.). Alexandria, VA: ASCD. This book presents a somewhat different model of supervision, in that it provides teachers with options about the kinds of supervisory and evaluative services they receive. Although many local variations exist, depending on district resources and needs, in general the differentiated model provides intensive development to nontenured teachers and to tenured teachers with serious problems. The rest of the faculty receive options about how they wish to foster their professional development. Most work in collaborative teams; some work with a more self-directed approach. In addition, the evaluation processes are differentiated, depending on tenure status and competence. The values critical to the differentiated supervision system include collaboration, inquiry, and continuous improvements (pp. 10–11).

Glickman, C. D., Gordon, S. P., & Ross-Gordon, J. M. (1998). *Supervision of instruction: A developmental approach* (4th ed.). Boston: Allyn & Bacon. If you are thinking about taking a district-level position as a reading specialist (or coordinator or supervisor), this would be a helpful text. It covers all aspects of educational leadership, and has a comprehensive section on supervision.

NOTES

1. Holonomy: Defined by Costa and Garmston (1994) as individuals acting autonomously while simultaneously acting interdependently (p. 3). For a more detailed discussion of holonomy, see Costa and Garmston's (1994) Chapter 7: Achieving Holonomy, p. 129.

CHAPTER ELEVEN

PLANNING AND PROVIDING PROFESSIONAL DEVELOPMENT

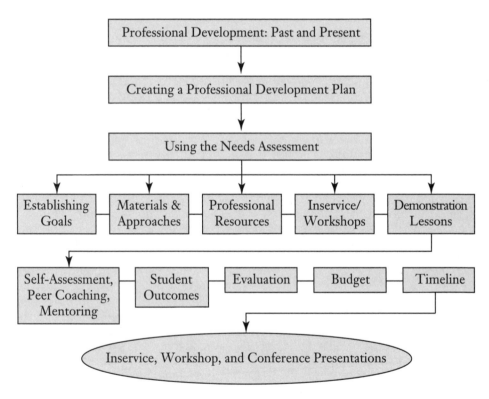

FIGURE 11.1 Chapter Overview

LEARNING GOALS

After reading, discussing, and engaging in activities related to this chapter, you will be able to:

1. design a professional development plan for your school or district based on a needs assessment;

2. as a part of the professional development plan, create and deliver a literacy inservice or workshop for teachers;

3. evaluate the effectiveness of the literacy inservice or workshop for teachers within the context of the professional development plan;

4. explain how the professional development of teachers exists within a social constructivist perspective;

5. Personal Learning Goal: In a three-minute brainstorming session, share what you know about professional development. Write a goal or a question that reflects something you want to learn as we explore these topics. Share this with others in your group.

Vignette

As Norma Chen pulled her SUV up to Emerson Elementary School, her eyes scanned the full parking lot, searching for a place to park. In front of the school, parents in their cars were already lining up to pick their children up after the final bell rang, and there were no parking places anywhere near the school. Running late for her inservice, Norma gunned the car and took off down a side street. Nearly a block from the school, she finally found a parking place. She opened the back of the van and removed her rolling cart, large bin of workshop materials, and a flip chart. Surveying the van's floor, she determined she had everything she needed, locked the car, loaded everything on the cart, and walked as quickly as she could to the school.

In the office, there was the usual end-of-the-day bedlam. Several parents were lined up at the front desk, the two secretaries were on the telephone, and Norma spotted the principal through her open office door, also talking on the phone while looking at her watch and sorting through papers on her desk. A teacher pushed by Norma and the waiting parents, holding the hand of a first grader with a bloody nose. As Norma stepped out of the way, the bell rang and several hundred children poured out of their classroom doors, into the hallway, and out of the school's front door.

Anxiously, Norma tried to get the attention of Mrs. Waters, the principal's secretary. "Hello! I'm Norma Chen and I'm here to do the inservice for your primary teachers. Could you please tell me where I'm supposed to be?"

Mrs. Waters picked up the daily bulletin on her desk as she ushered the bleeding child into the nurse's room, and said over her shoulder, "You're in the cafeteria, down the first corridor. Let us know if you need anything."

With that, Mrs. Waters disappeared and Norma was left to find her way to the cafeteria. Luckily, she found the custodian at the end of the hallway, and he directed her to the lunchroom. As Norma walked into the cavernous room, she sighed. No overhead projector was visible, no screen was there, and the cafeteria tables had already been folded up along the wall for the day. Looking at the clock on the wall, she realized that in fifteen minutes, she was to begin a mandatory reading workshop for sixteen primary teachers.

Thinking Points

1. Stop laughing . . . actually, what Norma has experienced to this point is not uncommon. What are the major tensions Norma is experiencing at this point?

2. What's the first thing she should do at this point to get ready for the inservice?
3. What could a reading specialist do to avoid problems of this nature?

Expanding the Vignette: Exploring the Tensions

Norma's worked in schools long enough to know that the custodian and the principal's secretary are her best friends in a time of crisis. So at this point she tracked down the custodian and asked him, very kindly, to please lower some of the cafeteria tables as soon as possible. She headed back to the office to ask assistance in locating an overhead and screen, and returned to the cafeteria to greet the teachers who were arriving with lesson plan books to complete and papers to grade. At this point, she realized that not only did she not have any water for herself but there were no refreshments or other comfort items available for the teachers. She also noticed that the handout that she'd sent to the school for duplication the previous week was nowhere to be seen. Things were not looking good for this inservice.

When the overhead arrived, the tables and benches were in place and the teachers had settled in, the principal hurriedly entered the cafeteria and headed directly toward Norma. She said, "Thanks so much for com-
ing over from District Office, Norma. Sorry that things were such a mess when you came into the school, but you know how that goes. Let's see . . . uh . . . you're doing comprehension today, right? Could you also bring in something about spelling? Our spelling scores are miserable right now and the teachers need help. Oh, and by the way, we found your handout. Sorry . . . it's being duplicated right now and will be here in a few minutes. In the meantime, how would you like me to introduce you? Is there anything you'd like me to say? Do you have everything you need?"

With that, the principal listened to a few facts about Norma's background, introduced her quickly, and left the cafeteria, not to return again. At the end of the two hour inservice, with little said about spelling and marginal involvement from the attending teachers, Norma packed up her things, glanced over the so-so evaluations the teachers completed, and headed for her car. She thought to herself, "I'm not doing this again. Something's gotta change."

Thinking Points

1. What additional tensions have you identified?
2. What do you think Norma could have done to avoid the problems she encountered?
3. Undoubtedly, you've attended many inservices during your teaching career. How would you characterize those that have been successful? How would you describe those that have been a waste of your time? What has made the difference?
4. What do you think should be the purpose of professional development for teachers? How do you think it should be designed?

PROFESSIONAL DEVELOPMENT: THE PAST AND THE PRESENT

We have not only attended a large number of inservices, workshops, and conference presentations, but we've also been on the presenting end for many of them. We've experienced both as participants and presenters those professional development opportunities that have been exciting learning experiences that have changed our thinking, attitudes, and our practice. We've also, both as participants and presenters, experienced the occasional times when we'd just as soon forget that we were ever there.

When education is well funded at the state and federal level, professional development monies are plentiful. In hard times, all too often, one of the first budget items to be slashed is professional development. This is unfortunate because those of us in education need to update our knowledge about current research, methods, approaches, and instructional materials on an ongoing basis if our students are to achieve at high levels. Reports issued by community groups, the government, researchers, and educational bodies all recommend sustained, high quality professional development to bring about educational reform (Sparks & Hirsh, 1997).

Traditionally, professional development, staff development, and inservice (we use the terms interchangeably) have consisted of sporadic presentations by "experts" who fly or drive in from somewhere, for an hour to a full day, to share new ideas, methods, and materials with the hope that the attending teachers and administrators will pick up an idea or two and return to the classroom enthusiastic about implementing them. Dennis Sparks and Stephanie Hirsch (1997) of the National Staff Development Council suggest that these sessions are usually evaluated in terms of a "happiness quotient"; that is, did everyone have a good time and learn something new? These types of sessions, while often enjoyable and informative, are usually aimed at "training teachers" rather than *educating* them, and, for the attending teachers, the main benefit may be the accumulated professional development hours or points that are tied to salary growth. As two people who have done our fair share of these types of inservice sessions, this is a bit hard to admit!

In reality, if we are expecting teachers to adopt new methods and implement new approaches, more needs to change than just a few activities or the purchase of new books. Instead, educating teachers and administrators is about affecting knowledge, attitudes, biases, practices, and, perhaps, even the particular culture that is at the heart of the school. Culture, as used here, refers to what the school is about—the beliefs of the stakeholders in the school and how those beliefs are in turn reflected by what goes on in each classroom everyday.

One of the primary reasons why "drive-in inservice" (analogous to fast food) isn't very effective is because, in a group of thirty teachers, there may be just a handful of people who really are interested in learning about the topic of the day. This is especially true when it is selected by an administrator or someone else who thinks the teachers *need* it, and when the inservice is mandatory to attend. Parker Palmer (1998) likens the transmission model of teaching to an IV bottle: "When we teach by dripping information into their passive forms, students [or teachers] who arrive in the classroom alive and well become passive consumers of knowledge and are dead on departure when they graduate [or leave]" (p. 42). This description of some presenters and teachers we have seen at inservices is not that far off.

Now, don't get us wrong. We strongly believe that effective professional development, including relevant, well-designed and presented inservices and workshops, can have a positive impact on teachers' attitudes and practices as well as on student achievement. And, an effective, one-time inservice can be very important in setting the tone for change. The critical factor is what constitutes a professional development effort, such as an inservice or workshop, and then what occurs after it. Ann Lieberman, a school reformer, argues for a "radical rethinking" of professional development. She suggests that, "What everyone appears to want for students—a wide array of learning opportunities that engage students in experiencing, creating, and solving real problems, using their own experiences, and working with others—is for some reason denied to teachers when they are learners" (cited in Sparks & Hirsch, 1997, p. 591).

By now, you're familiar with what we refer to as social constructivism and a sociocultural perspective. Within this theoretical construct, we believe that students in classrooms are individuals with their own backgrounds, strengths, talents, needs, cultures, and identities, and that teaching and learning exist for these students within particular contexts that must be understood and acknowledged if we are to reach them. In a constructivist classroom, students make sense of their world when their teachers pose relevant problems, encourage student inquiry, structure learning activities around important concepts, value their points of view, and assess their progress so that it is contextualized by the teaching (Brooks & Brooks, 1993; McLaughlin & Vogt, 1996).

Following this line of thought, the implications of social constructivism for professional development are "thus profound and quite direct: constructivist classrooms cannot be created through transmittal forms of staff development. Staff development must model constructivist practices for teachers if those teachers are expected to be convinced of the validity of those practices and to understand them sufficiently well to make them an integrated part of their classroom repertoires" (Sparks & Hirsch, 1997, p. 11). In this model, rather than having "knowledge" dripped in by "experts," teachers and administrators collaborate with each other, with researchers, and with their own students to make sense of teaching and learning within their particular contexts. Indeed, the richest professional development involves teachers as professionals and full stakeholders in determining the curriculum and organization of the school (Garmston, 1997).

A caution is in order at this point and it has to do with the notion of change. As teachers, we have all been affected by swinging pendulums and what seems like the never-ending call for educational reform. Sometimes it feels like we just figure out how to do the latest innovation or use the newest approaches with the most current materials, when along comes another wave that threatens to wash over us and undo everything we've been working to get established. (This happens almost as often at the university level as it does K–12, lest you think we as professors no longer experience this phenomenon.) When it happens, the new initiative is often purchased, mandated, and implemented before any of us understands what it's all about and, more importantly, whether it's appropriate for *our* students in *our* schools in *our* communities. Therefore, we caution that we not advocate change for change's sake or reform for the sake of reform. We implore you, as reading specialists and literacy leaders, to be knowledgeable about the research underpinnings for any new approaches or methods and be fully aware of the implications of the "the latest" for teachers and students before you jump on a bandwagon, pulling your fellow teachers on board. That said, we also urge that, as reading specialists, you lead from behind, nudging, encouraging, facilitating, modeling, and supporting the teachers with whom you work so that they may improve their teaching effectiveness.

In the next section, we recommend how you, as a school or district reading specialist, can use your needs assessment findings (Chapter 2) and your two-year plan (Chapter 3) to facilitate effective, relevant, and responsive professional development related to reading and language arts.

CREATING A PROFESSIONAL DEVELOPMENT PLAN

It may seem odd to you to be introducing a professional development plan after the comprehensive two-year plan is conceived. But remember that the two-year plan represents an overview or conceptual framework that provides a structure for all you do in your school related to reading and language arts. The two-year plan is about your school's (or district's) total literacy program. The professional development plan is about one aspect of that larger framework.

After you have conducted a needs assessment for your school (or district), and you've analyzed the results, no doubt there will be some areas of reading and language arts curriculum and instruction that will need attention. These need to be relayed to your staff, discussed, and reflected on. As a group, the staff will take the list of identified needs that have been culled by the literacy team, and decide on one or two primary foci for professional development for at least the next year. Although this vote represents a democratic process, be prepared for it to be a challenging task; some teachers will undoubtedly lobby strongly for one item while eliminating others. However, let your needs assessment and the other data you've collected guide you in helping the teachers and other stakeholders make the decision. This targeted goal for professional development is the one that you include in the school's (or district's) two-year plan. Consider your district and state reading and language arts standards as you formulate how to state the targeted need.

Using the Needs Assessment as a Guide for Professional Development Planning

After a professional development need has been determined, the literacy team brainstorms and investigates possible resources, instructional materials, speakers and workshop presenters, models of instruction, demonstration lessons, discussion groups, coaching opportunities, and possible student outcomes. This may require some library research (for professional books), looking through publishers' catalogs (also for professional books and resources), and/or a call to your district office and reading supervisor for assistance about locating speakers and instructional materials. At this point, don't focus too much on how things will be paid for, as budgeting takes place later in the planning process.

Goals. Establishing specific goals for the professional development plan is the first important step. We recommend that you not be overly ambitious with your goals. Prioritize what is most essential related to the targeted need and then write three or four goals that can be implemented, measured, and evaluated at the end of the time you allot for the professional development (at least one school year, often more).

Currently Used Instructional Materials and Approaches. If you didn't gather information about what teachers currently use and do during the needs assessment process, you may find it helpful to informally interview your staff about the instructional materials and approaches they're currently using to teach the targeted need.

Professional Resources. An important role of the reading specialist and literacy team is to review, evaluate, and then select a variety of references that can be used by all teachers and administrators (and instructional assistants, if you have them). Whatever the targeted need, there are articles, chapters, books, and instructional videos available to share and discuss it. Not all need to be purchased; use your public and university libraries as well as on-line resources such as the electronic journal *Reading Online* (available through the IRA Web site: www.reading.org). Be certain that you personally read and review any materials carefully that you distribute to others so that you can anticipate questions or concerns. However, don't expect that every teacher or administrator will devour each resource. Instead, you may wish to jigsaw sections of articles or chapters and then plan discussions about them to maximize participation. Provide study guides, graphic organizers, and other advance organizers to aid readers in synthesizing the texts you recommend. Remember that you're building background here—if you want your faculty to understand the approaches and methods you'll be recommending to them, it is very important to establish a research foundation for them, and that may require some assistance for them to be able to comprehend the research articles you provide.

Inservice and Workshops. It's important to remind you at this point that we're not advocating that the reading specialist and literacy team are responsible, all by themselves, for creating and then implementing all aspects of the professional development plan. Rather, it is highly likely that you will need to enlist the support of an expert (or two or three) in your district or from elsewhere to provide inservice workshops for your teachers. For example, you may wish to invite someone you have heard is an excellent presenter on your targeted need. This could be a kick-off activity or follow-up to the reading and discussion of the professional resources. There are also many reading council meetings, state reading conferences, and other inservice opportunities available through school districts, county offices, and state and national professional organizations (such as IRA and your state reading association). What's most important is to plan the inservice(s) around the assessed needs rather than on some new "thing" that everyone's talking about.

As you plan for inservicing teachers, don't forget about your administrators and instructional assistants. They need to be included so that all stakeholders are informed and aware of what you're trying to accomplish. It's also wise to hold at least one parent meeting at which you and the literacy team can discuss your targeted professional development goals, and ways in which parents can help their children become more proficient readers.

Demonstration Lessons.   You may recall that research suggests that "drive-in" inservices are not very effective in promoting changes in teaching when they're one-time events with little or no follow-up support. However, when teachers are assisted in implementing their new learning (just like their students) and instructional approaches are modeled and reinforced, they are more likely to adopt more effective teaching methods. Demonstration lessons in classrooms with "real kids" can provide this kind of support, assistance, and modeling. If we really believe in the methods we're touting, then we should be willing to go into our colleagues' classrooms, and demonstrate with students the techniques we've been talking about. Then again, demonstration lessons may not always go as expected, as you'll see in MaryEllen's Author Connection.

Author Connection: MaryEllen   Not long ago, I was working with a local school district on implementing reciprocal teaching (RT) as an approach to improving the comprehension of struggling 5th and 6th graders. Ten teachers, from several schools in the district, most unfamiliar with RT, volunteered to work with students in the after-school program, and committed to using reciprocal teaching and word study to improve the children's reading proficiency. I introduced reciprocal teaching at two inservice sessions attended by the ten project teachers. In addition, as a group we reviewed publishers' catalogues and ordered some great informational books about mummies, whales, tornadoes, and earthquakes, as well as a variety of narrative texts that we believed the students would enjoy reading at home.

The workshops went well and there was considerable buy-in on the part of the teachers. I began the first inservice, as I always do, with a research overview of comprehension skills and strategies. Then I took the teachers through a variety of texts so they could better understand their own meaning-making processes, provided reciprocal teaching prompt cards (laminated, even!), went through RT with the teachers, and by the end of the second inservice, I felt reasonably secure about turning everyone loose with their own students. Then it happened. One of the teachers said, "You know, I'd sure feel a whole lot more confident about reciprocal teaching if you could demonstrate the process with some kids." Keep in mind, I'd already modeled the process with the teachers, and we had engaged in reciprocal teaching discussions with the whole group and in small groups.

Without missing a beat, I replied, "Well, sure. No problem. I'll be happy to do that." Inside, I was thinking, "What have I just agreed to? Reciprocal teaching requires a degree of trust, and an understanding on the part of the kids of the four RT strategies (Predicting, Questioning, Summarizing, Clarifying). But how can I now tell these teachers I'm unwilling to model what I've been teaching them to do?" Plowing on, I suggested that all I needed was some students—"bring 'em on," I said. We agreed that the next day I would meet with six fifth graders, none of whom I had ever met, so that I could demonstrate to these teachers my expert skills in conducting a reciprocal teaching lesson.

The next day, after school, six intrepid and delightful fifth graders, the ten project teachers, and I all met in one of the teachers' classrooms. The students were polite, very compliant with the teachers' and my requests to put their chairs in a circle and to participate in a little reading and discussion. What I hadn't realized when I boldly stepped into this demonstration lesson was that all of these children were English learners. This was southern California, after all—and why hadn't I thought of that before? "Hmm . . .," I wondered. "How do I teach these students what the reciprocal teaching strategies are, how to use the prompt cards, and then work through a text together, all the while being observed by ten teachers? What was I thinking?" As I glanced up at the group of teachers before me, I realized that the next half hour was going to be a very humbling experience, and as I recall this lesson, I'm still feeling a bit embarrassed.

Group Inquiry Activity

1. If you had been MaryEllen, what would you have done to better prepare for this demonstration lesson?
2. With others in a group, brainstorm steps reading specialists can take to plan demonstration lessons that have a good chance of being successful.
3. What types of lessons are most appropriate for demonstration lessons? What types of lessons might be risky to teach as a demonstration?
4. If you find a demonstration lesson isn't going well, what should a reading specialist do?

Even if you are just going into a classroom and modeling a lesson for one teacher, remember to spend a few minutes getting to know the students. If possible, observe them while working with their teacher during a few periods over several days. Talk to them, read them a story, ask them to tell you about themselves, interact with some of the students on the playground, in the halls, or in the cafeteria. In other words, prepare yourself for the students and prepare them to work with you. You'll find demonstrations that are well planned will be enjoyable and productive, and you'll end up modeling what to do rather than what not to do.

One last comment about demonstration lessons: Depending on how you approach the teacher in whose class you'll be teaching, the lesson may be viewed as either helpful and needed or punitive. That is, some teachers may feel, rightly or not, that they've been singled out because of their poor teaching. Your demonstration lessons will be best received when you treat all teachers with respect, encourage the effective things that you're seeing them do, and then model as best you can how to improve their teaching. We don't think the reading specialist's position is to evaluate teaching as "good" or "bad"; rather, it is to assist teachers in providing the best teaching they can.

Self-Assessment/Peer Coaching/Mentoring. In Chapter 10, we discussed in detail the role of the reading specialist as cognitive coach and mentor. Now it's time to engage in that role. One of the best ways to assist teachers in making changes in their teaching, after you've provided the research foundations, inservice, and demonstration lessons, is to serve as a coach. In this role, you'll be conferencing, observing, and providing helpful feedback to a teacher who is working to implement the new approaches, methods, and materials.

It is important to reserve enough time for preconferencing, establishing an observation focus, reflection and conversation, and self-assessment for the teacher. Supportive, positive comments, encouragement, and constructive suggestions are all appropriate. Keep in mind that some teachers may resist your efforts to provide coaching. If this occurs, talk with the teacher and your principal if necessary. We suggest this with some caution because if your fellow teachers perceive that you are running to the principal with reports about their teaching, your effectiveness as a coach will be greatly diminished. So be discrete and highly professional in all of your interactions with faculty and the administration.

Student Outcomes.   Improved student outcomes, after all, are why we engage in professional development, and it's important throughout the process to keep student performance at the center. Depending on your established focus, you may wish to collect data about how students are acquiring the skills and strategies that are resulting from the teachers' professional development. For example, again using comprehension as the targeted need, you might ask teachers to administer the reading series' theme tests, especially noting student comprehension of the selections. You also may select some focus students in various grade levels and interview them about their strategy use, or create and conduct a strategy use survey. Informal reading inventories (see Chapter 4) and other assessments can also provide data, as well as end-of-year standardized tests. Not all professional development efforts will yield data on student outcomes, but if you can gather them, do so. After all, improving students' learning is what we're trying to effect with better instruction in reading and language arts.

Evaluation.   Your professional development plan must include a means for evaluating its success. Use the goals you established at the beginning of the planning process to guide your evaluation, and determine for each how you will collect and analyze data. For example, you may wish to include a survey of all participants (including teachers, instructional assistants, parents, students), interviews, and a report of student outcomes, if appropriate. On this type of survey, your data may be both quantitative (percentage of responses) and qualitative (written comments). Or you may wish to engage a few teachers in action research in which they collect anecdotal data (such as field notes) about how they have responded to the targeted need. Include a section on recommendations and discuss questions that need answers, such as: Should the established focus of the professional development continue? Have the goals been met? Is continued work necessary to fulfill goals? If so, what professional development efforts are needed to make progress in meeting the goals? Where should we (the school) go from here?

Budget.   Budgeting is never much fun, whether at home or school, but it's obviously very necessary to consider when planning professional development. After you have completed a draft of the professional development plan, list everything that you want to include that costs money—and we mean everything. For example, be sure to include the cost of books; duplication of articles; fees, travel, and expenses of speakers; conference fees, snacks or meals, and miscellaneous expenses.

Obviously, budgeting for professional development must be done in consultation with your site and/or district administrators. You may have a predetermined budget and your job is to allocate expenses wisely and stick to your limited amount of money. Or, you may be asked to prepare a budget with justification for each item. Whichever, a carefully planned and adhered-to budget will result in a more satisfying and effective professional development plan.

Time Line. The final step in creating a professional development plan is to write a time line, similar to what you did for the two-year plan, but with more detail. Keep in mind that, unlike your budget, the time line can be somewhat flexible, based on teacher and student response to your literacy team's efforts. We recommend that you set out the year, month by month, including the activities that teachers and administrators will engage in. Most likely you'll begin with discussions of the materials that are going to be read and shared, followed by inservices, workshops, and/or conferences, the discussion and sharing of information from these, demonstration lessons, and peer coaching opportunities, if relevant. See the professional development plan in Figure 11.2 for an example of a time line, as well as the other components discussed in this section.

ABC Elementary School Professional Development Plan: 2002–2003
Created by Sonia Begonia, Reading Specialist
The Literacy Team: (List Names and Grade Levels or other Affiliation)

Targeted Need: Improving Students' Comprehension
of Narrative and Expository Texts, Grades K–6

Goals of Professional Development
1. Establish a research foundation for, and understandings of the comprehension processes involved in proficient reading.
2. Provide all faculty and instructional assistants with relevant and effective inservice and follow-up support that focuses on instructional methods, materials, and approaches for teaching comprehension skills and strategies.
3. Use Informal Reading Inventories and miscue analysis to assess students' fluency, comprehension, and word recognition.
4. Improve students' comprehension of narrative and expository texts as determined by a variety of formal and informal measures.

Currently Used Instructional Materials and Approaches
As a literacy team, we will survey all faculty about current methods, approaches, and instructional materials used for teaching comprehension. We will interview selected faculty about how they teach comprehension and assess students currently. Our findings will be summarized and then reported at the first weekly staff meeting in October.

FIGURE 11.2 Sample Professional Development Plan

ABC Elementary School Professional Development Plan: 2002–2003 (continued)

Professional Resources

Purchase twelve copies (two for each grade level) of the following books:

Keene, E., & Zimmerman, N. (1997). *Mosaic of Thought: Teaching Comprehension in a Readers' Workshop*. Portsmouth, NH: Heinemann.

Harvey, S., & Goudvis, A. (2000). *Strategies That Work: Teaching Comprehension to Enhance Understanding*. York, ME: Stenhouse.

Purchase three copies (one for grades 3–6) of the following book:

McLaughlin, M., & Allen, M. B. (2002) book titled *Guided Comprehension: A Teaching Model for Grades 3–8*. Newark, DE: International Reading Association.

Purchase one copy for each faculty member:

Johns, J. J. (1997). *Basic reading inventory*. Dubuque, IA: Kendall/Hunt.

Duplicate and have ready for check-out ten copies of the article (note IRA policy regarding duplication for one-time use):

Suggested Activities for Professional Resources:

- During a school faculty meeting, review the Needs Assessment data related to comprehension instruction.
- Book-talk the new books your Literacy Team has selected.
- Invite staff members (including administrators and instructional assistants) to form grade-level discussion and study groups for the two professional books *Mosaic of Thought* and *Strategies That Work*. Start with *Mosaic of Thought*, a book that should be read chapter-by-chapter. Follow up with *Strategies That Work*, a resource with comprehension lessons.
- Offer an inservice on how to administer Informal Reading Inventories; include opportunities for teachers to analyze results; provide time for grade-level meetings to use finding to plan effective comprehension instruction.

Inservices and Workshops:

- Offer an inservice on comprehension skills and strategies, to establish a foundation of current research.
- Offer at least one workshop (with district reading specialist) on how to administer and analyze results from an Informal Reading Inventory.
- Offer one (or more) on how to use IRI's to assess comprehension, fluency, and word recognition.
- Survey faculty to see what additional inservice might be needed.
- Encourage and coordinate attendance at professional reading conferences, as budget will allow.
- Encourage teachers who have been implementing reciprocal teaching to share with other teachers during after-school workshop.

Demonstration Lessons:

- Offer and then schedule demonstration lessons on the following topics:
  - Administering an IRI
  - Teaching comprehension skills (e.g., main idea, cause/effect, drawing conclusions, etc.)
  - Comprehension strategies with DRTA's for narrative text and SQP2RS* for information/ expository text

*SQP2RS: An instructional framework for teaching comprehension strategies: Survey text; Generate questions; Make predictions of what will be learned; Read the text; Respond to the text, the questions, and predictions; Summarize key concepts. See Vogt, 2000 for more information about SQP2RS.

- Reciprocal teaching lessons
- Others, as requested

Self-Assessment/Peer Coaching/Mentoring

- Discuss possibility of videotaped comprehension lessons as opportunities for reflective self-assessment. Determine if anyone is interested in forming discussion groups to analyze and reflect on teaching effectiveness of comprehension lessons.
- Determine if any teachers are interested in or willing to establish peer coaching partners. If so, discuss how these might be organized and implemented.
- Establish mentors/coaches for teachers in years 1–3 of teaching.

Student Outcomes:

- Improvement in comprehension as measured by pre-post IRI passages, word recognition, and miscue analyses.
- Improvement in comprehension as measured by pre-post standardized test scores.
- Increase in number of students who are able to read grade-level texts.

Evaluation:

- Measures (IRI results) for evaluating comprehension growth in selected (from high, average, and low-performing) students for each grade level.
- Standardized test scores in comprehension for all students.
- Satisfaction measures (surveys, interviews) of teachers at end of first and second years.
- Evaluations collected at the end of all inservice workshops.
- Comparison of pre-post reading logs of students in grades 2–6.

Estimated Budget:

Professional resources for teachers and administrators (books)	$ 800.00
Duplicating of journal article	30.00
Materials for inservice	170.00
Honoraria for speakers	1500.00
Conference registrations	500.00
Total	$3000.00
Each year's budget (year's one and two)	$1500.00

Tentative Time Line:

Year One

September–October:

Distribute copies of *Mosaic of Thought* to grade-level teams. Organize study groups, determine a schedule, and begin reading the book. Be sure all members of literacy team are in the study group. Schedule afternoon inservice on how to administer the Informal Reading Inventory (IRI).

November–December:

Schedule demonstration for teachers wishing to see the administration of an IRI.
Schedule study groups for teachers wishing to discuss results and implications of IRI's they have administered.
Mosaic of Thought Study Group: Finish reading the book. At staff meeting, as a group, share main ideas and concepts from the book.
Literacy team: Offer an after-school inservice on comprehension strategies. Share copies of Dole, et al. article on effects of strategy instruction.

ABC Elementary School Professional Development Plan: 2002–2003   (continued)

January–February:
Schedule demonstration lessons on strategy instruction for any interested teachers.
Study group: Introduce *Strategies That Work*. Share ideas teachers have tried.
Model DRTA process for literacy team; encourage them to use it and discuss its effectiveness.
Schedule demonstration lessons on DRTA, using narrative text.

March–April:
Finish reading *Strategies That Work*. Share ideas teachers have tried. Discuss how the comprehension strategy instruction is working.
Schedule classroom observations for interested teachers.
Establish peer-coaching for observations. Offer to take classes of those who will be coaching.
Schedule school-wide (required) inservice for all teachers and administrators. Invite district reading specialist to assist literacy team in planning and implementing.

May–June:
Provide demonstration lessons on SQP2RS (for expository/information texts) for interested teachers.
Offer to cover classes so peer coaches can observe each other using SQP2RS.
During staff meeting, have teachers complete evaluation of the year's efforts in improving comprehension instruction.
When standardized scores become available spot-check them to see if there are any changes in comprehension scores.
Provide assistance in administering post-IRI's on selected students at each grade level (high achieving, average, and low-achieving). Look for areas of growth.
Administer a needs assessment related to comprehension for the following year.

Year Two
Fall Semester:
Form study groups to read McLaughlin & Allen's *Guided Comprehension: A Teaching Model for Grades 3–8*. Share the model and instructional activities with staff during faculty meeting.
Provide demonstration lessons on various activities. Implement peer coaching as necessary.
Review and revisit DRTA and SQP2RS.
Schedule conferences as needed.
Involve literacy team in plan 1–2 afternoon inservices (as needed) on activities and strategies from McLaughlin & Allen's book.
Target new teachers and those new to the school. Provide them with demonstration lessons, inservice, copies of the books read the previous year.

Spring Semester:
Assess overall comprehension plan at this point.
1. What is working well? How do we know?
2. What still needs further work? How do we know?
3. Which teachers are consistently and effectively teaching comprehension skills and strategies? How are their students performing?
Assess all students with IRI's, if time allows. If not, focus on struggling readers.
Compare IRI results with standardized test scores. Look for trends and any changes.
With literacy team, complete final evaluations of comprehension professional development plan.
With literacy team, conduct and evaluate results of new needs assessments.
With literacy team, establish a new two-year plan for professional development.

Group Inquiry Activity   Work with other group members and discuss the following questions:

1. As you were reading the professional development plan in Figure 11.2, did you think of any aspects that are absent? Are there any that are unrealistic? If so, what are they? What would you recommend be changed to make it more realistic for your present teaching context?
2. What is the relationship of the professional development plan (see Appendix F) to the two-year plan? Why is it necessary to create both? Which elements of the professional development plan should be included in a two-year plan? Why did you choose these?

PLANNING AND DELIVERING INSERVICES, WORKSHOPS, AND CONFERENCE PRESENTATIONS

It is beyond the scope of this book to write in detail about how to be a great public speaker. For that we encourage you to read the recommended readings listed at the end of this chapter, and if you've had no experience with speaking before an audience (other than your students), you might find it helpful to take a public speaking course or join your local Toastmasters Club. You probably have heard that statistic about how people are more frightened of public speaking than they are of most everything else. If you're in this category, help is available, so seek it out.

We both have had considerable experience in providing inservices, workshops, conference sessions, and other presentations related to various aspects of reading and language arts, yet we still get the jitters before we "go on" and there are inevitable problems that pop up, no matter how well prepared we are. Therefore, we'd like to offer some generic suggestions in this section, as well as some hints for success we've gleaned from our own experiences. In order to structure this information for you, we'll begin at the beginning of any workshop or other presentation you might provide for teachers.

From Taking the Request to Signing a Contract

As a new school or district reading specialist, most likely your first inservices and workshop sessions will be with the teachers at your own school or at a school in your district. You may know and work with some or all of the teachers who attend. This can be both positive and negative; you know the teachers so this is not a group of strangers, but it's usually a bit more difficult to present before your peers. Likewise, though you're presenting to a home crowd that should be friendly and supportive, there is some truth in the "prophet in his or her own land" phenomenon. For some reason, we all seem to take more seriously what the "experts" from the outside say rather than what our own peers and colleagues tell us. Don't let either of these throw you—if you're well prepared and have something of value to share that is relevant to the audience, and you present it in a credible, professional way, you'll be fine, even if you know every person in the room.

If the inservice is part of your school's professional development plan, then it is likely that you were involved in planning the topic, location, purpose of the meeting, audience, and so forth. A formal contract may not be necessary, but it's always good to get in writing exactly what is expected of you and of the teachers who will attend.

Group Inquiry Activity   As a group, think of an inservice you might provide for each of your schools. Brainstorm possibilities for flyers that you could use to promote the event. Sketch out some ideas and then share with others in your class. What appealing phrases or clip art could you include? Remember that you want to attract male teachers (or secondary), so go easy on things "cute"!

As a novice inservice provider, one of the most difficult things you'll do is negotiate a fee for the workshop. Once you gain some experience in your own school and district, you may find that people outside your community approach you about providing inservices for their teachers. If you're like we were, you'll be so happy that someone actually wants you to come to provide professional development that you'll almost be willing to provide your work for nothing! However, part of being a professional educator and a reading specialist is to determine (1) if it's ethical and legitimate for you to charge a fee; and (2) what that fee should be. You may have an obligation as part of your job to provide inservices to all the schools in your district. If so, then clearly you may not charge a fee or honorarium because you'll already be paid for the work you do. However, if this inservice is *on your own time* (and you'll not be paid by your own school district for the time you'll be working with the teachers), then it's perfectly ethical and appropriate for you to charge for your preparation and presentation time.

Obviously, we cannot suggest fees or rates for you, but we can recommend that you talk about fees with other people in your area who provide professional development in education. Keep in mind that your fee schedule will vary from others, depending on your experience in presenting, your educational level (credential, master's, or doctorate), and your willingness to plan lengthy (all-day or multiple-day) professional development in places some distance from where you live. Therefore, we recommend that you establish a fair fee schedule commensurate with your abilities, experience, and education, and then offer it when you are invited to make presentations. You may need to negotiate, but at least you'll present a professional and aboveboard appearance as a professional developer when you have established criteria for what your services are worth.

For those times when you are providing professional development as an independent contractor (not as an employee of your school district), you must secure a written contract from the school or district with which you're entering an agreement. This is not only for your protection (and the district's), but also for the Internal Revenue Service.

Planning and Organization of the Inservice

Reflect back on the relevant inservices and workshops you've attended that had a real impact on you and your teaching. Think about the opening, the organization, the speaker's skill at making transitions from one activity to the next, your engagement, your participation, and your collaborative work with others around you. These reflections will help you plan effective inservice opportunities for other teachers. While you plan and organize, we encourage you to consider each of the following:

1. *Prepare your opening:* Include the name of the school or district (even if it's your own) and, if possible, some anecdote about it. Make it personal. Thank those who have invited you and acknowledge any special assistance that you received from specific individuals.

2. *State your goals:* Clearly state your objectives and what you hope the teachers will take away from the inservice.

3. *Include an agenda:* We recommend that you provide a tentative agenda that is general or give one orally. For an example of an agenda that allows flexibility, see Figure 11.3.

ABC Elementary School
Inservice Day
February 18, 2002

Sponsored by your Literacy Team
Presented by Sonia Begonia, District Reading Specialist

8:30–8:45	Registration and Coffee
8:45–9:00	Welcome, Introduction, and Plans for the Day
9:00–10:30	Administering an Informal Reading Inventory
10:30–10:45	Break
10:45–12:00	Analyzing the Results of Informal Reading Inventories
12:00–1:00	Lunch
12:45–1:45	Using Results for Planning Instruction
1:45–2:00	Break
2:00–3:00	Implications for Teaching Vocabulary and Comprehension
3:00–3:30	Sharing Ideas, Wrap-Up, and Evaluation

FIGURE 11.3   Sample Inservice Agenda

Notice how this agenda lets participants know when the important things are going to happen (like breaks and lunch), but the topics allow the presenter to change plans as needed. When you reconvene after a break, briefly summarize what you've discussed in the previous session so that you can bridge to what is coming. Robert Garmston (1997) suggests that the first break after lunch (during an all-day inservice) should come no later than one hour after you all reconvene. We agree because the hour after lunch is the most difficult time to engage an audience, due to sleepiness, full stomachs, and a general letdown.

4. *Humor:* If there's one thing that's important to plan, it's humor. Now, you don't have to be a stand-up comedian to inject humor in your presentation. Cartoons, jokes (not shady or questionable), poems and stories about teachers' lives in the classroom, and anecdotes about your own teaching experiences (if funny) all can be used to generate smiles and laughs. Plan for humor and then also enjoy the moments when it occurs spontaneously. Practice telling jokes before friends and your family—jokes that fall flat don't count as "humor"!

5. *Content:* Do you remember teaching your first lesson when you were student teaching? Remember your first year? If so, you also probably remember planning way too much for what can reasonably be accomplished in an hour, half-day, or a school day. The same thing will happen as you begin to plan for inservices—it's almost guaranteed. As with children, it's best to overplan, but be prepared to let things go and not do all you've planned. Instead, include what's crucial; then have other activities ready to go if you have a quiet group or teachers who are knowledgeable about the topic and can move more quickly.

One other comment about the content of your inservice. Learn about your teachers and what they know about the topic you're presenting. It's important (always) to provide a brief research background for what you're sharing, but the operative word here is *brief.* Though most teachers are interested in hearing a little about research, all are eager to learn new instructional approaches and methods they can use "tomorrow," so be sure to include several practical ideas in your presentation.

6. *Activities:* Remember that many of the instructional techniques that work with students also work with adults, and you can scaffold their learning by building background, activating and reinforcing what they already know and do, reviewing what you've covered periodically throughout the day, and being very attentive to questions, puzzled faces, and the "aha's!" that you see. As in your classroom, vary the approaches and activities you use, and don't expect teachers to sit much more quietly than your kids!

Throughout the inservice, watch your audience carefully for signs of discontent and boredom, and, if necessary, stop talking and turn off or cover the overhead or LCD projector. Be honest about telling the teachers that you're sensing there's a problem, elicit what it is, and then respond to it accordingly, honestly and helpfully. Sometimes the problem has nothing to do with your presentation, but rather with something that's happened during a break or previously, even the day before. At other times, what you're saying may be "politically incorrect," contrary to district edicts. So it's always wise to check out what's going on, and then respond immediately to the concern, whether or not you can do anything about ameliorating it. Also remember that we all learn better by "participating and doing" than by "being told." Model the strategies you're teaching and take the audience through the various techniques as learners so that, when they try the activities in their own classrooms, they can feel successful.

7. *Conclusion, wrap-up, and evaluation:* Plan the ending of your inservice as carefully as you've planned the rest of it. A summary of your main points is always helpful, along with a story, joke, or poem that connects with your specific audience. Leave time for questions, especially if you didn't give participants time to ask questions throughout the presentation (our preference). In your conclusion, give the teachers something they'll remember, and conclude on a positive note, reinforcing how important the job is that they are doing everyday. Leave a few minutes at the end for everyone to complete an evaluation that you've created especially for the occasion. It's better that this is just not a "happiness survey" but something that will help you become a better presenter and that will enable you to plan for subsequent times when you may work with this group of teachers. See Figure 11.4 for a sample evaluation form for the inservice on how to administer and analyze results from an informal reading inventory.

Creating the Handout and Visual Aids

We're lucky today to have available to us computers, software, and easily accessible clip art that can help us create highly professional handouts and transparencies, as well as PowerPoint presentations. The following guidelines will, when used, provide for visual aids that greatly enhance and support the content you're presenting.

Handouts

1. Remember that we teachers like to have detailed handouts that include the most important information that's presented during an inservice. It's frustrating to take notes so fast and furiously that key points are missed. However, it's also unnecessary to have fifteen-page handouts. Outlines on which participants can fill in supporting information, PowerPoint handouts that replicate many of the slides shown, graphic organizers, numbered and/or bulleted key points, and brief summaries of how to use the instructional activities that are modeled, are all very helpful. Keep the text succinct, with easy-to-follow headings and subheadings. Organize the information in the order you present it.

2. Reproduce clean, clear copies of handouts. When things have been photocopied repeatedly, they look old and tired, and quite unprofessional. Number all pages, and include only typed materials—nothing handwritten.

3. In your handouts, include only original materials that you have created. *Never* reproduce another person's handout pages. This is unacceptable and it is considered plagiarism (unless permission is given). Also, *never* reproduce any material that is copyrighted unless permission is given—this is illegal. You can certainly use ideas, approaches, and methods that others have created if you cite the source, even if you don't copy it exactly or quote it directly. If it's someone else's idea, then give him or her

ABC Elementary School
Inservice Day, February 18, 2002
Presented by Sonia Begonia, District Reading Specialist

Inservice Evaluation

Please respond to each of the following statements by circling the number that best represents your feelings. Use the following scale.

Strongly Agree	Agree	No Opinion	Disagree	Strongly
1	2	3	4	Disagree
				5

1. This inservice met my expectations for the day.
   1   2   3   4   5

2. I feel confident about how to administer an Informal Reading Inventory.
   1   2   3   4   5

3. I feel confident about how to analyze the results of an IRI.
   1   2   3   4   5

4. I feel I can begin to match IRI results to my comprehension instruction.
   1   2   3   4   5

5. It would be helpful to meet with my grade level colleagues to do additional planning with the results of our students' IRI's.
   1   2   3   4   5

6. The pacing of today's inservice was appropriate.
   1   2   3   4   5

7. The activities we participated in today were helpful.
   1   2   3   4   5

8. The handout will help me remember and implement today's key points.
   1   2   3   4   5

9. One idea I will remember and implement from today's inservice is:

10. One concept or idea that is still unclear to me is:

11. I would like more assistance in learning how to:

12. Overall I would rate this inservice as:

Very Helpful	Helpful	Somewhat Helpful	Okay	Not Helpful
1	2	3	4	5

FIGURE 11.4   Sample Inservice Evaluation

credit for it. Also, always include a reference list at the end of the handout for any sources you've cited. It's a good idea to put your name on every page of your handout as a footer.

4. In your handouts, keep "cute-zi-ness" to a minimum. Teddy bears, butterflies, and bunnies may be appropriate for first graders, but they're not so cute for adults. We know that some primary teachers reading this may be gnashing their teeth at this recommendation, but other teachers will know exactly what we mean. There's nothing wrong with using appealing and engaging clip art illustrations of children, teachers, classrooms, books, schoolhouses, families, and so forth—let's just resist inserting things that are expressly feminine or overly cute.

5. Add a title page with your name, E-mail address, and/or phone number. With current technology, it's very easy to also include the name of the event, location, and date.

Visual Aids. Again, technology is enabling us all to have professional, engaging, and supportive visual aids for our presentations. The following suggestions will make them very effective.

1. Whether you use transparencies or PowerPoint, the fonts you use and the size of type are very important. Stick to standard, easily readable fonts (Times Roman or Ariel) for the text. Headlines work well with either of these, but you also may wish to use a bold Tehoma or even Kristin ITC for a little variety. However, avoid using several fonts in your visuals and handouts (often referred to as the "ransom note" approach). Just because they're available on your computer doesn't mean you need to use them.

2. For texts that will be projected, use 36–44 point type for the headlines and no smaller than 28 point type for the body of the text. Try to keep the ideas you're presenting on each slide to a minimum—three or four main ideas are plenty on one slide. In PowerPoint, you can display each idea one at a time through customized animation. The "cute-zi-ness" admonition also applies here. Use clip art, photos, cartoons, and so forth to enhance the slides, and try to establish a theme with them (such as children, books, content areas, classroom scenes, teachers, etc.). Be careful about including too many that are too big or distracting—remember that their purpose is to enhance and support the points you're making, not serve as the central focus.

3. Practice presenting with an overhead or LCD projector so that you're not walking or standing in front of the projected image. Watch your shoulder and hands—keep the space in front of the light free. Some presenters like to use pointers or other aids to refer to particular points. Darken or cover the projector if you are going to be talking for a lengthy period without changing the slide or transparency.

4. Organize transparencies in folders or binders according to the presentations you give. Using transparency covers protects the transparencies and lengthens their lives, though the covers need to be changed frequently because they get scratched. Power-Point presentations are easy to organize in a file and you can modify them quickly by "hiding" slides you don't wish to use for a particular presentation. If you are using PowerPoint, give yourself extra time for setup so that you have everything ready and running by the start time for the presentation. Watching a speaker fumble with cords, projectors, and the computer while mumbling things like, "Technology is only good if it works. . . ," does little to establish credibility and professionalism.

5. Seek permissions for any cartoons you reproduce and project, as well as book covers and contents. If the clip art you use is in the public domain (such as that available on Microsoft Word), you may use it without seeking permission or citing its source.

The Day of the Inservice

This section should actually be titled "the day before the inservice" because that's when many final details are completed and confirmed. If you're responsible for providing the refreshments (a must for any professional development event), confirm that they'll be delivered on time to the right place, or make sure you have everything ready to take with you. Load up your car the day before the event with nonperishable food, napkins and plates, snacks, and all other supplies (pencils, markers, post-its, etc.). In other words, everything should be ready at least twenty-four hours in advance. Call the school and/or district to confirm the time and place, and ask when the building will be open if the inservice is to be in the early morning. Ask about parking availability, parking passes, and where you may park to unload your car.

Also, be sure your handouts have been duplicated if they're to be provided by the district. (A hint: If the school or district is doing the duplicating, have the handout to the school, with your name, date and time of presentation, and contact number or E-mail, at least ten days before your presentation. Confirm that the handouts are ready two to three days prior to your presentation.) If you're printing the handouts yourself, give yourself (and the copy shop) plenty of time to do the photocopying.

Plan to arrive at the school or other location about an hour prior to the start of the inservice, earlier if you have considerable setup to do. Remember to check in at the office, letting the secretary and principal know you're there, and ask for help from the custodian if you need it. Many times, even though you've requested a particular room setup, it won't be right for you. Be prepared for tables that need to be moved, chairs that need to be wiped off or put in place, a microphone that needs to be found, an overhead that doesn't work properly (this is almost standard fare!), and/or the room is too cold, too hot, or poorly lit. Just be ready for anything, and be sure to bring a comfortable pair of shoes for the setup. After you have everything ready, walk around the room and check sight lines and sound from all four corners, making changes as necessary. Then . . . sit down and relax a few minutes, have a cup of coffee, review your notes, and make sure your presentation is ready to go. It's important to have this reflective time prior to the arrival of the teachers.

A Few More Hints for Success

Based on our experiences, we have a few more suggestions that may help you present a successful inservice.

1. Watch your time carefully. Don't try to cram everything into the last half-hour of the inservice if you get off-schedule. Speaking so fast that no one understands you and slamming one transparency after another onto the overhead (or flying through Power-Point slides) only results in frustration, for you and your audience. As the session is winding down, mentally decide what to omit and then relax and enjoy the conclusion. This management of content takes planning and practice. With experience, you'll learn how much you can include in a one-hour, two-hour, three-hour, or all-day inservice.

2. You'll find in every audience three to four teachers who are with you every step of the way. You can tell by their reactions because they're nodding, smiling, engaged, and participating. While it's important to watch for those who are looking bored and uninterested and try to enlist their participation, it's those who are engaged throughout the inservice who let you know that they've valued your time together. If you have the opportunity to thank them for their participation, do so—they'll appreciate that you noticed.

3. Last, be gentle with yourself. Even the most experienced and gifted speakers have "those days" when nothing seems to go right. Also, as you read your evaluations, even if you have 95 percent positive responses, you'll tend to dwell on the few negative comments that we all have received. If you can, read those first and learn from the remarks, if they're relevant. Then, focus on the positive comments you receive because these, most likely, will be the ones that will help you improve your presentations skills the most.

REVISITING THE VIGNETTE

Not long after her experience at Emerson Elementary School, the district reading specialist, Norma Chen, was asked to provide another inservice at another elementary school. This time, Norma was ready. She made sure of the following: (1) She was in close contact with the school's principal about the presentation; (2) She arranged in advance for refreshments for the teachers; (3) She coordinated with the school secretary what she needed for the session; (4) She made sure her handout had been received and duplicated prior to her workshop; (5) She clarified with the reading specialist and lead teachers some expectations for the inservice; (6) She sent an informal, simple (ten items on a Likert scale) survey for teachers to complete two weeks prior to the inservice, and she used the findings to plan the workshop; (7) She had all workshop materials prepared, gathered together, and loaded into her car the day before the workshop; (8) and she arrived a little over an hour prior to the start of the inservice. She was relaxed, confident, and ready to meet the attending teachers.

POINTS TO REMEMBER

In the past, professional development for teachers consisted primarily of unrelated inservice sessions that were selected by teachers based on their availability and interest.

There was little coherence within a school, and professional development opportunities often had little or nothing to do with the assessed needs of the teachers or their students. Today, professional development is considered to be part of a school's two-year plan for improving and sustaining effective literacy instruction. Based on a comprehensive needs assessment, a professional development plan includes not only inservices and workshops, but also research, texts, discussion groups, demonstration lessons, mentoring, and coaching. Designing inservice sessions, conducting workshops and demonstration lessons, and evaluating the effectiveness of professional development efforts represent a major responsibility of the reading specialist at both the school and district level.

PORTFOLIO PROJECTS

1. Based on the needs assessment findings for your school, design a professional development plan based on the model presented in this text. Share it with your principal or other administrator.

2. Design, deliver, and evaluate the effectiveness of a one-hour inservice or workshop related to a need identified in your two-year plan. Either give the inservice for others in your group of reading specialist candidates, or give it for teachers in your school. Reflect on how everything went and suggest changes or additions for a future workshop on the same topic.

3. Plan and provide a demonstration lesson on a literacy topic for a teacher in your school. After you have finished the lesson, reflect on it with the teacher, both in terms of how he or she might use what you presented in his or her teaching, but also what you could do next time to make the lesson more effective. Also, solicit and include in your written reflections suggestions or a critique from the teacher.

RECOMMENDED READINGS

Garmston, R. (1997). *The presenter's fieldbook: A practical guide.* Norwood, MA: Christopher-Gordon. This is a wonderful resource, one that we heartily recommend. It includes all the nuts and bolts about becoming an effective presenter in the field of education.

Robb, L. (2000). *Redefining staff development: A collaborative model for teachers and administrators.* Portsmouth, NH: Heinemann, National Staff Development Council. This professional organization's Web site includes a variety of resources related to planning and implementing programs of professional development: www.nsdc.org/educatorindex.htm.

PART IV

THE READING SPECIALIST: PROFESSIONALISM AND ADVOCACY

CHAPTER TWELVE

WORKING WITH FAMILIES AND ADULT LITERACY

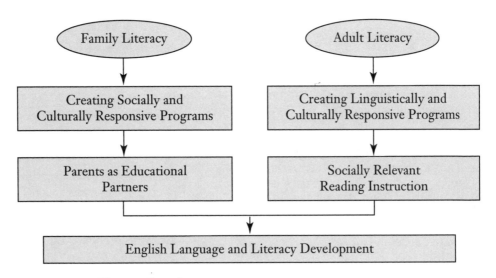

FIGURE 12.1   Chapter Overview

LEARNING GOALS

After reading, discussing, and engaging in activities related to this chapter, you will be able to:

1. discuss family literacy and its relationship to reading development in children;
2. describe components of effective family literacy programs;
3. locate resources and information about adult literacy programs;
4. compare models of adult literacy programs;
5. examine national data related to adult literacy in the United States.

Vignette

During the past year, Anne Law opened a private reading center in her community in a small, coastal community in the northeast. To establish a student clientele, she developed a relationship with the elementary schools in her local school district so that teachers in those schools could refer students with reading problems. Because she had young preschool twins, she left her full-time teaching job but wanted to continue working as a reading specialist. Therefore, she decided to devote herself half-time to her new venture, the reading center.

Early in the fall semester, Jorene Metzger sent Sarah, her ten-year-old daughter, to Anne for weekly reading instruction and tutoring. Jorene was upset because her fourth-grade child was reading at the second-grade level. Jorene was convinced that Sarah "had dyslexia" and that the school was not addressing the problem. So Jorene had Sarah tested at the local university, hoping to support her hypothesis. However, Jorene was disappointed when the university reported that Sarah's reading difficulties were mild. Next, she insisted that Sarah be tested to see if she could receive special education services in her school. As a result of the assessment, Sarah had been attending daily pull-out resource assistance in reading for nearly a year when she began working with Anne. When Jorene enrolled Sarah in Anne's reading center, her instructions were that she wanted her daughter's problems "fixed as soon as possible."

On taking an initial parent information survey, Anne discovered the following:

- *Sarah had an older brother in the sixth grade who, according to Jorene, was a "perfect student." He always received straight A's, had won a science fair prize in the previous year, and excelled at sports. In conversation with Anne, Jorene wondered in frustrated tones why Sarah couldn't be more like her brother.*
- *When Sarah wouldn't attempt her homework, her father routinely sat with her and completed the assignments for her.*
- *Jorene stated they had "done everything for Sarah." She expressed the belief that at least Sarah, the fourth grader, could reciprocate by "doing well in school."*
- *Jorene reported, somewhat reluctantly, that, while Sarah's father had completed two years in community college, she had dropped out of school at age fourteen.*

Thinking Points

1. What are several tensions that exist in this vignette?
2. What other information does Anne need to collect that will assist in her planning for Sarah?
3. What is the first step Anne should take? (Keep in mind that Jorene and her husband are now paying for Anne's expertise and services.)

Expanding the Vignette: Exploring the Tensions

While in her MA program, Anne learned about a variety of assessment instruments that provide important data that can guide the development of an instructional plan. Therefore, after an initial interview with Jorene and a brief discussion with Sarah's teacher (an ob-

servation of Sarah's classroom was deemed inadvisable at this point), Anne met with Sarah for the first time. During this session, she administered several assessments and talked to Sarah about her attitudes toward reading and writing. Together they established some short-term and long-term goals for their work together.

During the following session, Anne further assessed Sarah's reading, writing, and spelling. She also introduced a chapter book the two could read together, and began reading aloud the first chapter. At the conclusion of this session, Anne felt that trust had been established between herself and Sarah, and that they would work well together.

While she was pleased with her initial work with Sarah, Anne found she had been thinking a great deal about Jorene, Sarah's mother. In their initial interview, Jorene had expressed how fearful she was that Sarah would "end up like me . . . a pregnant teenager who dropped out of school . . . and who can't read." Anne knew how to proceed with Sarah in order to help her become a better reader—but she was also wondering if she couldn't assist Jorene in attaining some of her goals. However, she questioned whether this was even her business. Should she just leave well enough alone and focus all her efforts only on Sarah? Or was there anything she could—or should—do to help Jorene?

FAMILY LITERACY

In his classic text on the reading process, Huey (1908/1968) stated that, "It all begins with parents reading to children" (p. 103). Reading educators generally agree that parents may be the most important teachers that children will have—they're certainly the teachers that children will have for the longest period of time. However, as mentioned elsewhere in this book, Heath (1983) and others have found that the literacies that children engage in at home are not always harmonious with the literacies valued by the schools. Do you remember the comparison of Eric Torgerson and Carmen Coballes-Vega in Chapter 2, who as children brought rich but very different literacies to their classrooms? In part, to bridge the divide between home and school literacies, family literacy programs have been designed and implemented in communities across the country.

According to Lesley Mandel Morrow (1995), family literacy does not have a clear definition because it is a relatively complex concept, and there is little agreement about a set of criteria for evaluating effective implementation of family literacy services. In a brochure on the subject, the International Reading Association's Family Literacy Commission has this to say:

> Family literacy encompasses the ways parents, children, and extended family members use literacy at home and in their community. Sometimes, family literacy occurs naturally during the routines of daily living and helps adults and children 'get things done.' These events might include using drawings or writings to share ideas; composing notes or letters to communicate messages, making lists; reading and following directions; or sharing stories and ideas through conversation, reading, and writing. Family literacy may be initiated purposefully by a parent or may occur spontaneously as parents and children go about the business of their daily lives. Family literacy activities may also reflect the ethnic, racial, or cultural heritage of the families involved (Morrow, 1995, p. 8).

Educators increasingly have become convinced that family literacy programs can help parents support the literacy acquisition of their children. However, parents who lack schooling themselves, or whose primary language is other than English, may feel unqualified or inadequate to provide at home what children need to achieve in school. Homework assignments may be confusing, work schedules may prevent parents from being home when their children are out of school, or home cultures may dictate that academic education is the responsibility of the school, not the family. For these parents or caregivers, family literacy programs may serve as an important link to the school.

The Adult Education and Family Literacy Act, Title II of the Workforce Investment Act of 1998, suggests that family literacy programs integrate: (1) interactive literacy activities between parent and child; (2) training in parenting activities; (3) literacy training that leads to economic self-sufficiency; and (4) age-appropriate education to prepare children for success in school and life experiences. These family literacy programs generally work with both individuals and the family as a unit. Participants include parents, children, single parents, and other close family members. Federal programs within the U.S. Department of Education include the Even Start Family Literacy Program and Title I of the Improving America's School Act. Other participants may be found in Head Start programs under the U.S. Department of Health and Human Services, or in programs managed by various community organizations.

Many family literacy programs assist parents in improving their own literacy at the same time they're learning how to help their children be successful in school. Three programs that have become popular models are the Kenan Trust Family Literacy Project, the Missouri Parents as Teachers Program, and Parents as Partners in Reading. These three programs include common elements found in accepted family literacy services (Wagner, 1997, p. 11):

- assistance for parents beginning with their children's infancy;
- language play and interactive play as precursors to emergent literacy;
- books, print materials, and lessons appropriate to the literacy levels of family members;
- medical, social, and educational services that go beyond literacy learning activities;
- The development of feelings of self-efficacy in children and parents through success in literacy and *collaboration* (our emphasis) with others.

Collaboration here is the key. Rather than viewing the home as a "deficit environment," effective family literacy programs engage the parents as partners in the process of educating children. Considering these programs through the lens of "transmission," which defines the school or other community agency's role as transmitting how to be an effective parent misses the point. Rather, engaging parents in their own literacy development acknowledges that literacy isn't just "passed" from parent to child, but is more of an immersion process (Edwards, 1995). Studies have shown that, when parents use literacy in everyday ways, their children's literacy development is enhanced more than when they try to involve their children in add-on literacy tasks (Paratore, 1995). Literacy immersion begins with parents and other family members who are literate individuals.

The International Reading Association's Family Literacy Commission suggest that former models of family literacy programs that focused on "training the parents" are outdated. Instead, they state that neglected aspects of family literacy work include the following (Morrow, 1995, pp. 24–25):

- Parents or other caregivers working independently on reading and writing: As parents reduce dependence on their children for providing assistance with literacy (or language), the children are freed to concentrate their efforts on their own literacy development. In many families, especially where the home language is other than English or the parents are not literate, children are often the mediators for their parents, negotiating their way through many of life's events.
- Parents using literacy to address family and community problems: These might include issues such as immigration, employment, housing, taxes, and other events that are socially significant in the life of the family.
- Parents addressing child-rearing concerns through family literacy class: In a safe environment, parents can share their concerns about their children, and discuss how to access a variety of community resources.
- Parents supporting the development of their home language and culture: As parents develop their own literacy skills, they establish a foundation for their children's achievement, self-esteem, and appreciation for their own multicultural legacy.
- Parents interacting with the school system: The classroom is viewed as a place where parents can comfortably discuss school-related concerns, and explore their children's school experiences. They have a voice and are heard.

In order to implement family literacy programs that honor these aspects, we might focus on the following:

- Honoring and validating home languages and cultures;
- Exploring cultural issues related to literacy, learning, teaching, and educational systems and settings;
- Providing assistance in accessing medical, legal, and other community services;
- Supporting families as they gain proficiency in language and literacy.

When you reflect on all these elements, perhaps you can see that family literacy efforts that honor home cultures, parents, extended family members, and their children hold promise. Parents who are involved in their children's schools positively impact their children's academic achievement. In contrast, adults who themselves have not mastered basic literacy skills may have a more difficult time modeling for their children the literacy behaviors that will help them be successful in school.

Through family literacy programs such as these, we can put a stop to the "blame game," where parents are automatically deemed responsible for the difficulties their children experience in school. Taylor and Dorsey-Gaines (1988), in their study of literacy contexts of families in poverty, found that a child's poor academic performance may not be due to a lack of parental support for the child's literacy development. Rather, what puts their children at risk is that they do not have the social, political, and economic support for dealing with real-life challenges such as housing, health, and other financial and social needs.

Increasingly, schools and school districts are partnering with other community groups, such as community colleges, libraries, churches, and governmental agencies to provide family literacy programs. In the following Other Voices segment, you will read about one school district's attempt to introduce parents and extended family members to the family literacy program and other resources available in their community. Another goal of this event was to welcome parents and family members into the school. As you read, think about the various community members who came together to provide a supportive, welcoming environment for the people who participated in this family literacy event.

Other Voices: Cathy Williams

Cathy Williams is the Director of Elementary Curriculum in the Claremore Public Schools in Claremore, Oklahoma. This district has experienced rapid growth in its student population of English language learners. Most of these children come directly from Mexico, and many have parents who speak little or no English. To encourage parents to participate in school activities and in their children's literacy development, Cathy and her colleagues organized an Open House for the Hispanic families in the community. When asked how parents were invited to participate in this special evening, Cathy stated that notices about the meeting, written in Spanish and English, were posted where parents would see them, such as in the neighborhood grocery stores, check-cashing establishments, the library, gas stations, and the laundromat. They were also sent home with children, with Spanish on one side and English on the other. Cathy's description of a successful family literacy event follows.

As Director of Elementary Curriculum for a growing school district, the needs are ever-changing and the influx of students into our elementary schools who are English language learners has presented a new issue for parent and family literacy. To address this need in the Claremore School District, a committee composed of myself, two ESL teacher assistants, and other certified teachers and administrators meet each month to discuss issues and navigate the channels of funding and services available for ESL students in our district. At one of the early meetings, Edith Bryza, an elementary ESL assistant, suggested a family night for parents to come to the school and be introduced to the school and the programs offered. This was a great idea and she and the principal at the site where she is assigned developed a program for our Hispanic community. The Hispanic community is the largest of the ESL populations we currently serve.

The Open House for parents of ESL students took place in October. The evening was planned around the school and community as they are interrelated for students and families residing in Claremore. Representatives from most of the city services and school district were present. The mayor welcomed the families and a program by the ESL students was presented to parents. An interpreter was present and Lou Robertson, an elementary principal, presented an orientation to the ESL services in the school.

Booths were set up in the cafeteria to allow families to visit and receive information from various city services and community organizations. Among those with booths were the Fire Department, Red Cross, Rogers State University, Rogers County Health Department, Civil Defense, Police Department, and Claremore Super Recreation Center. Each booth provided literature and explained services and safety issues for families.

For example, representatives from the Department of Civil Defense office provided maps of the area and where shelters were located for weather emergencies. Claremore is situated in the middle of Tornado Alley, and several of the families in the community live in mobile homes or apartments. It was felt that safety issues for them were concerns that needed to be addressed. Accessing information on health and safety issues was addressed by the county health department and the Red Cross. The university has an adult education program for the GED and they also provide ESL classes for adults learning English. Enrollment and financial aid information was available.

One of the most visited booths was that of the Super Recreation Center. This facility has workout rooms, basketball courts, tennis courts, and an indoor Olympic pool. These are available at minimal or no cost to community members. The fees and access were provided so families could make use of the facilities in the city. The police and fire departments also sent representatives to provide a friendly and positive presence to our newest members of the Claremore community.

The librarian was having a book fair during the week of this meeting and she agreed to have the library open for parents to shop. We made sure we had library books in Spanish for parents to purchase as well as many in English. The district funds for ESL services appropriated money for the librarian to purchase books in both English and Spanish to establish a lending library for parents so they could read to their children at home. If parents cannot read in English they are encouraged to take books from the lending library and read to their children in Spanish. One of our district goals is to increase the time out of school that children read or are read to. This is one avenue that benefits these parents. Each elementary site has a lending library established and books will be added as additional funds are made available.

The evening was a huge success. Parents began arriving early and were very appreciative of the effort made on their behalf. The students performed and stole the show with songs and patriotic recitations. One of the fourth-grade teachers sang a medley of patriotic songs and the mayor made a short welcoming address to the parents and many extended family members. Local restaurants and grocery stores provided refreshments. Children received plastic fire hats, pencils, magnets, stickers, and other trinkets from the booths they visited.

Group Inquiry Activity   Consider each of the following definitions within the context of the family night in Cathy Williams's district:

Additive bilingualism: Rather than neglecting or rejecting students' language and culture, additive bilingualism promotes building on what students bring to the classroom, and then adding to it (Cummins, 1994; Echevarria, Vogt, & Short, p. 197).

Subtractive bilingualism: The learning of a new language at the expense of the primary language. Learners often lose their native language and culture because they don't have opportunities to continue using it, or they perceive that language to be of lower status. Loss of the primary language often leads to cultural ambivalence (Cummins, 1994; Echevarria, Vogt, & Short, p. 202).

Assimilation: The process by which members of a group become more like those of the majority group.

1. In what ways, if any, was the Claremore School District demonstrating an additive perspective toward bilingualism?
2. In what ways, if any, was the Claremore School District demonstrating an assimilative perspective?
3. From Cathy Williams's description of the family literacy event, what evidence can you find that indicates the school district does *not* subscribe to a subtractive perspective? In schools, classrooms, and community meetings, what types of instruction, activities, or attitudes imply a subtractive perspective? How would you recognize it? As a reading specialist, what can you do to counter this perspective?

Hopefully, the parents who attended the family night in Claremore School District will feel more comfortable now about attending other school events, such as parent conferences, PTA/PTO meetings, and Back-to-School Nights. Further, they may seek out other family literacy programs offered in the community. For more information about family literacy programs, please refer to the following:

- Even Start Family Literacy Program: U.S. Department of Education, 400 Maryland Avenue SW, Washington, DC 20202. www.ed.gov/offices/OESE/CEP/evenstrtquick.html
- National Center for Family Literacy: Waterfront Plaza, Suite 200, 325 W. Main Street, Louisville, KY 40202-4251. www.famlit.org
- Barbara Bush Foundation for Family Literacy: 1112 16th Street NW, Suite 340, Washington, DC 20036, www.barbarabushfoundation.com
- Reach Out and Read (ROR): In this program, physicians and nurses learn about literacy promotion as a standard component of pediatric care. They are trained in emergent literacy philosophy, and during well-baby visits give books to babies, infants, and toddlers, while speaking to parents about the benefits of reading aloud to their young children. In this project, reading specialists and medical personnel collaborate in a very unique way. ROR sites also serve as a clearinghouse for other

types of parenting information. Over 13,000 physicians and nurses are involved in Reach Out and Read, and there are currently 11,000 ROR sites in 50 states, plus Washington DC, Puerto Rico, and Guam. For information about Reach Out and Read, please see their Web site at www.reachoutandread.org or E-mail them for information at info@reachoutandread.org or call 617-629-8042.

Group Inquiry Activity   In a small group, take a piece of chart paper and divide it into a matrix with eight boxes. Head the vertical columns as follows: Focus/Purpose, Participants, Activities, Outcomes. Then, down the side of the boxes, write in four (or more) family literacy programs, projects, and/or events that your group members have been involved in. Fill in the boxes. When you're finished, discuss the following questions related to the events you've listed.

1. Were the purposes of the events related to a transmission model?
2. If so, how could they be changed or revised to focus more on the family's needs rather than the school's?
3. What are some family literacy classes, projects, or events that your school(s) could offer that would be socially, culturally, and linguistically relevant to the parents and families in your school?

A final thought about family literacy: As with other topics in this book, family literacy is complex, very important, and ever-changing. It's impossible in this chapter to list and discuss the many excellent district, community, state, and national family literacy projects and programs. As soon as we describe one in detail, there will be hundreds of others that we have slighted. Therefore, our approach to this topic was to share some principles of effective programs that have been identified in the research literature and by IRA's Commission on Family Literacy. It is our hope that you and other reading specialists in your district will take active leadership roles in creating and coordinating effective literacy programs for all citizens in your community, including parents and other family members. We encourage you to access the resources listed in this chapter to learn how to become involved in these critically important projects and programs.

ADULT LITERACY

In 1990, the governors of the United States reached an historic accord when they established a set of national educational goals for the year 2000. As part of the Goals 2000 initiative, Goal 6 was written as follows: "By the year 2000, every adult American will be literate and will possess the knowledge and skills necessary to compete in a global economy and exercise the rights and responsibilities of citizenship" (U.S. Congress, 1994). While there was universal approval of this goal, especially in the reading field, in reality, over the past decade, the bulk of resources and attention have focused on improving literacy instruction in grades K–12.

In the 1960s, the United States was considered to be one of the most literate countries in the world, with an estimated literacy rate of nearly 99 percent. At this time, in contrast, it was believed that many developing countries in the world had literacy rates of 50 percent or lower (Wagner, 1997, p. 2). In 1992, the first ever National Adult Literacy Survey (NALS) was conducted in the United States, with "adult" defined as those sixteen years or older. The NALS used test items that were similar to everyday life and they involved prose literacy, document literacy, and quantitative literacy. Representative data were gathered in twelve states (CA, FL, IL, IN, IA, LA, NJ, NY, OH, PA, TX, and WA), and for adults in prison. The NALS grouped the results into five levels that are now commonly used to describe adults' literacy skills. You will find examples of questions from the 1992 survey for each of the five levels in Figure 12.2.

The National Adult Literacy Survey was the most comprehensive study of its kind and its findings included both good news and bad. The good news was that approximately 95 percent of adult Americans could read a passage at the fourth-grade level or

Level	Prose	Document	Quantitative
1	Identify country in short article	Locate expiration date on driver's license	Total a bank deposit entry
2	Underline meaning of a term given in government brochure on supplemental social security income	Locate eligibility from table of employee benefits	Determine difference in price between tickets at two shows
3	Write a brief letter explaining error made on a credit card bill	Use bus schedule to determine appropriate bus for given set of conditions	Calculate miles per gallon using information given on mileage record chart
4	Explain difference between two types of employee benefits	Use table of information to determine pattern in oil exports across years	Using information presented in news article, calclate the amount of money that should go to raising children
5	Summarize two ways lawyers may challenge prospective jurors	Use a table depicting information about parental involvement in school survey to write a paragraph summarizing extent to which parents and teachers agree	Using calculator, determine the total cost of carpet to cover a room

FIGURE 12.2 Sample Items with Levels of Difficulty from the 1992 Adult Literacy Survey

better, suggesting there were few Americans who could be considered truly illiterate. However, reading at the fourth-grade level is not reading well enough. Nearly half of the people who were surveyed (out of 26,000) were reading at the lowest two levels of five.

The NALS found that, not surprisingly, adults with fewer years of schooling were more likely to fall in the two lowest levels of literacy than those who had completed high school. Of those with an eighth-grade education or less, 75 to 80 percent of those surveyed were in the lowest two levels. Some critics charged that the survey underrepresented adults from rural areas in the country (Byers, 1993), implying that the number of adults who experience reading problems may have been underreported.

In 2002, the National Assessment of Adult Literacy (NAAL) was administered by the National Center for Education Statistics (NCES). The results of this assessment provide the first measure in a decade of the nation's progress in meeting the national goal set for adult literacy. For the 2002 NAAL, literacy was defined as "Using printed and written information to function in society, to achieve one's goals, and to develop one's knowledge and potential" (National Assessment of Adult Literacy, NCES, Washington, DC). The purpose of the assessment was to describe the status of adult literacy, report on trends, identify relationships between literacy and adults' background, and develop partnerships with states. Again, the three literacy domains from the 1992 NALS were assessed. For the 2002 assessment, these were described as:

- Prose Literacy: The knowledge and skills needed to understand and use information from texts such as editorials, news stories, poems, and fiction;
- Document Literacy: The knowledge and skills needed to locate and use information contained in materials such as job applications, payroll forms, transportation schedules, maps, tables, and graphs;
- Quantitative Literacy: The knowledge and skills needed to apply arithmetic operations, either alone or sequentially, using numbers embedded in print materials.

For the 2002 assessment, NAAL assessed the English-language literacy abilities of adults aged sixteen and older in the United States, living in households, but not those living in group quarters, institutions (including prisons), or with no fixed address (homeless). Through a representative sampling process, adults in every area of the United States were selected for the assessment, but not in every state. As of this writing, results from the NAAL were not yet released. For more information about the National Assessment of Adult Literacy, please contact the National Center for Education Statistics, U.S. Department of Education, 1990 K Street, NW, Room 8008, Washington, DC 20006.

Adult Literacy Programs

According to the Division of Adult Education and Literacy in Washington, DC, Federal adult education programs served more than 4 million adults in 1997. However, the U.S.

Department of Education has estimated that between 40 and 44 million adults function at the lowest level of literacy (Kogut, 2001). Public libraries have increasingly offered adult literacy programs to meet the needs of the many adults who are not enrolled in government programs. In fact, during a Web search on the topic of adult literacy, we found over 533,000 sites! Of these, a great many were related to city, county, or state library adult literacy programs.

Two of the better-known adult literacy programs that have library affiliations are the not-for-profit organizations, Literacy Volunteers of America (LVA) and Laubach Literacy International. LVA is an integrated network of local, state, and regional literacy providers that give adults and their families the chance to acquire literacy skills. All sites are accredited by the LVA in order to bring consistency to the training of the legion of volunteers, and to the materials and approaches that are used. LVA currently delivers local literacy instruction to more than 80,000 adults and their families through a network of more than 350 volunteer literacy programs (Kogut, 2001).

Laubach Literacy International has 1100 member programs throughout the United States, with sixty-seven partner programs in thirty-six developing countries. It has its own publishing division and distributes adult educational materials to 46,000 literacy organizations. In early 2001, it was announced that the Literacy Volunteers of America and Laubach International were merging. For more information about either or both of these organizations, please go to their respective Web sites: www.literacyvolunteers.org and www.laubach.org.

It's important to note that adult literacy is the only field in education that uses large numbers of volunteers, and that has as its funding only a fraction of that which is allocated for K–12. Additionally, a growing body of research evidence indicates that pedagogical methods and materials that are effective for children may be quite inappropriate for adults. The majority of adults in a literacy program stay for no longer than six months before terminating the program, even though this amount of time is almost always insufficient for meeting academic and personal goals. Also, many adults reenter programs, a cycle that prolongs the duration of literacy acquisition over a long period of time (Venezky, Sabatini, Brooks, & Carino, 1996).

Group Inquiry Activity We are not surprised that adults have a difficult time remaining in these adult literacy programs. To get an understanding of how difficult this might be, choose a partner and briefly answer the following questions:

1. Have you ever started an exercise program or any other lessons and not followed through?
2. What's one thing you do poorly or with which you have always struggled?
3. Do you enjoy doing it? Why or why not?
4. How has it made you feel every time you had to do it?
5. How difficult would it be to work on that activity for at least an hour every day?
6. Do you think you could sustain it for one full year? Why or why not?

From research studies investigating adult literacy (Mikulecky, Albers, & Peers, 1994; Venezky, Sabatini, Brooks, & Carino, 1996; Wagner, 1997), we have learned the following:

- Metacognition plays an important role in interventions that support adults;
- There is little relationship between "seat time" (time spent in class) and performance gains;
- Much of adult education is "spread thinly" across many areas, rather than focusing on specific skill needs;
- There appears to be little transfer of general basic skills in reading, writing, and math, and that a better match may be needed between "functional context learning" and basic skills;
- There is a need for more research focusing on diagnostic instruments specially created and normed for adults;
- New models of remediation for adults need to be researched;
- Learners should be identified and instruction designed for their particular needs and circumstances; for example, English learners who are literate in their home language but not in English; English learners who lack literacy skills in both languages; learners who have competencies in math but not writing; adults with learning disabilities, and so forth;
- More research is needed on the effectiveness of family literacy programs and their impact on adults with limited literacy skills.

Clearly, children and the adults in their lives will benefit from well-designed adult literacy programs that assist the participants in gaining the skills and strategies needed for living full lives. To carry out this research agenda, in late 2001, Rutgers University in New Brunswick, New Jersey, in collaboration with the New Brunswick Public Schools, launched the new National Labsite for Adult Literacy Education. Collaborative research by teachers and faculty from Rutgers and the school district will lead to new approaches for addressing the literacy concerns of many of America's adults. We look forward to learning about their work over the next decade.

THE ROLE OF READING SPECIALISTS IN FAMILY AND ADULT LITERACY PROGRAMS

There are a number of ways that you can become involved in family and adult literacy programs in your community. At the district and school level, you and your literacy team can determine the need for a family literacy program, and, if warranted, organize one, even on a small scale. Remember what occurred in Claremore, Oklahoma!

If you want to pursue adult literacy as a career, we recommend that you contact your local community college and determine if there is an adult reading program in place. Increasingly, community college reading programs are requiring the instructors to have advanced reading certification, in addition to a master's degree.

If you wish to continue working in grades K–12, there are still ways you can become involved in adult literacy issues in your community. Contact your public library and see what programs are in place. You'll most likely find that the people who are administering the programs will welcome your expertise and assistance, perhaps with training volunteers, providing professional development, assisting with materials selection, and so forth. You will find these people to be an incredibly dedicated group.

The International Reading Association and its affiliates are another venue to explore. Traditionally, the local and state councils of the IRA have had as their primary focus the improvement of reading instruction and increased literacy for children and youth, primarily because the majority of members are elementary and secondary teachers and reading specialists. However, as awareness of adult literacy needs has increased, IRA and its affiliates have become more involved in research, dissemination of information, publications about and for adult literacy programs, and in taking positions related to the concerns of adults.

REVISITING THE VIGNETTE

Obviously, Anne Law, the reading specialist, must have as her first priority the children she's teaching, including Sarah. However, she also has the obligation to help Sarah's mom, Jorene, access community services related to family and adult literacy. Therefore, Anne provides Jorene with a contact at the local community college where she begins working toward her GED while receiving instruction in the reading program on campus, which is coordinated by a reading specialist who received her MA at the same time, in the same program, as Anne. As Jorene becomes involved in learning new skills and working toward a goal, she gradually becomes less intense about Sarah, who is making slow but steady progress with Anne's instruction. Anne works to support Sarah's primary instruction in the classroom, communicating on a regular basis with Sarah's teacher.

POINTS TO REMEMBER

Family literacy programs have gained the attention of the federal government, and a number have shown considerable promise. While they may be affiliated and administered by local or state community agencies, as well as the federal government, they are varied in the services they offer. In general, family literacy programs provide literacy instruction to children and adults, information about community resources, job-training skills, computer training, parenting skills, and other classes and workshops. Some family literacy programs exist within schools and school districts, and reading specialists can play a major role in creating and administering such programs. Newer models of effective programs include validation and support of home literacy and culture, and provisions for parents to engage meaningfully in their children's schools.

The Goals 2000 initiative in the United States targeted adult literacy as a major goal. The National Adult Literacy Survey (NALS) in 1992 indicated that a large number of American adults read at the lowest levels of literacy; levels deemed too low to be competitive in today's marketplace. In 2002, the National Assessment of Adult Literacy (NAAL) was administered to a sample of adults from throughout the United States. Results from this assessment have not as yet been reported.

Adult literacy programs, whether federally funded, state funded, or those that are staffed by volunteers, have demonstrated mixed results. There is a high rate of attrition and performance gains have been inconsistent. Further research is needed in identifying appropriate assessments, methods, and approaches for working with adults. The National Center on Adult Literacy, housed at the University of Pennsylvania, and the National Labsite for Adult Literacy Education at Rutgers University, are conducting important research in the area of adult literacy.

PORTFOLIO PROJECTS

1. Contact a family literacy organization, either nationally or locally. Determine what types of programs and services are available for families in your community. How many families are receiving services? Are there any data available about how effective the programs are in assisting parents and children? If so, what kinds of data are being collected? What kinds of outcomes are being measured?

2. Visit your public library to see what services are available for adults seeking literacy instruction. Find out who trains the volunteers and what kind of training they receive. What approaches are being used? What materials are being used? Based on a review of the research on adult literacy and learning, decide whether you think the adult literacy program is congruent with research findings. You may wish to get involved and volunteer yourself!

3. Contact a private reading center in your community. This could be a large commercial venture or a smaller center run by an individual. Formulate questions and seek answers regarding who the teachers are, what methods and approaches are used, what instructional materials are favored, and what, if any, data exist regarding the success rate of the students who attend. Write up your report and share it with others in your class.

4. If you can gain access, interview an adult in your community who is learning to read. Learn about his or her history and background. What kind of schooling experiences has this person had? What are his or her feelings about school and learning to read? As a sensitive reading specialist, what kinds of assistance and support might be helpful for this individual?

RECOMMENDED READINGS

The International Reading Association has published a number of very helpful resources that are also quite inexpensive. We've included them here and encourage you to share them with parents and families.

International Reading Association. (2000a). *Beginning literacy and your child: A guide to helping your baby or preschooler become a reader*. Newark, DE: Author.

International Reading Association. (2000b). *"Books are cool!" Keeping your middle school student reading.* Newark, DE: Author.

International Reading Association. (2000c). *I can read and write! How to encourage your school-age child's literacy development.* Newark, DE: Author. These are wonderfully complete but very accessible (twenty to twenty-four pages) booklets that are geared to parents. They include many important ideas and suggestions, and they're available in bulk at a very inexpensive cost. These would be wonderful to have available for parents when they visit the school.

Thomas, A., Fazio, L., & Stiefelmeyer, B. L. (1999). *Families at school: A Handbook for parents.* Newark, DE: International Reading Association. This is a wonderful guide originally created by educators who have been involved in a community family literacy program in Canada. The book is very "parent-friendly" and includes recommendations for finding family literacy programs, resources, inexpensive and easy-to-implement literacy activities, child observation checklists, and book lists. In our literacy center on campus at California State University, Long Beach, we provide this book for checkout, and it's always available for perusal while children are being taught. These authors have also published through IRA a helpful handbook for teachers titled, *Families at school: A guide for educators.*

The American Library Association (ALA) also has a very helpful Web site (http://www.ala.org) that has a number of helpful resources, including the Librarians Guide to Cyberspace for parents and kids (http://www.ala.org/parentspage/greatsites). Resources for Parents and Kids is another helpful resource, (http://www.ala.org/parents/index.html).

IRA also offers a series of brochures for parents. Single copies are free on request by sending a self-addressed stamped envelope to 800 Barksdale Rd., P.O. Box 8139, Newark, DE 19714-8139. These are also available in bulk. The titles include:

Get Ready to Read! Tips for Parents of Young Children
Explore the Playground of Books: Tips for Parents of Beginning Readers
Summer Reading Adventure! Tips for Parents of Young Readers
Making the Most of Television: Tips for Parents of Young Viewers
See the World on the Internet: Tips for Parents of Young Readers—and "Surfers"
Library Safari: Tips for Parents of Young Readers and Explorers

Morrow, L. M. (Ed.). (1995). *Family literacy: Connections in schools and communities.* Newark, DE: International Reading Association. If you really want to understand varied models of family literacy programs, we encourage you to read this book. Originally a project of IRA's Family Literacy Commission, this book includes chapters by authors involved in projects throughout the country. It includes detailed explanations, discussions, and recommendations.

Rasinski, T. V., & Padak, N. D. (Eds.). (2000). *Motivating recreational reading and promoting home-school connections: Strategies from the* Reading Teacher. Newark, DE: International Reading Association. This is a collection of articles from the *Reading Teacher* related to family literacy and parent involvement. You'll get a variety of perspectives and a wealth of ideas and activities for promoting family literacy programs.

CHAPTER THIRTEEN

MOVING THE FIELD FORWARD AS LEADERS, RESEARCHERS, AND ADVOCATES

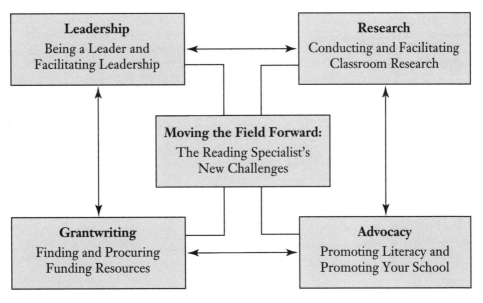

FIGURE 13.1 Chapter Overview

LEARNING GOALS

After reading, discussing, and engaging in activities related to this chapter, you will be able to:

1. define the characteristics of leadership as they apply to the reading specialist in school and community contexts;

2. explain the importance of establishing and maintaining professional affiliations, and locate the professional resources and publications related to literacy;

3. become familiar with the grant-writing process, the sources of funding, and external support for school personnel engaged in grant writing;

4. design and conduct classroom research and support teachers in research endeavors;

5. understand the role of the reading specialist as literacy advocate, and access advocacy resources and networks.

Vignette

When you walk into the office of Pat Ortiz, the reading specialist at Payne Elementary School in central Florida, you notice her diplomas on the wall near her desk. She has a master's degree in elementary education and a provisional license as a reading specialist while she finishes the last few classes for this additional degree. Pat is friendly and helpful to all of her colleagues, sharing ideas and support. She puts a weekly schedule of her work with students on her office door along with time slots for available conference times. She distributes a monthly literacy-related newsletter to all faculty and staff at Payne, and she has created a variety of forms that are used for referrals, assessment plans, and case reports. Pat notifies faculty about upcoming workshops, conferences, and local reading council meetings. She has established a lending library of books and journal articles, and keeps the faculty informed about new research.

At all times, Pat is careful to dress and act in a professional manner. She is never seen wearing jeans or sweatshirts to school, except on rare occasions when a special event warrants such attire. To Pat, this is an important aspect of being "a professional." Another part of being a professional is modeling her enthusiasm for literacy to others. She and several teachers, paraprofessionals, and one of the bus drivers share the latest novels they are reading with one another and openly discuss good books in the lounge and in the halls.

Thinking Points

1. What is your first reaction to Pat's ideas about professionalism?
2. If you were discussing professionalism with Pat what would you ask her?
3. What would you share with her?

Expanding the Vignette: Exploring the Tensions

One Wednesday evening in her graduate leadership, administration, and supervision class, Pat and her cohorts were discussing how rewarding it is to share their love of reading with their colleagues. They each talked about how they modeled this passion for their colleagues. However, Danielle appeared to be deep in thought as Pat described her beliefs about how her office should look, and how she should dress while at work. Danielle was clearly disturbed and said, "You know, I'm reluctant to hang my diplomas or 'dress up' within the casual atmosphere of school. I don't want to be perceived as arrogant." Several others in the class nodded their assent and expressed similar concerns about appearing "too professional."

Thinking Points

1. What additional tensions and questions have you identified in the vignette?
2. Why might individuals perceive these issues differently?
3. What other factors might be important for Pat and her cohorts to consider?

CONTINUING THE PROFESSIONAL JOURNEY

It appears we have come full circle, addressing some of the issues that concerned us as we began to write this book. "What does it mean to be a reading specialist?" "What does it mean to be a professional?" As individuals grow and change, they are forced to redefine their roles and their identities. Pat and her classmates are exploring these tensions as they begin their careers as reading specialists. They are asking themselves what it means to be a professional, an important question to raise. In this chapter, we will examine their concerns through our sociocultural perspective, emphasizing issues of leadership and professionalism. As you read the chapter, think about your responses to the questions in the vignette. We will revisit them at the end of the chapter.

The role of the reading specialist has changed dramatically in the last quarter century. Although some aspects of the job remain much the same, such as working with groups of struggling readers and assisting teachers in implementing new strategies, other tasks have emerged that require increased levels of expertise and professionalism. Mandates for high-stakes testing and calls for alignment with national, state, and local standards require reading specialists to focus beyond their schools and districts. This broadened perspective requires understanding the impact of external social and political forces on local instructional practices. As we discovered in Chapter 1, reading specialists find themselves responsible for leading initiatives to change teacher beliefs and behaviors. In response to limited local resources and demands for accountability, they are asked to seek and obtain external funds to support literacy initiatives. The one-day workshop has been replaced by more extensive long-term professional development. While this kind of professional support is consistent with lasting change, the reading specialist is expected to be knowledgeable about all the new trends and strategies that teachers might want to learn. At the same time, the media fan the fires of dissent, perpetuating the myth that the schools don't teach phonics and that children in the United States cannot read (McQuillan, 1998). Often, teachers and administrators look to the reading specialist for leadership in situations involving the need for advocacy.

The reading specialist today must, by necessity, form affiliations with networks of professionals and agencies that support the increased demands of the job. Instead of being able to answer all the questions—an impossible task—the reading specialist must know how to locate information and contact individuals with specialized expertise. The purpose of this chapter is to connect reading specialists with the human, technological, and material resources needed to meet the growing professional demands of the job. We have asked experts in different areas to share their specialized knowledge. As you read this chapter, you will hear from John Brekke, corporate consultant and an expert in leadership; Connie Erickson, educational grant writing consultant; and Michael Ford, Associate Dean at the University of Wisconsin, Oshkosh and nationally recognized expert in literacy advocacy. We have included Web sources and links to professional organizations. It is our hope that you will continue to seek new ways to connect with other professionals and to support those dedicated to increasing literacy levels in our schools and communities.

The Reading Specialist as Leader

Reading specialists often find it difficult to define their roles as leaders. As stated in Chapter 10, part of the problem relates to their position as quasi-administrators. They are on the front lines, implementing the changes mandated by others without the decision-making power of an administrator. If they attempt to coerce teachers, even in well-intentioned and pedagogically sound initiatives, they are doomed to fail. Today's definitions of leadership involve shared goals and collaboration. The leader is the one who invites and inspires others to "buy in" to a vision. A true leader seeks to help individuals discover their leadership potential and finds ways to foster those qualities. Often this means "leading from behind": mentoring, supporting, and encouraging others. Nowhere is this idea more critical than in a position such as that of the reading specialist.

Other Voices: John L. Brekke

The following excerpts are from a taped interview on leadership given by corporate consultant John L. Brekke for inclusion in this book. John's clients include the CEOs of a handful of the largest corporations in the United States. As a former educator and administrator in higher education, John draws on his experiences in the corporate and academic worlds to share his expertise with us.

On the Five Qualities of Effective Leaders

Leadership is one of those terms that I will not attempt to define, but I'll talk about the qualities of leadership, as I understand them. Years ago, leadership was defined in terms of competencies. I think *management* is defined in terms of competencies, and I think *leadership* has to do with qualities or characteristics of the people who are followed. I'm going to mention five of these qualities. They are certainly applicable to the world in which I work.

The five qualities I am going to talk about are derived from a variety of collated sources, including those firms that spend their lifetimes studying leadership, some academics who study this, and firms that specialize in placing leaders in senior management positions.

The first is **strategic thinking.** Strategic thinking, from my standpoint, simply means the ability to step back and take a look at the large picture; and, as a result of seeing that larger picture, to create a vision for the future of the organization. People who are strategic often talk about "implications thinking." If they are addressing a decision or trying to solve a problem, they readily ask, "What are the implications of the solution, of this decision, of this reorganization?" I think being strategic assumes the ability to act on the strategies that have been put in place.

The second quality or characteristic is **people-relatedness.** For many years we've heard of "management by walking around" within organizations whereby the bosses touched the lives of the individuals on a regular basis. And that's even more important today. What employees are really saying is, "I want to be recognized as a person who is contributing to the organization," or "I want to be seen as somebody who's valued by my boss and I want that boss, that person, to come to my area and have a conversation with me there."

The third quality or characteristic is really two words that have been, in the last few years, paired, **urgency and accountability.** I'm convinced these attributes are inextricably linked. The fast-paced nature of the workplace demands that decisions be made more quickly at the appropriate level. That is a very important qualifier . . . *decisions made more quickly, at the appropriate level, by people who are then held responsible.* It's a pretty simple formula. But it can get messed up rather quickly if decisions become too much of a deliberative thing or if bosses assume that they should be making all of the decisions. As long as people feel they have that authority to be making those decisions, regardless of where they are in that organization, then they expect that they will be held accountable.

Number four is what is called **cultural attention.** Employees are looking to the leadership and organizations to create organizations that are focused, provide opportunities for personal growth, demand personal excellence, and are employee-friendly. People understand that culture is constantly emerging and it's not haphazard. As organizations are being restructured today, cultures will emerge, even if you don't give attention to it. In time, you will be able to define what the behaviors are that support the culture of the organization. The challenge, of course, is to make sure that the behaviors are appropriate behaviors. Therefore, the cultural creation process is a very conscious and continuing effort by leaders within an organization.

The last attribute, or quality, is **coaching.** I am convinced that the most important thing leaders can do in this day and age is to devote themselves to coaching others. A couple of magical things happen. One is not unlike the process of teaching. I went to college and I went to graduate school and I supposedly learned some things for which I was qualified to teach. But, I really didn't learn that material until I was put into a position to teach. That's when it dawned on me that I better know this stuff. I better know this stuff at least well enough to be asking the provocative question in the classroom that would lead to the students learning. In like manner, those people who put themselves in the role of a coach—coaching others—much more consciously understand what leadership is all about.

Group Inquiry Activity   The five principles of leadership John described were presented in the context of the corporate world although they are relevant to the world of the reading specialist. In your group, for each of the five principles, describe a situation in which a reading specialist could apply it in a specific school setting.

1. Strategic Thinking
2. People-Relatedness
3. Urgency and Accountability
4. Cultural Attention
5. Coaching

John's ideas about leadership demonstrate that leaders in corporations, too, recognize the role of cultures within organizations. The sociocultural perspective has shifted us away from the rigid definitions and boundaries we drew around concepts such as leadership. We are also discovering new ways to envision mentorship as a much more egalitarian relationship, often involving shared support in attaining goals. An outgrowth of these ideas is that, increasingly, compromise is no longer viewed as the best way to solve problems. When two people compromise, both sacrifice a portion of their goals. In effect, it's a lose–lose proposition, such as when teachers have to lose part of their teaching identities in order to adopt a new strategy being imposed on them. No wonder they resist.

Newer forms of leadership stress approaching seemingly contradictory goals by finding ways to produce win–win situations. Reading specialists who understand this stop trying to "get" teachers to do things their way. They sit down with the teachers and find ways to support what goes on in the classroom and find compatible strategies that foster change in nonthreatening ways, much like the middle-school reading specialist we described in Chapter 8. If a teacher loves drill and practice, you might show him how to add a new strategy or dimension to extend that drill and practice with some meaning-oriented follow-up strategies. That's a win–win situation. It will serve to keep the reading specialist credible and valuable to teachers.

The Role of Reading Specialist as Professional
Author Connections: Brenda and MaryEllen

Historically, a course in leadership, administration, and supervision is taken at the end of the master's degree or certification program. Both of us notice that something important happens as our students in this course progress through the semester: They become professionals in ways that are readily apparent but difficult to describe. These individuals change their perceptions of themselves and cross a threshold from literacy teachers to literacy professionals—*reading specialists*. If ever there were proof that identity is socially constructed it occurs in this class. As the weeks pass and students engage in passionate discussions involving real-life problems that are situated in their schools and communities, their sharing takes on deeper dimensions. The group develops cohesiveness as the teachers become more and more willing to take risks with their peers by sharing problems that occasionally elicit tears and by confiding what they still don't know or understand. We find these to be the teachable moments; living vignettes that provide us with the kinds of authentic group problem solving that can make or break a reading specialist. Many of these have inspired the vignettes and examples in this book.

When we were students in our graduate supervision course in the old days, we discussed professionalism as "trait theory." "This is what a professional looks like." "This is how a professional dresses." "This is how a professional acts." Our textbooks even reminded us about good grooming, including perfume, hair, and makeup! If you had asked us to define professionalism, we would have rattled off a set of attributes with a fair degree of confidence. How ironic that the more we have come to learn about social constructivism, the less we are able to define professionalism as a static construct. We are not so sure we know what it means to be a professional because it (like so much else) seems to depend on the context.

For example, in the popular media not long ago there were discussions about who could call themselves "professionals." Up to this point, the term had been reserved for those with advanced degrees and specialized certification, such as doctors, lawyers, CPAs, dentists, and so forth. Over time, others who considered themselves to be professionals claimed the right to the title: bus drivers, custodians, and, yes, teachers. So the question, "What is a professional?" depends on who's asking and who's answering. Each person will answer the question based on a variety of culturally and socially constructed beliefs and values, further shaped by life experiences and the context of the school and community in which the person teaches. Is it possible that Pat, in this chapter's vignette, will be perceived as a professional in one school or community and as an elitist in another? We suspect that it is more helpful to define a professional by what the person does than by what the person "is."

Group Inquiry Activity *Think–Pair–Share* On your own, write your answers to the following questions. Share your ideas with a partner and create a Venn diagram comparing and contrasting your ideas.

1. Describe how you would model "professionalism" in your school and community.
2. How would you describe what the reading specialist (as a professional) does within this context?
3. What are the beliefs and cultural influences from your childhood and adult experiences that influenced your answer?
4. Which attitudes, beliefs, and needs of your school influenced your answer?
5. Which aspects of your university experience shaped your answer?

As you negotiated ideas and definitions of professionalism you may have found these questions limited in scope, dealing with external and superficial aspects of professionalism. To assist you in reflecting on what a professional does in the role of reading specialist, we developed a few questions. We hope you will consider them with regard to your particular social and cultural context.

Questions for the Reading Professional

1. How does a literacy professional interact with administrators? With colleagues?
2. In what ways is a literacy professional in the role of reading specialist like and unlike other classroom teachers?
3. What are the obligations of a professional with regard to dissemination and implementation of ideas and strategies? Is there any difference between the ways peer teachers interact in a shared lesson and the way a reading specialist and a teacher might interact in a shared lesson?
4. Is there a kind of "professionalism" that distinguishes a reading specialist from his or her peers?
5. What is the obligation of the professional with regard to:
   - remaining current in literacy-related research and practice;
   - the balance between working with students and helping teachers;
   - the necessity of engaging in advocacy for literacy;
   - belonging to professional organizations and developing presentations;
   - sharing expertise with teachers and in what manner;
   - securing external funds;
   - reading, understanding, and disseminating journal articles, Web site lists, and other resources;
   - leading professional development;
   - engaging in community outreach and service?

We hope you will add to the list of questions over the course of your career. Professionalism is not a static concept. You need not be so concerned about defining the word *professionalism*. It is more helpful for you to ask, "How did the idea of 'professionalism' come to mean what it does to me?"

As reading specialists and professionals, we believe that we should be engaging in each of the behaviors listed in the previous section. Therefore, what follows are some suggestions for how to become involved in those that have not been previously discussed in this book: Involvement in Professional Organizations, Writing Successful Grant Proposals, and Advocacy.

INVOLVEMENT IN PROFESSIONAL ORGANIZATIONS

As a reading specialist you have the right to be served by professional organizations, but, as a professional, you also have the obligation to serve your chosen association. Membership in local councils, state associations, and IRA provides reading specialists with the opportunity to participate in what Gee (2001a, 2001b) describes as "affinity groups." Recall that affinity groups are formed by individuals who share a common goal, culture, or interest, and have a common discourse or way of using language when they interact within the group. Especially in small communities, reading specialists often feel like isolates. Active membership in literacy organizations allows for sharing of problems and insights that advance the collective expertise. Large associations such as the

International Reading Association and many state associations provide a wealth of on-line information, access to research and practitioner journals, and opportunities to attend outstanding conferences.

Opportunities for service and leadership within local, state, and IRA councils are plentiful. We hope you will feel an obligation to serve these organizations by assuming leadership roles, engaging in committee work, and sharing your ideas and innovative teaching strategies through presentations and journal articles. Reading specialists often volunteer for special events such as Reading in the Mall, Books for Babes (for new mothers in the hospital), Book Drives, or Young Author's Conferences—all of which are regularly sponsored by various local and state reading associations. Both of us have served as presidents of our local and state reading associations and in 2004–2005, Mary Ellen will serve as IRA president. We mention this not only because we want to reinforce or encourage your participation, but also because we have found that it's virtually impossible to "burn out" when you're involved with other professionals who remain committed to improving literacy. Professional organizations are an important and effective support group. We hope you will investigate the opportunities for professional affiliation and growth offered by the literacy-related organizations listed in the next section.

Professional Organizations for Educators

International Reading Association (IRA).   This professional organization, with a membership of over 84,000 literacy professionals, serves as a clearinghouse for reading research and provides information through conferences and publications. The goal of IRA is to improve the quality of literacy instruction for all and to promote lifelong literacy learning throughout the world. IRA serves as the parent organization for over 1200 local and state reading councils with 300,000 affiliates in more than sixty countries. On the IRA Web site (www.reading.org) you will find information on how to become involved in your state associations and local reading councils. The free electronic journal of IRA, *Reading Online* (www.readingonline.org) has a wealth of cutting edge articles. In addition to *Reading Online*, publications of IRA include *The Reading Teacher, The Journal of Adolescent and Adult Literacy, Reading Research Quarterly, Lectura y Vida, The Thinking Classroom*, and the quarterly magazine, *Reading Today*. IRA also has a large publishing division and each year it introduces a wide variety of new book titles related to reading and language arts. You also might find the IRA position statements to be of use in your school and district. These are available at no cost for one copy and a minimal cost for multiple copies. The IRA Position Statement on the Roles of the Reading Specialist can be found in Appendix I.

National Reading Conference (NRC).   This important research organization has as its members university researchers and teacher educators, graduate students, and reading specialists, all of whom share an interest and commitment to conducting and disseminating the results of cutting-edge literacy research. NRC's Web site (www.nrc.oakland.edu) has links to white papers that synthesize research addressing key topics in literacy. NRC publications include the annual *Yearbook of the National Reading Conference* and *Journal of Literacy Research*.

National Council of Teachers of English (NCTE).   This organization is dedicated to improving the learning of English and Language Arts in all areas of education, and its members include elementary and secondary English teachers, reading specialists, and others interested in English education. On the Web site (www.ncte.org) there are many opportunities available to teachers for professional growth and a forum to discuss issues related to the teaching of English. There also is a free weekly newsletter of ideas, articles, and connections for those who teach reading/language arts (www.ncte.org/inbox/currentissue.html). Publications of NCTE include *Language Arts, Voices from the Middle*, and *The English Journal*.

American Library Association (ALA).   Members of ALA include teachers, reading specialists, media specialists, and librarians. The organization addresses areas of diversity, professional development, literacy programs, equal access, and protecting intellectual freedom (www.ala.org). ALA also honors outstanding children's authors and illustrators each year with the Newbury and Caldecott Awards.

Association for Supervision and Curriculum Development (ASCD).   The members of this organization are professionals with the common goal of providing excellence in education and creating success for all learners (www.ascd.edu). The primary journal of ASCD is *Educational Leadership*, and the Association is known for its videotapes and books that are available through its publishing division.

College Reading Association (CRA).   The College Reading Association provides a forum for those interested in examining aspects of college and university reading education programs and general topics related to reading and literacy (http://explorers.tsuniv.edu/cra/). Publications include *Reading Research and Instruction, CRA Yearbook*, and a biannual *Monograph Series*.

Computer-Using Educators (CUE).   The goal of this organization is to promote the use of technology throughout all areas of education from preschool to college (www.cue.org).

National Middle School Association (NMSA).   This 20,000-member organization (www.nmsa.org) serves professionals, parents, and others who are interested in the educational and developmental needs of young adolescents (ages 10–15). Its publications include *The Middle School Journal* and a monthly magazine entitled *Middle Ground*. The organization holds an Annual Literacy Leaders Institute.

National Staff Development Council (NSDC).   NSDC is the largest organization dedicated to ensuring the academic success of students through staff development and school improvement. The organization is a resource for high quality staff development programs and instructional materials (www.nsdc.org/educatorindex.htm).

Teachers of English to Speakers of Other Languages, Inc. (TESOL).   The mission of TESOL is for its members to be able to communicate effectively in diverse settings and respect the language rights of others (www.tesol.edu/index.htm).

Although not an organization, another helpful Web site is "Teacher Vision" (www.teachervision.com). This comprehensive site serves as a resource link for all areas of education. The resources include technology connections, lesson plans, and more.

It is important that reading specialists remain informed of the current research and practice in literacy through the major publications in the field, particularly *The Reading Teacher* (elementary), and *Journal of Adolescent and Adult Literacy* (adolescent through adult), *Reading Today*, and *Reading Online*, all publications of the International Reading Association (IRA). Sharing articles and current news about literacy issues with colleagues is an essential role of all reading specialists.

WRITING SUCCESSFUL GRANT PROPOSALS

Securing outside funding for special literacy projects is becoming a commonplace task for reading specialists. Numerous Web sites support teachers in locating funds for specific purposes and guide them through the writing process. We list a few of these sources for you at the end of this chapter. We also urge you to read Jim Burke and Carol Prater's (2000) very informative book on grant writing. You can locate other resources through organizations such as the International Reading Association, your state Department of Public Instruction, or agencies such as the Cooperative Educational State Agencies (CESA).

Other Voices: Connie Erickson

Because of her expertise at writing grants and assisting teachers and schools in securing funds, we asked Connie Erickson to share her best advice about successful grant writing. Connie began writing grants more than ten years ago as a young media specialist right out of college. Within the last few years, she left her school district in rural Wisconsin to become a full-time educational grant consultant for CESA #11.

I was in the grocery store with my five-year-old son Daniel and was just ready to pay our bill when I realized that I had forgotten my checkbook. Daniel watched as I dug through my purse, looking for my credit card or cash, when he declared to the young cashier "Oh, that's ok. My mom will just write you out a grant." If only it were that easy!

It is no secret that writing grant proposals can be a time-consuming and complicated process. Successful grants are most often done in a collaborative manner, involving as many of the stakeholders as possible. Gathering people together and meeting deadlines requires organization and patience at the same time. While this may be enough to deter the average person from stepping into the grant-writing arena, most educators have a leg up on the process from the start: Teachers work like this each and every day!

Grants are so much more than money. Learning how to develop and write successful grant proposals can provide opportunities for your students and school districts that traditional funding cannot afford. Many schools have historically looked for grant funding to support "things" such as computers, books, and facilities. In fact, more and more funding sources are awarding grants to projects that strengthen professional development, provide new learning experiences for teachers and students, and promote a stronger relationship between school and community resources.

Despite the fact that each grant program will have its own guidelines, these helpful hints should help get your proposal started:

1. Determine Your Outcomes
   - What problem or need do you hope to address in the grant? Design the project backward from these outcomes.
2. Begin with Data; End with Data
   - What data do you have to support your need?
   - Find current research to support your project idea. You do not have to reinvent the wheel, but you can't simply jump on someone else's bandwagon either.
   - Assess everything, using a variety of methods that will provide feedback on your project's objectives and goals.
3. Do Your Homework
   - Attend workshops and contact people who have worked on grants before to gather information on the process.
   - Learn about funding sources and guidelines.
   - Ask for last year's winning grant proposals.
   - Create a time line with deadlines.
4. Gather District Support for the Project
   - Make sure that key administrative personnel are aware of your proposal. Invite and encourage help from district leaders in the beginning: You may need their support during the implementation phase.
   - Many grants require matching or "in kind" funds from your district. Depending on the grant, items such as volunteer time, transportation expenses, and even facility costs may be used.
   - Circumstances can exist where districts are limited to the number of federal and state applications that they can apply for. Be sure to ask.
5. Follow the Rules
   - Warning: About one third of all grant proposals are thrown out because they do not follow directions. Review the guidelines and have others do the same.
   - Do not assume anything about the grant evaluators: Spell everything out for them.

- Do not edit your own work. Have outside people read and evaluate your proposal. If they do not understand it, chances are the grant evaluators will probably have questions as well.
- Stay true to your goals. Do not stray.
- Do not send anything extra. Keep it concise.

ROLE OF THE READING SPECIALIST IN SUPPORTING CLASSROOM RESEARCH

It has only been within the last ten years that large numbers of teachers have begun to see themselves as researchers. Until that time research was seen as the province of the university, not the school. When teachers began to recognize research as a process with four basic components, asking a compelling question, gathering data systematically, analyzing the data, and translating their insights into classroom practice, they realized research was at the heart of reflective practice. Good "kid watchers" do it every day. The difference is that systematic data gathering around a specific question transforms reflective practice into inquiry.

The reading teacher has the potential to be a catalyst in the process of fostering classroom research, collaborating with a teacher or a group on research planning, and conducting research together. The process might start during a casual conversation in which a teacher mentions a new project, strategy, or question. The reading specialist might reply, "What an interesting idea. What do you think about conducting classroom research together to investigate this?" The ideal is when a group of teachers share an interest in a common question and decide to engage in a group research project. Topics for classroom research might arise from teacher study groups formed during the implementation of the two-year plan. Just as we are on the alert for the "teachable moment" with our students we must be aware of the "researchable moment" when we can foster classroom research.

Reading specialists can collaborate with teachers to:

- develop a clear research question, one which can lead to data collection, and define terms used to frame the research. The question can be open-ended and need not require statistical data. For example, a teacher might ask, "How will daily sustained silent reading increase the amount of voluntary recreational reading I observe in my classroom?";
- locate related research and be able to provide a rationale for the study; explain why the research is important; share articles in publications such as *The Reading Teacher* to locate articles on the topic;
- select and develop systematic observational and performance data that are appropriate to the question and preserve the integrity of complex, situated classroom events. For example, if you want to find out whether a certain strategy will improve children's story writing, but you are only measuring spelling and grammar, your methods are inadequate for answering your question. Collecting writing samples

from a child over time and comparing patterned elements in them is a much more authentic and informative approach to the question. In the case of our question about the effects of SSR on voluntary reading, the teacher could designate one day a week in which she counts the number of books being read during times of free choice;

- the next step is to analyze the data. In our SSR example, perhaps the teacher finds that recreational reading has increased dramatically, and she has the data to prove that;
- the final step is a "So what?" process. Now that the teacher knows the impact of SSR on amounts of recreational reading, what will she do in her classroom? The choice seems clear. She will most likely continue with the practice of SSR.

The process could end when "So What?" is answered, but we suggest you invite teachers to go one step further and publish their findings. The reading specialist can help a teacher or group start by writing an article about the research project for the local council newsletter. However, we suggest you attempt to write for your state reading journal or a similar publication. We also suggest you study articles from the publication to which you will submit your work. What is the structure of these articles? What kinds of discourses are used? What kinds of articles and topics seem to "fit" in this publication? The two of you or the study group can meet weekly to work on the writing project. We have witnessed how thrilling it is for a teacher to see his or her name on that first article. The process changes individuals and the way they view themselves as professionals. This sort of mentorship by the reading specialist is very much in the spirit of leadership advocated by John Brekke in his advice to us.

THE READING SPECIALIST AS LITERACY ADVOCATE

As political forces and various constituency groups attempt to advance their agendas for school reading programs, IRA has recognized the need for literacy educators to develop a strong collective voice to explain and defend their practices. State and local literacy organizations acknowledge that these debates often take place in local arenas. Therefore, it is essential to join local and state literacy groups that collect and disseminate research, information, and materials that can be used to address school boards, politicians, and the media.

Other Voices: Michael Ford

Michael Ford, Associate Dean of the College of Education and Human Services at the University of Wisconsin, Oshkosh, is a nationally recognized leader in issues related to advocacy. Michael received a grant from the Gertrude Whipple Professional Program through the International Reading Association to compile Advocacy for Best Practice: Resource Materials for Reading Educators. *This rich resource contains research-based information to defend sound practice, transparencies and other materials to aid educators in making presentations, and a variety of supportive resource material. We asked Mike to share some ideas about advocacy with you.*

It wasn't until their local school district threatened to eliminate the Reading Recovery program they had helped to secure and implement that three teachers, Barbara Keresty, Susan O'Leary, and Dale Wortley, found the need to become political. They came together, organized, prepared, and successfully fought for the survival of the program in which they deeply believed. They reminded many of us that when teachers become activists they can impact policy decisions. They wrote of their story and strategies in *You Can Make a Difference: A Teacher's Guide to Political Action* (Heinemann, 1998).

This battle, like most others, reminds reading specialists that the most important advocacy efforts take place at the local level. Even when proposed policy changes at the state and federal level have the power of impacting local reading programs, advocacy through local representatives may be the best way to influence decisions being made beyond the building or district level.

With increasingly public and political scrutiny of reading programs, many reading specialists find themselves defending practices as often as they do implementing them. It is important to be reminded of a few key guidelines for effective local advocacy efforts.

- First, pick your battles wisely. Some critics are more interested in arguing than they are in the arguments. Save your time and energy for those families and stakeholders who have genuine concerns about local reading programs. Respond to critical issues with receptive audiences to maximize the impact of your efforts.
- Secondly, be able to anticipate what the opposing side is going to say and then prepare your response accordingly. When critics choose to indict local programs using aggregated data and generalized information indicting programs everywhere, local advocates must clearly respond with accurate local data, program descriptions, and specific documentation.
- Finally, network with others. Join local and state organizations that bring you into contact with material and human resources that can assist local advocacy efforts. When frustrated by how your single voice is marginalized, join with others to help turn up your volume.

Group Inquiry Activity

1. What, if any, groups or individuals have tried to influence reading instruction in your own district, community, or states? Who are these people and what is their agenda? What is their background? Why are they trying to influence reading instruction? Who has their ear?
2. What has been the response to these individuals of your school board? Of your local reading council? Of your local and state politicians?
3. If you are involved in your local reading council, do you have a legislative or advocacy chairperson? If not, what can you do to help establish such a position? If you are not involved in your local reading council, get involved! This is *your* professional organization!

Mike Ford has assembled a wealth of information on the Wisconsin State Reading Association (WSRA) Web site (www.wsra.org). The materials can be easily adapted to address specific local issues. If you need materials to use in a presentation to your school board or a parent or community group, Mike's materials are essential. The WSRA advocacy link also includes Mike's list of "Ten Books for the Bookshelf of Every Reading Advocate." Titles include the book he mentioned in the Other Voices segment, as well as books by Jeff McQuillan (1998), Denny Taylor (1998), and David Berliner and Bruce Biddle (1995). As educators, we are grateful to Mike and the others who have devoted a great deal of time and energy to supporting teachers in advocacy endeavors.

We are all so busy educating children that we sometimes forget to be proactive in letting the public know what we do well and why we do it. Allen Berger (1997) reminds us to think about the publications we read about our schools and literacy, *The Reading Teacher, Language Arts*, and other practitioner publications. Now think of where we encounter negative articles on schools and literacy education. These are often found in the newspapers and magazines that come into our homes.

Are we educators just talking to each other in our state and IRA publications? Maybe so, but that's not all bad. These professional materials inform our thinking and our practice. However, there is much we can do with what we know and what we've experienced. Berger (1997) suggests we write editorials and articles and send them to mainstream publications *before* we are under attack. This makes so much sense to us that it is surprising we often fail to think about it. His advice on how to write an article for a newspaper is to turn the usual journal article upside down. A journal article doesn't present *findings* until near the end. It starts by describing what happened in the past, followed by what is happening in the present, and giving suggestions for the future. Berger suggests you begin your article for the public by telling what you found out and then telling how it connects with past research (p. 8).

He also recommends that teachers read and edit one another's drafts. In addition to articles, the reading specialist can suggest writing a joint or collaborative editorial. Projects such as these transform teachers into advocates and published professionals. They transform and energize reading specialists, too.

REVISITING THE VIGNETTE

Thinking Points

1. Think about how you addressed Pat's struggle with defining herself as a professional.
2. Are there any additional insights you gained as you read and discussed the ideas in this chapter?
3. What advice would you give Pat if you were in her graduate course in leadership, administration, and supervision?

Final Author Connection: Brenda and MaryEllen

Writing the final paragraphs in a book such as this is an emotional experience, and as you read these final words, we hope that you now share our commitment to developing culturally responsive literacy programs. Few would argue that our students need to be lifelong learners, able to read, critically evaluate, and navigate through a variety of communication symbols and systems. One can only guess at the changes the fifteen-year-olds of today will encounter in their lives and work. There are many challenges for the reading specialist in addition to creating the kind of schools that will prepare these students for the future.

We are pleased to leave you with the thoughts of our friend and colleague Marty Ruddell, past president of the National Reading Conference and professor of reading education at Sonoma State University.

Other Voices: Martha Rapp Ruddell

On Literacy, Teaching, and Changing the World

Many years ago, while at the IRA World Congress in Australia, I had dinner with Ed Fry [a respected and long-time reading expert], and some advanced graduate students in reading. In the course of the conversation, Ed turned to the graduate students and asked them, "In your career as a reading educator, how do you plan to move the world forward by a quarter of an inch?" He then commented that when we're young we all want to Change the World, when in fact the most any of us can do is move it forward in very small increments.

I remember thinking at the time how *right* he was, and how profoundly optimistic and hopeful. Every time I think of it, his comment reminds me of the lessons I learned as a new teacher, and which have been reinforced throughout my teaching career: (1) I could *not* save every child that needed saving; (2) I could not make every teacher in the school good and fair and reasonable; (3) I could not make negative influences and circumstances of my students' home lives go away; (4) I was not always the perfect teacher; (5) I did not like all students equally; (6) I could not make fear and hate and other bad things go away; and on and on and on. On the other hand, I could save *some* kids. I could do everything possible to help all my students become fluent, avid readers and learners. I could make my classroom an oasis of tolerance and respect, where all students were sheltered from fear and hate and meanness. I could maintain my commitment to being a good teacher and my staunch belief that kids really do want to learn. I could hold firmly to the high academic and personal standards I set for my students and myself in my classroom. And I could continue my own learning throughout my career.

That's my "quarter of an inch"; that's how I have Changed the World.

I now challenge you. How in your career as a reading specialist do you plan to move the world forward by a quarter of an inch?

POINTS TO REMEMBER

This chapter explored some other expanding and emerging roles of the reading specialist. Some of the challenges inherent in trying to define what it means to be a professional and a leader in social constructivist terms were discussed. John Brekke offered thoughts on leadership congruent with the collaborative models of problem solving and learning we advocate for the schools. Connie Erickson provided valuable, practical guidance on grant writing. Reading specialists were given a list of professional organizations and publications and Mike Ford delivered a compelling argument for becoming locally active in advocacy initiatives. This chapter contains a variety of resources that are valuable to reading specialists and can be shared with colleagues. Finally, Marty Ruddell issues a challenge for your future as a professional literacy leader—as a *reading specialist*.

PORTFOLIO PROJECTS

1. Think about how you would define the terms *professional* and *leader*. Consider your experiences, the cultural contexts that influenced you, your beliefs, and your current school culture. How do these factors shape your definitions? Choose one of the two terms and map it relative to the factors above.

2. Think about one of the needs you identified in your needs assessment. Is there a need for which you might write a grant? Find a small grant through one of the information sources listed and write a summary of a grant proposal.

3. Think about a classroom problem or question you have in your teaching. Using the steps from this chapter and referring to one or more of the resources listed, write a two- to three-page classroom research proposal you plan to carry out in the future.

4. What are the social and political issues related to literacy in the community and the state? Develop a plan outlining the steps you will take to become a knowledgeable and active advocate for literacy.

RECOMMENDED READINGS

Arhar, J. M., Holly, M. L., & Kasten, W. C. (2001). *Action research for teachers: Traveling the yellow brick road.* Upper Saddle River, NJ: Merrill/Prentice-Hall. This is a comprehensive text on designing, planning, implementing, and evaluating action research. Using the metaphor of Oz as a path of discovery, the book is detailed and very readable.

Cooperative Children's Book Center (CCBC), 4290 Helen C. White Hall, 600 N. Park Street, Madison, WI 53706. This center for children's literature annually reviews and recommends thousands of children's books from around the world. It is also an excellent resource for intellectual freedom and provides resources for dealing with censorship issues (www.education.wisc.edu/ccbc).

Ford, M. (2001). *Advocating for best practices: Resource materials for reading educators.* Compiled by M. Ford, Chair, Advocacy Committee of Wisconsin State Reading Association with support from the Gertrude Whipple Professional Program International Reading Association (www.wsra.org).

Grant Update. Free newsletter sends grant announcements directly to your E-mail. Tips on grant writing for beginners (www.grantupdate. com).

NEA: FREE Education Resources. The official directory of federal grant programs in education.

U.S. Department of Education. Information on millions of dollars of grants of all sizes (www.ed.gov).

LITERACY
HISTORY PROMPTS

If you have never created a literacy history, we urge you to do so. You'll be amazed at what you learn about your own literacy development, and how it impacts you today as a reader and writer. The following literacy prompts may assist you in remembering, reflecting, and creating the literacy history (McLaughlin & Vogt, 1996).

- What are your earliest recollections of reading and writing?
- Were you read to as a child? By whom? What do you remember about being read to?
- Did you read or write with siblings or friends?
- Did you have books, newspapers, and/or magazines in your home? Did you subscribe to any children's magazines? Did your parents or other family members maintain a personal library? Did they read for pleasure?
- Can you recall seeing family members making lists and receiving or sending mail? Did you send or receive mail (e.g., birthday cards, thank-you notes, letters) when you were a child?
- Did you go to the library as a child? If so, what do you remember about going to the library? When did you get your first library card?
- Can you recall teachers, learning experiences, or educational materials from elementary, middle, and secondary school? How did these influence your literacy development?
- Do you remember the first book you loved (couldn't put down)? Do you remember reading/writing as a pleasurable experience? If so, in what ways? If not, why not?
- How did you feel about reading in elementary school? Junior high? High school? Did your reading/writing ability impact your feelings about yourself as a person? If so, how?
- Did you read a certain type of book (i.e., mysteries, biographies) at a particular age? Why do you think you made such choices?
- What is your all-time favorite children's book? Novel? Nonfiction work?
- Are you a reader/writer now? If so, describe yourself as a reader; if not, why do you suppose this is so? What are you currently reading? Writing?

EXAMPLES OF TWO SCHOOLS' VISION STATEMENTS

The first example is the vision statement of Bret Harte Elementary in the Long Beach (California) Unified School District.

VISION STATEMENT

We believe that all students can learn and want to learn. They come to school with their own special experiences and knowledge. Students become literate by building on these experiences and knowledge and by receiving developmentally appropriate instruction. This provides the basis for students' progress from emergent to fluent readers and writers. In order to become members of a literate community, students need:

- A print-rich environment
- Modeling of proficient reading, writing, listening, and speaking
- Opportunities for daily practice: independent, directed, and collaborative
- An environment that encourages risk-taking and accepts approximations
- Opportunities to publish, share, and respond to writing
- Access to technology, which enhances communication.

The second example was written by Christine Wright, a graduate student at the University of Wisconsin, Oshkosh.

VISION STATEMENT

We believe that the primary purpose of reading is comprehension. The major goal of reading instruction is the development of strategic readers who know the reading process and who can construct meaning and apply the necessary strategies to learn from a variety of print and non-print materials. It is a developmental process in which students progress at their own rate.

An effective reading program is dictated by the district curriculum which is aligned with the state standards and is student centered. Teachers are professionals who recognize multiple literacies and multiple communities and honor this in instructional goals. It is crucial, however, that family members, the wider community, and students themselves take active roles in the students' reading development.

Reading instruction encompasses the entire curriculum across all content areas, and effective lessons include pre-reading, reading and post-reading activities. Evaluation of reading growth can be assessed through a variety of objective and subjective methods. It should be emphasized that teacher judgment based upon daily observation and analysis of reading behaviors is a very important evaluative instrument. For an effective reading program to occur, staff development is essential. An effective reading program develops readers who can and will read. Reading is a life-long activity that will enrich students' understanding of themselves and the world. Reading is the best practice for learning to read.

ASSESSMENT PROFILE FOR STANDARDS

GRADE K–5 READING/LANGUAGE ARTS ASSESSMENT PROFILE

(Adapted with permission from an Oshkosh Area School District document; Deb Zarling, District Reading Cordinator)

Oshkosh Area School District Grade K-5 Reading/Language Arts Student Assessment Profile

Name: _____ Grade: _____ Year: 20_____ - 20_____

School: _____ Teacher: _____

School: _____ Teacher: _____

Support Teacher: _____

Overall Proficiency Level	Qtr. 1	Qtr. 2	Qtr. 3	Qtr. 4
• Reading/Language Arts				

Reading Strategies		Qtr. 1	Qtr. 2	Qtr. 3	Qtr. 4
• Understands concepts of print/text structure					
• Uses meaning to make predictions					
• Demonstrates phonological awareness					
• Combines a variety of word recognition strategies					
• Notices and self corrects errors					
• Reads with fluency and expression					
• Uses a variety of reference materials independently (e.g., Word Wall, atlas, almanac, etc.)					
• Establishes a purpose for reading and varies reading rate appropriately					
• Interprets figurative language					
• Expands vocabulary					
	Proficiency Level				

Comments:

_____

_____

Reading Responses		Qtr. 1	Qtr. 2	Qtr. 3	Qtr. 4
• Retells orally					
• Summarizes text					
• Responds to text in a variety of ways					
• Asks and answers questions to clarify understanding of text					
• Interprets text structure					
• Identifies and makes connections among texts					
	Proficiency Level				

Comments:

_____

_____

Text Reading Level				Qtr. 1	Qtr. 2	Qtr. 3	Qtr. 4
• Circle measure used:	DRA	QRI III	Flynt-Cooter				

Oshkosh Area School District Grade K-5 Reading/Language Arts Student Assessment Profile

Writing	Qtr. 1	Qrt. 2	Qrt. 3	Qrt. 4
• Uses the writing process				
• Applies ideas and content				
• Applies organization				
• Applies voice				
• Applies word choice				
• Applies sentence fluency				
• Applies conventions				
Proficiency Level				

Comments:

_____

_____

Oral Language	Qtr. 1	Qrt. 2	Qrt. 3	Qrt. 4
• Uses oral language to communicate				
• Listens effectively				
Proficiency Level				

Comments:

_____

_____

Attitudes and Interest Toward Literacy	Qtr. 1	Qrt. 2	Qrt. 3	Qrt. 4
• Demonstrates a positive attitude toward literacy				
Proficiency Level				

Comments:

_____

_____

PROFICIENCY LEVELS

A = Advanced - A proactive learner who demonstrates in-depth understanding through application of knowledge and shows initiative to extend learning.

P = Proficient - An actively engaged learner who independently communicates and applies knowledge.

B = Basic - A guided learner who seeks assistance and begins to communicate and apply knowledge.

M = Minimal - A dependent learner who relies on assistance from others to gain and apply knowledge.

CONCEPT ACHIEVEMENT

★ = Exceeds expectations   X = Meets expectations   ✓ = Below expectations   □ = Not yet taught

SAMPLE NEEDS ASSESSMENT SURVEY

This is a survey created by a graduate student for her course in leadership and supervision. Note that you will want to tailor your survey statements for your own school context. Also, you may find you get a higher return rate if you can have your colleagues complete the survey during a faculty meeting. Remember to get approval from your principal before you distribute the survey to teachers!

Dear Teachers,

I am currently in the reading specialist credential program at CSULB. One of my assignments is to conduct a school-wide needs assessment of our reading/language arts instructional program. With your help I will be able to do my homework! This is an anonymous survey, but I would like to know some information about you. Also feel free to add comments.

Please return the completed survey to my box by April 21. Thanks in advance for your support!

Kristen Jones, Room 33

I am a: ☐ Teacher   Grade level: 1 2 3 4 5 6
         ☐ Specialist
         ☐ Administrator

I have been teaching for: 1–2 yrs.   3–5 yrs.   6–8 yrs.   9–12 yrs.   13+yrs.

Page 1

Reading/Language Arts Needs Assessment Survey

Barton Elementary School

Directions: Please circle the number that reflects your feelings about the following statements. Note that "5" represents strongly agree.

	Strongly Agree		Unsure/Unknown		Strongly Disagree
Instructional Materials					
I have access to relevant district and state materials (e.g., standards/frameworks).	1	2	3	4	5
Appropriate texts and support materials are available to me.	1	2	3	4	5
The school library is sufficiently stocked with books and resources my students need.	1	2	3	4	5
I have an adequate number of books in my classroom library.	1	2	3	4	5
Our adopted reading series is appropriate for my students' needs, including ELL's.	1	2	3	4	5
Reading Assessment and Instruction					
I have adequate access to assessment instruments that I can use with my students.	1	2	3	4	5
I feel confident when using assessment instruments.	1	2	3	4	5
I feel confident about how to align my instruction with district standards.	1	2	3	4	5
I feel confident in managing flexible groups for my literacy instruction.	1	2	3	4	5
My students have adequate opportunities to read independently.	1	2	3	4	5
My students have adequate opportunities to write independently.	1	2	3	4	5
Our instructional block of time for reading and language arts is adequate.	1	2	3	4	5
I'm able to use a variety of instructional methods and approaches for teaching reading.	1	2	3	4	5

	Strongly Agree		Unsure/Unknown		Strongly Disagree
I feel confident in my ability to provide for the literacy needs of my students.	1	2	3	4	5
We have adequate parent involvement and support at our school.	1	2	3	4	5
Our grade level team has adequate planning time.	1	2	3	4	5

I would benefit from professional development in the following areas:

_____   Phonological processes (phonemic awareness/phonics)
_____   Comprehension skills and strategies
_____   Spelling and vocabulary development
_____   Curriculum and standards alignment
_____   Improving reading in the content areas
_____   Writing and district rubrics
_____   Selecting, administering, and evaluating results from assessments
_____   Flexible grouping and management
_____   Other: _____

Comments (use other side you if wish):

SAMPLE NEEDS ASSESSMENT SUMMARY

Jefferson Elementary School Literacy Program

Summary of Strengths:
- Students exceed the target growth points on the state test by 68 points.
- Teachers continually attend inservices to improve their literacy instruction.
- The school has adequate resources to meet objectives.
- Teachers are committed to literacy program improvement.
- Teachers conduct numerous assessments to determine student's literacy abilities.

Summary of Needs: The teachers, including special educators, agree or strongly agree with their ability to teach comprehension strategies, to identify students' needs through running records, and to read aloud to the students daily. The majority of the teachers feel that the school doesn't help parents support literacy in the classroom. This is an area that needs significant attention. Other areas that need to be addressed include the reading series, intervention, English learners, technology, and classroom libraries.

Needs	Strengths	Weaknesses
The adopted reading series matches the needs of our students. The reading program interventions are effective.	The majority of the teachers feel the series does match the needs of the student population. The majority also feels that program interventions are effective. To examine further how the series is meeting the needs of all students and how interventions are applied, additional information would be needed.	Forty percent feel that the series does not meet the needs of the students. This may indicate that many student needs are not being met by the reading series. Often teachers need to supplement materials or other alternatives because their students' needs are not being met through the reading series.
Instructional materials used for intervention for struggling readers and writers are effective.	The majority of the teachers feel that they have sufficient materials needed to assist students' needs. Further investigations would be needed to determine the effectiveness of the materials.	39% feel that they do not have enough materials to assist struggling readers and writers. We need to know what materials teachers need.

Needs	Strengths	Weaknesses
The current reading program meets the needs of English Language Learners.	38% feel that the needs of English Language Learners are being met in the classroom.	The majority of the teachers do not feel that the reading program meets the needs of ELL's. The school's population consists of 68% ELL.
Collaborations among grade levels are frequent and productive.	Many 1st grade teachers feel they don't collaborate enough. The other grade levels were inconsistent with their responses or felt their grade level did not collaborate or meet consistently.	The majority of teachers felt their grade level didn't meet consistently. We need to determine how to meet more frequently and more productively.
The needs of Special Education students are met with our current literacy program.	30% feel that they are meeting the needs of special education students and 17% had no opinion. This area needs to be looked into further to determine if the question was fully understood and to examine how the needs are being met.	The majority believe the reading series isn't meeting needs of special education students. We need to determine what skills and strategies need to be implemented for these children.
Additional reading strategies for Social Studies and Science texts are needed.	Many teachers report they do need additional reading strategies for SS/Science.	32% report they need more strategies; the majority had no opinion. The question needs clarification to see why so many have no opinion.
Providing students with adequate Technology instruction and support.	39% feel comfortable using technology in the classroom. These teachers need to provide assistance to those that feel inadequate teaching with technology.	The majority of teachers do not feel comfortable using technology in their rooms. Inservice is needed for helping teachers implement technology and access the Internet.
Classroom libraries have a sufficient number and variety of books.	The majority of teachers feel they have a sufficient number of books in their classroom libraries.	38% don't feel they have enough books in their classroom libraries. Some teachers may not be aware of how many books are sufficient for meeting students' reading needs.
Parent support for literacy is adequate.		The majority of teachers feel that parent support is inadequate. The faculty need to discuss ways to help the parents become more involved and comfortable in the academic environment.

Conclusion: The results of the Needs Assessment Survey indicate there is not consensus regarding some of the areas of strength. The areas of need identified in this report are those in which approximately $\frac{1}{3}$ or more of the teachers expressed concerns. There were a large number of responses that indicated "No Opinion." For these survey items, more detailed investigation is needed. Professional development is needed to assist teachers and administration in regard to the perceived lack of parent involvement in the literacy program.

SAMPLE TWO-YEAR PLAN

This two-year plan was created by a graduate student based on a needs assessment that she conducted during her course in supervision and leadership at CSULB. It is appropriate for presentation to administrators and the school board as well as faculty. It's also a "working" document, intended to guide instruction related to a targeted need. All identifying data have been changed and pseudonyms are used throughout.

ABC Elementary School
Two-Year Literacy Plan
2002–2004

Submitted by Susan Johnson
Reading Specialist

District and School Demographics
XYZ Unified School District is a large, urban school district in California, serving grades K–8. In the district there are 85,000 students. The diverse student population consists of the following groups: Hispanic (62%); African American (13%); White (18%); Asian (6%); Pacific Islander (1%). The District consists of 43% English-Only designated students; 37% English Language Learners; 13% redesignated English Fluent students; and 6.5% English Fluent non-native students. At the Elementary and Middle School level, 50% of the students receive free lunches; 39% pay full-price, and 9.5% receive reduced-fee lunches.

ABC Elementary School
ABC Elementary School is a large, K–6 urban school in the XYZ Unified School District. There are 950 students with a demographic population mirroring that of the district. The calendar is traditional, and there are 33 full-time teachers with an average class size of 28. There is a Principal, Vice Principal, two Reading Specialists, and three special education teachers. During recent years, the Parent/Teacher Organization (PTO) has floundered and currently only 13 parents on average attend meetings which are held after school.

Vision Statement

Every student at ABC Elementary School will be inspired to develop a love of reading through immersion in a literacy-rich environment. Reading and language arts instruction based upon current research and theory will be provided by knowledgeable, caring teachers. All students will receive developmentally appropriate literacy instruction based upon assessment of their needs and strengths. Our goal is to ensure that all ABC students leave our school as literate, life-long readers and writers.

Literacy Team Members

Grade K: Mrs. Alvarez, Teacher
Grade 1: Mr. Overlie, Teacher
Grade 2: Miss Dana, Teacher
Grade 3: Miss Myers, Teacher
Grade 4: Mrs. Abbas, Teacher
Grade 5: Miss Gerlock, Teacher
Grade 6: Mr. Elliot, Teacher
Reading Specialist: Mrs. Begonia
Reading Specialist: Mr. Johnston
Special Education: Mr. Ramirez
Vice Principal: Mrs. McGuire
Parents: Mrs. Capella
         Mrs. Gomez
Student Representative (6th grade): Anthony Gonzalez

Summary of Needs Assessment Survey

Developmental Reading: Instructional Practices

Identified areas of strength:

- Providing students with an appropriate developmental reading program (84%)
- Program support for school-wide SSR (Self-Selected Reading) (84%)
- Consistency across grade levels with teaching methods (69%)
- Alignment of developmental reading program and district standards for reading/language arts (76%)

Identified area of weakness:

- Only 45% of teachers believe that students are progressing satisfactorily in the developmental reading program

Instructional Resources

Identified areas of strength:

- Current reading series meets the needs of students (62%)
- Teachers have sufficient materials that come with the series (58%)
- The library supports content covered in the classroom (72%)
- Teachers feel they have sufficient books in their classroom libraries (75%)

Identified areas of weakness:

- Sufficient informational texts for teaching content area reading (42%)
- Current reading series adequate in addressing content area reading (25%)
- Adequate resources for teaching English language learners (42%)

ABC Elementary School Two-Year Literacy Plan, 2002–2004   (continued)

Intervention
Identified areas of strength:
- Teachers know how to access support for struggling readers (69%)

Identified area of weakness:
- Although teachers know how to access support for struggling readers, only 30% had used the Student Study Team (SST) to get the support.

Professional Development
Identified area of strength:
- Professional development opportunities are plentiful (64%)
- Requests for professional development: guided reading, independent workstations and flexible grouping, and literature discussion circles

Written Comments
- A common theme emerged from written comments: Teachers feel very strongly that tutoring and intercession should continue for all students that qualify.

Current Program Description
Developmental
- All classes have grade level materials for the adopted reading series.
- Some teachers use the reading series for guided and shared reading; others use level books. Core literature is available for all classrooms.
- Twelve teachers participated in a study group reading *Mosaic of Thought* and *Strategies that Work*.
- All teachers have received a copy of John's *Basic Reading Inventory*, but they haven't been trained in how to use it.
- K–3 teachers all use the Bumblebee (pseudonym) commercial phonics program.
- Teachers in all grades are required to use the Bumblebee (pseudonym) spelling program.
- Students are assessed with District Benchmark Tests, retellings, and writing prompts.

Recommendations:
- Revisit the adopted reading series materials. Review uses of the series and discuss need for continuity in the reading program. Include materials in curriculum mapping of language arts.
- Teachers who participated in the reading strategies study groups will lead grade level study group.
- Training for all teachers on use of the *Basic Reading Inventory*.

Recreational
- All classes have scheduled times for SSR. These times range from 15–45 minutes.
- Library times are scheduled weekly for all classes. Times range from 25–45 minutes.
- The school participates in the Governor's Reading program. Last year ABC Elementary won for reading the most books in the district.

Recommendations:
- Inservice teachers in effective methods for engaging all students during SSR.

- Inventory classroom libraries to determine adequate numbers of informational and expository texts.

Intervention and Remedial
- Summer intercession is recommended for all students reading one or more years below grade level. Intercession is taught by district reading specialists.
- There is no standard program for intercession; instruction is based on assessed student needs.
- The district no longer pays for after-school tutoring.
- The two Reading Specialists work with bilingual students with reading difficulties, perform assessments, provide demonstration lessons, and teach children for half of the day.
- The special education teacher and her assistant teach students who have an IEP on file at the school.
- Students are seen one-to-one and in small groups.
- First grade teachers have received professional development in identifying and teaching a commercial intervention program for at-risk children.
- Two teachers in each grade (3–5) have received professional development in how to provide effective intervention for older readers.

Recommendations:
- Continue training in sheltered English techniques for all teachers. Hold regular meetings on how to effectively meet the needs of the school's English learners.

Instructional Materials
Recommendations:
- Inventory the adopted reading series. Make sure all classrooms have appropriate and sufficient support and materials.
- Continue emphasis on building classroom resources for instruction in the content areas.
- Create a professional library that is easily accessible and contains resources for reading and writing strategies, including assessment resources.
- Provide intercession teachers with relevant materials.

Technology Resources
Recommendations:
- Recently, the school was awarded a grant to implement a Science/Technology Lab. During this implementation, the school will upgrade its technology capabilities.
- Survey teachers about their technology needs and knowledge.

Professional Development Plan

Targeted Need:
Improving Students' Comprehension of Expository and Informational Texts
in the Content Areas, Grades K–6

Goals:
1. Investigate and establish a research foundation for and understanding of teaching expository and informational texts using the content areas in the language arts block.

ABC Elementary School Two-Year Literacy Plan, 2002–2004   (continued)

2. Provide all faculty and instructional assistants with relevant and effective inservice(s) and follow-up support that focus on instructional methods, materials, and approaches for teaching the content areas in the language arts block.
3. Improve students' comprehension of expository texts as determined by a variety of formal and informal measures.

Suggested Activities
- During a faculty meeting, discuss needs assessment data and draft of two-year plan related to comprehension instruction.
- Invite all staff members (including administrators and instructional assistants to form grade-level discussion groups for two professional books: *Mosaic of Thought* (Keene & Zimmerman) and *Strategies That Work* (Harvey & Goudvis). Teachers who have formerly participated in a study group will be facilitators.
- Offer and schedule demonstration lessons on the following topics: administering an IRI, teaching comprehension skills (e.g., main idea, author's viewpoint, text structure, cause/effect, etc.)
- Offer and schedule demonstration lessons on comprehension strategies for informational text, including SQP2RS and VSS.
- Discuss possibility of videotaping comprehension lessons as opportunities for reflective self-assessment.
- Determine if teachers are interested in establishing peer-coaching partners. If so, discuss how these might be organized and implemented.
- Focus new teacher support efforts on our targeted need. This will support first and second year teachers.

Inservices and Workshops
- Offer one workshop with an outside speaker on comprehension skills and strategies to establish a foundation of current research.
- Offer at least one inservice (district reading specialist) on how to administer and analyze results from an Informal Reading Inventory. Schedule follow-up meetings to share findings.
- Offer one or more workshops to help English language learners access expository and informational texts.
- Encourage and coordinate attendance at local and state reading conferences, and IRA. Research grants for registration fees.
- Encourage teachers who have been integrating content into the language arts block to share with other teachers during an after-school workshop.

Anticipated Student Outcomes
- Improvement in expository text comprehension as measured by pre-post IRI passages, word recognition, and miscue analysis (sampled in each grade level).
- Improvement in expository text comprehension as measured by pre-post SAT-9 standaridized test scores (all students).
- Increase in number of students passing grade-level nonfiction benchmark tests.

Evaluation of Professional Development Efforts
- Measures for evaluating expository text comprehension growth in students (benchmarks, IRI's, SAT-9 scores)
- Satisfaction measures of teachers (surveys, interviews) Teachers' reflections on demonstration lessons
- Evaluations collected at the end of all inservices and workshops
- Comparisons of pre-post reading logs of students in grades 2–5

Tentative Schedule

Year One

September–October
- Present needs assessment data from spring and literacy team's recommendations.
- Present two-year plan for approval of faculty (after approval of administration).
- Offer workshop by outside speaker on topic of targeted need to kick off professional development plan.
- Register interested teachers for upcoming conferences
- Offer after-school inservice on administering IRI's

November–December
- Form grade-level teacher-as-reader groups using the professional resource books; schedule after school discussions with refreshments
- Offer inservice by district readings specialists and new-teacher mentors related especially to needs of English language learners
- Offer inservice for administrators on how to conduct and analyze results from an IRI.
- Provide demonstration lessons on IRI's and schedule group discussions on analyzing results.

January–February
- Coordinate peer coaching groups
- Coordinate videotaping of lessons
- Continue teachers-as-readers group of professional resources
- Offer first after-school inservice on how to teach comprehension skills and strategies through SQP2RS and VSS

March–April
- Schedule and facilitate coaching opportunities for peer-coaches
- Cover classes for peer coaches
- Schedule after-school meetings to discuss how things are going
- Offer follow-up workshop by district reading specialist to support teaching of comprehension skills and strategies
- Assist teachers in preparation for SAT-9

ABC Elementary School Two-Year Literacy Plan, 2002–2004   (continued)

May–June
- Assist teachers in sampling students with IRI assessments
- Assist in analyzing results from IRI's
- Facilitate peer coaching and cover classes
- Offer final inservice to discuss and model comprehension strategies that have been identified as areas of concern.
- Collect and analyze school's post-assessment data
- Distribute needs assessment survey for year two

Year Two
September–October
- Meet with Literacy Team to analyze needs assessment data
- With literacy team, make adjustments in two-year plan
- Organize study groups for reading *Guided Comprehension: A Teaching Model for Grades 3–8* (McLaughlin & Allen)
- Facilitate after-school workshop for planning second year of professional development for targeted need.

November–June
- Based on needs assessment data and literacy team recommendations, revise plan and schedule activities

Anticipated Supplies/Materials/Resources

Supplies and Materials: Office supplies for inservices (pens, markers, flip charts, paper, overhead transparencies, note pads); duplicating of handouts; videotapes for discussion groups; refreshments for all meetings and workshops

Professional Resources: Multiple copies of professional texts

Estimated Budget for Year One:

Professional Resources:	$ 600
Supplies and materials:	250
Honoraria for outside speaker:	500
Duplication of handouts:	150
Conference registrations:	500
Refreshments:	150
Other:	150
Total:	$2300
Total Available:	$5000

LEARNER ASSESSMENT PROFILE (LAP)

Learner Assessment Profile (LAP)
Identifying Information

Name	Date of Birth	Date of Report
Parents	Phone	
School	Grade	Teacher

Background: Home and Community

The School and Classroom

Assessment Information		
Assessment	Date	Findings
Analysis of Assessment		

Match or Mismatch with Present Instructional Context

Matching Areas:

Areas of Mismatch:

What Might Achieve a Closer Instructional Match?

Recommendations

Additional Comments

Profile Prepared by _____ Date _____
                              Reading Specialist

Observations and Insights during Instruction
Date: _____ Location:
Date: _____ Location:
Date: _____ Location:
Date: _____ Location:

CLASSROOM ASSESSMENT PROFILE

For ease of use, we recommend that you create a Classroom Assessment Profile that runs horizontally across an $8\frac{1}{2}'' \times 11''$ or $11'' \times 14''$ piece of paper. This represents one way to organize your assessment data.

Student	Assessment/Date	Findings	Comments

IRA POSITION STATEMENT:
Teaching All Children to Read:
The Roles of the Reading Specialist (2000)

ROLES OF THE READING SPECIALIST

Teaching all children to read requires that every child receive excellent reading instruction and that children who are struggling with reading receive additional instruction from professionals specifically prepared to teach them. Teaching all children to read also requires reading specialists in every school because the range of student achievement in classrooms, with the inclusion of children who have various physical, emotional, and educational needs, requires different educational models from those of the past.

In order to provide these services, schools must have reading specialists who can provide expert instruction, assessment, and leadership for the reading program. Reading specialists are professionals with advanced preparation and experience in reading who have responsibility for the literacy performance of readers in general and struggling readers in particular. This includes early childhood, elementary, middle, secondary, and adult learners. Learners can be in public, private, and commercial schools, or in reading resource centers or clinics.

The Association's recommendations for the roles of the reading specialist in the three specific areas mentioned above include the following:

1. Instruction—The reading specialist supports, supplements, and extends classroom teaching, and works collaboratively to implement a quality reading program that is research-based and meets the needs of students.

2. Assessment—The reading specialist has specialized knowledge of assessment and diagnosis that is vital for developing, implementing, and evaluating the literacy program in general and in designing instruction for individual students. He or she can assess the reading strengths and needs of students and provide that information to classroom teachers, parents, and specialized personnel such as psychologists, special educators, or speech teachers in order to provide an effective reading program.

3. Leadership—The reading specialist provides leadership as a resource to other educators, parents, and the community.

Single copies of *Teaching All Children to Read: The Roles of the Reading Specialist* are available free on-line or by mail. Download a copy of the brochure in PDF format, or send a self-addressed, stamped No. 10 envelope to: Position Statements, International Reading Association, 800 Barksdale Road, PO Box 8139, Newark, DE 19714-8139, USA. To purchase multiple copies visit the Association's Online Bookstore.

REFERENCES

Adams, M. J. (1990). *Beginning to read: Thinking and learning about print*. Cambridge, MA: MIT.

Aldinger, L., Warger, C. L., & Eavy, P. (1992). *Strategies for teacher collaboration*. Ann Arbor, MI: Exceptional Innovations.

Allington, R. L. (2001). *What really matters for struggling readers: Designing research-based programs*. New York: Addison-Wesley Longman.

Allington, R. L., & Walmsley, S. (Eds.). (1995). *No quick fix: Rethinking literacy programs in America's elementary schools*. Newark, DE: International Reading Association.

Alvermann, D. E. (2001). *Effective literacy instruction for adolescents*. Executive summary and paper commissioned by the National Reading Conference. Available at: www.nrc.oakland.edu/documents/2001/alverwhite.PDF

Alvermann, D. E., Hinchman, K. A., Moore, D. W., Phelps, S. F., & Waff, D. R. (Eds.). (1998). *Reconceptualizing the literacies in adolescents' lives*. Mahwah, NJ: Erlbaum.

Alvermann, D. E., Smith, L. C., & Readence, J. E. (1985). Prior knowledge activation and the comprehension of compatible and incompatible text. *Reading Research Quarterly, 20*, 420–436.

Anderson, R. C. (1984). Role of the reader's schema in comprehension, learning, and memory. In R. C. Anderson, J. Osborn, & R. J. Tierney (Eds.), *Learning to read in American schools. Basal readers and content texts*. Hillsdale, NJ: Erlbaum.

Anderson, R. C., Hiebert, E. H., Scott, J. A., & Wilkinson, I. A. G. (1985). *Becoming a nation of readers: The report of the Commission on Reading*. Washington, DC: National Institute of Education.

Anderson, R. C., & Pearson, P. D. (1984). A schema-theoretical view of basic processes in reading comprehension. In P. D. Pearson (Ed.), *Handbook of reading research* (pp. 225–295). White Plains, NY: Longman.

Anderson, V., Chan, C., & Henne, R. (1995). The effects of strategy instruction on the literacy models and performance of reading and writing delayed middle school students. In K. A. Hinchman, D. J. Leu, & C. K. Kinzer (Eds.), *National Reading Conference Yearbook, 44* (pp. 180–196). Chicago: National Reading Conference.

Au, K. H. (1993). *Literacy instruction in multi-cultural settings*. New York: Harcourt Brace.

Au, K. H. (1998). Social constructivism and the school literacy learning of students of diverse backgrounds. *Journal of Literacy Research, 30*, 297–319.

Au, K. H. (2000). A multicultural perspective on policies for improving literacy achievement: Equity and excellence. In M. L. Kamil, P. B. Mosenthal, P. D. Pearson, & R. Barr (Eds.), *Handbook of Reading Research, Vol. III* (pp. 835–851). Mahwah, NJ: Erlbaum.

Au, K. H., Garcia, G. G., Goldenberg, C. N., & Vogt, M. E. (2002). *Handbook for English language learners: Resources for universal access*. Boston: Houghton Mifflin.

Au, K. H., & Raphael, T. E. (2000). Equity and literacy in the next millennium. *Reading Research Quarterly, 35*(1), 170–188.

Ayres, L. R. (1998). Phonological awareness of kindergarten children: Three treatments and their effects. In C. Weaver (Ed.), *Reconsidering a balanced approach to reading* (pp. 209–255). Urbana, IL: National Council of Teachers of English.

Banks, J. A. (1994). *An introduction to multicultural education*. Boston: Allyn & Bacon.

Bartlett, F. C. (1932). *Remembering*. Cambridge, England: Cambridge University Press.

Barton, D., Hamilton, M., & Ivanic, R. (Eds.). (2000). *Situated literacies*. New York: Routledge.

Bauman, J. F., Hoffman, J. F., Moon, J., & Duffy-Hester, A. M. (1998). Where are teachers' voices in the phonics/whole language debate? Results from a survey of U.S. elementary teachers. *The Reading Teacher, 51*, 636–650.

Bean, R. M., Cassidy, J., Grumet, J. E., Shelton, D. S., & Wallis, S. R. (2002). What do reading specialists do? Results from a national survey. *The Reading Teacher, 55*(8), 736–744.

Bean, R. M., Cooley, W., Eichelberger, R. T., Lazar, M., & Zigmond, N. (1991). In-class or pullout: Effects on the remedial reading program. *Journal of Reading Behavior, 23*(4), 445–464.

Bean, T. W. (2001, December/January). An update on reading in the content areas: Social constructivist dimensions. *Reading Online 4*(11). Available at: http://www.readingonline.org/article/art_index.asp?HREF=/handbook/bean/index.html

Bear, D., Templeton, S., Invernizzi, M., & Johnston, F. (2000). *Words their way: Word study for phonics, vo-*

cabulary, and spelling (2nd ed.). Upper Saddle River, NJ: Merrill/Prentice-Hall.

Beck, I. L., & McKeown, M. G. (2001). Text talk: Capturing the benefits of read-aloud experiences for young children. *The Reading Teacher, 55*, 10–20.

Berger, A. (1997). Writing about reading for the public. *The Reading Teacher, 51*, 6–10.

Berliner, D. C., & Biddle, B. (1995). *The manufactured crisis.* New York: Longman.

Blachman, B. A. (2000). Phonological awareness. In M. L. Kamil, P. B. Mosenthal, P. D. Pearson, & R. Barr (Eds.), *Handbook of reading research, Vol. III* (pp. 483–502). Mahwah, NJ: Erlbaum.

Blachowicz, C., & Fisher, P. J. (2002). *Teaching vocabulary in all classrooms* (2nd ed.). Upper Saddle River, NJ: Merrill/Prentice-Hall.

Blevins, W. (1998). *Phonics from A–Z.* New York: Scholastic.

Bond, G. L., & Dykstra, R. (1967a). The Cooperative Research Program in first-grade reading instruction. *Reading Research Quarterly, 2*, 5–142.

Bond, G. L., & Dykstra, R. (1967b). *Coordinating center for first-grade reading instruction programs.* (Final Report of Project No. X-001, Contract No. OE5-10-264). Minneapolis: University of Minnesota.

Boomer, G. (1992). Negotiating the curriculum. In G. Boomer, N. Lester, C. Onore, & J. Cook (Eds.), *Negotiating the curriculum: Education for the 21st century.* Bristol, PA: Falmer Press.

Boutte, G. S., LaPoint, S., & Davis, B. (1993, November). Racial issues in education: Real or imagined? *Young Children*, 19–23.

Boutte, G. S., & McCormick, C. B. (1992, Spring). Authentic multicultural activities: Avoiding pseudomulticulturalism. *Childhood Education, 68*(3), 140–144.

Bracey, G. W. (1997). *Setting the record straight: Responses to misconceptions about public education in the United States.* Alexandria, VA: Association for Supervision and Curriculum Development.

Britzman, D. (1986). Cultural myths in the making of a teacher: Biography and social structure in teacher education. *Harvard Educational Review, 56*, 442–456.

Brooks, J. G., & Brooks, M. G. (1993). *In search of understanding: The case for constructivist classrooms.* Alexandria, VA: Association for Supervision and Development.

Bruner, J. (1983). *Child's talk: Learning to use language.* New York: W. W. Norton.

Buber, M. (1970). *I and thou.* (Walter Kaufman, Trans.). New York: Charles Scribner's Sons.

Buehl, D. (2001). *Classroom strategies for interactive learning* (2nd. ed.). Newark, DE: International Reading Association.

Burke, J., & Prater, C. A. (2000). *I'll grant you that: A step-by-step guide to finding funds, designing winning projects, writing powerful grant proposals.* Portsmouth, NH: Heinemann.

Byers, A. (1993). National Adult Literacy Survey overlooks rural illiteracy. *Rural Clearinghouse Digest, 1*(1), 1–3.

Cairney, T., & Ruge, J. (1998). *Community literacy practices and schooling: Towards effective support for students.* Canberra City, Australia: Commonwealth Department of Employment, Education, Training, and Youth Affairs.

California Department of Education. (1999). *Reading/Language Arts Framework for California Public Schools.* Sacramento, CA: Author.

Calkins, L. M. (1983). *Lessons from a child: On the teaching and learning of writing.* Exeter, NH: Heinemann.

Cambourne, B. (1988). *Learning and the acquisition of literacy in classrooms.* Portsmouth, NH: Heinemann.

Carlson, T. R. (Ed.). (1972). *Administrators and reading: A project of the International Reading Association.* New York: Harcourt Brace.

Center One. (1998). *The needs assessment.* Washington, DC: ORBIS Associates.

Chall, J. S. (1967). *Learning to read: The great debate.* New York: McGraw-Hill.

Chall, J. S. (1983). *Stages of reading development.* New York: McGraw-Hill.

Chomsky, N. (1999). *Profits over people: Neoliberalism and global order.* New York: Seven Stories Press.

Clay, M. (1991). *Becoming literate: The construction of inner control.* Portsmouth, NH: Heinemann.

Clay, M. (1985). *The early detection of reading difficulties: A diagnosis survey and recovery procedure.* Portsmouth, NH: Heinemann.

Clymer, T. (1963). The utility of phonic generalizations in the primary grades. *The Reading Teacher, 16*, 252–258.

Cochran-Smith, M. (1995). Uncertain allies: Understanding the boundaries of race and teaching. *Harvard Educational Review, 65*(4), 541–570.

Cochran-Smith, M., & Lytle, S. (1990). Research on teaching and teacher research: The issues that divide. *Educational Researcher, 19*(2), 2–11.

Cogan, M. (1973). *Clinical supervision.* Boston: Houghton Mifflin.

Colvin, C., & Schlosser, L. K. (1997/1998). Developing academic confidence to build literacy: What teachers can do. *Journal of Adolescent and Adult Literacy, 41*, 272–281.

Cooper, J. D. (1999). *Project Success: An intervention model for grades 3–6.* Paper presented at the Research Institute of the California Reading Association, Long Beach, CA.

Cooper, J. D. (2000). *Literacy: Helping children construct meaning* (4th ed.). Boston: Houghton Mifflin.

Cooper, J. D., & Pikulski, J. J. (2000). *A research-based framework for Houghton Mifflin Reading: A legacy of literacy.* Boston: Houghton Mifflin.

Comber, B. (2001). Classroom explorations in critical literacy. In H. Fehring & P. Green (Eds.), *Critical literacy: A collection of articles from the Australian Literacy Educators' Association* (pp. 90–102). Newark, DE: International Reading Association.

Costa, A. L., & Garmston, R. J. (1994). *Cognitive coaching: A foundation for renaissance schools.* Norwood, MA: Christopher-Gordon.

Costa, A. L., & Garmston, R. J. (2000). *Cognitive coaching: A foundation for renaissance schools* (2nd ed.). Norwood, MA: Christopher-Gordon.

Cummins, J. (1979). Linguistic interdependence and the educational development of bilingual children. *Review of Educational Research, 49*(22), 51.

Cummins, J. (1981). The role of primary language development in promoting educational success for language minority students. In California State Department of Education, *Schooling and minority students: A theoretical framework* (pp. 3–49). Los Angeles: National Dissemination and Assessment Center.

Cummins, J. (1984). *Bilingualism and special education: Issues in assessment and pedagogy.* San Diego, CA: College-Hill.

Cummins, J. (1990). Reflections on "empowerment." *California Association for Bilingual Education Newletter, 12*(3), 7, 11.

Cummins, J. (1994). Primary language instruction and the education of language-minority students. In C. Leyba (Ed.), *Schooling and language minority students: A theoretical framework* (2nd ed.). Los Angeles: Evaluation, Dissemination, and Assessment Center.

Cunningham, J. (2000). RRQ Snippet: How will literacy be defined in the new millennium? *Reading Research Quarterly, 35*, 64–65.

Cunningham, J. W. (2001). The National Reading Panel report. *Reading Research Quarterly, 36*(3), 326–335.

Cunningham, J. W., Many, J. E., Carver, R. P., Gunderson, L., & Mosenthal, P. B. (2000). Snippets: How will literacy be defined? *Reading Research Quarterly, 35*(1), 64–71.

Delgato-Gaitan, C. (1996). *Protean literacy: Extending the discourse on empowerment.* London: Falmer Press.

Delpit, L. D. (1995). *Other people's children: Cultural conflict in the classroom.* New York: New Press.

Derman-Sparks, L., & A. B. C. Task Force (1989). *Anti-bias curriculum: Tools for empowering young children.* Washington, DC: National Association for the Education of Young Children.

Dermody, M., & Speaker, R. (1995). Effects of reciprocal strategy training in prediction, clarification, question generation, and summarization on fourth graders' reading comprehension. In K. A. Hinchman, D. Leu, & C. K. Kinzer (Eds.), *National Reading Conference Yearbook, 45.* Chicago: National Reading Conference.

Diaz-Rico, L. T., & Weed, K. Z. (1995). *The cross-cultural, language, and academic development handbook.* Boston: Allyn & Bacon.

Dickinson, D. K., & Smith, M. W. (1996). Long-term effects of preschool teachers' book readings on low-income children's vocabulary and story comprehension. *Reading Research Quarterly, 29*, 104–122.

Dillon, D. R. (2000). *Kids insight: Reconsidering how to meet the literacy needs of all students.* Newark, DE: International Reading Association.

Dillon, D. R., O'Brien, D. G., Moje, E. B., & Stewart, R. A. (1994). Literacy learning in secondary school science classrooms: A cross-case analysis of three qualitative studies. *Journal of Research in Science Teaching, 31*, 345–362.

Dolch, E. W. (1942). *Basic sight word test.* Champaign, IL: Garrard.

Dole, J. A., Brown, K. J., & Trathen, W. (1996). The effects of strategy instruction on the comprehension performance of at-risk students. *Reading Research Quarterly, 14*, 481–533.

Dole, J. A., Duffy, G. G., Roehler, L. R., & Pearson, P. D. (1991). Moving from the old to the new: Research on reading comprehension instruction. *Review of Educational Research, 61*(2), 239–264.

Downing, J. (1962). *Experiments with an augmented alphabet for beginning readers.* New York: Educational Records Bureau.

Dudley-Marling, C., & Murphy, S. (1997). A political critique of remedial reading programs: The example of Reading Recovery. *The Reading Teacher, 50*, 460–469.

Durkin, D. (1974–1975). A six-year study of children who learned to read in school at the age of four. *Reading Research Quarterly, 1*, 9–61.

Durkin, D. (1978). What classroom observations reveal about reading comprehension instruction. *Reading Research Quarterly, 14*(4), 481–533.

Dyson, A. H. (1993). From invention to social action in early childhood literacy: A reconceptualization through dialogue about difference. *Early Childhood Research Quarterly, 8,* 409–425.

Dyson, A. H. (1994). Viewpoints: The word and the world—Reconceptualizing written language development or, Do rainbows mean a lot to little girls? In R. B. Ruddell, M. R. Ruddell, & H. Singer (Eds.), *Theoretical models and processes of reading* (4th ed., pp. 297–322). Newark, DE: International Reading Association.

Echevarria, J., & Graves, A. (1998). *Sheltered content instruction: Teaching students with diverse abilities.* Boston: Allyn & Bacon.

Echevarria, J., Vogt, M. E., & Short, D. (2000). *Making content comprehensible for English language learners: The SIOP model.* Boston: Allyn & Bacon.

Edwards, P. A. (1995). Combining parent's and teachers' thoughts about storybook reading at home and school. In L. M. Morrow (Ed.), *Family literacy: Connections in schools and communities* (pp. 551–568). Newark, DE: International Reading Association.

Edwards, P. A., Pleasants, H., & Franklin, S. (1999). *A path to follow: Learning to listen to parents.* Portsmouth, NH: Heinemann.

Ehri, L. (1994). Development of the ability to read words: Update. In R. B. Ruddell, M. R. Ruddell, & H. Singer (Eds.), *Theoretical models and processes of reading* (4th ed., pp. 323–358). Newark, DE: International Reading Association.

Elley, W. B. (1992). *How in the world do students read? IEA study of reading literacy.* The Hague, Netherlands: International Association for the Evaluation of Educational Achievement.

Faltis, C. J. (1993). *Joinfostering: Adapting teaching strategies to the multicultural classroom.* New York: Maxwell Macmillan International.

Feeley, J. T., & Rhodes, C. S. (1995). A new look at the materials selection process. In S. B. Wepner, J. T. Feeley, & D. S. Strickland (Eds.), *The administration and supervision of reading programs* (2nd ed., pp. 111–129). Newark, DE: International Reading Association.

Fitzgerald, J. (2001). Can minimally trained college students help young at-risk children read better? *Reading Research Quarterly, 36,* 28–47.

Flesch, R. (1955). *Why Johnny can't read.* New York: Harper & Brothers.

Flood, J., & Lapp, D. (1994). Developing literacy appreciation and literacy skills: A blueprint for success. *The Reading Teacher, 45,* 608–616.

Florio-Ruane, S. (1994). The future teachers' autobiography club: Preparing educators to support learning in culturally diverse classrooms. *English Education, 26*(1), 52–56.

Fox, B. J. (2000). *Word identification strategies: Phonics from a new perspective* (2nd ed.). Upper Saddle River, NJ: Merrill.

Freire, P. (1970). *Pedagogy of the oppressed.* New York: Continuum.

Friend, M., & Cook, L. (1997). *Interactions: Collaboration skills for school professionals* (2nd ed.). White Plains, NY: Longman.

Fries, C. C. (1963). *Linguistics and reading.* New York: Holt, Rinehart, & Winston.

Fullan, M. (1993). *Change forces: Probing the depths of educational reform.* New York: Routledge.

Garmston, R. (1997). *The presenter's fieldbook: A practical guide.* Norwood, MA: Christopher-Gordon.

Gee, J. P. (1990). *Social linguistics and literacies: Ideology in discourses.* Philadelphia: Falmer Press.

Gee, J. P. (1996). *Social linguistics and literacies: Ideology and discourses* (2nd ed.). London: Taylor & Francis.

Gee, J. P. (2001a). Identity as an analytic lens for research in education. *Review of Educational Research, 25,* 99–125.

Gee, J. P. (2001b, December). *Reading in "New Times."* Plenary address presented at the National Reading Conference, San Antonio, TX.

Gilmore, P. (1986). Sub-rosa literacy: Peers, play, and ownership in literacy acquisition. In B. Schieffelin & P. Gilmore (Eds.), *The acquisition of literacy: Ethnographic perspectives* (pp. 155–168). Norwood, NJ: Ablex.

Glickman, C. D., Gordon, S. P., & Ross-Gordon, J. M. (1998). *Supervision of instruction: A developmental approach* (4th ed.). Boston: Allyn & Bacon.

Godina, H. (1996). The canonical debate: Implementing multicultural literature and perspectives. *Journal of Adolescent and Adult Literacy, 39,* 544–545.

Goldberg, M. (2001). *The bee season.* San Francisco: Knopf.

Goldenberg, C. (1993). Instructional conversations: Promoting comprehension through discussion. *The Reading Teacher, 46*(4), 316–326.

Goldfield, B., & Snow, C. E. (1992). What's cousin Arthur's daddy's name? The Acquisition of the knowledge about kinship. *First Language, 12,* 187–205.

Goldhammer, R. (1969). *Clinical supervision: Special methods for the supervision of teachers.* New York: Holt, Rinehart, and Winston.

Goodman, K. (1986). *What's whole about whole language.* Portsmouth, NH: Heinemann.

Goodman, K. (1994). Reading, writing, and written text: A transactional sociopsycholinguistic view. In R. B. Ruddell, M. R. Ruddell, & H. Singer (Eds.), *Theoretical models and processes of reading* (4th ed., pp. 1093–1130). Newark, DE: International Reading Association.

Goswami, U. (2000). Phonological and lexical processes. In M. L. Kamil, P. B. Mosenthal, P. D. Pearson, & R. Barr (Eds.), *Handbook of reading research, Vol. III* (pp. 251–265). Mahwah, NJ: Erlbaum.

Gray, W. S. (1915). Standardized oral reading test. *Studies of elementary school reading through standardized tests* (Supplemental Educational Monographs No. 1). Chicago: University of Chicago Press.

Gutman, A. (1999). *Democratic education* (2nd ed.). Princeton, NJ: Princeton University Press.

Guzman, R. (1986). A definition of sheltered English as it applies to level III and transitional students at T. J. Quirk Middle School. In National Council of Bilingual Education Web document 300860069. *Facilitating transition to the mainstream: Sheltered English vocabulary development.* NCBE Homepage. Available at: http://www.ncbe.gwu.edu

Haberman, M. (1996). Selecting and preparing culturally competent teachers for urban schools. In J. Sikula (Ed.), *Handbook of research in teacher education* (pp. 747–760). New York: Simon & Schuster.

Haggard, M. (1982). The Vocabulary Self-Collection Strategy: Using student interest and word knowledge to enhance vocabulary growth. *Journal of Reading, 27,* 203–207.

Hansen, R. A., & Farrell, D. (1995). The long-term effects on high school seniors of learning to read in kindergarten. *Reading Research Quarterly, 30,* 908–933.

Hanzl, A. (2001). Critical literacy and children's literature: Exploring the story of Aladdin. In H. Fehring & P. Green (Eds.), *Critical literacy: A collection of articles from the Australian Literacy Educators' Association* (pp. 84–89). Newark, DE: International Reading Association.

Harris, T. L., & Hodges, R. E. (1995). *The literacy dictionary: The vocabulary of reading and writing.* Newark, DE: International Reading Association.

Harste, J. C. (1994). Literacy as curricular conversations about knowledge, inquiry, and morality. In R. B. Ruddell, M. R. Ruddell, & H. Singer (Eds.), *Theoretical models and processes of reading* (4th ed., pp. 1220–1242). Newark, DE: International Reading Association.

Hartman, D. (1995). Eight readers reading: The intertextual links of proficient readers reading multiple passages. *Reading Research Quarterly, 30,* 520–551.

Harvey, S., & Goudvis, A. (2000). *Strategies that work: Teaching comprehension to enhance understanding.* York, ME: Stenhouse.

Heath, S. B. (1982). What no bedtime story means: Narrative skills at home and school. *Language and Society, 11,* 49–76.

Heath, S. B. (1983). *Ways with words: Language, life, and work in communities and classrooms.* Cambridge, UK: Cambridge University Press.

Heath, S. B. (1994). The children of Trackton's children: Spoken and written language in social change. In R. B. Ruddell, M. R. Ruddell, & H. Singer (Eds.), *Theoretical models and processes of reading* (4th ed., pp. 208–230). Newark, DE: International Reading Association.

Henk, W. A., Moore, J. C., Mariak, B. A., & Tomasetti, B. W. (2000). A reading lesson observation framework for elementary teachers, principals, and literacy supervisors. *The Reading Teacher, 53(5),* 358–369.

Hiebert, E. H. (2001). Keynote presentation to California State University reading faculty. Long Beach, CA: California Institute for Reading Reform.

Hiebert, E. H., Pearson, P. D., Taylor, B. M., Richardson, V., & Paris, S. G. (1998). *Every child a reader.* Ann Arbor, MI: Center for the Improvement of Early Reading Achievement (CIERA), University of Michigan.

Hiebert, E. H., & Taylor, B. M. (2000). Beginning reading instruction: Research on early interventions. In M. L. Kamil, P. B. Mosenthal, P. D. Pearson, & R. Barr (Eds.), *Handbook of Reading Research, Vol. III* (pp. 455–482). Mahwah, NJ: Erlbaum.

Hinchey, P. H. (2001, May). Learning to read the world: Who—and what—is missing? *Reading Online, 4(10).* Available at: http://www.readingonline.org/newliteracies/lit_index.asp?HREF=/newliteracies/hinchey/index.html

Hoffman, J. (1992). Critical reading/thinking across the curriculum: Using I-Charts to support learning. *Language Arts, 69,* 121–127.

Huey, E. B. (1908/1968). *The psychology and pedagogy of reading.* Cambridge, MA: MIT Press.

Hynd, C. R., Qian, G., Ridgeway, V. G., & Pickle, M. (1991). Promoting conceptual change with science texts and discussion. *Journal of Reading Behavior, 34,* 596–601.

International Reading Association. (1992; 1998). *Standards for reading professionals.* Newark, DE: Author. Available at www.reading.org

International Reading Association. (1997). *The role of phonics in reading instruction: A position statement of the International Reading Association.* Newark, DE: Author. Available at: www.reading.org

International Reading Association & National Council of Teachers of English. (1996). *Standards for the English Language Arts.* Newark, DE: International Reading Association. Available at: www.reading.org

Ivey, G. (1999). Reflections on struggling middle school readers. *Journal of Adolescent and Adult Literacy, 42,* 372–381.

Kamil, M. L., Intrator, S. M., & Kim, H. S. (2000). In M. L. Kamil, P. B. Mosenthal, P. D. Pearson, & R. Barr (Eds.), *Handbook of reading research, Vol. III* (p. 771–788). Mahwah, NJ: Erlbaum.

Keene, E., & Zimmerman, S. (1997). *Mosaic of thought: Teaching comprehension in a reader's workshop.* Portsmouth, NH: Heinemann.

Keresty, B., O'Leary, S., & Whortley, D. (1998). *You can make a difference: A teacher's guide to political action.* Portsmouth, NH: Heinemann.

Klenk, L., & Kibby, M. W. (2000). Remediating reading difficulties: Appraising the past, reconciling the present, and constructing the future. In M. L. Kamil, P. B. Mosenthal, P. D. Pearson, & R. Barr (Eds.), *Handbook of reading research, Vol. III* (pp. 667–690). Mahwah, NJ: Erlbaum.

Klesius, J. P., & Griffith, P. (1996). Interactive storybook reading for at-risk learners. *The Reading Teacher, 49,* 552–560.

Kogut, B. (February, 2001). National literacy volunteer organizations authorize merger discussions. A press release from Laubach Literacy International.

Kos, R. (1991). Persistence of reading difficulties: The voices of four middle school students. *American Educational Research Journal, 28,* 875–895.

Kotter, J. (1996). *Leadership change.* Boston: Harvard Business School Press.

Krashen, S. D. (1984). *Writing: Research theory and application.* Oxford, England: Pergamon Press.

Krashen, S. D. (1985). *The input hypothesis: Issues and implications.* New York: Longman.

Krashen, S. D. (1998). Comprehensible output. *System, 26,* 175–182.

Johns, J. J. (1997). *Basic reading inventory.* Dubuque, IA: Kendall/Hunt.

LaBerge, D., & Samuels, S. J. (1974). Toward a theory of automatic information processing in reading. *Cognitive Psychology, 6,* 293–323.

Ladson-Billings, G. (1995). Toward a theory of culturally relevant pedagogy. *American Education Research Journal, 32,* 465–491.

Lalik, R., & Hinchman, K. (2001). Critical issues: Examining constructions of race in literacy research: Beyond silence and other oppressions of white liberalism. *Journal of Literacy Research, 33*(3) 529–561.

Lazar, A. (2001). Preparing white preservice teachers for urban classrooms: Growth in a Philadelphia-based literacy practicum. In J. V. Hoffmann, D. L. Schallert, C. M. Fairbanks, J. Worthy, & B. Maloch (Eds.), *National Reading Conference Yearbook, 50* (pp. 558–571). Chicago: National Reading Conference.

Leftwich, S. (2001, December). Using the ABCs Model to help preservice teachers involved in a community reading project. Symposium presented at the Fifty-First Annual Meeting of the National Reading Conference, San Antonio, TX.

Leu, D. J. (2000a). Developing new literacies: Using the Internet in content area instruction. In M. McLaughlin & M. E. Vogt (Eds.), *Creativity and innovation in content area teaching* (pp. 183–205). Norwood, MA: Christopher-Gordon.

Leu, D. J. (2000b). Literacy and technology: Deictic consequences for literacy education in an information age. In M. L. Kamil, P. B. Mosenthal, P. D. Pearson, & R. Barr (Eds.), *Handbook of reading research, Vol. III* (pp. 743–770). Mahwah, NJ: Erlbaum.

Lewis, C. (2001). *Literacy practices as social acts: Power, status, and cultural norms in the classroom.* Mahwah, NJ: Erlbaum.

Linn, R. L. (1993). Educational Assessment: Expanded expectations and challenges. *Educational Evaluation and Policy Analysis, 15*(1), 1–16.

Lipson, M., & Wixson, K. (1997). *Assessment and instruction of reading and writing disability: An interactive approach* (2nd ed.). New York: Longman.

Long, R. (1995). Preserving the role of the reading specialist. *Reading Today, 12*(5), 6.

Luis, S. F. (1997). *The role of state departments of education in complex school reform.* New York: Teachers College Press.

Luke, A. (1994). *The social construction of literacy in the primary school.* South Melbourne, Australia: Macmillan Education.

Luke, A., & Freebody, P. (1999, August). Further notes on the four sources model. *Reading Online.* Available at: http://www.readingonline.orgpast/past_index/asp?HREF=/research/lukefreebody.html

Luke, C. (1999). Media and cultural literacy studies in Australia. *Journal of Adolescent and Adult Literacy, 42,* 622–626.

Maeroff, G. I. (1993, March). Building teams to rebuild schools. *Phi Delta Kappan, 74*(7), 512–514.

Many, J. (2001). Assessment and instruction in a graduate literacy class: Reflecting what I'm learning in what I do. *Journal of Adolescent and Adult Literacy, 47,* 566–579.

Manzo, A. V. (1969). The ReQuest procedure. *The Journal of Reading, 13,* 123–126.

Mazurkiewicz, A. J., & Tanyzer, H. J. (1966). *Easy to read i/t/a program.* New York: Initial Teaching Alphabet Publications.

McCaleb, S. P. (1994). *Building communities of learners.* New York: St. Martin's Press.

McGee L. M. (1992). An exploration of meaning construction in first graders' grand conversations. In C. K. Kinzer & D. J. Leu (Eds.), *The National Reading Conference Yearbook, 41* (pp. 177–186). Chicago: National Reading Conference.

McGee L. M., Courtney, L., & Lomax, R. (1994). Supporting first graders' responses to literature: An analysis of teachers' roles in grand conversations. In C. K. Kinzer & D. J. Leu (Eds.), *National Reading Conference Yearbook, 43* (pp. 517–526). Chicago: National Reading Conference.

McGill-Franzen, A. (2000). Policy and instruction: What is the relationship? In M. L. Kamil, P. B. Mosenthal, P. D. Pearson, & R. Barr (Eds.), *Handbook of reading research, Vol. III* (pp. 835–851). Mahwah, NJ: Erlbaum.

McLaughlin, M., & Allen, M. B. (2002). *Guided comprehension: A teaching model for grades 3–8.* Newark, DE: International Reading Association.

McLaughlin, M., & Vogt, M. E. (1996). *Portfolios in teacher education.* Newark, DE: International Reading Association.

McQuillan, J. (1998). *The literacy crisis: False claims and real solutions.* Portsmouth, NH: Heinemann.

Meek, M. (1983). *Achieving literacy: Longitudinal studies of adolescents learning to read.* London: Routledge & Kegan Paul.

Mehan, H. (1979). *Learning lessons: Social organization in the classroom.* Cambridge, MA: Harvard University Press.

Mikulecky, L., Albers, P., & Peers, M. (1994). *Literacy transfer: A review of the literature* (Technical Report No. TR94-05). Philadelphia: University of Pennsylvania, National Center on Adult Literacy (ERIC Document Reproduction Service No. ED374340; CE067321).

Mitchell, C. (1991). Preface. In C. Mitchell & K. Weiler (Eds.), *Rewriting literacy: Power and the culture of the other* (pp. xvii–xxvii). Toronto, Canada: OISE Press.

Moje, E. B. (2000). Critical issues: Circles of kinship, friendship, position, and power: Examining the community in community-based literacy research. *Journal of Literacy Research, 32*(1), 77–112.

Moje, E. B., Young, J. P., Readence, J. E., & Moore, D. W. (2000). Reinventing adolescent literacy for new times: Perennial and millennial issues. *Journal of Adolescent & Adult Literacy, 43*(3), 400–410.

Moll, L. C. (1994). Literacy research in community and classrooms: A sociocultural approach. In R. B. Ruddell, M. R. Ruddell, & H. Singer (Eds.), *Theoretical models and processes of reading* (4th ed.). Newark, DE: International Reading Association.

Moll, L. C., & Gonzales, N. (1994). Critical issues: Lessons from research with language-minority children. *Journal of Reading Behavior, 26*(3), 439–456.

Moore, D. W., Alvermann, K. A., & Hinchman, K. A. (Eds.). (2000). *Struggling adolescent readers: A collection of teaching strategies.* Newark, DE: International Reading Association.

Moore, D. W., Bean, T., Birdyshaw, D., & Rycik, J. (1999). *Adolescent literacy: A position statement for the Commission on Adolescent Literacy of the International Reading Association.* Newark, DE: International Reading Association.

Moore, M., & Wilson, H. B. (1927). *A peep into fairyland: A child's book of phonics games.* Moore-Wilson Readers. Boston: D. C. Heath.

Morrow, L. M. (1995). Family literacy: New perspectives, new practices. In L. M. Morrow (Ed.), *Family literacy: Connections in schools and communities.* Newark, DE: International Reading Association.

Morrow, L. M., & Asbury, E. (1999). Best practices for a balanced early literacy program. In L. B. Gambrell, L. M. Morrow, S. B. Neuman, & M. Pressley. *Best practices in literacy instruction* (pp. 49–67). New York: Guilford.

Nagy, W. (1988). *Teaching vocabulary to improve reading comprehension.* Urbana, IL: National Council of Teachers of English, and Newark, DE: International Reading Association.

National Center for Education Statistics. (2001). *Internet access in public schools and classrooms.* Available at: http://nces.ed.gov/pubsearch/pubsinfo.asp?pubid=2001071

National Council on Education Standards and Testing. (1992). *Raising standards for American education.* Washington, DC: U.S. Government Printing Office.

National Council of Teachers of English. (1974). *Students' rights to language, College Composition and Communication* (pp. 2–3). Urbana, IL: National Council of Teachers of English.

National Reading Panel. (2000). *Teaching children to read: An evidence-based assessment of the scientific research literature on reading and its implications for reading instruction.* Washington, DC: National Institute of Child Health and Human Development, National Institutes of Health.

Nieto, S. (1996). *Affirming diversity: The sociopolitical context of multicultural education.* New York: Longman.

Nieto, S. (1999, December). *Language literacy and culture: Intersections and implications.* Paper presented at the Forty-ninth Annual Meeting of the National Reading Conference, Orlando, FL.

O'Brien, D. (2001, June). "At-Risk" adolescents: Redefining competencies through the multiliteracies of intermediality, visual arts, and representations. *Reading Online 4*(11). Available at: http://www.readingonline.org/article//HREF=/newliteracies/obrien/index.html

O'Brien, D. G., & Stewart, R. A. (1992). In E. K. Dishner, T. W. Bean, J. E. Readence, & D. W. Moore (Eds.), *Reading in the content areas: Improving classroom instruction* (3rd ed., pp. 30–40). Dubuque, IA: Kendall-Hunt.

Ogle, D. (1986). K-W-L: A teaching model that develops active reading of expository text. *The Reading Teacher, 39,* 564–570.

Ogle, D., & Fogelberg, E. (2001). Expanding collaborative roles of reading specialists. In V. J. Risko & K. Bromley (Eds.), *Collaboration for diverse learners: Viewpoints and practices* (pp. 152–167). Newark, DE: International Reading Association.

Okagaki, L., & Sternberg, R. (1993). Putting the distance into students' hands: Practical intelligence for school. In R. R. Cocking and K. A. Renninger (Eds.), *The development and meaning of psychological distance* (pp. 237–254). Hillsdale, NJ: Erlbaum.

Padilla, A. M., Lindholm, K. J., Chen, A., Duran, R., Hakuta, K., Lambert, W. E., & Tucker, G. R. (1991). The English-only movement: Myths, reality, & implications for psychology. *American Psychologist, 46,* 120–130.

Pailliotet, A. W. (1998). Deep viewing: A critical look at visual texts. In J. L. Kincheloe & S. Steinberg (Eds.), *Unauthorized methods: Strategies for critical teaching* (pp. 123–136). New York: Routledge.

Palinscar, A. M., & Brown, A. (1982). *Reciprocal teaching of comprehension-monitoring activities* (Tech. Rep. No. 269). Champaign, IL: Center for the Study of Reading, University of Illinois.

Palinscar, A. M., & Brown, A. (1984). Reciprocal teaching of comprehension·fostering and monitoring activities. *Cognition and Instruction, 1,* 117–175.

Palmer, P. J. (1998). *The courage to teach: Exploring the inner landscape of a teacher's life.* San Francisco: Jossey-Bass.

Paratore, J. R. (Summer, 2000). Grouping for instruction in literacy: What we've learned about what works and what doesn't. *The California Reader, 33*(4), 2–10.

Paratore, J. (1995). Implementing an intergenerational literacy project: Lessons learned. In L. M. Morrow (Ed.), *Family literacy: Connections in schools and communities* (pp. 37–53). Newark, DE: International Reading Association.

Patterson, L., Cotten, C., Pavonetti, L., Kimball-Lopez, K., & VanHorn, L. (1998). The shared "ah-ha experience": Literature conversations and self-organizing complex adaptive systems. In T. Shanahan & F. V. Rodrigeuez-Brown (Eds.), *National Reading Conference Yearbook, 48* (pp. 143–156). Chicago: National Reading Conference.

Patty, D., Maschoff, J. D., & Ransom, P. (1995). *The reading resource handbook for school leaders.* Norwood, MA: Christopher-Gordon.

Payne, S. (2001). *McGuffey readers.* Online. Available at: ww.nd.edu/~rbarger/www7/mcguffey.html

Pearson, J. W., & Santa C. M. (1995). Students as researchers of their own reading. *Journal of Reading, 38*(6), 462–469.

Pearson, P. D. (1998a). Standards and assessments: Tools for crafting effective instruction? In J. Osborn, & F. Lehr (Eds.), *Literacy for all: Issues in teaching and learning* (pp. 264–288). New York: Guilford.

Pearson, P. D. (1988b). Standards in the Language Arts. In J. Flood, S. B. Heath, & D. Lapp (Eds.), *Handbook of teaching literacy in the communicative and visual arts* (pp. 763–775). New York: Macmillan.

Pearson, P. D., & Fielding, L. (1991). Comprehension instruction. In R. Barr, M. L. Kamil, P. B. Mosenthal, & P. D. Pearson (Eds.), *Handbook of reading research, Vol. II* (pp. 815–860). New York: Longman.

Phillips, L. M., Norris, S. P., & Mason, J. M. (1996). Longitudinal effects of early literacy concepts on reading achievement: A kindergarten intervention and a five-year follow-up. *Journal of Literacy Research, 28,* 173–195.

Pikulski, J. J. (1995). Preventing reading failure: A review of five effective programs. *The Reading Teacher, 48,* 30–39.

Pinnell, G. S., Fried, M. D., & Estes, R. M. (1990). Reading Recovery: Learning how to make a difference. *The Reading Teacher, 43,* 283–295.

Pressley, M. (2000). What should comprehension instruction be the instruction of? In M. L. Kamil, P. B. Mosenthal, P. D. Pearson, & R. Barr (Eds.), *Handbook of reading research, Vol. III* (pp. 545–562). Mahwah, NJ: Erlbaum.

Pressley, M., Allington, R., Morrow, L., Baker, L., Nelson, E., Warton-McDonald, R., Block, C., Tracey, D., Brooks, G., Cronin, J., & Woo, D. (1998). *The nature of effective first grade instruction.* Unpublished paper. National Research Center of English Learning and Achievement. State University of New York, Albany.

Pressley, M., Johnson, C. J., Symons, S., McGoldrick, J. A., & Kurita, J. A. (1989). Strategies that improve children's memory and comprehension of text. *Elementary School Journal, 90,* 3–32.

Pressley, M., & Woloshyn, V. (1995). *Cognitive strategy instruction that really improves children's academic performance.* Cambridge, MA: Brookline Books.

Progoff, I. (1975). *At a journal workshop: The basic text and guide for using the intensive journal.* New York: Dialogue House Library.

Purcell-Gates, V. (1993). Issues for family literacy research: Voices from the trenches. *Language Arts, 70,* 670–677.

Purcell-Gates, V. (2000, July). The role of qualitative and ethnographic research in educational policy. *Reading Online 4*(1) Available at: http://www.readingonline.org/article/gates/HREF=/article/purcell-gates/index.html

Quatroche, D. J., Bean, R. M., & Hamilton, R. L. (1998). *The role of the reading specialist: A review of research.* A Report of the Commission on the Role of the Reading Specialist. Newark, DE: International Reading Association.

Quatroche, D. J., Bean, R. M., & Hamilton, R. L. (2001). The role of the reading specialist: A review of research. *The Reading Teacher 55*(3), 282–294.

Radencich, M. C. (1995). *Administration and supervision of the reading/writing program.* Boston: Allyn & Bacon.

Radencich, M. C, Beers, P. G., & Schumm, J. S. (1993). *A handbook for the K–12 reading resource specialist.* Boston: Allyn & Bacon.

Ramos-Ocasio, A. (1985). An interpretation of a theoretical concept and its applicability to an ESL classroom setting. In National Council of Bilingual Education, Web Document 300860069. *Facilitating transition to the mainstream: Sheltered English vocabulary development.* NCBE Homepage. http://www.ncbe.gwu.edu

Raphael, T. E. (1984). Teaching learners about sources of information for answering comprehension questions. *Journal of Reading, 27,* 303–311.

Rawls, W. (1961). *Where the red fern grows.* Garden City, NY: Doubleday.

Readence, J. E., Bean, T. W., & Baldwin, R. S. (2001). *Content area literacy: An integrated approach* (7th ed.). Dubuque, IA: Kendall/Hunt.

Resnick, D. P., & Resnick, L. B. (1985). Standards, curriculum, and performance: A historical and comparative perspective. *Educational Researcher, 14*(4) 5–20.

Rhodes, L. K., & Shanklin, N. L. (1993). *Windows into literacy: Assessing learners, K–8.* Portsmouth, NH: Heinemann.

Risko, V., & Bromley, K. (Eds.). (2001). *Collaboration for diverse learners: Viewpoints and practices.* Newark, DE: International Reading Association.

Robb, L. (2000a). *Redefining staff development: A collaborative model for teachers and administrators.* Portsmouth, NH: Heinemann.

Robb, L. (2000b). *Teaching reading in middle school: A strategic approach to teaching reading that improves comprehension and thinking.* New York: Scholastic.

Robinson, F. P. (1946). *Effective study* (2nd ed.). New York: Harper & Row.

Robinson, H. A., & Rauch, S. J. (1965). *Guiding the reading program: A reading consultant's handbook.* Chicago: Science Research Associates.

Rodriguez, R., Prieto, A., & Rueda, R. (1984). Issues in bilingual/multicultural special education. *Journal of the National Association for Bilingual Education, 8*(3), 55–65.

Rosenblatt, L. M. (1978). *The reader, the text, the poem: The transactional theory of literary work.* Carbondale, IL: Southern Illinois University Press.

Rosenblatt, L. M. (1994). The transactional theory of reading and writing. In R. B. Ruddell, M. R. Ruddell, & H. Singer (Eds.), *Theoretical models and processes of reading* (4th ed., pp. 1076–1092). Newark, DE: International Reading Association.

Ruddell, M. R. (2001). *Teaching content reading and writing* (3rd ed.). New York: John Wiley.

Ruddell, M. R. (In press). At-risk students. In B. Guzetti, & J. Johns (Eds.), *Literacy in America: An encyclopedia.* Newark, DE: International Reading Association.

Ruddell, M. R., & Shearer, B. A. (2002). "Extraordinary," "tremendous," "exhilarating," "magnificent:" Middle school at-risk students become avid word learners with the vocabulary self-collection strategy (VSS). *Journal of Adolescent and Adult Literacy, 45,* 352–363.

Ruddell, R. B. (2002). *Teaching children to read and write: Becoming an effective literacy teacher* (3rd ed.). Boston: Allyn & Bacon.

Saleebey, D. (1997). Constructing the community: The emergent uses of social constructivism in economically depressed communities. In C. Franklin & P. Nurius (Eds.), *Constructivism in practice: Methods and challenges* (pp. 291–310). Milwaukee, WI: Families International.

Salinger, J. D. (1962). *Catcher in the Rye*. Boston: Little, Brown.

Semali, L. M., & Watts-Pailliotet, A. (Eds.). (1999). Intermediality and why study it in U.S. schools? In L. M. Semali & A. Watts-Pailliotet (Eds.), *Intermediality: The teachers' handbook of critical media literacy* (pp. 1–4). New York: Westview.

Schallert, D. L., & Roser, N. I. (1989). The role of reading in content area instruction. In D. Lapp, J. Flood, & N. Farnum (Eds.), *Content area reading and learning: Instructional strategies* (pp. 25–33). Englewood Cliffs, NJ: Prentice-Hall.

Schmidt, P. R. (1998a). The ABC model: Teachers connect home and school. In T. Shanahan & F. V. Rodriguez-Brown (Eds.), *National Reading Conference Yearbook, 47* (pp. 194–208). Chicago: National Reading Conference.

Schmidt, P. R. (1998b). The ABCs of cultural understanding and communication. *Equity and Excellence in Education, 31*(2), 28–38.

Schmidt, P. R. (1999). Know thyself and understand others. *Language Arts, 76*(4), 332–340.

Schmidt, P. R. (2001a). Emphasizing differences to build cultural understandings. In V. J. Risko, & K. Bromley (Eds.), *Collaboration for diverse learners: Viewpoints and practices* (pp. 210–230). Newark, DE: International Reading Association.

Schmidt, P. R. (2001b). The power to empower. In P. R. Schmidt & P. B. Mosenthal (Eds.), *Reconceptualizing literacy in the new age of multiculturalism and pluralism* (pp. 389–433). Greenwich, CT: Information Age Press.

Schmidt, P. R., & Pailliotet, A. W. (2001). Introduction. In P. R. Schmidt & A. W. Pailliotet (Eds.), *Exploring values through literature, multimedia, and literacy events: Making connections* (pp. 1–9). Newark, DE: International Reading Association.

Shannon, P. (1999). Every step you take. *The Reading Teacher, 53*, 32–35.

Shannon, P. (2000). "What's my name?": A politics of literacy in the latter half of the 20th century in America. *Reading Research Quarterly, 35*(1) 90–107.

Shearer, B. A. (2000). Student-directed written inquiry: Transferring ownership to students. In M. McLaughlin & M. E. Vogt (Eds.), *Creativity and innovation in content area teaching* (pp. 209–230). Norwood, MA: Christopher-Gordon.

Shearer, B. A. (2001, December). *Oral history project of the National Reading Conference: Excerpts from an interview with Robert Dykstra*. Poster session presented at the National Reading Conference, San Antonio, TX.

Shearer, B. A., Ruddell, M. R., & Vogt, M. E. (2001). Successful middle school intervention: Negotiated strategies and individual choice. In J. V. Hoffmann, D. L. Schallert, C. M. Fairbanks, J. Worthy, & B. Maloch (Eds.), *National Reading Conference Yearbook, 50* (pp. 558–571). Chicago: National Reading Conference.

Shefelbine, J. (1995). *Syllabic unit approach*. Paper presented at the meeting of the Asilomar Regional Reading Conference, Monterey, CA.

Slavin, R. E., Madden, N. A., Dole, L. J., & Wasik, B. A. (1996). *Every child, every school: Success for All*. Newberry Park, CA: Corwin.

Smith, F. (1987). *Joining the literacy club*. Portsmouth, NH: Heinemann.

Snow, C. E., Burns, S., & Griffin, P. (1998). *Preventing reading difficulties in young children*. Washington, DC: National Academy Press.

Snow, C. E., & Dickinson, D. K. (1991). Some skills that aren't basic in a new construction of literacy. In A. Purves & T. Jennings (Eds.), *Literate systems and individual lives: Perspectives on literacy and schooling* (pp. 175–213). Albany, NY: State University of New York Press.

Snow, C. E., & Goldfield, B. (1982). Turn the page, please: Situation-specific language acquisition. *Journal of Child Language, 10*, 559–569.

Soriano, F. I. (1995). *Conducting needs assessments: A multidisciplinary approach*. Thousand Oaks, CA: Sage.

Soto, G. (1997). *Buried onions*. New York: Scholastic.

Sparks, D., & Hirsh, S. (1997). *A new vision for staff development*. Alexandria: Association for Supervision and Curriculum Development and Oxford, OH: National Staff Development Council.

Spindler, G., & Spindler, L. (1987). *The interpretive ethnography of education: At home and abroad*. Hillsdale, NJ: Erlbaum.

Stahl, S. A., & Vancil, S. J. (1986). Discussion is what makes semantic maps work in vocabulary instruction. *The Reading Teacher, 40*, 62–67.

Stanovich, K. (1986). Matthew effects in reading: Some consequences of individual differences in the acquisition of reading. *Reading Research Quarterly, 21*, 360–407.

Stauffer, R. G. (1969). *Directing reading maturity as a cognitive process*. New York: Harper & Row.

Stevens, L. P. (2001). *South Park* and society: Instructional and curricular implications of popular culture in the classroom. *Journal of Adolescent and Adult Literacy, 44*, 548–555.

Street, B. V. (1996). *Social literacies: Critical approaches to literacy development*. New York: Longman.

Strickland, D. (1995). Whole language. In T. L. Harris & R. E. Hodges (Eds.), *The literacy dictionary: The vocabulary of reading and writing* (pp. 279–281). Newark, DE: International Reading Association.

Sullivan, M. W., & Buchanan, C. D. (1963). *Programmed reading series.* New York: McGraw-Hill.

Sulzby, E. (1994). Children's emergent reading of favorite storybooks: A developmental study. In R. B. Ruddell, M. R. Ruddell, & H. Singer (Eds.), *Theoretical models and processes of reading* (4th ed., pp. 244–280). Newark, DE: International Reading Association.

Sutherland, E. (1988). *Simpson's contemporary quotations.* Boston: Houghton Mifflin.

Tancock, S. (1995). Classroom teachers and reading specialists examine their Chapter 1 reading programs. *Journal of Reading Behavior, 27*(3), 315–335.

Tatum, B. (1997). *Why are all the black kids sitting together in the cafeteria?* New York: Basic Books.

Taylor, B. M., Graves, M. F., & van den Broek, P. (Eds.). (2000). *Reading for meaning: Fostering comprehension in the middle grades.* Newark, DE: International Reading Association and Teachers College Press.

Taylor, B. M., Short, R. A., Frye, B. J., & Shearer, B. A. (1992). Classroom teachers prevent reading failure in low achieving first grade students. *The Reading Teacher, 45*, 941–945.

Taylor, B. M., Short, R. A., Shearer, B. A., & Frye, B. (1995). First-grade teachers provide early reading intervention in the classroom. In R. Allington & S. Walmsley (Eds.), *No quick fix: Rethinking literacy programs in America's elementary schools* (pp. 159–176). New York: Teachers College Press.

Taylor, D. (1998). *Beginning to read and the spin doctors of science.* Urbana, IL: National Council of Teachers of English.

Taylor, D., & Dorsey-Gaines, C. (1988). *Growing up literate: Learning from inner city families.* Portsmouth, NH: Heinemann.

Teale, W. H., & Martinez, M. G. (1996). Reading aloud to young children: Teachers' reading styles and kindergarteners' text comprehension. In C. Ponticorvo, M. Orsolini, B. Berge, & L. B. Resnick (Eds.), *Children's early text construction* (pp. 321–344). Mahwah, NJ: Erlbaum.

Templeton, S., & Morris, D. (2000). Spelling. In M. L. Kamil, P. B. Mosenthal, P. D. Pearson, & R. Barr (Eds.), *Handbook of reading research, Vol. III* (pp. 525–543). Mahwah, NJ: Erlbaum.

Thomas, W., & Collier, V. (1997/1998). *School effectiveness for language minority students.* Fairfax, VA: George Mason University. National Clearinghouse for Bilingual Education.

Thorndike, E. L. (1917). Reading as reasoning: A study of mistakes in paragraph reading. *Journal of Educational Psychology, 8,* 323–332.

Thorndike, E. L. (1921). *The teacher's word book.* New York: Teachers College Press.

Tompkins, G. E. (2001). *Literacy for the 21st century: A balanced approach* (2nd ed.). Upper Saddle River, NJ: Prentice-Hall.

Tovani, C. (2000). *I read it, but I don't get it: Comprehension strategies for adolescent readers.* Portland, ME: Stenhouse.

U.S. Congress. (1994). *Goals 2000* (P.L. 103-227). Washington, DC: U.S. Government Printing Office.

Valencia, S. W., Hiebert, E. H., & Afflerbach, P. P. (1994). *Authentic reading assessment: Practices and possibilities.* Newark, DE: International Reading Association

Valencia, S. W., & Wixson, K. (2001). Inside English/language arts standards: What's in a grade? *Reading Research Quarterly, 36*(2), 202–217.

van den Broek, P., & Kremer, K. (2000). The mind in action: What it means to comprehend in reading. In B. M. Taylor, M. F. Graves, & P. van den Broek (Eds.), *Reading for meaning: Fostering comprehension in the middle grades* (pp. 1–31). Newark, DE: International Reading Association and Teachers College Press.

Venezky, R. L., Sabatini, J. P., Brooks, C., & Carino, C. (1996). *Policy and practice in adult learning: A case study perspective* (Technical Report No. TR96-07). Philadelphia: University of Pennsylvania, National Center on Adult Literacy.

Vogt, M. E. (1989). *The congruence between preservice teachers' and inservice teachers' attitudes and practices toward high and low achievers.* Unpublished doctoral dissertation, University of California, Berkeley.

Vogt, M. E. (1997). *Intervention strategies for intermediate and middle school students: Three models (that appear) to work.* Paper presented at the Research Institute of the Annual Conference of the California Reading Association. Anaheim, CA.

Vogt, M. E. (1998). *Read-2-Succeed: An intervention model for middle school students.* Paper presented at the Research Institute of the Annual Conference of the California Reading Association. Sacramento, CA.

Vogt, M. E. (2000). Content learning for students needing modifications: An issue of access. In M. McLaughlin & M. E. Vogt (Eds.), *Creativity and innovation in content area teaching.* Norwood, MA: Christopher-Gordon.

Vogt, M. E., & Verga, M. (1998). Improving comprehension: Developing strategic readers. In C. Cox (Ed.), *Current research in practice.* Los Angeles: Los Angeles County Educational Consortium for the Improvement of Reading.

Vogt, M. E., & Vogt, K. D. (1999). Electronic journals: Encouraging reflection in preservice teachers. In S. Gardner & T. Fulwiler (Eds.), *The journal book: For teachers in technical and professional programs* (pp. 80–91). Portsmouth, NH: Boynton Cook/Heinemann.

Vygotsky, L. S. (1978). *Mind in society.* Cambridge, MA: Harvard University Press.

Wade, S. E., & Moje, E. B. (2000). The role of text in classroom learning. In M. L. Kamil, P. B. Mosenthal, P. D. Pearson, & R. Barr (Eds.), *Handbook of reading research, Vol. III* (pp. 609–627). Mahwah, NJ: Erlbaum.

Wagner, D. A. (1997). *Toward the goal of adult literacy.* Philadelphia, PA: National Center on Adult Literacy, University of Pennsylvania. APA Online: American Psychological Association.

Walker-Dalhouse, D., & Dalhouse, A. D. (2001). Parent-school relations: Communicating effectively with African American parents. *Young Children, 56,* 75–80.

Warger, C. L., & Rutherford, R. (1996). *Social skills instruction: A collaborative approach.* Reston, VA: Foundation for Exceptional Innovations.

Watts-Pailliotet, A. (2000, July). Welcome to the New Literacies department. *Reading OnLine, 4*(1). Available at: www.readingonline.org/newliteracies/lit_index.asp?HREF.wattspailliotet1/index. html

Wellins, R. S., Byham, W. C., & Wilson, J. M. (1991). *Empowered teams.* San Francisco: Jossey-Bass.

Wepner, S. B., Feeley, J. T., & Strickland, D. S. (Eds.). (1995). *The administration and supervision of reading programs* (2nd ed.). Newark, DE: International Reading Association and Teachers College Press.

Wepner, S. B., & Seminoff, N. (1995). Evolving roles and responsibilities of reading personnel. In S. B. Wepner, J. T. Feeley, & D. S. Strickland (Eds.), *The administration and supervision of reading programs* (2nd ed., pp. 22–38). Newark, DE: International Reading Association and Teachers College Press.

Wilkinson, L. C., & Silliman, E. R. (2000). Classroom language and literacy learning. In M. L. Kamil, P. B. Mosenthal, P. D. Pearson, & R. Barr (Eds.), *Handbook of reading research, Vol. III* (pp. 337–355). Mahwah, NJ: Erlbaum.

Willis, A. I., & Meacham, S. J. (1997). Break point: The challenges of teaching multicultural education courses. *Journal of the Assembly for Expanded Perspectives on Learning, 2,* 40–49.

Wolfe, L. (1992). Reading potential through bilingual education. In S. Bredekamp & T. Rosegrant (Eds.), *Reading potential: Appropriate curriculum and assessment for young children* (pp. 139–144). Washington, DC: National Association for the Education of Young Children.

Wolfram, W. (1991). *Dialects and American English.* Englewood Cliffs, NJ: Prentice-Hall.

Wong-Fillmore, L. (1991). *The classroom as a setting for social learning.* Paper presented at the Celebrating Diversity Conference, Oakland, CA.

Wood, M., & Prata Salvetti, E. (2001). Project story boost: Read-alouds for students at-risk. *The Reading Teacher, 55,* 76–83.

Xu, H. (2000). Preservice teachers in a literacy methods course consider issues of diversity. *Journal of Literacy Research, 32*(4), 505–531.

Yaden, D. B., Rowe, D. W., & MacGillivray, L. (2000). Emergent literacy: A matter (polyphony) of perspectives. In M. L. Kamil, P. B. Mosenthal, P. D. Pearson, & R. Barr (Eds.), *Handbook of reading research, Vol. III* (pp. 425–454). Mahwah, NJ: Erlbaum.

Yinger, R. (1985). Journal writing as a learning tool. *Volga Review, 87*(5), 21–33.

Yopp, H. K. (1992). Developing phonemic awareness in young children. *The Reading Teacher, 45,* 696–703.

Zeichner, K. M., & Liston, D. P. (1996). *Reflective teaching and the social conditions of schooling.* Mahwah, NJ: Erlbaum.

INDEX